The Other British Isles

The Other British Isles

*A History of Shetland, Orkney, the Hebrides,
Isle of Man, Anglesey, Scilly, Isle of Wight
and the Channel Islands*

DAVID W. MOORE

McFarland & Company, Inc., Publishers
Jefferson, North Carolina, and London

LIBRARY OF CONGRESS CATALOGUING-IN-PUBLICATION DATA

Moore, David W., 1951–
The other British Isles : a history of Shetland, Orkney,
the Hebrides, Isle of Man, Anglesey, Scilly, Isle of Wight
and the Channel Islands / David W. Moore.
p.   cm.
Includes bibliographical references and index. ,

ISBN-13: 978-0-7864-2143-5
ISBN-10: 0-7864-2143-6 (illustrated case: 50# alkaline paper)

1. Islands—Great Britain—History.
2. Great Britain—History, Local.   I. Title.
DA668.M66   2005   941'.00942—dc22   2005014049

British Library cataloguing data are available

Cover map ©2005 Clipart.com

Manufactured in the United States of America

McFarland & Company, Inc., Publishers
Box 611, Jefferson, North Carolina 28640
www.mcfarlandpub.com

Acknowledgments

No book is an island, entire of itself, with apologies to John Donne, and so it is with this one, hewn from a trans-oceanic compilation of readings, on-site observations, and archive and museum materials. The uniqueness of Britain's offshore islands lies in being Britain's offshore islands, and this book would have been impossible to write without the memorable trips to reach them. In the matter of historiography not all islands are equal in the matter of their own histories in print — some are well covered but for others there is a paucity of suitable information. It was a matter of relief and pleasure therefore to find money spent on artifact collections, reference rooms, museums and preservation of historic sites. I am grateful to all those responsible since critical insights came from simply being on location.

Several "background" books lightened my load on challenging questions, notably those by Barry Cunliffe and Aubrey Burl on prehistory, Hubert Lamb's work on climate in history, and Mike Ashley's encyclopedic inventory of British monarchs, a significant time-saver logging the multitude of rulers in the marginal medieval kingdoms. I am grateful also for a number of splendid works written on specific island themes, some available only in the islands, and I hope I managed to do justice to their scholarship. A reading list is given at the end of the book.

Special thanks are due to my former students Angela Martinez and Priscilla Yamano for assistance on research and early drafts. Minh Carter of Golden West College Library defied (my) credulity on several occasions by finding books through inter-library loan requests on obscure subjects from the deep trove of American university and college libraries. Suggestions and advice were given by colleagues and friends, and I would like to acknowledge Linda Borla, Ken Reay, Frank Heron, Peter Griggs and Ian Corrie in that regard. Not least I thank my wife Bethy and children Sally, Peter and Kylie in their forbearance of my appetite for this particularly magical history tour.

David W. Moore,
Golden West College,
California,
Summer 2005

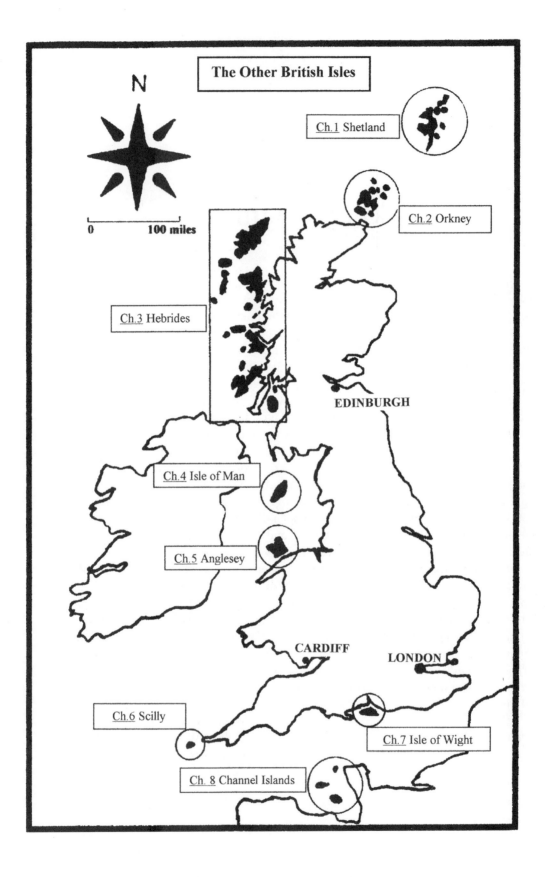

The Other British Isles

N

0   100 miles

Ch.1 Shetland

Ch.2 Orkney

Ch.3 Hebrides

EDINBURGH

Ch.4 Isle of Man

Ch.5 Anglesey

CARDIFF

LONDON

Ch.6 Scilly

Ch.7 Isle of Wight

Ch. 8 Channel Islands

Contents

List of Maps

Preface

British history is not what it used to be. Valid questions about selection and organization of material were raised decades ago, not least of them questions about histories of England masquerading as British history. England and Britain are not synonyms and the horizons of Shakespeare's "blessed plot" have rolled back to accommodate other parts. Yet there is more to it than adding Scotland and Wales to the mix. Britain is an archipelago nation, though history readers might be forgiven for not appreciating it: such is the ease with which the off-islands slip through the fingers of historical reporting. Although small pieces of history individually, the outer-island aggregate is not insignificant. Over half a million people make homes there, and their earliest habitations are among the oldest anywhere in Europe. Accessory to the main event at best and sometimes ignored altogether, the offshore assumes center stage here.

The UK Ordnance Survey counts a mightily impressive 6,289 offshore islands around mainland Britain,[1] ranging from the likes of the Isle of Wight with 132,000 residents to thousands of tiny islets and rocks that are little more than resting perches for tired seagulls. The names compose creative couplets like Man and Muck, Eigg and Rum, Sark and Scilly, Yell and Hoy, Skye and Fair Isle, Rona and Rockall, and so on, but this book is not a gazetteer. It explores only those islands supporting significant populations over millennia. Eight groupings of archipelagoes and single islands present themselves, stretching over 800 miles from north to south: Shetland, Orkney, the Hebrides, Isle of Man, Anglesey, Scilly, Isle of Wight and the Channel Islands. It is an untried permutation. A number of histories have been written about specific islands but none has attempted such a range in one sweep or narrated the entire period of occupation. Thomas Jefferson argued that the tree of liberty should be refreshed from time to time and so it is with history, not with the blood of tyrants in this case but the fuel of new perspectives.

There are marked differences between mainland and islands—more intimate communities, a different experience of history, a plethora of languages. A variety of sub-cultures have ebbed and flowed off Britain's shore since the dawn of farming. England's Stonehenge may get the attention but the lesser-known prehistoric treasures of Orkney's Skara Brae and Maes Howe comprise some of the most remarkable Neolithic evidence anywhere in Europe. Its dynamic community once stood at the

1

far-northern head of an important zone of ritual monuments and sea trade. Several thousand years later the Romans were so impressed with the Isle of Wight that they built at least seven villas within its confines, inducing a bustling hive of activity, a nodal center for continental exchange. A thousand years after that, the Isle of Man was at the epicenter of an influential Irish Sea realm, embracing the Hebrides, though it barely gets a mention in the rush to explain the Norman conquest of England. These Celtic islands were breeding grounds of a unique British Norseness, the Scandinavian impact more pervasive than nationalistic Scottish and Welsh histories typically allow. Medieval courts at Aberffraw on Anglesey and Loch Finlaggan on Islay once pulsed with the adrenaline of their powerful communities and a retinue of poets and musicians, but nary a mention appears in standard histories. The Channel Islands meanwhile harbored a peculiar Anglo-French culture, last remnants of a cross–Channel feudal empire begun with William the Conqueror, beleaguered for centuries in a tug-of-war: French-speaking but recognizing English monarchs as their heads of state.

At least six different languages other than English were spoken for centuries offshore, unifying extraneous communities and fostering unique identities. This is a conservative estimate, formulated from knowledge of speech that lasted long enough to be chronicled. Four of them are Celtic languages— Scots Gaelic, Manx, Welsh and Cornish — spoken respectively in the Hebrides, Isle of Man, Anglesey and Scilly Isles. The others have a mixed heritage — the Dgernesiais and Jèrriais of the Channel Islands are Norman-French dialects while Norn once spoken in Shetland and Orkney was a form of Old Norse. If we were to take the round date of A.D. 1000, then only on the Isle of Wight would a strain of English have been heard and even this, foreign to the modern ear.

There is a strong macro dimension to this study, an acknowledgment of the wider context in which the islands evolved. The objective is to illuminate historical events, not isolate them. In this respect the book belongs to that genre of histories that have broken the nation-state mold. Hugh Kearney's pioneering *The British Isles: A History of Four Nations* (1989) was one of the first, proposing England, Scotland, Wales and Ireland as a historical unit in which various cultures struggled for supremacy and survival for thousands of years. Norman Davies' *The Isles: A History* (1999) likewise broke with convention, overturning English exclusivity, rewriting William the Conqueror as Guillaume le Conquérant to the annoyance of purists, de–Englishing an age when the ruling class spoke a form of French, placing the scepter'd isle within a wider Europe. Both strategies invigorate the subject, addressing English, Welsh, Scots and Irish as inhabitants of a cultural region, without negating England's eventual dominance. Britain and Ireland feature not as self-contained islands, entire of themselves, but as pieces of the continent, no less diminished by it, but "a part of the main" nonetheless. So it is with the smaller islands.

Inspiration came by going there, by visiting most of the islands in this book, living up to that hackneyed but still critical phrase about the importance of the "three L's" to the telling of history: location, location, location. Francis Bacon did not idly recommend the inductive method as a road to truth. Field observations are invaluable. Geography is a historical document and I credit it as a primary instructional experience, tramping through what A.J. Toynbee called in *A Study of History*, in another context, "the intelligible fields of study." There are absolutes in history, things happened, and confirmation is found by going to see what is left. A history that is composed entirely indoors is an anorexic history.

The sight of Iona, a sixth century holy island in the Inner Hebrides, caught even the not-easily-impressed Dr. Johnson by surprise. "To abstract the mind from all local emotion would be impossible ... and foolish," he wrote on his 1773 tour of the Hebrides, moved to be on ground he felt "dignified by wisdom and virtue."[2] It may be isolated in today's demographics but Iona once was a much-visited fount of British Christianity. Aubrey Burl, a leading authority on megalithic monuments, painstakingly located, measured and listed around four hundred stone circles in Britain, Ireland and Brittany but was not so jaded by it all as to ignore the aesthetics. Phobull Finn, an oval ring on North Uist in the Outer Hebrides, he described as "one of the loveliest settings of any stone circle, strangely beautiful on its hillside of bracken and heather overlooking Langass Loch and distances of tiny lochs, machair bright with water lilies, marsh marigolds and orchids, overflown by lapwings, thinly whistling dunlins and oystercatchers."[3] The compass of ancient habitat can still be a living thing. Anyone who has witnessed midwinter sunset at Maes Howe or walked around the amphitheater of hills in which sits Islay's Loch Finlaggan, home of the medieval lordship of the isles, will testify to it. To see the cylindrical towers and round turrets of Muness Castle on Unst in Shetland, most northerly castle in the British Isles, is to appreciate the far reach of the castle phenomenon: Shetland may be remote but it is a part of Europe. To see German World War II evidence on British territory, on Guernsey and Jersey, a unique phenomenon of itself, is invaluable to discussion of the Channel Islanders' predicament, torn between resistance and collaboration under Nazi occupation.

Sentiments about how we experience small islands differ but many have commented on their human-like feel, the familiar way they slip about our shoulders. The British writer John Fowles thought they related "to the human body closer than any other geographical conformation of land."[4] When American author John McPhee returned to the Hebridean isle of his ancestors Colonsay, he found its physical perspectives similar to its human ones, "less a small town than like a large lifeboat" he observed, where "friend and enemy dwell in the same skin."[5] Perhaps it's the resolute separateness of islands that feeds our singularity, although how we experience that insularity may stand in stark contrast. Small islands evoke liberating feelings in some and trigger claustrophobia in others. To modern American travel writer Paul Theroux, they are "the ultimate refuge — a magic and unsinkable world."[6] A century earlier his Victorian explorer equivalent Sir Richard Burton likened them to prisons, wishing for a swallow's wings to escape. Some have seen islands as a threat (or an antidote) to civilization itself, unleashing primitive instincts as in William Golding's *Lord of the Flies*. Daniel Defoe's *Robinson Crusoe* has been variously interpreted as imperialistic or redemptive, a desert island experience with a personal awakening.

Contemporary island life is a medley of rural simplicity and urban sophistication. The latter is mostly present where there are well-heeled new residents and regular tourists. All the islands endured despotic landowners for centuries, many of them disinterested absentees whose vice-like grip on resources and inheritance dis-possessed countless generations of any chance of self-improvement. Memorabilia can be found aplenty in island bookshops but the nostalgia-loaded imagery of a cozy idyll masks the harshness of working lives and spartan conditions. The island tem-perament defies generalization. Exclusivity and intransigence are often presumed, a disconnect from the march of time, as in much-publicized corporal punishments handed out in the courts of the Isle of Man in the 1970s, padlocking of gates to chil-dren's playgrounds on Sundays by the Lord's Day Observance Society in the Outer Hebrides, or banning of automobiles on Sark in the Channel Islands. Equally it's hardly a surprise to discover that close-knit communities guard their secrets. Paul Theroux found that "everyone knew where everything was" on islands "and if you didn't [then] you had no business there."[7] On the other hand islanders can be expan-sive and worldly, as the innovative global marketing of offshore financial and corpo-rate services in the Channel Islands and Isle of Man demonstrate, a strategy earning both rich country economic profiles by 2000. Insularity and innovation are not mutu-ally exclusive. Faraway Orkney had the first public library in Scotland in 1693. By 1900 smuggling Scilly had reinvented itself as a major supplier of commercial flowers to London's Covent Garden. The open-air rock music festivals on the Isle of Wight in 1969 and 1970 attracting hundreds of thousands of paying fans were unprece-dented, pulling in more visitors over two weekends than in millennia.

Living where land and sea meet drives a special dynamic; the people share per-ils, benefits, values, and beliefs, a phenomenon Barry Cunliffe, Oxford Professor of European Archaeology, defines as an "oceanic mentality" in his *Facing the Ocean: The Atlantic and Its Peoples* (2001), a study of kinship among peoples of the Atlantic seaboard. Geography does condition mindsets and as such should not be underes-timated. The bond may be constructive as in the megaliths of the fourth millennium B.C., or contentious, if the tales of the marauding Viking *Orkneyinga Saga* are any guide. In the later 20th century it has brought the smaller islands together in cama-raderie through sports. A bi-annual Inter-Island Games was first held on the Isle of Man in 1985 with seven sports and fifteen small islands participating. The event has since gone from strength to strength and the Shetland Games 2005 anticipate fifteen sports and twenty-four competing islands, many from Britain's offshore but others as far flung as St. Helena and the Falkland Islands in the South Atlantic, insular in competitive entry but as one in their exceptionalism.

---

    1. Ordnance Survey Geo Facts (http://www.ordnancesurvey.co.uk/).
    2. *Samuel Johnson and James Boswell: A Journey to the Western Islands of Scotland and The Journal of a Tour to the Hebrides,* Levi, Peter ed. (Penguin Classics, 1984), 141.
    3. Aubrey Burl, *A Guide to the Stone Circles of Britain, Ireland and Brittany* (Yale University Press, 1995), 152.
    4. John Fowles, *Islands* (Little, Brown, 1978), 12.
    5. John McPhee, *The Crofter and the Laird* (Noonday Press, 17th printing 1995), 48–49.
    6. Paul Theroux, *The Happy Isles of Oceania: Paddling the Pacific* (Putnam, 1992), 503.
    7. Paul Theroux, 433.

1

Shetland: "Ultima Thule"?

"In later years a new age will come in which the Ocean shall relax its hold over the world and a vast land shall lie open to view ... and Thule will not be the last country on earth"— Seneca *Medea*

The 14-hour ferry service from Aberdeen on the northeastern coast of Scotland to Shetland is the longest scheduled in British waters, affording enough time to reflect on cruder vessels once braving these hostile seas. A force nine gale is one thing with modern stabilizers and heated cabins but quite another in a Viking galley where the only protection was sealskins and the instant anesthetic of a North Sea wind. The overnight voyage is fleeting in summer with a late dusk dimming of the sky around midnight known locally as the *simmer dim*. In the winter months, ships' lights pierce a vast northern darkness. Shetland was conceived some 12,000 years ago, in the retreat of the last Ice Age. As rising seas flooded peninsular Europe, a hundred or so hilltops survived to break the waves along the 60th parallel, but its mapping fate is to be forever misplaced. Most map scales don't accommodate its far-northerly position, dragging the archipelago 200 miles south to be boxed ignominiously off Scotland. About 15 islands are inhabited and most of the 22,000 residents (2001 UK Census) live on the biggest of them, named Mainland. Nominally Scottish, Shetland derives its name from the Old Norse *Hjaltland*, and the principal town Lerwick (Norse: *Leir-vik*) maintains a Scandinavian inclination: *The Shetland Times* runs a Norwegian news digest column, Icelandic dictionaries sell in bookshops, and streets are named for St. Olav, King Erik and King Harald. Norse place-names are everywhere — Hammavoe, Burravoe, Trondra, Lunnasting, Sullom Voe, Jarlshof, to name a few.

Shetland holds the all-time UK record for wind speed, tracked at 194 mph on January 1, 1992, and the weather can be harsh with rain-lashed gales an everyday threat. Fortunately the warming wash of the North Atlantic Drift, a Gulf Stream extension, has a modifying effect and winter temperatures are less severe than imagined, though without those currents it would be as cold as Moscow. A denuded rolling interior of dark heather clad hills provides little respite from the wind with tree foliage conspicuously absent, blankets of dark peat moorland thickened millennia

SHETLAND

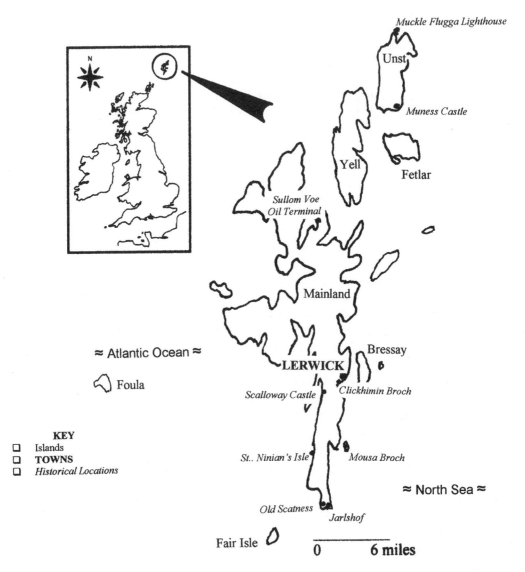

Muckle Flugga Lighthouse

Unst

Muness Castle

Yell

Fetlar

Sullom Voe
Oil Terminal

Mainland

≈ Atlantic Ocean ≈

Bressay

⌂ Foula

LERWICK

Scalloway Castle

Clickhimin Broch

KEY
- Islands
- **TOWNS**
- *Historical Locations*

St.. Ninian's Isle

Mousa Broch

≈ North Sea ≈

Old Scatness

Jarlshof

Fair Isle

0   6 miles

ago. The sea is omnipresent, coastlines so indented by cliffs and small wave-lashed
fjords that no spot is more than four miles away from it. Separation from the rest of
Britain has produced natural history differences—there are no voles, a subspecies of
wren has evolved, and half the world's population of Great Skuas (seagulls) breed in
countless seabird colonies along the coasts. The diving scavenger habits of the skuas
elicit a mixed reaction, but a more positive response is accorded to Shetland ponies,
smallest of the horse family yet hardy enough to be a high demand harness animal.
Shetland has little cultivable land, and crops struggle. This is sheep country, and
another export strain with a far-flung fame, Shetland sheepdogs, keep order.

The Early Settlers

Bands of hunter-gatherers colonized newly vegetated northern lands during the centuries of post-glacial warming and may have explored what became Shetland, but the evidence is long since drowned. In a warmer Neolithic Age, birch and pine forest cover extended to Orkney,[1] the neighbor archipelago to the south, and Shetland probably had woods and certainly more arable land than now. The Neolithic denotes the period when agriculture emerged, and in Shetland's case this would mean the later fourth millennium B.C. Evidence of it survives because the land was never intensely domesticated, a happy state of affairs for archaeologists. Contractors working on the runway at Sumburgh Airport on the southern tip of Mainland in 1977 came across human remains near the control tower. Forensic analysis revealed 18 adults and children interred with grave goods. Radiocarbon dating placed their lives between 3235 and 3135 B.C., over 5,000 years ago. At least 60 Neolithic stone-using farming sites have been identified to date; Val Turner's recent book details finds[2] and research and discovery is ongoing.

The material evidence presents multi-island farm communities growing oats and *bere* (an early form of barley), herding livestock and fishing. The presence of cattle and sheep is some testament to their ingenuity; the animals were probably tethered down and ferried to the islands in little oval skin-covered wicker-frame *curraghs* or coracles, commonly ascribed as the shipping of that era. The early inhabitants fashioned hardware from readily available steatite or soapstone, schist and sandstone. Some of it is displayed in the Shetland Museum in Lerwick — plowshares, sharpening tools, querns for grinding grains, fishing-line weights, pots and lids, hammers, arrows, and axes. Some technology was exported. "Made-in-Shetland" polished axeheads have shown up in digs in Orkney and Scotland, and Shetland steatite was widely traded for millennia. Marine resources kept Shetlanders busy too as bone, blubber and oil were utilized for domestic purpose and shellfish and mackerel shoals in the vöes supplemented diet.

In the same vicinity as the 1977 human finds at the foot of Mainland is Jarlshof, prehistoric and medieval Shetland in microcosm. A 19th century gale ripped away its sandy cover and over 4,000 years of continuous settlement has been unearthed, dwellings built and rebuilt by countless generations of farmers and fishers. The Norse name (Jarlshof = "Earl's hall") is misleading. Jarlshof is named for a nearby 17th century house included by Sir Walter Scott in his 1822 novel *The Pirate*, but these homesteaders were there in the second millennium B.C., perhaps even earlier, building small oval-shaped stone walled dwellings with conical turf roofs. An interior wheelhouse design developed over time, so-called because alcoves or rooms were set off a communal area like spokes around a wheel-hub. Their livestock was sheltered within the living space, too precious to be left unprotected. The Norse eventually settled there and Jarlshof was still important in the 16th century, when Stewart earls had a medieval hall built. Early Shetland farm dwellings generally stood separately or in mini-clusters, less nucleated than modern villages.

Farmsteads provide one insight and mortuary methods offer another. Interment has long been a preoccupation of the living. Shetland has no elaborate chambered tomb megaliths or large-stone complexes as does Orkney, which may infer smaller or less organized populations, but effort and time were expended on interment nevertheless. Neolithic Shetlanders built heel-shaped stone cairns, temple mounds in effect, to describe burial space. An entrance façade was sometimes added to enhance appearance, and these stonewall structures may have had timbered roofs. The best known, at Stanydale in western Mainland, is described as a temple. Excavated field boundaries and three ruined dwellings in the vicinity indicate a temple-village, occupation of which is dated to the later Neolithic. Such structures represent a long-term investment by communities and as such are a good sign of successful sedentary economic life. The largest standing stone left is on Fetlar, the tall thin Ripple Stone, maybe a kind of ancient navigational aid, though rising sea levels have changed coastlines and that interpretation is not a certainty. The graves and stones register some sort of sanctification of space, a theme encountered with even more intensity on Orkney, and considered in more depth in that chapter.

If the later Neolithic has given up some of its secrets, the subsequent Bronze Age does not. Long stretches of mysterious time appear in prehistoric Shetland, particularly the later second millennium B.C. Bronze was never worked during the Bronze Age, and the bronze objects that have shown up are dated to the Iron Age. There are veins of copper but no proof they were worked. At least part of this dark age may be explained by climate deterioration. A combination of falling temperatures and rising precipitation is known to have occurred in Britain and Ireland from around 1200 B.C., and some sites were likely abandoned as surface water led to decomposition and carbonization of vegetation. Blanket peat bog progressively carpeted island interiors, hardly propitious for tree growth or farming, and soil acidity reduced food production to redistribute settlement. We can only speculate as to how it impacted political arrangements and beliefs, but catastrophe may help explain why Shetlanders became clustered in and around the tall cylindrical stone tower-houses known as *brochs* by the last millennium B.C., sited along coasts away from peat-bound interiors.

The Broch Dwellers

The *broch* is peculiar to the Highlands and Islands zone of Scotland, a region hard hit by climatic change. Around 500 have been mapped. All are in areas blighted by peat and deficient in timber but well supplied with stone. The builders and occupants left no written record, the fact that the brochs sheltered animals and humans is about as much as can be said with any certainty. Were they homes of seafaring people who fished more than they farmed, or of land-based farmers who feared raids by sea pirates? We may never know. What is clear is that they were a new phenomenon, a taller adaptation of so-called Atlantic roundhouses, compact circular farmsteads found through upland Atlantic Europe. Some *brochs* date in conception back to the later Bronze Age. The Celtic word equates with the Germanic *borg* or fort, but the military connotation is misleading. The towering height of *brochs* may infer colossal insecurity, but evidence does not support especially chaotic or warlike times. Perhaps they were the high-minded celebratory symbols of recovery after the catastrophe that destroyed their ancestors? What can be concluded is that they were at the core of farming communities and functioned in accordance with those interests. Their distribution is at least partly explained by better grazing land along the coasts. They were there long before the Romans came to Britain, built before and during the period of prehistory now labeled Celtic (from c. 600 B.C.). Many have credited construction to Picts (they are still called "Pict hooses" by some) because brochs are found in areas assumed Pictish, but such claims are more convenient than they are definitive. Archaeology reports *broch* abandonment before the word *Picti*, a Roman epithet for northerly British tribes from A.D. 297, was even coined.

Scores of *brochs* have been located down the length of Shetland in a chain from Burrafirth on northerly Unst to the foot of Mainland. The best, indeed the best to be seen anywhere, is on the sheltered lee-side of solitary Mousa ("Moosa") Island. The 46-foot sandstone sentinel is immediately visible to the modern visitor, looking like a derelict cooling tower from some forgotten Industrial Revolution plant. Powerful winds have whipped around it for millennia, and the fact it is still standing is tribute to the efficacy of its cylindrical design. Mousa features in two medieval Icelandic sagas. In *Egil's Saga* a couple fleeing from Norway were shipwrecked on Mousa Island and married and wintered there. In *Orkneyinga Saga*, Mousa features as a hideout for Erlend the Young and his lover, the mother of Harold Maddadarson, Earl of Orkney. Eventually the enraged earl caught up with them, but "it was not an easy place to attack"[3] and Harald gave up, although he did grant permission for the elopers to have a happy ending, or so the saga goes. A *broch* also stood at Jarlshof but it is buried beneath the Stewarts' medieval hall. Nearby at Old Scatness, the Shetland Amenity Trust and University of Bradford (England) have excavated another. At least a thousand years of pre-*broch* occupation has come to light and crescent shaped symbols on pebbles stones and silver coinage indicate a Pictish and Norse presence after abandonment. It is the thought of such protracted continuity that is compelling — the *broch* being but one (interesting) phase within millennia of settlement in one place.

The most accessible *broch* is at Clickhimin, positioned on an island in a small loch (lake) on the southern outskirts of Lerwick. Reachable by a short causeway, it is somewhat incongruous in its modern surrounds of housing tract and a leisure center. Yet even in its semi-ruinous state, parts of walls still stand 32 feet high. A farming community lived there in the early first millennium B.C. and the *broch* evolved out of oval-shaped hut dwellings (as did those at Jarlshof and Old Scatness) with interior galleries and a stairway within its circular exterior wall by A.D. 100. Excavations in the 1960s generated great interest when sling stones and Greek influenced pottery designs were found. The finds are dated to the fifth or fourth century B.C.[4] Apparently far-flung Shetland was not quite so far off the beaten track.

True North

The Mediterranean world and metal-rich Atlantic Europe were in regular trade contact in the last millennium B.C. and a Greek mariner, Pytheas of Massalia, circumnavigated Britain in the fourth century B.C. He may have visited Shetland. We know of his voyage only through secondhand sources since his own report *Peri Tou Okeanu* ("On the Ocean") is lost to posterity. Massalia — the ancient Greek colony that is now Marseilles — was in the market for Cornish tin and Baltic amber, one possible reason for his voyage. His careful celestial observations and mathematical calculations indicate scientific interest too. Ancient narrators considered him worthy of inclusion in their histories but were unconvinced by his claim to have traveled to the ends of the habitable world, reporting it as an interesting yarn rather than scientific discovery. Modern scholars accord him more respect, noting his solar observations of position and path as later geographers' method for calculating longitudinal lines.

Pytheas's redactors wrote of a place six sailing days north of Britain and one day south of frozen seas, where the sun went down for only two or three hours at night, a place Pytheas termed "Thule." The name and place excited imaginations. Virgil phrased it "Ultima Thule" and Seneca immortalized it as the last place on earth, a synonym for the precipice of the world. Thule became fused with the Hyperboreans of classical myth, revered as the seat of those legendary dwellers beyond the north wind, the superhuman order believed to be on top of the universe. His actual whereabouts remains a mystery. Was he experiencing a "simmer dim" in Shetland? Or was he even further north in the Faeroe Islands, Iceland, Greenland, or even off the Norwegian coast? Strabo (c. 64 B.C.–A.D. 21), an Asiatic Greek scholar who sought to synthesize the geographical knowledge of his time, discusses Pytheas, but was not impressed by his northerly claim. "The things Pytheas said about it [Thule] and other places nearby are fabrications," he decided, "as is clear from [his] comments about familiar areas. He lied about most of these, as was said earlier, so it is clear he is an even worse liar about out-of-the-way places."[5] Poor Pytheas. Strabo gave him scant credibility. Posterity has been kinder. The arctic Thule people, ancestors of the modern Inuit, kept the name alive — there is a Thule district of Greenland — and there is no doubt about the pub that greets thirsty sailors disembarking in Lerwick's small boats harbor: "The Thule."

During the A.D. 80s a Roman fleet circumnavigated Britain under orders from Governor Julius Agricola. There is no evidence that these sailors landed on or even saw Shetland, but some second century Roman items are on display in the Shetland Museum — fragments of fine glass cups from Clickhimin, pieces of Samian-ware pots, and two vases of Emperor Hadrian — with trade contact the likely explanation for their presence. By the early fifth century when the Romans left Britain for good, the *brochs* were no longer epicenters. The structures were abandoned though not necessarily the sites, as Jarlshof demonstrates. Whether Shetland was the elusive Thule remains unresolved, but in the post–Roman era it lay on the northern edge of Pictish territory.

Picts and Christians

Association with the Picts is in the form of inscribed memorial stones that archaeologists designate as Pictish. A seventh century stone found on Mainland at

Mail, depicting an axe-wielding, tunic-wearing figure with a dog-like head, resembles other "Pictland" stone carvings, and early Christian stone-cross slabs found at Papil and West Burra also bear a Pictish design. A pair of inscribed pebble stones thought to be Pictish was found at Old Scatness in 1998. The Picts were a late Roman and post–Roman tribal confederation occupying parts of northern Britain, and since Shetland finds are not extensive, they will be discussed more fully in the Orkney chapter. The few finds there are, however, at least suggest Shetland was part of a wider realm. The surest indicator of that is the presence of Christianity.

Adventurous monks sailing north from Orkney introduced the Mediterranean originated faith either before or during the eighth century. Among early centers were Mail, Lunna, and St. Ninian's Isle. The latter, a tiny monastic isle hooked to midwestern Mainland by a shell-sand isthmus, is of special interest. It is dedicated to Ninian, a fourth century Romano-British (Welsh?) monk, who founded a monastery in Galloway in southwestern Scotland over three centuries earlier (397). It's unlikely he traveled as far as Shetland, but according to the eighth century Anglo-Saxon scribe Bede it was he who converted southern Picts,[6] so perhaps his stature with them helped carry his name north. The low ruins of a 12th century church can still be seen on the isle. Beneath it are traces of an earlier chapel, one that may go back to the eighth century. Excavations in 1955 directed by Professor O'Dell of the University of Aberdeen dug up a nave, apse, and altar plus seven post-stones, five of which were carved with Pictish symbols. Three years later in 1958 came one of those moments all archaeologists hunger for when a larch box buried beneath a broken sandstone cross was found with a significant deposit of value. A local schoolboy working on the dig as a volunteer turned it over. Within it lay 28 decorated silver objects— a treasure hoard of bowls, dishes, a spoon, sword pommel, cones, brooches, and the jawbone of a porpoise. The contents are dated to c. 800. It is thought they were buried beneath the floor of the earlier chapel and were gifts to the early church. A favored explanation is that it was hidden there during Viking attacks, but to the chagrin of Shetlanders it's no longer in Shetland hands, housed instead in the National Museum of Scotland in Edinburgh. There is a replica set in Lerwick's Shetland Museum.

Vikings

As Shetland came within the Christian fold, it also became part of an expanding pagan Norse empire. Bands of Viking Norsemen (*vikingr* = "hit-and-run raider") were active around the Shetland and Orkney coasts from the ninth century. Many of them came from southwestern Norway during the time of Harold Haarfager (Harald Finehair), a late ninth century king who unified Norway by defeating other petty rulers. Those dispossessed and displaced from this upheaval sought new economic opportunities across the North Sea. A mix of exiles and émigrés, they have long been misrepresented in history: the horned helmets belong in Wagnerian opera. Modern opinion divides over the bloodthirsty terrorism attributed to them, a reputation arguably exaggerated in documentation by their Christian victims. Monastic scribes were unlikely to feel charitable toward thieving pagans. Tales of *berserkers* working up a battle-frenzy, fighting impervious to pain, have thrilled and appalled for centuries. Skeptics note that the horrors described by medieval clerics employ a similar proselytizing tone to that of St. Augustine in his response to heathens sacking early fifth century Rome. Of course there is truth to it, monasteries were sacked, but we should not overlook the probability of locals looting ecclesiastical property also. The church's lay benefactors had their enemies at home too. A revisionist version of events accommodates archaeological evidence, noting Norse roles as migrant farmers, sea traders and town builders (they began the first Irish towns), presenting them as wealth creators as well as plunderers of it.

One aspect rarely disputed about Vikings is seamanship and shipbuilding skills. The Viking ship defined the Viking age above all else. Galleys ranged from sleek warships (the famed longships) to broader craft capable of shipping settlers, possessions, livestock and trade-goods. Hulls were clinker-built; that is, they were constructed from overlapping planks joined with iron rivets, sterns elegantly curved to cope with heavy rolling seas. The prows on the best warships depicted heads of snakes or dragons. Powered by sails and oars, the average of them carried 60 fighting men. They navigated northern waters with apparent ease by observing bird flight, wind and wave direction, and sun compass, set to follow sun shadows when cloud cover permitted. If the wind blew unexpectedly from the wrong direction then they went in the wrong direction! They must have been used to that. These were open boats with no below-decks and those on board were largely unprotected from the elements. Hides and skins provided a minimal cover. Ominously, as they neared foreign shores, no inlets or rivers were closed to them; their shallow drafts and determined crews saw to that.

Norse settlement on Shetland was well underway by 900, the best known at the aforementioned Jarlshof, but also at Underhoull and Sandwick on Unst, all three fittingly coastal. The newcomers quickly acclimated as herders. Fishing was as instinctive as drawing breath, and rich breeding seas may have been another colonization incentive. Unfortunately artifacts are disappointing in their quantity. A brooch and fine bone combs are all that is on display in the Shetland Museum. Clibberswick is the best-documented Viking period grave but it was dug up as long ago as 1863.[7] Nothing much remains of their turf and timbered dwellings above ground and we are dependent on excavation of foundations: typically rectangular with a central hearth for peat fires, easy to differentiate from earlier circular and oval designs. The livestock housed at one end made a smelly form of central heating (still no chimneys yet) but the best protection against rustling. Recent incomplete investigations of stone and turf enclosures on the Kame of Isbister, a barely accessible rocky promontory off the north coast of Mainland once thought a monastic retreat, revealed signs of a substantial sedentary Norse population (around 100) and the strong suggestion of a Viking ship burial site.

The impact on Shetland is open to interpretation since the extent of the pre–Norse population is not clear. It is unlikely to have been more numerous than in Neolithic times, possibly less because of *broch* abandonment. We should not rule out maritime contact between Shetland (or Orkney) and the Scandinavian shores before the Viking phase of history. Scenes of mayhem and slaughter have been the popular view but not necessarily the accurate one. Whether Vikings saw themselves as an invading cultural force is also debatable, even though that is what history generally reports. Co-existence is not implausible. Each instance of settlement needs to be addressed on its own evidence, rather than generalized rushes to judgment. The results from the Old Scatness dig, for example, suggest less outright demolition and more occupation in a continuing settlement, even if it did take fighting to secure residence. Norse houses excavated in the 1960s at Underhoull near an old *broch* were found above a Pictish period settlement of round houses. What is probable is that surviving Pictish Shetlanders became secondary to the dominant Norse population: that much is clear in the impact on language. A form of Old Norse called Norn became the speech of Shetland, though how long it took to wipe out the earlier Pictish (Celtic?) language is not understood. Norn is the least known of medieval British tongues, although it lasted until the early 20th century. As part of the Germanic subgroup of languages, its closest relatives are Icelandic and the speech of the Faeroe Isles, both Scandinavian colonies. Modern Shetland speech or "Shetlandic" is a Scots-English dialect, but many words of Norse origin live on in flora and fauna, place-names and farm and marine terminology.

Christianity was present when the Norse arrived, as we have seen, although exactly how influential it was is again unclear. It seems unlikely there were rich pickings from monastic settlements and hermitages, St. Ninian's treasure notwithstanding, and the faith may have waned as traditional Scandinavian beliefs prevailed. According to saga, a great grandson of Harald Finehair, Olaf Tryggvasson (King Olaf I) of Norway, appeared in Orkney in 995, to declare for Christianity, ordering all to follow likewise on pain of death.[8] Yet fifty years or more passed before we know with any certainty that Christianity had returned to Orkney and by extension to Shetland. The revival had more to do with King Olaf II (r. 1015–1028) and his acclaimed effort to convert fellow–Norse, a move likely related to his determination to secure political unity. A singular Christian society was easier to rule than groups of individualistic pagans. Olaf II's death in battle is submerged in folklore (he became St. Olaf) but an instrumental factor in turning more and more Norse from the old beliefs. New churches were built, old Christian sites re-adopted and diocesan organization imposed. Shetland was included in the new diocese of Orkney with an archdeacon appointed to represent the bishop in Shetland. One of his first acts was to levy a tithe or church tax, and a *teind* barn (the building used to store goods collected as tithe payment) has been identified at Tingwall on Mainland.

A Norwegian Dependency 1194–1379

Bergen, a port on the Norwegian coast some 220 miles east, was the political and commercial center of medieval Norway, and Shetland was a useful link in the chain reaching from it to colonial Norse in the Faeroe Islands, Iceland and Greenland. Norse knowledge of those places may well have been learned from seafaring Shetlanders. Shetland's orbit remained firmly Scandinavian during the 13th and 14th centuries, even as Orkney grew closer to Scotland. A reason lies in an uprising in 1194 when Shetlanders led by an Orkney *jarl* (earl), Harold Maddadarson, conspired against Sverre Sigurdarson, a Faeroese opportunist who had taken the Norwegian throne. Conspiracies such as this were not unusual, part of an ongoing process of checking power, but unfortunately for the Shetlanders, it was Sverre who won. As a reprisal, he detached Shetland from the Orcadian earldom and ruled it directly, demanding that the church submit to his leadership too, provoking bitterness until his death in 1202.

Shetland was more than just a friendly haven for Norse en voyage to Iceland. Contacts with a wider German-speaking world grew as news of its prime location in rich fishing grounds spread. Ocean currents create excellent feeding conditions for cod, haddock, whiting, mackerel and herring and Hanseatic merchants began to show up bringing salt, textiles, beers and spirits to trade for wool and dried fish. Business with the *Hansa*, an association of Germanic towns formed for mutual commercial interests, helped Shetland's economy progress from self-sufficiency mode to one with a greater element of foreign exchange. It has been a popular boast that Amsterdam, a Hanseatic city, was built on money made from Shetland herring.

Political boundaries in Britain meanwhile were in flux. Forces accumulated to change destiny there long before the rise of King Sverre. Duke William of Normandy invaded southern Britain in 1066 and a new Norman-French elite uprooted the Anglo-Saxon establishment. Ireland, which had escaped Roman conquest, was not immune either. The first of the French Plantagenet kings of England, Henry II, sent a conquering army there in 1171. A little over a century later, Scots nobles fought Edward I to preserve their independence, maintaining a Scottish realm with papal blessing in 1328. The original tribal kingdom of the Scots, begun in the fifth century on the Argyll coast, was not strong enough to rule the new polity, and Norman-French originated families (first Bruce and then Stewart) assumed dynastic kingship. Norman-French influence would be pervasive for the next few centuries and Scotland, like its English neighbor to the south, had a ruling class with French antecedents. Their ascendancy was sustained through primogeniture, in which property inheritance was reserved to the first-born son. The effect was large estates under ruling dynasties with inheritors accepting titles of dukedoms and earldoms from their kings, confirmation of rank in a society increasingly commanded by this landed aristocracy.

The shift from a Norse to a Norman-French patriarchy became evident in the Northern Isles—a collective term for Shetland and Orkney—when intermarriage between influential families from Caithness in northern Scotland and those in Orkney produced a Scots-Norman earl of Orkney in 1379: Henri St. Clair or Henry Sinclair. The earl was also invested with the title lord of Shetland and the two archipelagos were reunited for the first time in almost two centuries. Sinclair had to recognize kings of Norway as his liege lord for his island fiefdom, but in reality Norwegian influence was on the wane. Shetland and Orkney were moving more and more into the Scottish sphere.

A Scottish Fief

Norway lost its independent status in 1397, when the Union of Kalmar united it with Denmark and Sweden under the Danish Crown, in a calculated move to resist the Hanseatic League in the Baltic Sea trade. Kalmar probably did not impact the islanders much. German and Scandinavian merchant and fishing vessels continued to visit. A much more consequential change came in 1468, when a hard-up Danish king, Christian I, pawned both archipelagoes to Scotland to pay the dowry for his daughter's marriage to James III of Scotland. Denmark's intention was always to redeem Shetland and Orkney at some later date, but while overtures to this effect were made for the next 300 years, Scotland never entertained them, and caught in a new net, islanders faced different definitions of land tenure and inheritance. The custom of property subdivision among all siblings had created a patchwork of small lots, but the new politics demanded one predetermined landowner to consolidate power. Centuries of Norse *udal* custom whereby freemen owned their land *allodially* (absolutely) were under threat. The change didn't happen overnight, but by the 17th century the premise on which land was held had been profoundly altered, dissolving the old social structure.

Some explanation of the prevailing *udal* custom is necessary. As Christianity spread the thrall or slave underclass diminished and *udal* freeholds increased. *Udal* custom permitted tenure in perpetuity, allowing settlers the right to enclose and till land without obligation to a superior. Only the communal grazing pasture or *scattald* was taxed and *scat* (duty) paid to rulers. Inheritance extended rights to all siblings with daughters allotted portions half that of the sons. Small land-lots proliferated, hardly conducive to growth in our own age but in medieval Shetland it generated equitable land distribution, less rigid social hierarchies, and kinfolk stayed together. In the islands, as in traditional societies anywhere, economics was subordinate to community interest. Disputes fluctuated according to political and economic circumstance, but most were heard at the *lawting*, an open-air parliament at which free men could influence legislation. Tingwall or "the place of the court," a village between Lerwick and Scalloway, is a modern place-name reminder. *Udal* custom extended to seashores and to tidal water, a provision never abolished in modern law, though eroded in a 1958 British court judgment concerning ownership of the St. Ninian's Treasure. Such "sea-rights" continue to raise legal questions.

The challenge of Scots annexation was about accommodating legal concepts that defined land less in terms of community value and more in a military context. The pivotal feudal power relationship was between lord and vassal. Fiefs were units of land held by vassals from lords conditional on annual fulfillment of obligations, duties often spelled out in military service. Feudalism raised armies and had been around at least a half millennium in this form before it reached Shetland. It was a way to defend territory in an age with little centralized authority. Feudalism grew in Scotland under David I (r. 1124–1153) when he encouraged continental knights to settle in areas where he faced problems, but since the Northern Isles lay outside his realm, Norse customs in Shetland and Orkney remained constitutionally intact. A 1567 Scots law appeared to permit their continuation[9] but enactment itself suggests that traditions were under attack or review. No such law had been necessary before. The Shetlanders were vulnerable from the moment Scots brandished written title. *Udal* land was typically held in unwritten freehold. Property deeds as much as weapons dispossessed Shetlanders. The compliant became landholding tenants obligated by services and payments to their new lairds (a Scots-English term for landlords); those not suitably deferential lost their lands altogether. Some of the biggest villains in this transition, at least villains in Shetland and Orkney folklore, were members of two of Scotland's most prestigious feudal families—Bruces and Stewarts.

The Stewarts: Castles and Infamy (1564–1615)

The Stewarts were the successors of Bruce as Scotland's ruling dynasty. The name derives from the appointment of an Anglo-Norman knight, William Fitz-Allan, to the office of steward during the rule of David I. Fitz-Allan was among the first to be invited to settle and as such was in at the inception of feudal Scotland. The first to become directly involved with Shetland and Orkney was Robert Stewart, an illegitimate son of James V, granted the crown estates of the Northern Isles by his half-sister Mary Queen of Scots in 1564. The position of sheriff was thrown in too. He extended his influence by forcing a later transfer of land with Adam Bothwell, Bishop of Orkney. The former Catholic bishopric had been broken up after the Scottish Protestant Reformation of 1560. In 1581, during the reign of James VI, Robert was given the title earl of Orkney and lord of Shetland, despite pleas to the king about his scurrilous land grabbing. The new earl mostly left administration of Shetland to his equally unpopular half-brother, Lawrence Bruce, a Perthshire laird, who took over the sheriff duties. The admission of this "foreign" office was of itself subjugation. Sheriffs were originally Anglo-Saxon tax collectors or *shire-reeves,* but the office developed larger supervisory responsibilities within Norman-French fiefdom, and Shetland (or Zetland as documentation then called it) had become a subject fief.

The Scots physically imposed themselves in ways the Norse did not, building great stone castles bigger in floor space than *brochs,* grander than the dwellings of the native elite, visual proclamation of a new command society. The infrequent visits of old by the Norse kings did not begin to compare. Lawrence Bruce had Muness Castle built out on Unst's wild southwestern coast in 1598. The most northerly of all British castles, its gaunt looking stone keep survives with a curious Z plan design intact, as if contoured to stand in a wind tunnel. Two Norman-style cylindrical towers were set at diagonal opposites with round turrets in alternate corners and the gunholes positioned to cover castle and courtyard. The defenses did not work so well, however; privateers sacked the place a few decades later. The biggest castle was built by the same architect for Patrick Stewart, inheritor of his father's titles and lands, at Scalloway, a medieval port on western Mainland. The imposing tower house still overlooks the sea, the lord of all it surveyed. Only Shetland's insular geography could counter its centralizing impact. The dispersed nature of multi-island settlement preserved some autonomy, the sea always an arbiter in archipelago politics.

Earl Patrick Stewart took his governance more seriously than his father, intensifying conflict with Shetlanders, but he inherited debts as well as titles and therein lies the root of his local infamy. The unfortunate heirloom was compounded by his taste for spending. Despite meager funds he embarked on another building project, a new palace at Kirkwall in Orkney. Work on Scalloway began in 1599, taking five years to complete, and even in its current state of decay the castle is well worth a look. The surviving tower keep was the earl's residence and a lot more comfortable for him than it appears now with long-gone timbered floors and plaster-covered walls once adorned with woven tapestries and shuttered rooms warmed by peat fire. On a second floor the earl had his own private suite with fireplace, a novel feature in the islands, courtesy of chimney invention, and an en suite latrine closet. Obviously he desired more than defense and put his architect and masons to work on a level of domestic comfort and style unprecedented in Shetland. It is a Renaissance building of sorts.

Earl Patrick recognized Norse customs, at least when it was in his interest to do so. *Scat* was still payable in fish-oil (used for lighting), butter and woolen cloth; and fines punishing physical assault were unchanged, variable according to parts of the body hit. It was the earl who received payment. Smaller offenses continued to be dealt with in each locality and the *lawting* met in Scalloway Castle. There is no evidence to suggest that these courts were improperly run, but as the earl accumulated more debt he used his rank to advocate whichever legal tradition was fiscally advantageous— Norse or Scots. It was this arbitrary manipulation of both judicial systems that got him into trouble. His new penal code increased the number of offenses for which land forfeiture or even death was the punishment. Complaints reached the royal court in Edinburgh. He exercised his prerogative as liege lord by enforcing feudal right to make use of neighbors' tenants in castle construction, allegedly without offering food and drink in return. Local histories report that blood and human hair were used to mix mortar, and whatever the truth of it the stories are a measure of his unpopularity. He was wasteful of resources. Available driftwood was seized for his purpose and an entry in the Court Book of Shetland 1604 records 32 fathoms of peat to heat the castle, another extravagance by inference.

During his earldom the Scottish and English crowns merged to form the United Kingdom (1603) and James VI of Scotland became James I of the United Kingdom of Britain and Ireland. An early decision of the new regime worked against him when the bishopric lands were restored to the Church and the loss of revenue impacted his already hard-pressed purse. The king was not unfriendly but his patience ran thin as the earl's quarrelsome behavior became too outrageous to ignore. In 1608 the earl directed servants to ransack the house and property of William Bruce of Sumburgh, then followed this up by leading a force in an armed raid on Lawrence Bruce's castle at Muness. It was simpler for the king to deal with his fractious vassal than answer the combined wrath of his enemies, and in 1609 Earl Patrick was seized and imprisoned, firstly in Edinburgh and then in Dumbarton.

His imprisonment spelled the beginning of the end of Norse custom in the Northern Isles. A Scottish Act in 1611 abolished what it called "the foreign laws" of Orkney and Shetland, and the extent to which it was precipitated by Earl Patrick's self-serving dual-law practice was made explicit: "Some persons bearing powers of magistracy have these divers years bygone taken upon them to judge the inhabitants … making choice sometimes of foreign laws and sometimes with the proper laws of the kingdom [Scotland] as they find matter of gain and commodity."[10] It is worthy of note that two years earlier James I sought to suppress equally "foreign" Gaelic practices in the Hebrides with the Statutes of Iona (1609). There is a wider context. Both laws sought to bring offshore islands in line with what the Scots king considered a state of civility, although islanders doubtless saw it as servility. The king was determined to assert his prerogative as fountain of justice and landowner supreme, notions that would not have sat well with Shetlanders accustomed to *lawtings* and *udal* rights.

Meanwhile Earl Patrick, impenitent to the last, sent instructions from prison to his son to recover his Orkney estate, knowing it could not be won without a fight. The insurrection of young Robert Stewart did get some support among locals, so not all were anti–Stewart, but he was unable to hold Kirkwall against old enemies, the earl of Caithness and bishop of Orkney. The failed rebellion cost both Stewarts their lives. Robert was hanged in Edinburgh in January 1615 and Earl Patrick was beheaded the following month. James Law, Bishop of Orkney, was installed as the crown's representative in the islands. The despotism persisted anyway as a succession of crown administrators used the law for their own ends and outsiders arbitrarily acquired land. Earl Patrick's removal seems to have changed little in that regard. Shetland was too remote for anyone in higher authority to care much.

The Growth of Lerwick

Scalloway Castle remained the administrative headquarters of Shetland for the rest of the 17th century, serving as law court and quartering parliamentary soldiers during Oliver Cromwell's English Commonwealth in the 1650s. The castle gate was the official site for legal proclamations. By the early 18th century it was in much need of repair and its demise spoke for the village of Scalloway. In 1766 the castle passed to Sir Lawrence Dundas, whose successors were made earls and later marquises of Zetland. They were mostly absentee landlords. When Patrick Neill visited Scalloway in 1806 (*A Tour through some of the islands of Orkney and Shetland*) he found only a few scattered houses in the vicinity of a rundown castle. There was no inn and he noted the paltry provisions of residents. Scalloway's poverty probably spoke for much of the archipelago although the emergent market and harbor at Lerwick was an exception on occasion. Snug within the protective shelter of Bressay Sound, it was already the new center when Neill visited. Fierce Norse king Harald Hardraada rested there during the epic year of 1066 before his defeat and death at the battle of Stamford Bridge, but it had only a handful of residents until Dutch herring fleets began to drop anchor. The temper of the port can be rated by a 1625 court judgment on complaints of prostitution, drunkenness, theft and murder. Since successful markets were rowdy affairs in most places, it seems that Lerwick had found new vigor by the 17th century.

A fort was planned to protect Lerwick's anchorage in 1653 but it is unclear whether it was constructed. During the second Dutch War, a trade war between England and the Dutch Republic, one was built on Bressay Sound in 1665 for Charles II, but it was abandoned in 1668 when that war ended. Dutch warships sacked Lerwick five years later during the third Dutch War, this one caused by Charles II's support of a

French invasion of the Dutch Republic, but market and port recovered. A century later the fort project revived during the later phase of the American War of Independence. The Scots-born renegade and American privateer John Paul Jones led daring raids into British waters in 1778 and 1779 to provide a fresh reason to beef up defenses. The alliance in 1781–1782 of the French, Spanish and Russian navies in the so-called Armed Neutrality (threatening to take up arms if Britain tried to revive failing efforts to hold on to its rebellious American colonies) added more incentive. In the event, Fort Charlotte, named for George III's queen, was unfinished when the 1783 peace treaty was signed and the independent USA recognized. Fort Charlotte has had a fairly uneventful life subsequently. The original armament was removed in 1855. The buildings survive in modified form, having been used for non-military functions for the developing town. It was Lerwick's jail and courthouse from 1837 to 1875 and a customhouse and coastguard station. A variety of guns were mounted on the seaward battery between 1861 and 1910, but no enemies engaged their fire. A British Territorial Army unit and Army cadet force were using the premises more recently.

Acculturation

The fortification of Lerwick was another step in the process of pulling Shetland within the orbit of British politics, but cultural and trade links with Germanic Europe still remained strong in the 18th century. When Shetlanders interacted with Norwegians, Danes, Germans and Dutch, they did so in their own variant of Germanic speech. A new combination of factors had accumulated to undermine this orientation by 1800, however, with maybe one third of the population by then of Scots descent and speaking a Scots-English dialect. Since this community included the political and clerical establishment, other Shetlanders were obligated to learn English, even if they spoke in Norn among themselves. Norn was not written down. Surviving medieval documents are written in Norwegian, weakening Norn's legitimacy at a time when printing presses augmented use of English. Further, when Scots and English parliaments united in 1707, a century after the union of crowns, Shetland came directly within London's legislative jurisdiction. British mercantilist laws saw to it that trade policy protected British interests and trade was increasingly conducted with Britain on British terms. English was the language of business.

Reports of Norn's demise are found when the lesser-known outposts of the British Isles became objects of scholarly tourism in the Age of Enlightenment, as the intellectually curious sought travel for personal enrichment. One such adventurer, a Scottish clergyman, Reverend George Low from Forfarshire, sailed to the Northern Isles to research and study natural history (*A Tour through the Islands of Orkney and Shetland*, 1774) but became fascinated by Norn speech and pursued that instead. He found no texts in Orkney other than a version of the Lord's Prayer and had to sail north to Shetland to find people on Foula who recognized it. A century later, thousands of Norn words had been recorded. Early 20th century scholars such as Hugh Marwick of Orkney and Jakob Jacobsen of the Faeroes carefully compiled a lexicon covering the speech of everyday Shetland, and Jacobsen's *An Etymological Dictionary of the Norn Language* had reached W by the time of his death. It was published posthumously 1928–32 and the Shetland Islands Council republished it in 1993. Visitors hearing Shetland speech for the first time may be under the impression that it's still spoken but contemporary "Shetlandic" is really a Scots-English dialect with variations in pronunciation. Norn is gone but not forgotten.

Maritime Matters

If the islands surrendered some cultural autonomy in the transition from Norn to English, the long arm of London governance did not encourage economic independence either. The sea is inseparable from Shetland life and a 1712 British protectionist law to reduce salt imports ruined (intentionally) the centuries-old whitefish-for-salt exchange with German merchants. The enactment of such mercantilist measures was intended to further British economic interests, but for Shetlanders it had negative repercussions, the principal of which was restriction of choice. Fishing had been a subsistence staple from the first settlement — much of it inshore — and fish fried in oatmeal or boiled in broth was supper for countless generations. The herring fleets took advantage of rich resources from medieval times for commercial advantage, but the new restrictive legislation ended that business. However, in the 18th century the sub-Arctic ice pack was greater than it is now, and in a little ice age[11] fish scarcity adversely impacted food stocks and trade probably would have been reduced anyway. Potato cultivation provided a welcome protein substitute, productive even on Shetland's limited arable land with seaweed and manure added as fertilizer. This diversification was sufficient to boost an otherwise fluctuating population from 15,000 (c. 1750s) to 22,000 by 1800. On the other hand potatoes were not very exportable (being grown everywhere in Britain) and the economy remained rooted in subsistence.

Commercial whaling provided some wage-earning respite. Whales, seals and walrus were hunted back to at least the 12th century but with rising 18th century demand for whalebone and whale oil, the activity expanded at an unprecedented rate. The landing of whales in Shetland led to conflicts over proceeds between lairds and captors, the former pulling feudal rank and the latter defensive of old customs. The bigger enterprise was to hunt whales in distant Greenland waters. It demanded more resources than cash-starved islanders could muster independently but at least it was a significant employer. The islands harbored a rich reservoir of tough seafarers and whaling expeditions originating in British ports sailed to Shetland to find crews. The French Revolutionary and Napoleonic wars interrupted prospects for a while as men found themselves pressed into service on war frigates, but when it all ended in 1815, whaling grew greater than ever before. Around 1400 Shetlanders earned wages in Greenland whaling at its 19th century peak. When the Norwegians introduced an explosive harpoon in the 1860s, even greater harvests beckoned. The work was perilous whatever the technology. Fears of entrapment in ice flows, howling winds of 30 and 40 knots, treacherous breakers and jagged rocks were constant. The story of one ill-fated expedition is related in the Shetland Museum.

The whaling ship *Diana* left Hull, England, on 19th February 1866 to anchor in Lerwick on the 25th of the same month, spending weeks recruiting before departing with a crew of fifty. On arrival in Greenland seas icebergs contrived to trap the ship in a dreaded vise-like grip and the crew remained incarcerated in this Arctic prison for six horrific months. Each man went on weekly rations of three lbs. of biscuit and ¾ lbs. of beef. It was not enough; 13 perished before the ship eventually got free. Nine of the dead were Shetlanders.

Ships from the outer world were not welcomed unreservedly. Religious elders feared exposure of younger Shetlanders to outside-world influences and what were viewed as corrupting bad habits and attitudes brought into the islands. Islanders signed on despite dangers and moral objections. They did so because whaling made good sense financially — it was waged — and because seafaring was in the blood. In a good season they could earn enough to set up their families for the winter. The same reasons lured Shetlanders tens of thousands of miles south to the Falkland Islands in the 1950s to hunt Antarctic whales. Christian Salvesen, a Norwegian company operating out of Leith, the port of Edinburgh, set up a whaling base there in 1908 after the shrinkage of Arctic stocks. Costs and conservation pressures ended the enterprise in the 1960s. Meanwhile deep-sea fishing recovered in the 19th century and several Shetland family businesses grew and prospered out of it, excepting the merchant-laird involvement to be discussed. In the 20th century the ever-present herring and mackerel fishing were lucrative.

If interaction with the mores of worldly Britain aroused suspicion among some Shetlanders, lines of communication still grew. A regular shipping passage to Leith was underway in the 18 century. The service sailed via German ports initially, but direct sailings increased from the 1750s as Shetland ponies were exported for haulage work in northern English coalmines. Services to Aberdeen increased too. Not all the maritime endeavors were economically motivated. Shetland had its strategic uses. When the British Admiralty sought to monitor the Russian fleet in the 1850s and set up better navigational aid for ships en route to the White Sea, a lighthouse was projected for the northern tip of Unst. The first light of the marvelously named Muckle Flugga lighthouse shone out as the Crimean War between Britain and Russia began in 1854. The permanent structure was completed in 1858, after peace was signed. The logistics of Victorian lighthouse construction are impressive to contemplate anywhere around rocky British coasts, but at almost 61°N Muckle Flugga has no peers. A temporary iron barrack with tons of blocks and tackles plus water, cement, lime, coal, stone and glass had to be hauled up a 200-foot rock in ferocious weather. It was not uncommon for waves to crash right over the rock summit in the pounding winter seas. At 64 feet, Muckle Flugga is taller than Mousa Broch. The credit goes to National Lighthouse Board Chief Engineer David Stevenson and his brother Thomas,[12] father of famed author Robert Louis Stevenson. R.L. Stevenson accompanied his father as a youngster on at least one trip to Unst, and it is possible that *Treasure Island* (1883), written when he was in his thirties, drew inspiration from a childhood memory of it. The claim is feasible in that the fictional isle's shape does correspond to Unst's contours; otherwise the latitudes are far removed from the exotic climes in which he envisaged Long John Silver and the marooned *Hispaniola*.

The Merchant-Lairds

Pre-capitalist practices persisted in Shetland, even as mainland Britain indus-trialized and urbanized. Any commercial opportunities were pursued by those with the monetary resources to do so, but any chance native-born islanders had of capi-talizing were shackled by archaic land and fishing laws favoring the feudal lairds. The Scots Crown that introduced them was obsolete, having merged with England in 1603, but the laws persisted, keeping power in the hands of a few. Bonded tenants were still obligated to hand over sea-catches under threat of eviction, an arrange-ment advantageous to profit-inclined lairds. These merchant-lairds, as they were called, prospered, not only from whaling, but also herring and other sea bounty. The export prices to British markets were often favorable because mercantilist law lim-ited foreign competition. The costs were favorable too because fishers were typically paid in goods rather than cash, such "truck wages" calculated according to retail prices and items purchased wholesale, a profitable ruse in itself. In the meantime bonded and cash-deprived fishermen had to lease boats and lines, effectively own-ing and earning nothing. Production was a mix of capitalist intent by feudal means.

Raw wool was also a marketable resource and lairds who saw the commercial viability of sheep farms thought nothing of evicting tenants from holdings to make it happen. To compound problems of the poor, the potato blight that devastated Ire-land in the later 1840s impacted Shetland too. The unhappy combination of an enslav-ing truck system, land evictions, and crop failure distress pushed some to leave, many in the third quarter of the 19th century, the intensity consistent with a wider world of migratory movement. Shetlanders sailed away to mainland Britain, North Amer-ica and the Antipodes. It is thought there are more people of Shetland descent in New Zealand than there are in Shetland.

Enterprise and Reform

Nevertheless, the entrepreneurial energy of the new industrial age did not entirely bypass Shetland. There were exceptions. Arthur Anderson, co-founder of the great P & O (Peninsular and Oriental) Steam Navigation Company, ancestor of the same company whose ships still service Shetland, is notable, although he had to leave the islands to find success. Born in 1791, in a house preserved in his memory near Lerwick, he volunteered for naval service in the Napoleonic War in 1808, having been "press-ganged" (drafted) earlier and released on the understanding he would join up when 16.[13] A basic education in letters helped him secure a position as a ship's clerk and it was to shipping he turned for employment in London after the war was over in 1815. He became a ship owner in partnership with others in the 1830s, pro-moting a steam-driven service to Spain and Portugal, the peninsula part of the even-tual enterprise. A government contract to carry the mail to Alexandria, Egypt was won in 1840 and when the same service extended to India two years later, the ori-ental connection was born.

His global interests did not make him forget Shetland. Indeed his wider world experiences probably made him all the more determined to modernize its anachronistic economic system. In 1836 Anderson published *The Shetland Journal*, a short-lived newspaper in which he blasted the ways in which feudal obligations and the merchant-lairds' monopoly limited enterprise. The following year he turned sermon into practice by setting up the Shetland Fishery Company, introducing new fish curing methods, a portent of things to come, but he could not break the merchant-lairds' stranglehold or tradition in the short term. Shetlanders were still starved out of the cash economy. The paper folded after ten years. Anderson was a great liberal in the Victorian English sense, pinning his beliefs in self-improvement and the necessity for successful entrepreneurs like himself to use their wealth to help make it happen. He invested in local education and built homes for widows of fishermen and others. His social benefactions survive. The first Shetlander to sit as an MP (Liberal) in the British House of Commons, elected for the Orkney and Shetland constituency, he died in 1872. Within two decades, the kinds of reforms he had visualized were enacted.

The "truck system" was outlawed in the 1870s, after intense lobbying by British labor unions. In 1890, an Edinburgh court ruled against the lairds on division of proceeds from landed whales, although by then alternative lighting meant that whale oil demand was in decline. In a national atmosphere of democratic reform, local government by election replaced archaic patriarchal practices in the 1880s. Shetland was not excluded. Two representative councils were set up — one for the county of Zetland (as Shetland was still called) and one for the borough of Lerwick — and a measure of self-government was official for the first time since the days of the *lawtings*. Lerwick Town Hall was built in 1884 and the nearby County Buildings followed. The 1886 Crofters Act was restorative too, giving landed tenants some rights on rent and tenure. The sparse cultivable land and rough pasture was subdivided into more and more crofts (a specifically Scots-English word for small rented landholdings), in effect a return to the land lots of yore. Scottish crofts are mostly clustered in agriculturally marginal areas, and Shetland decidedly falls into that category. It remains one of the main crofting regions, together with the northern Hebrides. We will encounter it again with reference to the Hebrides, so suffice to observe here that the modern Shetland crofter is a true descendant of Jarlshof, a jack-of-all-trades survivalist making the most of what the habitat can offer. Whatever material deprivations presumed by strangers, crofters have recovered a measure of autonomy and independence, non-quantitative values in island culture.

Faded black and white photographs of hardy 19th century women in shawls tending livestock and children, scarves tightly wrapped about heads, baskets on their backs filled with fish or peat, waiting for men to return from the sea, are images analogous to all Britain's offshore islands. Women were also the backbone of domestic manufacturing. On islands where sheep outnumbered people, it's not surprising that knitting was long a staple activity. A demand for knitted woolen sweaters was stimulated by 15th and 16th century Dutch shipping crews, and by the 17th century thickly tufted box bed covers known as *taatit rugs* were regularly made. The deep-sea whalers and sealers expanded markets in the 18th century until factory production eventually challenged hand-knitting output. Lace making was also productive. Arthur Anderson sent lace hosiery to Queen Victoria in a publicity stunt for Shetland fine lace products, and this cottage industry grew too for a while until likewise checked by machines and alternative fibers. Patterned knitwear was given a boost by the Fair Isle sweater phenomenon in the early 20th century. The Fair Isle style of hand-dyed colors in geometric banded patterns began on the tiny sheep isle of the same name in the 17th century, but it was nobility sporting the V-necked multi-colored pullover version on 1920s golf courses that turned it into a fashion statement for casual wear. The pattern's popularity has survived the test of time and is still knitted throughout the isles. The real Fair Isle holds workshops on how to hand-spin, weave and dye the said garment. Other fine quality lace and wool products still find customers with a textiles trades association representing the interests of modern specialist businesses.

Military Maneuvers

As Europe internally combusted in the first half of the twentieth century in warfare and then economic depression and then more warfare, with all the vicissitudes involved, Shetland experiences were no exception. Over 600 died in World War I, a big loss per capita. In the inter-war period whaling was no longer viable and the traditional standbys of fishing, crofting and knitting could not compete with wider world attractions for the young. Emigration continued. World War II literally began with a bang in Shetland. A bomb dropped by the *Luftwaffe* in November 1939 on Sullom, Northmavine, is thought to be the first to hit British territory. As Hitler's air war intensified in 1940 the new top-secret gizmo of radar proved critical in defense against German bombers. It began in 1935 under the direction of physicist Robert Watson-Watt, and in the war a network of ground-based radar stations called Chain Home linked Britain from Scilly to Shetland in an effort to improve air surveillance and direct interceptions. The Shetland radar was specifically intended to detect U-boat activity.

News of Nazi occupation of Norwegian territory in April 1940 brought the war that bit closer, Bergen being nearer than Edinburgh. British defense services poured into hastily set-up bases in numbers matching permanent residency, but their presence did not deter *Luftwaffe* missions and there were casualties; fishing boats were sunk with crew left adrift for days in life rafts. Over 3,000 Shetland men and women eventually served in World War II, and as might be expected many were in the naval services. The Norwegian Navy also used Shetland as a war base. Indeed Nazi-occupied Norway occupied Shetlanders' minds more and more as the war progressed and a special opportunity arose to pay a friendly compliment a millennium after Norse settlement. As Nazi presence intensified, Shetland fishing boats sailed bravely to land supplies, weapons and saboteurs, and to liberate refugees. The Norwegian Resistance named the operation "Shetland Bus" and over 300 grateful individuals were "bussed" to safety through the duration of war. In the spring of 1940, however, prospects seemed dire. UK intelligence units were crippled in their ability to get Scandinavian information after the fall of Norway and "Shetland Bus" began as an exercise to rectify that problem. It was placed under the direction of a British intelligence officer Major L.H. Mitchell and his deputy RN Lt. David Howarth.

A BBC radio newsman in the early days of that medium, Howarth wrote an account of the whole venture after the war.[14] There is also a small museum dedicated to it in Scalloway, port base of many "Shetland Bus" missions. Fishing vessels were granted a level of immunity in the naval war, affording an opportunity for refugees posing as crew to slip through checkpoints without alerting suspicion. The US Navy provided submarine chasers for the missions from 1943.[15]

Among Howarth's truth-is-bolder-than-fiction adventures is one of a daring plan in late October 1942 to try and cripple the German battleship *Tirpitz*. After *HMS Rodney* and *King George V* sank the *Bismarck* off southwest Ireland in May 1941, the *Tirpitz* was the best battleship left in the German Navy. Anchored at Trondheim on the north Norwegian coast, it posed a problem as *Bismarck* had done, tying up Britain's home fleet in readiness. Since ships were urgently needed elsewhere, the need to sink it intensified. A plan emerged to ship 20-foot-long torpedo "chariots" into enemy waters, where two-man crews would steer them into target position, using electric motors. Warheads would then be unscrewed, time fuses set, and with a quick exit the crewless warheads left to do their detonating work. A modest fishing boat named *Arthur*, of a type familiar around Trondheim, was given the task of transporting the "chariots." Passage through a checkpoint was secured with the declared purpose of a peat cargo delivery. It got within five miles of the *Tirpitz* with the deadly arsenal undetected, then all went wrong. The towing lugs weakened by *Arthur's* pitching at sea tore off and the torpedoes sank beyond retrieval.[16] The crew was forced to abort the mission, but one of them, an Englishman, Able Seaman Robert Evans, was captured, interrogated and later executed. The Nazi admiral responsible for his death was later charged at the Nuremberg trial for war crimes.[17] The *Tirpitz* did not have the last word, however. Barracuda dive-bombers with pilots trained at HMS Urley on the Isle of Man disabled it in April 1944.

Howarth readily concedes that "Shetland Bus" was peripheral but comes up with good arguments to prevent it from going to a watery grave in history books. The operation was not just about a few hundred bussed out. Nearly 400 tons of ordnance were bussed in and put to good use in sabotage attacks. Radio operators were landed to transmit information on Nazi activities. By 1943 the code breaking team in London's Bletchley Park had cracked the "Enigma" codes of the German armed services and all radio transmissions were valuable weapons. At the end of the war the Shetland operation had 60 functioning in Norway. These implants fortified the Norwegian Resistance too and made the Germans fear armed rebellion. Howarth muses that there must have been German soldiers stationed in small isolated garrisons for whom final capitulation in 1945 at least spelled release from vengeful Norwegian guerrilla action. Ten German divisions were held in Norway until the Allied invasion of Europe in 1944. As Howarth points out the "Shetland Bus" base of around a hundred operatives was a link in a chain that ultimately tied down more than a quarter of a million German soldiers.

Shetland carried on playing a subversive role in the ensuing Cold War. RAF Saxa Vord, situated on far northernmost Unst overlooking Muckle Flugga lighthouse, was operational in that regard and the radar mast towers are still visible. As part of NATO's defenses it kept an ear and eye on Soviet shipping and aircraft from 1957, feeding data into the UK's air command system. The Official Secrets Act masks whatever it achieved as an early warning station and spy post, but its positive impact on the local economy can be measured by the shocked reaction to a 1999 Ministry of Defense downsizing announcement. A 70 percent "draw-down" of personnel was planned over two years, and since the housing estate for Saxa Vord families at Setters Hill was the most concentrated settlement north of Mainland, the decision aroused fears for the Unst economy.

Oil Bonanza

The hopes of those wishing progress on Shetland have had much to feed on in the second half of the twentieth century. Economic reconstruction arrived in assorted ways through land law reform, merchant navy jobs, increased farm and marine output, tourism, and suddenly in the form of a single bonanza: North Sea oil. Sullom Voe, meaning perversely "a place in the sun," is maybe the oddest Shetland sight of all, Europe's largest oil and gas terminal. Built in 1978 to handle a million barrels of crude per day and fed by pipelines from the Brent and Ninian offshore fields beneath the seabed east of Shetland, its flare stack burning off excess can be seen from afar. At a cost of £1.2 billion and with hired labor numbering 7,000 it was the world's biggest construction project at that time. The workforce (nicknamed "bears") was housed in two purpose-built construction villages and the rowdy tales rival those of "navvies" building Britain's railways in the Victorian Age. Islanders flocked in to find wages too.

The North Sea[3] oil and gas extraction made the UK the biggest oil producer in the European Union in the 1970s, a dramatic turnaround for a nation hitherto wholly dependent on imports. OPEC price hikes in 1973 pressured western oil consumers to look for non–OPEC reserves and the North Sea, among other places, helped counteract the cartel's pricing power. It brought Shetland unprecedented prosperity for 25 years with lower levels of unemployment and leaps in public services. After decades of depopulation, the population rose by 57 percent to reach 27,000 in 1981. Service sector activities boomed. The effects are there in modern housing tracts, new schools, supermarkets, leisure centers, interisland ferries and better roads. The archetypal Shetlander, working and living on a croft close to the foreshore, surrounded by his farm and fishing equipment, rusted old cars and rotting upturned boat-hulls, had new neighbors. More oil discoveries followed to the west of the islands, but the boom is now over. Its proportion of overall value to the Shetland economy fell to just under 20 percent by 1998,[18] although one-fifth of all output is still a healthy contribution. New extraction techniques drain fields faster, and Sullom Voe production was down to about 600,000 gallons a day by 2002. The population has fallen too (by about 20 percent) but remains higher than pre-oil boom times.

Fishing Modernization

A more familiar Shetland business is fishing, and the industry has seen major advances in catching methods. Families once sailed out to fix nets and return with a herring catch in the next day or so. Now factory ships are gone for weeks as radar traces shoals and huge nets trawl up vast numbers. Some catches are frozen and canned at sea. Conservationist outcry at such mass production and stock decimation triggered European Union wild catch quotas, regulatory agendas that frustrate and anger Shetland fishing interests. The Shetland Fishermen's Association fumes over prospects for fishing family livelihoods while environmentalists fret over the knock-on ecological impact of depleted sand eel stocks on seabird colonies. Sand eels have been fished commercially from the mid–1970s. Since the much publicized "cod wars" between Iceland and Britain from 1958 to 1976 over fishing zone limits, cod and skate stocks in British waters have generally been lower. Herring and mackerel have fared better and modern processing plants in Lerwick testify to it. The local feeling is that it would do even better if *udal* rights over foreshore and seabed were restored, giving Shetlanders more control over their own waters.

On a positive note, oil monies have helped fishing by providing seed money for modernization. The Shetland Islands Council has invested large sums of its oil revenues to revitalize the industry. The Shetland Islands Council was born in the 1974 reorganization of UK local government with a merging of the two Victorian councils. A centerpiece of its fishing investment is the North Atlantic Fisheries College in Scalloway, an industry-managed institute opened in 1992. Its mission is in training and research in new fish catching, processing and farming techniques. Fish catching and processing are the traditional mainstays of the industry but salmon, shellfish and halibut farming, or aquaculture as it is called, is a rejuvenating new element. Aquaculture was such a growth industry internationally in 2000 that forecasts suggested it might eventually supply most of the fish people eat. Regular fish farm supply has led to an increase in supermarket demand in western countries—so much so that supply may outstrip demand. Shetland accounted for about one-third of all the salmon farmed in the UK in 2000 and 40 percent of Scottish mussel farming. Halibut and cod farming are in the research and development stage. Fishing overall employed about one-in-five of the working population in 2000. Some 700 years after Hanseatic merchants dropped anchor, fishing remains a staple. Intense competition and conservation rules continue to render prospects unpredictable, though, and spokespersons for the industry often express unease.

Contemporary Politics & Society Outlook

The oil boom triggered local political ambitions too, energizing aspirations of home-rule, at least by a dedicated few. A movement burned briefly in the 1980s, helped by a wider Scottish Nationalists' campaign, a key slogan of which was "It's Scotland's Oil." Shetland attitudes toward Scottish nationalism have been ambivalent, at least according to the quantifiable evidence. In 1979, Shetlanders together with Scots at large voted to reject a separate Scots parliament. Britain's third political party, the Liberal Democrats, has held the constituency of Orkney and Shetland for the UK parliament since the 1950s with convincing majorities. The long-serving MP (Member of Parliament) Jo Grimond (1950 to 1983) was sensitive to the fact that islanders did not necessarily identify with mainland Scottish issues and sought "opt-out" clauses in Scottish devolution proposals. In 1979 it never materialized but 20 years later opinions had shifted. Devolution, meaning transfer of some legislative powers to separate parliaments in Scotland, Wales and Northern Ireland, a form of federalizing what has long been a unitary system of government, revived under Tony Blair's New Labor of the 1990s. In Scotland's case, initiatives finalized proposals in 1999 and Edinburgh got its own elected parliament. Shetland support for it was less emphatic than Scotland as a whole. In the preceding 1997 referendum on twin proposals for a separate parliament and limited taxation powers, Shetlanders voted "yes-yes" at 62 percent and 52 percent respectively. The Scots' overall "yes-yes" votes were a more enthusiastic 74 percent and 63 percent.

While Shetland residents are no longer the exclusive community of the past, it's not given either that they see themselves in the same breath as mainland Scots. The relationship is still tempered by geography and a modern desire to recognize the non–Scots heritage. There is no Gaelic or Scots tartan in Shetland. Instead locals dress up as Vikings in the annual *Up-Helly-A'* festival and drag a galley through the streets for ceremonial burning. Nevertheless in accordance with the wishes of two-thirds, they are represented in Edinburgh, with their own MSP (or Member of the Scottish Parliament), separate from Orkney. The first election winner was a Liberal Democrat, party-consistent with the Westminster choice. The separatist Scottish Nationalist candidate polled only 14 percent of the votes. As the 21st century progresses, new technologies will further erode separateness. Even remote Foula out to the west, once the most isolated community in Britain, has electricity, thanks to an aero-generator using wind and waterpower. The new mediums of electronic data transfer, text messaging, video conferencing and interactive TV with wire line and wireless bind virtual and physical worlds ever more closely. There is much talk in the internet age of the "death of distance" and it is feasible to do business and live in faraway places. Clean air, low crime, uncrowded schools, and a quality infrastructure (created by the oil boom) may attract new settlers. The unemployment rates remain beneath the national Scottish average. Despite a fall-off in absolute numbers with the passing of the oil boom, the number of Shetlanders has risen as a percentage of Scotland's total (declining) population. In 1999 two large red Plexiglas bus shelters stood on Unst near Baltasound amid the peaty solitude, looking as if they'd been airlifted from some identikit housing estate on the edge of an English city and dropped carelessly into nowhere. Practically the size of a London bed-sit, they stand waiting for an as yet unseen flood of newcomers, bright plastic boxes on an ancient landscape.

---

1. Lamb, Hubert, *Climate, History and the Modern World*, second ed. (Routledge, 1995), 134.

2. Turner, Val, *Ancient Shetland* (Batsford Books, 2003).

3. *Orkneyinga Saga*, Pálsson, Hermann, and Edwards, Paul, trans. (Penguin Classics, 1981), Ch. 93, 190.

4. Roseman, Christina Horst, *Pytheas of Massalia: On the Ocean Text*, Translation and Commentary (Ares, 1994), 152.

5. *Strabo: Geography*, Jones, Horace Leonard, trans. (Harvard University Loeb Classical Library, 1969), Bk. IV, 5.5.

6. *Bede: The Ecclesiastical History of the English People*, McClure, Judith, & Collins, Roger, eds. (Oxford University Press World's Classic Series, 1994), 114-115.

7. Graham-Campbell, James, & Batey, Colleen E., *Vikings in Scotland: An Archaeological Survey* (Edinburgh University Press, 1998), 64.

8. *Orkneyinga Saga*, Ch. 12, 37.

9. Donaldson, Gordon, ed., "Abolition of Norse Law in Orkney and Shetland," in *Scottish Historical Documents* (Neil Wilson Publishing, 1974), 177.

10. Donaldson, "The Scottish Act of 1611," 177.

11. Lamb, 217.

12. Bathurst, Bella, *The Lighthouse Stevensons* (Perennial Books, 2000), 203.

13. Shetland Museum online collections, "Arthur Anderson" (http://www.shetland-museum.org.uk/bod/arthur_anderson. txt, 11 Jan. 2003).

14. David Howarth, *The Shetland Bus: A WWII Epic of Escape, Survival and Adventure* (Lyons Press edition, 2001; originally published by Thomas Nelson, 1951).

15. Howarth, 210-211.

16. Howarth, 155.

17. Howarth, 162.

18. Shetland Islands Council Development Department online, "Shetland Structure Plan 2001-2016," (http://www.shetland.gov.uk/splan/bus.htm, 2001 report).

2

Orkney: "Land of Saga"

His [Svein Asleifarson's] drinking hall was so big, there was nothing in
Orkney to compare with it ... he would go off plundering in the Hebrides
and Ireland on what he called his spring trip, then be back home just
after midsummer, where he stayed till the cornfields had been
reaped and the grain was safely in. After that he would go
off viking again"— The Orkneyinga Saga, c. 1200

There can be few places in the western world with a greater sweep of hands-on history than Orkney. Visited and named by Pytheas of Massalia on his fourth century B.C. voyage, the archipelago lies within sight of the northern Scottish coast, far flung from the modern center of British gravity. Yet a thousand years ago it was at the heart of a Norwegian sea-realm and four millennia before that harbored one of the great centers of megalithic culture. In Orkney you don't need to go looking for prehistory, you're standing on it. The rocky coast looks forbidding when approached across the choppy Pentland Firth with the imposing two-legged sandstone sea stack Old Man of Hoy looming starboard, but Orkney takes on a gentler look on disembarkation, undulating, treeless and green. There is a greater feel of drowned landscape than Shetland. Its soft hills slope seaward and with the exception of Ward Hill on Hoy, at 1570 ft. the highest point in both Orkney and Shetland, the topography is of low relief. A roaring wind adds sound bite. When the clouds roll back this is Britain's big sky country with 360 degrees of horizon, alternating bays, lochs and moorland. The glacial inheritance is more generous than Shetland and the fertile moraine supports agriculture. About 17 of the 90 or so islands and islets are inhabited, the 2001 census reporting a population of 19,245. The administrative center is Kirkwall, a Norway-facing port on the eastern coast of Mainland, biggest island of the group, its skyline dominated by the rusty red sandstone bulk of its medieval Norse cathedral, St. Magnus's.

ORKNEY

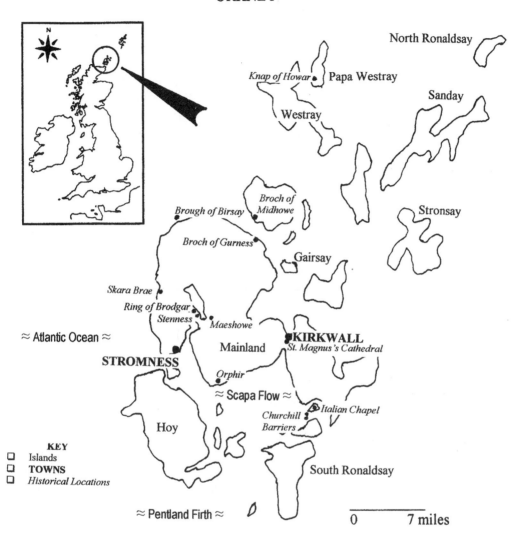

Neolithic Villages

Early bands of Mesolithic hunter-gatherers may have found resources to their liking but pre-historical pride of place goes to a farming settlement named Skara Brae. Located on the Bay of Skaill in western Mainland, it is one of Europe's best-kept Neolithic secrets, a Bedrock for-real reborn in modernity. Fierce storm tides ended its long hibernation in 1850 by washing away a grassy dune blanket, and full excavation got underway in 1927 when Australian archaeologist Gordon Childe began research. The findings indicate occupation from c. 3100 B.C. with a revitalization project undertaken about halfway through the impressive six centuries of habitation. Visitors are led down a trail to the coastal site with signposts checking off famous historical events in reverse order: the 1969 moon landing, 1876 telephone invention, the date of the first Crusade, the Roman Empire, the Great Wall of China, the pyramids of Ghiza, until there it is: Skara Brae, earliest of them all at 3100 B.C.!

The uncovered dune is hard up against the beach now with a protective sea wall to combat further erosion. Skara Brae was a semi-subterranean housing tract, its dwellings not so much individual houses as prehistoric condominiums, set off a maze of sandstone slab passages and alleyways. About ten dwellings are exposed with walls up to nine feet high. Floors were of mud clay (not the sand of today) and roofing was timber or whalebone framed, covered with animal skins, heather and turf. The slow deterioration of stone over millennia has left us pieces of stone furniture to gaze at incredulously — built-in furnishings recognizable to the modern eye such as dressers, storage alcoves, bed frames, seats and fireplaces. Conveniences extended to water closets and a drainage system of sorts, 3,000 years before that of the Romans, usually credited as the first plumbers in Britain.

Skara Brae villagers grew barley and oats, grazed cattle, sheep and pigs. Beyond the settlement wild boar and deer roamed uncultivated land with a variety of fowl, ducks, gulls, auks, and shellfish there for the taking. The menu reads like a veritable cornucopia of the north. Archaeology attests to honey, herbs, crab apples, wild cherries, blackberries and hazelnuts.[1] Strabo tells us in *Geography* (c. A.D. 23) that Pytheas of Massalia claimed Orcadians ate herbs, fruit, roots, and had "grain and honey drink" (mead or barley beer perhaps), thinking it was another Pytheas "tall story" about frozen climes, but then Strabo did not understand the Gulf Stream warming effect. The Neolithic climate was a few degrees warmer than now and the beach would have been further away from the village. There was rich foliage of birch and pine forest[2] and grasses, flax and wool provided fiber for textiles. The Orcadians' lives were not without comforts. Village artisans worked flint, stone, bone and antler into tools, shaping clay bowls for domestic use and votive tributes.

Skara Brae was not alone. Other evidence has come to light, some of even greater antiquity. Two oblong dwellings discovered by chance in the 1930s at the Knap of Howar on the Isle of Papa Westray date to c. 3600 B.C., making them the oldest standing buildings in northern Europe; they were in use for half a millennium thereafter. On the shore of Harray Loch near the Standing Stones of Stenness at least 15 ruins have been excavated since discovery in 1984, the oldest of which is c. 3300 B.C. Unlike Skara Brae these houses were free standing but with similar central curbed hearths, built-in box beds and stone dressers. Special interest is accorded to a bigger barn-like central building which accounts for the whole settlement being named Barnhouse. Thought to have some relationship to the nearby Stenness ceremonial site, this village was inhabited at the same time as Skara Brae but abandoned earlier. Another settlement named Stonehall, a few miles distant in the parish of Firth, was in continuous use for centuries in the later Neolithic period. Interaction between these places must be presumed. We know Skara Brae used hematite tools for finishing leather products, and the nearest supply was ten miles away on the Isle of Hoy.[3] Different sea levels at that time meant a different interisland geography, but the sea channels were highways for these islanders, sailing back and forth in their small oval shaped coracles, workaday craft of choice for thousand of years. Skara Brae is not sited for defense and no weapons have been found.

Scholars have searched for clues as to Skara Brae's fate c. 2500 B.C. Professor Childe favored a huge sandstorm inundating the site, but the modern view is that no single drama was responsible. Evidence suggests that villagers left of their own volition. During its lifetime the rabbit warren of homes either became encased within drifting sand and village compost (a novel but putrid form of weatherproofing and wind shelter) or they deliberately back-filled their own dwellings with the same, forcing it into disuse, though why they would do that is not known. One reasonable hypothesis[4] has it that as lives increasingly focused on megalith sites in the vicinity — the chambered tomb of Maes Howe and stone circles of Stenness and Brodgar — a new regional order emerged. New generations moved out to smaller farmsteads and nucleated communities such as Skara Brae and Barnhouse deferred to a higher regional organization expressed in the megaliths.

Horizon Breakers of the Third Millennium B.C.

If Neolithic farming was productive enough to feed generations in villages then it could make available surplus labor for other projects. History is about the struggle to secure stability and ease in this life, and having reached that point Neolithic farmers in Atlantic Europe were moved to move stone as testimonials to their achievement. Megaliths in the form of chambered tombs and stone circles were progressively built from Scandinavia down to the Iberian Peninsula between 3200 and 2000 B.C. Though they were once thought the work of itinerant eastern Mediterranean craftsmen, later 20th century radiocarbon dating methods deflated old assumptions. England's Stonehenge and Ireland's Boyne Valley tomb complex, both c. 3000 B.C.— to cite famous examples— began much too early to be based on Mycenaean Greek imports. Some megaliths predate the beginning of Egyptian dynasties (2700 B.C.) and are older than the pyramids, beginning as constructs of Atlantic European latitudes, not Mediterranean culture. They were the triumph of architects, masons, quarrymen, sculptors, fetchers and carriers, Neolithic folks the late celebrated Orcadian author George Mackay Brown aptly termed "the horizon breakers."

Before examining the Orkney evidence, some general comments are appropriate. Experts in various disciplines have measured, analyzed, categorized and theorized megaliths to man-hours impressive as that of their original construction. Out of a myriad of theories, unifying aspects emerge. Firstly there is a clear pattern of association between megaliths and pastoral agriculture. The survivors in the British Isles are in stone-using upland areas, on offshore islands, places with good grazing pasture. According to human bone analysis, meat was at least as important as grain in the Neolithic diet. Secondly megaliths served spiritual and community needs. They were sanctuaries for the dead and civic arenas for the living. Thirdly they were not single-phase structures but public works projects developed over extensive time demanding the considerable effort, cooperation and devotion of generations.

After the builder's demise, myths about megaliths' mysterious powers became so powerful that early Church councils and synods denounced them, condemning worshippers. In the 16th century scholars began to try to unravel their meaning and by the 18th century the structures were subclassified in Celtic vernacular as *menhirs* (long stones), *cromlechs* (stone circles) and *dolmens* (burial chambers), considered relics of an ancient though newly identified Celtic culture. William Stukeley, an English physician and antiquarian who undertook field studies of the great English stone circles at Avebury and Stonehenge, sought to reconcile the fact of megaliths with biblical stories and ancient accounts of druids in Celtic Europe. He came up with a pseudo-history in 1724, in which the stones represented sacred symbols of God's early work, before divine authority passed on through druids, "the sons of Noah," to Christianity. A follower, Henry Hurle, founded the Ancient Order of Druids in 1781, and the image of hooded druids in long robes presiding over congregations and working magic potions was institutionalized. There is no doubt people venerated the stones long after the fact of megalithic culture, but it is also the case that their antiquity preceded Celts and druidism by millennia.

Maes Howe Chambered Tomb (c. 2750 B.C.)

Orkney possesses an extraordinary concentration of megaliths in close proximity around the lochs (lakes) of Harray and Stenness on Mainland. Three of them are outstanding — the chambered passage tomb of Maes Howe and the *henges* of Brodgar and Stenness. Situated at the top of a northern axis of offshore megaliths stretching south through the Hebrides and Man to Anglesey, they were part of a wider axis described by archaeologist Barry Cunliffe as "Boyne-Orkney"[5] since there are parallels between Orkney's megaliths and those of Ireland's Boyne Valley. The innards of the great grassy mound that covers Maes Howe, over 100 feet wide and 26 feet high, was first excavated in 1861. A later radiocarbon analysis of peat from the surrounding ditch dated its origin to 2750 B.C., a period well within the frame of Skara Brae habitation. A carving on a corner pillar in the inner sanctum of the tomb is stylistically similar to those at Skara Brae, serving notice of that affiliation. The stone was quarried about six or seven miles away and somehow dragged to the site. Hardworking masons packed small flat stones between neatly cut stone slabs to build the tomb upwards in corbel fashion. It moved Stuart Piggott, the late eminent University of Edinburgh archaeology professor (a Gordon Childe protégé), to describe the architectural skills employed as among the most splendid of prehistoric Europe.[6] The central gallery with three sepulchers set off it is reached down a narrow stone passage, aligned to catch the filtered light of a midwinter sunset. The aforementioned central building at Barnhouse village was also astronomically aligned, except that it faced the rising sun of a summer solstice; "a light which gladdened the living, just as the rays of winter solstice pierced the realm of the dead" as Professor Sherratt of the University of Oxford put it.[7]

What distinguishes Maes Howe is its communal accommodation. This was not the tomb of one individual but a memorial to many ancestors. Interment accommodation was limited nevertheless so presumably it was those with elite status who were dignified. Death exerts its own kind of authority, and ancestor worship was a practical expression born out of concern for the living, protection of the ancestors provided protection in life. Maes Howe, Stenness and Brodgar are in close proximity and obviously stand within a region of profound meaning to their builders. Perhaps priest-kings were inaugurated there, mediators between the "other world" of the dead and that of the living; there is no shortage of speculations about purpose. If they defined one sanctified space then there were others such as Finstown where burial chambers at Cuween and Wideford together with the settlement of Stonehall have been found. Does sepulchral preservation tell us anything about their beliefs? Neolithic peoples were intensely religious. They invested meaning in their universe and appear dominated by their beliefs, a reason for expending much time and effort constructing edifices like Maes Howe. Unfortunately the energy expended still doesn't tell us much about theology. We cannot assume for example that ethical behavior, as in our own monotheistic religions, played a part in securing an afterlife, if indeed that was sought. We can only presume that part of the purpose was pragmatic, as in traditional cultures today, dealing with daily survival — the moods of nature — trying to secure some well being in this life.

The Henges

Only two miles to the west of Maes Howe are four uprights known as the Stones of Stenness, towering remains of a once grand Neolithic stone circle of twelve great *menhirs* organized in an ellipse within an encircling *henge*. *Henges* involved the construction of earthen banks and/or ditches to encase a variety of stone rings. The Stenness builders erected the stone ring first c. 3000 B.C. It would have been hard to maneuver stones once the *henge* was dug. Neolithic Orkney was wooded and pine was available for log levers, tracks and cribs to drag and erect stone slabs. Shards of pottery, cremated bones and fire evidence have been found in the small central area, indicative of ritual usage. Remarkably another splendid stone circle stands within sight of Stenness. The huge and exact circle of *menhirs* of the Ring of Brodgar was built on what is now gently sloping land close to salt-water Stenness and fresh water Harray, both further from the sea than today. At least 60 tall stones once stood proud within a rock cut ditch. Twenty-one withered relics survive, each between six and twelve feet high. Giant Brodgar was raised around the time of Skara Brae's demise and was the last of the great sites at the heart of Orkney. Stenness was already in place and human remains laid to rest in Maes Howe for several centuries. In addition about a mile to the northwest of Brodgar are the remains of yet another *henge*, the Ring of Brookan. Its site housed a Maes Howe–type passage grave also but there is little to be seen beyond some scattered small stones and a grassy mound and ditch, yet once it too was part of this great open-air Neolithic pantheon.

The *henges* raise plenty of questions about Neolithic theology, and we are left to conjecture division of material and spiritual worlds. It is logical (for us) to associate earthly circles with heavenly spheres — sun and moon brought to earth — and astronomical alignments are compelling; orientations respect summer and winter solstices. Many *henges* were built at points of convergence with lunar and solar alignment (Brodgar's position seems particularly sensitive to surrounding hills, water and sky), perhaps as a means of predicting celestial events such as eclipses. The Neolithic and Bronze Age Europeans were avid students of the heavens and megalithic association with calendars and the zodiac is enthusiastically advocated by modern commentators, but it meets with skepticism in some. The fact is it is easier to figure out how they built them than to establish why. Ultimately it is reasonable to view them as expressions of big considerations, celestial and terrestrial. They were temples for ritual and ceremony; there was enough room at the Ring of Brodgar for hundreds to gather. All communities develop icons of one sort or another for unification and solidarity. The stones are protective of something but they are mute brooding fossils from a world that keeps its secrets.

Bronze Age Mysteries

The Ring of Brodgar was built when single graves were starting to become more common, a phenomenon linked to the emergence of Bronze Age beaker culture. Named for distinctive drinking goblets imported from continental Europe (from c. 2300 B.C.), typically found at single-grave burial sites, beakers are closely associated with Stonehenge and Avebury in southern England. The beaker finds on Orkney are meager — just a few of the coarse grooved corded-ware type, a design begun in the Eurasian steppes where twisted cord was wrapped around the beaker's upper half to produce parallel lines. A few excavated beakers hardly make a case for new settlers, but their presence does indicate an immigration of artistic ideas, a product of widening trade contacts.

The Orkney climate became cooler, wetter and stormier through the later second millennium B.C. with blanket peat forming over arable land. The forests were in retreat. The Neolithic clearance of woodland for pasture and resources may have already denuded the landscape and helped bog formation. Chaos must have ensued. There are no records of it but we can imagine that those moving on to better land threatened those already there and in a time of upheaval, grand structures like Maes Howe, Stenness and Brodgar were abandoned. Communal burial chambers were no longer built or used and cremation practices were adopted, indicative of shifts in beliefs, a religious reformation even? The same pattern is evident in Shetland. The epoch of the megaliths faded away.

Brochs *in a Celtic Age*

Recovery and reorganization is evident by the last millennium B.C., a timeframe associated in wider European prehistory with Iron Age Celts. New fields and boundaries were marked out and another wave of imposing construction evolved — that of the *brochs*. The dry-stone tower *brochs* dominated the Orcadian seashore as well as Shetland. As many as 120 were already standing or in construction by 100 B.C. with a significant concentration in the Eynshallow Sound area between Mainland and the Isle of Rousay; three are known on the Evie coast and six on Rousay's shore. Those at Gurness and Midhowe are still in sufficiently good repair to warrant inspection. Such density can only be explained by a productive and prospering economy. The Gurness excavations and to a lesser extent Midhowe reveal that the *broch* itself, the tower structure, was at the core of a larger village development. This "*broch* village" layout, unique to Orkney, suggests appreciable population density. Professor Piggott once described the Iron Age Britons of Scotland as "Celtic Cowboys," more nomadic than their southern Briton neighbors, yet the Gurness "*broch* village" reveals a sedentary life with barley grown, pigs and goats kept, cattle and sheep too. Dogs were used for herding. Cottagers spun and wove. There was fishing, wildfowling on the shores and marshes. The hunting of red deer was still pursued.[8] Life appears stable and secure.

The late T.G. Powell thought that the Latin-named *Orcades* (etymology uncertain) or "Orca people" of Orkney, encountered by Julius Agricola's exploratory fleet of the A.D. 80s, were a single Brittonic Celtic tribe.[9] Note that historical linguists subdivide Celtic speech in Britain and Ireland into a q–Celtic or Gaelic mode, associated with Ireland, and a p–Celtic or Brittonic mode, associated with Britain. The rationale determining these distinctions is discussed in the Hebrides chapter. Powell thought that Orkney names had a p–Celtic element to them but conceded that the proof is scant. His hypothesis places Orkney into the same Celtic sub-group as the Welsh. So while Orcadians may have been Celts, there is no evidence that they (or Shetlanders for that matter) were Gaels. As to their contact with the Romans he cites Roman historian Tacitus, who reported their willingness to give allegiance to Rome, presumably after seeing Julius Agricola's navy and looking to win political favors. Otherwise there is no hard evidence of Roman occupation, only a few pottery shards and jewelry fragments. Any encounter appears fleeting.

The *broch* abandonment after A.D. 100 cannot be fully explained. It may have stretched over centuries. There is no apparent catastrophic event. All that can be said is that the farming settlements became more dispersed again. The centuries between the *brochs* and Norse arrival are a challenge. Documentary evidence is sparse. Orkney is mentioned only in the context of interaction with outsiders, either Scots or Norse. We know that Roman presence in northern Britain unified native opposition and accelerated migratory movement. By the time of the legions' departure in 410, several new confederations had emerged. One was Dálriada, a kingdom formed by migrating Scots from Ireland (the Latin *Scotti* = Irish), the genesis of Scotland. The Gaelic-speakers crossed the sea in the fifth century to colonize what is now Argyll or "coast of the Gaels" in western Scotland. According to the *Annals of Ulster* a king of the Dálriada Scots, Aidan MacGabran, made a visit to Orkney in A.D. 580. If true then it might be taken as a measure of Orkney's importance. His journey would have taken him north through "Pictland," defined by archaeological finds as a territory stretching from the Firth of Forth on the eastern Scottish seaboard to Orkney and Shetland, meaning it was an expedition to the Picts, though whether friendly or not is unclear.

Pictish Orkney

The Picts are a puzzle. There are abundant theories about them but scant documentary evidence. The presumption is that their name derives from skin-dyed tattoos (Latin verb *pingo*: to paint), first used by Romans in A.D. 297[10] to describe rebellious northern Britons. Some interpret Pict as a synonym for non–Romanized Celtic Britons—those inhabiting far northern parts Romans never colonized. Others extrapolate it from *Pritan*, a Celtic word for Britain used by Pytheas in the fourth century B.C. Such a definition envisages a much older culture, pre–Roman Celtic or even non–Celtic. We have a lot of speculation but not many facts. Orkney was a part of Pictland but we cannot name a single Orkney Pict!

The best case for Pictland is in archaeological evidence. Pictish rock artists chiseled human, animal and geometric shapes in a fashion not found elsewhere in the British Isles. Over fifty stylized symbols have been identified, ideographs that developed separately from Celtic design and are not to be confused with Irish *ogham* writing, a non-pictographic form of stone inscription that is almost certainly Roman influenced. It compares with Scandinavian styles apparently, a not implausible connection since northern Britons and Norse did not have to wait until Vikings for cultural interaction. Fauna inscriptions show salmon, goose, eagle, wolf, wild boar, deer, reindeer, and fantastical beasts. Inspiration has been credited to Roman mythological tradition since the heads of Pictish animal symbols point right and inscriptions follow a left-to-right reading pattern, the top line downward of Roman writing, an argument diminishing an ancient indigenous culture. The symbols themselves are unique and are thought to represent tribal names—"the salmon-folk," "the deer-folk" and so on — just as modern surnames may derive from human occupations. In this vein *Orcades* may derive from the island of "orcs" or wild boars, meaning that Orcadians were "boar folk." Men are drawn wearing gown-like tunics that look suspiciously like Roman togas but the women are shown as hunters, encouraging speculation about the matriarchal nature of their society, quite an un–Roman feature. Object motifs include crescents and v-rods, serpents, hammers, swords, spears, combs, and mirrors. Some of these motifs are found in Orkney, as we shall see; hence its inclusion within the Pictish realm.

Orkney's sixth century cultural make-up appears a fusion of Celtic and Pictish inputs, but place must be accorded also to its insularity. There is one documented insight into the nature of its political relationship with Pictland. The source is Adomnán of Iona, a seventh century abbot, who tells of a meeting between Scots saint Columba and Bridei, king of the Picts, in 558.[11] A sub-king of Orkney was discussed, from whom Bridei had taken hostages. One of Columba's monks, Cormac Ua Liatháin, had gone to Orkney, and Columba wanted assurances that he would come to no harm. If King Bridei had gone to the trouble of capturing Orcadians then maybe Orkney was difficult to control? Cormac returned to Iona some time later, so it seems that it was an unsuitable retreat for one reason or another. We might take from this that Orkney was a province within a confederate Pictland, its rulers subject to a higher king on the mainland, explaining Columba's visit to Bridei, yet powerful in their own domain. A Pictish high king list chronicled by 10th century monks survives, but other than confirming Pictland as an entity separate from that of the Scots, it tells us little else and nothing about Orcadian rulers.

We have to examine the physical evidence to glean anything else. By the fifth century a pattern of individual farms had developed out of nucleated *broch* settlements, and archaeology reveals dwellings to be small sturdy farmsteads built of stone and turf, exemplified at Gurness, where a Pictish house was built after *broch* abandonment, and Buck Quoy in Birsay. If the diminutive Gurness "shamrock" house is a guide, so-called because four small chambers circled a central room, then decline had occurred, possibly an economic effect of Roman withdrawal. On the other hand occupants still enjoyed recreational pastimes. A Buck Quoy stone gaming board is in the Orkney Museum in Kirkwall, its surface marked out as if for some checker game. By the seventh century most of Pictland had heard the Christian message, and Orkney nomenclature helps in determining the spread of early Christian sites. The *papae* or priesthood is found in surviving place-names like the small outlying isles of Papa Westray and Papa Stronsay, homes to tiny monastic cells presumably. Material proof survives in the form of stone cross slabs and some iron hand bells used to rally the flock. The Orkney Museum in Kirkwall has a Pictish inscribed cross slab from St. Boniface Kirk on Papa Westray.

Birsay Bay on Mainland's northeastern coast seems to have been a major power base, particularly the Brough of Birsay, a tidal island and natural defensive site. Traces have been found of Pictish houses, although none are visible above ground. A Pictish picture stone was dug up and a replica cast is on display on the island. Carved in the seventh or eighth century, the inscriptions display a Pictish crescent and v-rod, a swimming porpoise, an eagle and three warriors in stately robes (togas?). The latter may depict a Pictish Orcadian ruler with his loyal retinue, the closest we get to see these mystery people. Later Norse sites set over the Pictish foundations pose the challenge of distinguishing one from the other. However, the fact that incoming Norse established a presence may be enough to support its importance. The Vikings were usually interested in finding good locations!

Pictland faced two threats in the ninth century and both proved deadly. One came from overseas in the form of Vikings, and the other involved Dálriada. Both destroyed the tribal confederation and were contributory to Scotland's rise. Vikings crushed northern Pictish warriors in 839, killing the Pictish king Uven; then in 843, Kenneth MacAlpin, king of the Dálriada Scots, benefiting from weakened Pictish resistance and eager to expand his own territory, delivered the decisive deathblow. The last king on the chronicled Pictish king list, Drust IX, was slain in battle and a new expanded Scot-land was born, centered on Perthshire. Pictish authority disappeared, as mysterious at the death as it had been at the outset. Meanwhile the Brough of Birsay was greatly impacted by the Viking incursion and several oblong stone and sod buildings with barns and byres had been built by c. 850. What happened to the Birsay Picts is not known. Were they still living there when Vikings arrived, or had they already abandoned the place? Did the Vikings massacre or assimilate? James Graham-Campbell and Colleen Batey, whose comprehensive report on Viking archaeological finds in Scotland re-appraises preconceptions, lean toward the former. They reason that if Birsay were an important Pictish power-base then the Norse would have had to use force to take it.[12] Recovery of Pictish styled bone combs and pins may mean that women at least were spared for Norse husbands. A small monastic community there was probably routed and pre–Christian religious practices again became the norm.

A Viking Colony

There is no better place offshore to contemplate Vikings than Orkney. Most place-names are of Scandinavian origin, it's the home of *Orkneyinga Saga*, a unique account of British Norse culture, and the archipelago has more pagan Norse graves than anywhere else in Scandinavian Scotland. The contents of one boat grave found at Scar on the Isle of Sanday are displayed in the Orkney Museum —fine brooches, rivets, a sickle, a wooden needle case and an iron sword— possessions of a tall man who died in his thirties, an elderly woman with jewelry an indication of high rank, and a ten-year old child, each prepared for Valhalla, great hall of Odin, god of war. The clinker-built oak ship was probably built in Scandinavia, and the three of them were conceivably first-generation immigrants. Five Viking treasure hoards have been found to date, most famously that of Skaill in western Mainland where over 100 items were unearthed in 1858, including nine silver penannular "thistle" brooches, 14 silver necklets and 27 silver armlets. The cache was probably part of a ritual offering and is dated to the mid–10th century.

Displaced by ninth century political changes at home, the Vikings leapt from dragon ships to charge ashore mob-handed and indulge their special brand of gratuitous violence, or at least that is one version of it. Another is that having arrived as hit men, they liked what they saw, returning with livestock and household goods. Some brought families and others took Pictish wives. They all introduced a new language, Norn, which became the speech of Orkney as it did Shetland. Expanding Norway was an independent entity from the 11th through 13th centuries, and Orkney was pivotal as a colony and service center. Merchant ships came and went with cargoes of flour, dried fish, fish oil, gold and silver jewelry, amber, iron and woolen goods, timber, furs, sealskins, walrus tusks and Shetland steatite. The Norse preferred soapstone hardware to pottery. It may be marginalized on British maps, boxed away in the top right, but not in Norse navigational terms. Medieval documents named Orkney and Shetland as *Nordr-eyjar* or "Nordreys" (Northern Isles) to distinguish them from the Hebrides and Isle of Man, called *Sudr-eyjar* or "Sudreys" (Southern Isles). It is only in this context that the modern Scottish county of Sutherland makes any sense, nonsensical for a place name so far north but logical when thought of as south land of Orkney. Orkney was at the heart of the Norwegian sea-realm.

The Orkneyinga Saga and the Orkney Earldom

Transition from Pictish Orkney is like passing from famine to feast, from a history with no-names to one with a banquet of personalities. Credit is due to an unknown 13th century Icelandic scribe who recorded the words of skalds (court-poets) and others, dropping colorful Viking names on every page of *Orkneyinga Saga*, the oldest account extant of seafaring life in the British Isles. It was written c. 1200, maybe by a contemporary of Snorri Sturluson, the composer of *Heimskringla Saga*, story of the kings of Norway, and *Egil's Saga*, which contains a reference to Mousa Broch, Shetland. Since monks documented oral tradition and Icelanders were converts by the 13th century, we can assume that the scribe was a cleric.

He begins at a point three or four centuries before his own time, relating survivalist tales akin to those of a more recent American Wild West, except they are set in a pioneering sea frontier. The sagas (from an Old Norse verb *segja*: to speak) were part celebration of a shared past, part entertainment, and part Christian message, complete with Old Testament style hereditary trees. Icelanders were Norse émigrés and the author probably visited, returning to Iceland with a fund of local tales to immortalize characters such as Thord Dragon-Jaw, Einar Belly-Shaker, Sigmund Fish-Hook, Harald Smooth-Tongue and Thorfinn Skull-Splitter! Dialogue may be fabricated and events sometimes confused with elsewhere, but the action is credible. It involves individuals and places corroborated in other evidence, a more plausible "near-history" than the Germanic *Beowulf* or Welsh *Mabinogion*, other British vernacular sources of not dissimilar vintage. Although it opens with the supernatural in the form of Kari (god of storms), Frosti (frost), Snaer (snow) and Logi (flame) it's mostly about mortal heroics. Men don't fight dragons as in *Beowulf* or transmogrify as in *Mabinogion*; magic that occurs is clearly God's work within a proselytizing Christian context, but that message is not overwhelming.

The saga events unfold from the reign of powerful Norse ruler Harald Haarfager (Harald Finehair), first of the recorded Norwegian kings, who won authority over warring petty kings in a decisive sea-fight near Stavanger in 872. Those who refused to submit fled, and their property was confiscated. The saga tells us he sacked Orkney and Shetland to teach Vikings already settled there a lesson for challenging him, gifting them to a loyal henchman, Rognvald Eysteinsson, as compensation for his son's death in battle.[13] The tale does not negate archaeological evidence of mid-9th century Norse settlement and allows us to consider Viking infighting as another dimension of marauding and hostilities. Rognvald gave the title of *jarl* to brother Sigurd, who stayed on in the islands, and the earldom of Orkney began (c. 875). It is said both men were descended from Gor, brother of Nor, heroic founder of Norway, giving Orkney credible pedigree in Norse mythology, but it did not prevent their mortality. Sigurd died from an infection and Rognvald was killed by Harald Finehair's sons, burned alive in his longhouse, early casualties of the internecine warfare that rages through the *OS*.

As a Norse dependency the Orkney earldom included Shetland and Caithness on the adjacent British mainland, but Norse kings were infrequent visitors and earls were left to their own devices, intermarrying with Pictish and Scots nobility to consolidate their position. Orkney was a quasi-independent state for several centuries, reaching its zenith in the 11th century, during the earldoms of Sigurd the Stout and son Thorfinn II (the Mighty), sea lords with fierce reputations through the Hebrides to the Irish Sea. Earl Sigurd (c. 987 to 1014) used his war fleet to exact tributes from as far away as the Isle of Man. An alliance with the Scots king expanded his authority over northern Britain and his stature was such that toward the end of his life the king of Norse Dublin, Sitric Silkenbeard, approached him for help in a war to retrieve Dublin from the Celtic high king Brian Bóru. Sigurd was enticed by the promise of becoming an Irish king himself, but the invasion failed and he died in battle at Clontarf in 1014, as did Brian Bóru. In his wake, his son, the formidable Thorfinn the Mighty, dominated from the 1030s to c. 1060. The saga describes him as "unusually tall and strong, an ugly looking man with a black head of hair, sharp features, a big nose and bushy eyebrows,"[14] a pagan "raven-feaster," a force who imposed his will over islands and coasts from Shetland to the Irish Sea. Later in his life, tiring of fighting, the saga says that Thorfinn sought redemption from Viking ways by traveling to Rome (c. 1050) to plead for absolution, and on his return home to the Brough of Birsay he dedicated a church and monastery, possibly at a spot where Christian Picts once prayed.

Archaeology cannot corroborate his Rome trip, but there are foundations of an 11th century church on the windswept islet. The ruins of a church — nave, chancel, and apse — stand beside excavated Norse longhouses and its Romanesque layout of evenly proportioned lines is still visible. Fragments found around the site suggest small glazed windows and plastered internal walls, which may have been painted and hung with colorful tapestries, the interior not as bleak as imagined. Whether Thorfinn's newfound Christian zeal came from conscience or pressure to join the wider political community is a matter of debate. The conversion of King Olaf II (r. 1015–1028) was influencing Norse politics by his time. Paganism was an individualistic pursuit, anyone could conduct rites, whereas Christianity was organized by an authoritative patriarchy, and as such helped to centralize power. Whatever the case, the Birsay church and monastery was his lasting legacy, to be the seat of the bishopric of Orkney before that distinction was lost to Kirkwall. It is also the burial place of St. Magnus, the *OS* figure whose life and death encapsulates the popularization of Christianity in Orkney.

St. Magnus the Martyr (c. 1080s–1117)

Magnus Erlendsson, grandson of Thorfinn the Mighty, tasted the Viking life as a young man, sailing to the Irish Sea on an expedition led by colorful Norwegian king Magnus "Bare-Legs" Olafsson in 1098. The accolade Magnus is common in Norse nomenclature deriving from *magna*, Latin script for "the great." Bare-Legs was deserving of it. Chronicles and sagas have him as a formidable cloaked Viking who led men and ships down western Britain to the Irish Sea, likely after renegade Norse, those owing him tribute. We know of his expedition through his *skald* Bjiorn Cripplehand, who gleefully tells of terrorizing the Hebrides on the voyage south. As part of his war band young Magnus Erlendsson had impressive credentials of his own — the old "raven-feaster" was his grandfather after all — but in the event he was not a chip off the old block when it came to fighting and killing. According to the

OS he was unwilling to kill those with whom he had no quarrel, preferring to chant psalms in one battle in the Menai Straits, Isle of Anglesey.[15] His companions saw such piety as cowardice and he fled the expedition. It proved a wise move. Bare-Legs was killed in action not long after in Ulster (1103).

Magnus Erlendsson sailed home to co-rule the earldom with cousin Hakon Paulsson for several years before they became estranged and the islands divided. The OS tells of a meeting on Egilsay (c. 1117) where Hakon's fleet and men heavily out-numbered Magnus. The assembled chieftains demanded that one of the two earls must die to unify the islands and according to Holdbodi, a Hebridean Norse farmer and ally of Magnus, Earl Hakon's reaction was: "better kill him then. I don't want an early death; I much prefer ruling over people and places."[16] Hakon ordered a standard-bearer to kill his cousin, but the man refused, so his cook Lifolf carried out the dire deed, weeping as he struck Magnus over the head with an axe. Magnus, true to Matthew's Gospel, turned the other cheek and forgave his executioner. Magnus the Martyr was born and the saga reported two miracles. A green field grew on the spot where he had fallen on Egilsay and a bright heavenly light shone out over his first resting place at the little church on the Brough of Birsay founded by his grandfather, the "raven feaster."

Prayer to the bones of St. Magnus reputedly cured the sick and insane, and Earl Rognvald Kali Kolsson, a nephew of Magnus Erlendsson, ordered a new church to house his remains, winning himself tribute and power in the process. Work on the new church began c. 1137 at the port settlement of Kirkwall, a growing beneficiary of Norse trade. Rock was quarried in a great fervor of cathedral building in 12th century Europe, as much stone moved to the glory of God as for the Egyptian pyramids. Christianity had come of age. The stout sandstone Romanesque pillars holding up St. Magnus's Cathedral stand witness that Orkney was part of a greater Christendom. Building also began on a fitting residence next door for a new bishop, William the Old (1102–1168). The original bishopric was centered at Birsay, but now there would be a new bishop's palace in Kirkwall, a magnificent stone hall with a timbered floor and high timber roof, thought to be similar to the archbishop's hall at Nidaros (Tröndheim) in Norway. An archbishopric was established there in 1152 and the Orkney bishopric came under its diocesan wing. Pilgrimages to saintly relics were lucrative business. Kirkwall had a market and the church secured its status as Orkney's premier settlement at the expense of more exposed Birsay. One long street, was what early 19th century traveler Patrick Neill found 500 years later, in his *Tour through some of the islands of Orkney and Shetland* (1806), still Scandinavian in its aspect, houses positioned with their gables to the street.

St. Magnus's Cathedral was the biggest religious edifice seen in Orkney since the megaliths, both about a transcendent power but the cathedral was now the potent force. The old stones lay redundant, though they did provide occasional use. Earl Harald Maddadarson and some of his men were caught in a snowstorm in 1153 and took shelter in what was left of Maes Howe, an unnerving experience send-ing two of the party insane.[17] Runic inscriptions in the tomb testify to a Norse pres-ence at some stage, 24 groups of which stand at the entrance to Maes Howe. The Viking runes, letters of an ancient Germanic alphabet made by cutting straight strokes, mostly communicated charms and messages, somewhat equivalent to our own graffiti. One at Maes Howe tells lewdly of the beautiful Ingibjorg, "many a woman has had to lower herself to come in here whatever their airs and graces," and the drawing of a panting dog nearby leaves no illusions. Another spoke of a great treasure once hidden there. In the new Christendom runes like megaliths became redundant, replaced by Latin script, instrument of a new higher authority.

Svein Asleifarson — Archetypal Viking

The *OS* earls are frequently eclipsed in Orcadian heroics by one Svein Asleifarson, a happy-go-lucky adventurer and throwback to pillaging days of yore. He is the quintessential Viking of the popular imagination, living when the 12th century earldom was divided between three earls— Rognvald Kali Kolsson, Earl Harald Maddadarson and Earl Erlend Haraldsson–getting in and out of scrapes in the tales, surviving the constant feuding in reality. His farmstead was on Gairsay, a small island off northeastern Mainland, where he wintered and entertained, his drinking hall bigger than anyone else's. After sowing his barley and oats in the spring he left for trips to the Hebrides and Ireland, returning to reap and bring in the grain, then "he would go off raiding again, and never came back till the first month of winter was ended. This he used to call his autumn viking."[18]

The charismatic Svein is at his irrepressible best in a tale of Yuletide celebrations at Orphir, a high status settlement and home of Orkney earls on the sheltered Scapa Flow coast of Mainland. It is now the site of the Orkneyinga Saga Center. Christianity had not dampened earthly appetites, and the Christmas ale had to be the strongest brew of the year. Earls went to great lengths to get the best malted beer and all were expected to imbibe; anyone staying sober might take advantage of the others. As the drinking progressed the party switched from silver cups to Viking horns but one of them, Svein Breastrope, became agitated by the thought that the other Svein was drinking from a horn smaller than his own and a larger one was offered to Asliefarson to bring him up to par. He took it but thrust it impudently into Breastrope's hands instead, an incendiary action bound to upset the man further. Breastrope muttered he would kill Asleifarson but Vespers intervened, a timely reminder of new spiritual duties, and the drunken Vikings staggered off for evening service to an adjacent church. The earl led the way. After the service Asleifarson, fearing Breastrope's deadly threat, got ahead of him and hid in the shadows. As Breastrope exited the church, he got his blow in first, striking him on the forehead with his axe. Breastrope struck out in blind fury, killing one of his kinsmen by mistake, before collapsing dead himself. In the confusion that followed a friend pulled Asleifarson aside and he made his customary escape,[19] one of many in the saga. The foundations of the Orphir longhall are still visible but the church where they attended Vespers has been destroyed twice over. Once it was circular, inspired possibly by the rotunda of Jerusalem's Church of the Holy Sepulcher. Europeans journeyed there after 1099 in the first Crusade, and one of the many pilgrims, according to the *OS*, was Earl Hakon Paulsson, seeking atonement for St. Magnus's murder. He lived at Orphir and the church may have been built on his return, sometime before his death c. 1123. A grain mill has been found nearby also.

Svein Asleifarson also played host after sea trips, and at one of his Gairsay feasts Earl Harold Maddardarson urged him to give up the Viking life; "most troublemakers are doomed to be killed unless they stop of their own free will," he counseled. Svein's response was that he would take just one more autumn trip; "Hard to say which comes first, old fellow," replied the Earl, "death or glory." Svein managed both. His next trip proved his last! Having failed to exact as much in the Hebrides, where he had friends, he and his band went looking for richer pickings further south in Ireland, sailing until they reached Dublin, the Norse colony begun in the ninth century. The Dubliners, who surrendered initially, played an old trick, digging pits outside and within their settlement during the night, covering them with branches as to trap an animal. There was no escape this time. In the morning the unsuspecting Svein fulfilled all expectations by crashing headlong into the trap where he and his men were set upon and hacked to pieces (c. 1171). The butchery moved the saga narrator to lament: "that apart from those of higher rank than himself, he was the greatest man the world has ever seen."[20]

End of the Norse Earldom

Earl Rognvald had met his end earlier in 1158, murdered by a rebellious chieftain in Caithness, and buried at St. Magnus's, the cathedral he had begun. Earl Harald Maddadarson became sole ruler but was involved in a failed plot to overthrow Sverre of the Faeroe Islands, new king of Norway. He was fortunate to keep Orkney, having to agree to forfeit of lands and tax penalties. Shetland came under direct Norwegian rule as we have seen. Harald (d. 1206) is the last earl named in the OS and the male line of Thorfinn the Mighty appears extinct by 1231. Thereafter the earldom passed through an heiress to the Scots earl of Angus. Norway was wracked by dynastic feuds and wars with its neighbors and Orkney entered a political twilight, its entrepôt importance diminished, hovering on the fringe of Scots intrigues.

A case in point developed when Margaret (1283–1290), the so-called "Maid of Norway," appeared to bring the Norse and Scots realms closer. Her father was Norwegian king Eric II and mother the daughter of Scots king Alexander III. Alexander wanted his infant granddaughter recognized as legitimate heir following the untimely death of his son in 1284, and when he died in a riding accident two years later preparations were made to bring young Margaret to Scotland for coronation. It was not to be. She took sick on the sea journey and died in Orkney in 1290 aged seven years. The little fishing village of St. Margaret's Hope on South Ronaldsay commemorates her memory. Succession problems for the Scots kingdom mounted as candidacy was contested and it was not resolved until the hard fought victory by Scots-Norman noble Robert le Brus (Bruce) over Edward I of England at Bannockburn 24 years later (1314). A new Scots dynasty eventually emerged under the Stewarts in 1371 and the realms of England, Scotland and Norway remained distinct.

Scots Annexation

Orkney was in political limbo in the 14th and 15th centuries, associated with the Scots kingdom through earls of Angus and Strathearn but not in it because officially Norse kings still held suzerainty. Norway was by now past the apex of its influence and its rulers no longer enforced their will. A Scots-Norman noble, Henri St. Clair (Henry Sinclair), acquired the earldom in 1379 and invested lord of Shetland to reunite the Nordreys. This same earl, according to Sinclair descendants, crossed the North Atlantic in the 1390s to land in what is now Nova Scotia. The claim is not impossible (Norsemen had done so in earlier centuries and such a voyage may have become part of local nautical knowledge) but is unproven. Wracked by 14th century plagues, Norway lost its independence to become part of a wider Danish kingdom in 1397 under the Union of Kalmar. Orkney was included. It is hard to imagine that Orkney escaped the epidemics given the way the contagion devoured seafaring communities.

The political destiny of Orkney turned on the decision of Christian I of Denmark to cede it with Shetland to Scotland in 1468, part of a royal dowry. It was Denmark's original intention to redeem the Nordreys, and for its part Scotland seemed ambivalent initially. In 1524, it toyed with mortgaging them to the Danish for hard cash, for example, but this never materialized. The change of proprietorship had a drastic effect on island elites, as Orcadian communities lost land to incoming Scots. By 1600 practically all the higher clergy were Scots, de facto agents of the Scots crown. Bishop Robert Reid upgraded the Bishop's Palace at Kirkwall in 1541, having a high circular tower added at the northwestern corner, but it proved the last refinement. Scottish Protestants led by fire-and brimstone Calvinist preacher John Knox abolished the Church of Rome in Scotland in 1560 and the Catholic bishopric estate in Orkney was broken up. Documentary sources point to more angst over changing land law than over religious faith. There is no reference to heretics of either persuasion burning in Reformation fires of condemnation, though this does not mean that atrocities were not committed or that transition was easy. The old church must have lingered on in the hearts of the people.

The Stewart Earls (1564–1615)

Orcadians were progressively concerned with reconciling their customs and institutions with alien Scots law in the 16th century. Disenchantment expressed itself in the face of the Stewart earldom, approved by the Scots Parliament in 1564. The Stewart earls Robert and Patrick made their presence felt in Orkney more so even than Shetland. Alarm bells sounded the moment Robert Stewart put up permanent residence at Birsay, near the old Pictish/Norse power base. The size and grandeur of his palace, built between 1569 and 1574, set him apart from his neighbors and helped lay the foundations of his unpopularity; the ruins can still be seen. It wasn't long before he had made a thorough nuisance of himself, according to later charges made against him, raising taxes and rents, confiscating land and manipulating legal procedures to his own advantage. Complaints led to a summons to Edinburgh Castle in 1575 and removal from the earldom. He was a courtier with useful connections, however, and his nephew James VI reinstated him in 1581. His title and despotic traits were fully inherited by son Patrick.

Earl Patrick Stewart has been long held in detestation in local lore, but it is worthy of note that like his father, he ruffled the feathers of the elite, rather than the poor, whose circumstances were unchanged. Determined to create his own princely impression, he had a Renaissance palace built in Kirkwall, an extension of the old Bishop's Palace that came into his father's hands along with other bishopric estates after 1568. The architectural consistency with Stewart properties in Shetland is noticeable with the corbel turrets, decorative gun loops, and grand main staircase with classical straight flights suggesting the same architect and master mason at work. Kirkwall's great hall is bigger than that of Scalloway and it was in this hall that Earl Patrick dispensed his reputedly cruel brand of justice. He really had little time to enjoy his stylized creations, though; his debts, administrative mischief and extortionist skullduggery saw to that, landing him in trouble with James VI. Kinship did not excuse mischief. The Scots king became James I of the United Kingdom in 1603 but was keen to maintain credibility in Scotland, and Earl Patrick was imprisoned in Edinburgh Castle within a few years. He was not so easily subdued, however, and plotted from prison to have his son Robert raise an armed force and recover lands and collect taxes and rent. The plan did not go well. His son had to retreat to his grandfather's palace at Birsay in 1614 and the insurrection failed, conspiring only to earn both men death sentences. When the perfidious earl faced the executioner in 1615, it was because he had incited treasonous rebellion, not because of the charges that led to his incarceration.

One Orkney historian, W.P.L. Thompson, interprets the Stewart earls' tragedy less in terms of the petty tyranny associated with them and more as the critical event weakening any chance of Orkney (or Shetland) retaining some political autonomy. He argues that by disregard of due process, the Stewart earls drew attention to the exceptional Norse laws and undermined any prospect of progression with those customs and institutions intact.[21] A Scottish Act rescinded what it called "the foreign laws of Orkney and Shetland" in 1611 and Orkney's destiny was to become a dependent Scots province rather than a self-governing state under English sovereignty like the Isle of Man, Jersey or Guernsey. Much could be made of this twist of fate, but James I's homogenizing offshore policy was motivated by Hebridean events as well as Stewart malpractice, as we shall see in the next chapter. Acculturation was in the wind whatever the Stewart earls' behavior.

Land Law Upheaval and Jacobites

Udal land tenure conferred absolute ownership rights in perpetuity in the same way it had on Shetland, a practice with roots commonly ascribed to the Norse but perhaps originating earlier. Kin maintained possession of land for centuries by equitable inheritance. The custom was not always sacrosanct. An early 10th century

Orkney earl, Einar, withdrew the privilege and treated islanders as tenants, though the reform died with him c. 920. By the 11th century crown, church, and earls all claimed lands, but the remainder (a not insignificant percentage) was *udal* land. *Udallers* had no social obligations with respect to their property, and their freemen status was secure provided they paid *scat*, a tax on communal pasture. Under incoming Scots law, however, ownership was reserved to the king (in theory) with everyone else a tenant, liable for payment of services and dues. The application of Norman primogeniture, where the first-born (not other siblings) inherited to maintain large estates, was enormously destructive of social and political customs. The new estates were closely obligated to the king, and although the multi-island geography may have helped some *udallers* hang on to small plots, many were unable to meet rising taxes by the 17th century and obliged to become bonded tenants, subordinate to new superiors.

In a tumultuous 17th century when the English Parliament struggled with the Stuart monarchy (note, as kings of the UK from 1603, the convention is to use Stuart rather than Stewart), Orkney was not unaffected. A Scottish laird, the earl of Montrose, raised hundreds of Orcadians and Shetlanders to fight for the royalist cause after Charles I's execution in 1649, but the mission was doomed from the outset. Montrose overestimated the extent of royalist sympathy in the Highlands and his force was surprised and routed by Scots covenanters (anti-establishment Lowlanders) at Carbisdale in northeastern Scotland in 1650. Montrose was captured and killed. Parliamentary forces ended up occupying Orkney, the first time an English force had done so. After 1688, when James II was deposed in London in favor of a constitutional monarchy based on Protestant succession, supporters of the Stuart cause lingered among loyal Catholics in northern Scotland. Jacobites, a term derived from supporters of James (Latin = Jacobus), were well represented in Orkney, especially among smaller lairds who disliked their new feudal superiors, the earls of Morton. In 1714, the prince of Hanover, a German state, had been invited by the English Parliament to assume the UK crown — George I — and the earls of Morton became staunch Hanoverians to the anger of loyal Jacobites. However the islanders were not in unison on the issue. After the grandson of James II ("Bonnie Prince Charlie") failed to wrest the crown back for the Stuarts, being defeated in battle at Culloden in the Highlands in 1745, an Orkney naval captain, Benjamin Moodie of Melsetter, went after Orcadian Jacobites, burning several of their homes to the ground. Apparently Jacobites from Burray had killed his father some 20 years earlier. Orkney, it seems, possessed at least some of the schisms of Scotland itself, where a growing nonconformist class challenged the Jacobite elite.

Economic Challenges

Orkney's economy remained largely unreconstructed at this juncture, whatever the political allegiances. As land enclosures and crop rotations began to take root in southern Britain, medieval run-rig land distribution was the norm. Farms as we might visualize them did not exist. Run-rig, an Anglo corruption of Gaelic *roinn ruith* meaning a division of spoils, is a term for what is open-field strip farming elsewhere, involving division of rigs or arable strips in an attempt to ensure that all got a share of good land and bad land. A run was a series of rigs. Rigs held by one family typically intermingled with others in the same community, a by-product of *udal* inheritance where land was constantly sub-divided among siblings. Oats and barley grew on fertile rigs while poorer land was left for pasture, itself subject to periodic reallocation. Ox-teams and plows, where they existed, were communally owned, but mostly plowing and harvesting were hand tool activities. On such unconsolidated land there was little opportunity to experiment, as the goal was community subsistence not self-interest; anyway lairds held the title deeds, not *udallers*, so there was little incentive to change.

It was the seashore that dominated the economy in 1800, or more specifically kelp on the seashore (the activity originated on Scilly as we shall see in Chapter 6) sold to glass and soap manufacturers in industrial centers reachable by sea. Kelp is an alkaline ash made by burning seaweed, a commodity plentiful on Orkney. Production began in 1722 on Stronsay; "to the eye of a passing mariner the smoke from the kilns gave it the appearance of an active volcano."[22] It flourished during the later 18th and early 19th centuries as estate tenancies were expanded to provide more kelp workers, a negative by-product of which was reduction in the number of independent farmers. Orkney was one of Britain's main centers for kelp production and the "merchant lairds" who sold it lived well, making small fortunes when the Napoleonic War reduced foreign imports between 1800 and 1815. Profits bought the lairds inclusion in the London social scene, their wives importing fine fabrics to keep up with fashions, a far cry from the miserable poverty of kelp workers and smoky stench of kilns. A "kelp riot" occurred in 1762 with farmers claiming cattle deaths from kiln inhalations, but when the free trade lobby in England began to win its way after 1815 and duties fell to permit imports, the industry declined and lairds lost money. It revived for a while as a source of iodine later in the Victorian Age but finally ended in the 1930s after a life of 200 years. Abandoned kilns are still to be seen on Orkney coasts.

The community traditionally addressed pauperism through charity, but 19th century British Poor Law legislation placed the burden of poverty relief on local parish rates, a more formalized system empowering already-powerful lairds to mete out social justice. Lairds determined who were the deserving poor and who were not and it served only to intensify the inflexibility of the patriarchal society. Those able to leave did so, but exodus was a protracted process in Orkney, unlike the rapid experience engendered by land clearances in parts of the Hebrides and Highlands.

A manufacturing sector of sorts did exist. Woolen textiles sustained generations in work although since property rights were surrendered during Scots annexation it never raised living standards much above subsistence. Imported Baltic flax helped linen manufacturing grow in the 18th century and tens of thousands of yards of finished cloth were exported by 1800. Production was organized on a "putting-out" basis. The merchant-lairds purchased the flax and had their agents distribute it to cottagers to work at home. The finished cloth was collected when a fresh supply of flax was delivered. The mostly female work force was paid in kind (or "truck") as well as cash, sometimes because there was a money shortage but also because it kept costs down for lairds. Any payment was better than nothing if land and sea harvests were poor, but wageless workers only perpetuated the poverty cycle. The industry failed to maintain its competitive edge when factory processes developed elsewhere and Baltic flax became difficult to obtain. Linen production was finished in Orkney by the 1830s. Some women found alternative work weaving imported straw for fashionable ladies' bonnets. Stromness was the main production center. It lasted until the 1850s when other fabrics became more popular and demand fell away.

Stromness was a hamlet in 1700 but a growing port by 1800, growing in response to whaling and commercial fishing activities and serving the British and Atlantic trade more directly than Norway-facing Kirkwall. Hundreds of Orcadians were recruited each summer in Stromness for Davis Straits whaling expeditions, the same expeditions joined by Shetlanders. The local waters offered opportunities for commercial fishing too, especially with growing British urban demand (particularly London), but insidious merchant-lairds owned sea proceeds as well and the activity never realized its potential.

Agricultural Transformation

It was transportation improvements that helped induce change. Regular steamship services with Scotland began in the 1830s and by 1848 Orkney was exporting 8,000 live cattle annually to new mainland markets. The opening of the Highland Railway to the northern Scottish port of Thurso in 1874 helped cattle and sheep exports rise higher. Meanwhile land enclosure and drainage in the third quarter of the 19th century helped cereal output. There was tenancy displacement but the 1886 Crofters Act (as in Shetland) gave survivors greater security from arbitrary eviction. Land courts dealt with grievances and went some way to preventing lairds from being sole beneficiaries of land wealth. However the Crofters Act only helped those who had land; the landless became paupers or emigrated. The population fell by a third between 1850 and 1950. A croft provided only a minimal lifestyle. There were 3,000 of them in 1900, but by the 1980s only a few hundred were scattered around the islands. Ultimately rural depopulation reformed land distribution as large estates became less economically viable. The 20th century trend was toward more equitable farm sizes. As land sales increased, small owner-occupier farms replaced the tenancies and crofts of old. Beef production, dairying, and sheep farming became major parts of Orkney agribusiness.

Although 19th century island dwellings changed little with homes of stone, driftwood, straw and turf with earthen floors still common, Orkney progressed in other quality of life matters. A grammar school in Kirkwall developed as part of the cathedral establishment, and in 1560 the Reformed Church of Scotland (Protestant) demanded a school in every parish, although few were built in the first instance. The Scottish Society for the Propagation of Christian Knowledge set up schools in the smaller islands during the 18th century. Presbyterianism grew in strength in the 19th century, although without the same religious intensity as Lewis in the Outer Hebrides for example. As regards enlightenment, Kirkwall boasts Scotland's first public library, dating to the 17th century. Lairds had their own private libraries. It was 19th century farm income that radicalized society. A new middle class formed as cash relationships overrode feudal bonds and the lairds sold up, some dropping their merchant roles. Orkney had its first democratic government by the 1890s, though this reform seems to have had more to do with imposition from above — the UK Local Government Act of 1889 — than it did with grassroots populism. Self-sufficient and ruggedly insular, Orcadians were not accustomed to looking toward government as a cure-all. Nonetheless by 1900 some recovery of autonomy had begun for those who had survived the land rationalization, an autonomy laid on a foundation of farm capitalism.

Enmity, Endurance and Endeavor

After Serbian nationalist Gavrilo Princip pulled his trigger and shot dead the heir to the Austro-Hungarian Empire in 1914 to begin World War I, the British Grand Fleet anchored in Scapa Flow, a sheltered strip of water at the heart of the Orkney archipelago. It was chosen for strategic position. The Baltic Sea, where the German Navy was based, was not so distant. The Royal Navy did not provide artillery to protect the anchorage, and the only defense was block ships sealing off the entrance. Fears of naval attack receded after the Battle of Jutland in 1916 and Orkney was not threatened. However, when the fleet returned in 1939 at the outset of World War II, the anchorage was no better defended than it was in 1914, and this war came much closer to home. A little over a month after declared hostilities, on October 14, 1939, the German submarine U-47 slipped unseen into island waters hoping to surprise a fleet of British warships. It found instead only a single ship — *HMS Royal Oak* — whose anti-aircraft battery was poor defense against an underwater enemy. Having evaded the block ships of Kirk Sound, the sub fired a salvo of torpedoes at the *Royal Oak* to sink her in less than six minutes: fatalities numbered 833. Orcadians were aghast at the horror. Action brought reaction. Winston Churchill visited Scapa Flow and ordered eastern approaches permanently closed to protect the fleet. A major civil engineering company, Balfour Beatty, was given the contract to build what became the Churchill Barriers.

It proved quite an assignment — the first reconfiguration of geographical endowment in Orkney's history. The Churchill Barriers utilized more quarried rock than the megaliths and involved 300,000 tons of concrete facing blocks. Fortunately lightning did not strike in the same place twice because it took over four years to complete and by the time it was done the submarine threat had dissolved. Yet it was not wasted effort. Five islands had become connected with causeways and a good arterial road covers the 25 miles south of Kirkwall down to the southern tip of South Ronaldsay, a journey possible only by boat previously, bringing welcome economic stimulus. Dune colonization is another consequence, and sand once carried into Scapa Flow is now deposited on the eastern side of the barriers trapping the old block ship hulks.

World War II POW Camp 60

Out of this innovation came another. The war helped to meet the Churchill Barriers' labor demand in the form of forced prison camp workers, and one prison camp has left Orkney with a unique memorial. The camp in question housed Italian prisoners of war captured at Tobruk and Benghazi, prisoners of Field Marshall Montgomery's North African campaign in 1942. Italian POWs were sent to three camps in Orkney, all of them small islands in the Churchill Barriers' chain, 700 split between two camps on the larger island of Burray with another 500 imprisoned on the bleak little isle of Lamb Holm. All were forced labor in the block-casting yards. It is from Camp 60 on Lamb Holm that the chapel emerged.

Camp 60 consisted of 13 cheerless corrugated iron "Nissen" huts, housing POWs from the Sixth Anti-Aircraft Regiment of the Mantora Division of the Italian Army and from the Italian Tank Corps. To occupy their free time, inmates busied themselves planting flowers, making concrete paths, tables and benches, and setting up a makeshift theater inside the recreation hut. One of them, Domenico Chiocchetti, a native of Moena in sub–Alpine northern Italy, sculpted a figure of St. George, working it from imprisonment materials— barbed wire covered with cement. It survives at the entrance to the former POW camp. His coup de grace was to transform two unlovely corrugated huts into a Mediterranean-style chapel in the most un–Mediterranean of settings. The project was inspired by a prison visit from an Italian padre, Fr. Gioachino Giacobacci, in September 1943. The British camp commander gave his blessing and Chiocchetti gathered a small band of POW volunteers to encase the huts in a thick cement coat to disguise the unsightly tubular exterior. Cement pillars, an archway and ornamented belfry were built over the doorway to improve the entrance, with Gothic windows on either side of the doorway added to give lightness and color. Gold colored curtains were purchased from a firm in England to furnish a more intimate interior, paid for out of the welfare fund and hung on either side of the altar. The centerpiece is a *Madonna and Child* based on a painting by Nicolo Barabini entitled *Madonna of the Olives*. Chiocchetti carried a tiny copy of it in his pocket, given him by his mother when he left for war.

The prison camp was dismantled when the war ended, but the chapel was spared. It fell into disrepair until a group of interested Orcadians took the trouble to track down Chiocchetti in Italy in 1960. Keen to see his work again, he returned to Orkney to supervise restoration. As the only Camp 60 building left it is an odd sight in the midst and mist of remote Scapa Flow sand dunes. Chiocchetti died in 1999 but not before more exchanges of Orcadians and Italians had taken place and the lesson registered that old enmity can be forgotten with a little creative encouragement.

Regeneration

There was little in the 1950s and 1960s to prepare peripheral agrarian Orkney for the changes of the last quarter of the 20th century. Commercial farm growth came with a social cost, and Orkney did not escape the depopulation that occurred in other Scottish islands. In the wake of land reorganization and less labor-intensive farming practices the islands were in demographic decline. The population fell from over 21,000 in 1951 to only 17,000 in 1971, its lowest level since the 18th century. A regeneration came in the shape of an unlikely oil bonanza, courtesy of a petroleum-dependent West searching to counter OPEC oil price hikes in the early 1970s, applicable to Shetland too as we have seen. British Petroleum exploration struck oil 110 miles off Aberdeen in what became the massive Forties field, and Orkney was an important player in the North Atlantic economy again, for the first time since the days of the Norse empire. The census of 1981 reported an increase in residency to 19,000.

The Flotta oil terminal, from the Old Norse for "flat," located in Scapa Flow, is at the heart of the Orkney part of the operation. The Piper and Claymore platforms, started up in 1976–77, have been its most productive feeds. Flotta still provided 14.7 percent of total Orkney production by-value in 1995[23] and although tonnage levels were down from the mid–1980s peak with most of the large North Sea fields 70–90 percent depleted, it was still sufficient to make oil a leading contributor to the economy of 2000. The multiplier effect in all the ancillary services has diversified the economy, and in decades when Scotland's population marginally declined (1971–1991) the percentage living in Orkney (and Shetland) rose. Although fears of decline have returned in a post-oil era with a fall of nearly 2 percent giving rise for concern, it is still not as severe a drop as in the Outer Hebrides, which lost nearly 11 percent of its population between 1991 and 2001.

Oil bonanza apart, the recent economic story has been more about diversification and renewal than root-and-branch transformation. The economy of 2000 was still led by the farm sector. Agriculture contributed 14.5 percent of total production by-value in 1995[24] even when poor summer weather had reduced productivity. The BSE crisis or "mad cow disease" of the later 1990s did not help business by lowering beef prices (there was a low incidence of BSE in Orkney) but the overall prognosis is still positive, at least more so than other offshore islands. Agriculture is a controversial and volatile activity in the European Union, but Orkney's industry is modernized technologically and visitors hoping to see a traditional farming lifestyle will be disappointed, at least on Mainland. Of the other primary sector activities, fishing and fish farming account for less than 10 percent of total output by value, an indicator of reduced place, though with "water, water everywhere" and small inshore fisheries the activity is still visible. Local resources remain a wellspring for other commercial pursuits. Spring water is the life source of the Highland Park Distillery at Kirkwall, an enterprise began in 1798 as an illegal whisky still and legally operational since 1825. A proportion of the malt is kilned in the traditional way and local peat is used for part of the drying process, cut from the company's own moss at Hobbister Hill near Scapa.

Much of the rest of the economy is spread evenly through a variety of government and private services. Orkney does not have the romantic allure of the Isle of Skye, but tourism has shown encouraging signs in recent years. Significantly banking, finance and insurance constituted over 5 percent of the mid–1990s productivity pie, more than 1 percent higher than the Scottish economy as a whole.[25] In an age of electronic communication, these kinds of tertiary businesses are now feasible in remoter spots like Orkney and a clean environment, low crime and plenty of room for the home office can attract incomers. Concern has been voiced that new "white collar lairds" do not help local employment, their businesses often freelance and owner-operator, but Orkney's unemployment figures were generally favorable against Scottish national figures (1997: only 4 percent compared with 6.5 percent in Scotland as a whole) with some negative fluctuation in the early years of the new century.

To Be Scots or Not to Be: That Is the Question?

For a while the oil boom galvanized local politics, inspiring feelings of economic self-confidence, even to the level of a "home-rule" Orkney and Shetland movement. A secessionist candidate polled 14.5 percent of the vote in the 1987 UK Parliamentary elections, a result partly explained by the Scottish National Party's decision not to run against him. The SNP itself was rejuvenated by oil, running on jingoistic slogans like "It's Scotland's Oil," although the investment reality was rather more international than the propaganda had people believe. Many North Sea oil companies are American. Secessionist feelings have not strengthened, if more recent polls are a guide. Scottish devolution is another matter. A long-promised UK Labor Party reform, devolution aimed to deflect Scots nationalism into a federal Britain rather than a dissolved Britain. In 1999 Scots got their own parliament in Edinburgh but Orcadians did not massively support it. In a 1997 referendum on the twin questions of an independent Scots parliament and limited income tax powers for that assembly, Orcadians voted "yes-no," a response even more lukewarm than Shetland where at least a "yes-yes" vote was secured. It was certainly less heartfelt than Scotland at large. For the record 57 percent of Orcadian voters supported devolution against a more resounding 74 percent national support. On the other question 53 percent rejected giving a Scots parliament the right to vary income tax levels. What Orkney's leaders want is greater control over local resources, and whether they win that in Westminster or Edinburgh may be immaterial. There has been some skepticism that an Edinburgh parliament may prioritize the needs of urban Scotland. Perhaps devolution has not devolved far enough for Orcadians.

British party politics do not travel well in the offshore islands. In the Orkney Islands Council members sit as Independents, not as Conservatives or Labor. A free spirit is expressed in the choice of representatives for UK parliaments too. The urban-life oriented policies of Britain's main two parties are unappealing to Orcadian voters, and the third political party of Liberal Democrats dominates representation for both further flung governments. Orkney and Shetland are linked as one constituency for the UK Parliament in Westminster and split in two for the Scottish Parliament in Edinburgh. At the time of writing the incumbent MP and MSP are both Liberal Democrats. Loyalty to the Liberal cause is deep-rooted, stretching back to the Victorian Age when the Liberals were the party of self-help capitalism. The stress on the individual rather than the state struck a chord with nonconformist islanders;

furthermore Liberals stood in opposition to Anglican Tories, long negatively associated with the patriarchal lairds.

The strength of loyalty to the Liberal agenda is well illustrated in the career of Jo Grimond. The rise of the Labor Party cost the Liberals dearly in the first half of the 20th century, and it had lost all of its Scottish seats by 1945. The tide turned in 1950 when Jo Grimond, later described as "the greatest politician never to become Prime Minister," won the Orkney and Shetland seat for the Liberals. His victory was totally against the national grain with the party on its knees after the election results, having polled only 2.5 percent of the national vote, strangled by a "business or union" appeal by Conservatives and Labor. The appeal did not convince islanders evidently. The eponymous Grimond, born in Fife, Scotland, took up residence in Orkney and lived there for 43 years until his death in 1993, his name synonymous with the place. Grimond understood that Orcadian interests did not necessarily parallel those of Scotland and sought "opt-out" clauses in devolution proposals. He was Liberal Party leader for 10 years and an Orkney and Shetland MP for 33, serving under nine prime ministers in his House of Commons career. Admiring crowds thronged St. Magnus's Cathedral to hear his funeral oration. Island voters have stayed with the Liberals in their various incarnations subsequently. The Liberal Democrat candidate took 51.5% of the popular vote in the 2005 election.

Modern Orcadians are relatively quiet about their cultural personality, but they clearly feel a separate identity. Community centers, clubs and societies keep the flame alive and a mass football game played in the Kirkwall streets on New Years Day persists (called simply the *Ba'*), attributed by some to a tale in *Orkneyinga Saga*. Alternatively it's not difficult to find omens of the mainstream. The number of non–Orkney born councilors sitting on the Orkney Islands Council has risen, for example, and over 15 percent of Orcadians are non–Scottish born, a higher percentage than the Hebrides. Although there is renewed interest in Norn speech, the live language itself is long lost. A controversial local decision in recent times was school centralization. Two secondary high schools at Kirkwall and Stromness serve the archipelago and children aged 12 and above on the outer islands, once educated in their island parishes, come into Kirkwall and board at a hostel. Some of the outer islands experienced population decline of over 20 percent between 1991 and 2001 and since four out of every five Orcadians live on Mainland the decision was inevitable. Nevertheless for diehard natives it destroyed one of the last seeds of inter-island diversity. One small consolation for those who mourned its passing is that celebrated islander literati like George Mackay Brown, whose angular weather-beaten face looks proudly from book covers in island bookshops, and Eric Linklater, the self described "peasant with a pen," did not live to see it. Their writings did much to capture the old idiosyncrasies. Where a new generation will be found sensitive to that heritage is open to question. Young Orcadians pack their bags and leave to find higher education and prospects and many never return. Unless emigration is reversed then the pre-oil decline trend will resume. Brown's loyalty to Orkney was such that he apparently never saw Shetland until an old man!

1. Clarke, David, and Maguire, Patrick, *Skara Brae* (Historic Scotland publication, 1996), 20–23.

2. Lamb, Hubert, *Climate, History and the Modern World* second ed. (Routledge Press, 1995), 134.

3. Clarke and Maguire, 25.

4. Clarke and Maguire, 27.

5. Cunliffe, Barry, *Facing the Ocean: The Atlantic and Its Peoples, 8000* B.C.–A.D. *1500* (Oxford Univ. Press, 2001), 211.

6. Piggott, Stuart, *Scotland Before History* (Polygon, Edinburgh, 1992), 149.

7. Sherratt, Andrew, "The Transformation of Early Agrarian Europe," in *Prehistoric Europe*, ed. Barry Cunliffe (Oxford University Press, 1997), 195.

8. Fojut, Noel, *The Brochs of Gurness and Midhowe* (Howie and Seath Ltd. Historic Scotland series, reprint 1996), 5.

9. Powell, T.G.E. , *The Celts* (Thames & Hudson, 1980), 202.

10. Ireland, S., ed., "Panegyric on Constantius Caesar, delivered A.D. 297" in *Roman Britain: a Sourcebook* (Routledge, 1986), 127

11. *Adomnán of Iona: Life of St. Columba,* Sharpe, Richard, trans. (Penguin Classic, 1995), Bk. II 42, 196.

12. Graham-Campbell, James, and Batey, Colleen E., *Vikings in Scotland: An Archaeological Survey* (Edinburgh University Press, 1998), 11.

13. *Orkneyinga Saga* Palsson, Hermann, and Edwards, Paul, trans. (Penguin Classics, 1981), Ch. 4, 26.

14. *Orkneynga Saga*, Ch. 20, 50.

15. *Orkneyinga Saga*, Ch. 39, 84.

16. *Orkneyinga Saga*, Ch. 49, 94.

17. *Orkneyinga Saga*, Ch. 93, 188.

18. *Orkneyinga Saga*, Ch. 105, 215.

19. *Orkneyinga Saga*, Ch. 66, 124–127.

20. *Orkneyinga Saga*, Ch. 108, 217–218.

21. Thompson, W.P.L., *History of Orkney* (Mercat Press, 1987).

22. Willis, Douglas, *Crofting* (John Donald, Edinburgh, 1991), 37.

23. *Orkney Economic Review No. 18* (Orcadian Ltd, 1998), 1.4, 4.

24. *Ibid.*

25. *Ibid.*

3

The Western Isles: "Hebridean Odyssey"

"I had desired to visit the Hebrides or Western Isles of Scotland for so long, that I scarcely remember how the wish was originally excited" — Samuel Johnson, *A Journey to the Western Isles of Scotland, 1775*

There is no such thing as bad weather, someone wryly observed, only inadequate clothing, and it is with such thoughts that a journey through the Hebrides ("Heb'-rid-eez"), infamous for its inclement moods, might be contemplated. English writer and raconteur Samuel Johnson declared the weather "not pleasing" in his travels there in 1773 but managed to enjoy it in retrospect and it was a Hebridean tempest in 1829 that inspired Mendelssohn's musical tribute *Fingal's Cave* (Isle of Staffa). Named *Ebudae* in the first century A.D. by Alexandrian Greek geographer Claudius Ptolemy and correspondingly *Hebudes* in Latin by Pliny the Elder, the root may lie in Greek mythology with *Erebus*, embodiment of darkness, and the *hesperides* (Greek *hespera* = west), deities who lived in the far western ocean. The noun accommodates more than 500 islands scattered off Scotland's wild Atlantic coast, ranging in size from little Rockall — a euphemism for nothing much — to pendulous Lewis and Harris. The Clyde islands of Bute and Arran are added, not strictly Hebrides nominally but elemental in the same offshore experience historically. About one-fifth are inhabited and despite an exodus in recent centuries, more than 50,000 still call them home.

Outer Hebrides and Inner Hebrides

Geographers separate them into outer and inner groups, a division not necessarily convenient for historians but useful as an introduction. The Outer Hebrides of Lewis/Harris, North and South Uist, Benbecula and Barra stretch 130 miles from the Butt of Lewis to Barra Head. These Western Isles, to use the bland modern descriptor, are virtually one "long island" thanks to modern causeway and ferry

THE HEBRIDES

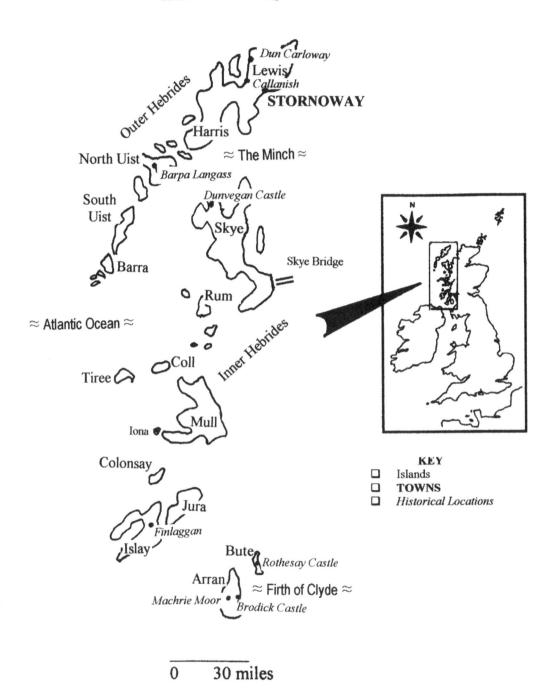

0   30 miles

service connections. Like a fish skeleton with its flesh eaten by fjords, the northerly chunks of Lewis and Harris form the broader upper torso with the Uists and others as the tail. Geology has not been that kind. Beneath a ground cover of peat moss, heather, and grass is some of the world's oldest rock, crushed, melted and folded for millennia to form the hard crystalline rock known as Lewisian Gneiss but the ground holds little or no metal and more acres are fit for grazing than for cultivation. This is Britain's last frontier, and residuals of traditional life persist. It may be the UK but English is not necessarily the language of choice. Scots Gaelic, a minority language descended from ancient Irish settlers, revived in recent times and the greatest concentration of its speakers is found in the Outer Hebrides. Indeed resistance to English — language and other cultural manifestations — has been a preoccupation for centuries. The biggest town is Stornoway (Lewis), with around 8,000 inhabitants, biggest not only in the Hebrides, but in northwestern Scotland.

The Inner Hebrides — principally Skye, Mull, Islay and Jura — are much less homogenous, scattered over a 150 mile range from north to south. Skye (from a Norse word for cloud — *skuy* — its perennial cover) is the furthest north of them, popular with tourists and relatively populous and bridged to mainland Kyle of Lochalsh since 1995. Mull, a windy isle of open moorland, is the second largest in the group, and lying off its southwestern edge is Iona, well-visited island cradle of British Christianity. Islay ("Aye-luh"), home of the medieval lordship of the isles and a major producer of single-malt whisky, is a little less accessible but worth the effort. Jura (from Norse *dyr-ey* = deer island) is even more secluded with more deer than residents, reachable only by ferry from Islay, its woodlands and private estates a popular retreat for the Edwardian hunting, shooting and fishing fraternity. On a completely different note George Orwell wrote *1984* there. Bleak and windswept Coll and Tiree are more isolated and the ferry service to Colonsay is infrequent.

The islands of Arran and Bute located in the Clyde estuary to the east of the long Kintyre peninsula share the same Gaelo-Norse heritage as the Hebrides. Arran is the bigger. Its 5,000 residents live in a micro–Scottish landscape with gorse-clad volcanic-looking summits up north and low green farmland in the south. The principal town Brodick is named from the Old Norse *breidr-vik* or broad bay. Bute with over 7,000 became a holiday island in Victorian times attracting trippers from Glasgow sailing "doon the watter" on Clyde steamers.

First Farmers

Human occupation stretches back to c. 7000 B.C. as post-glacial sea levels rose to create western Scotland's trademark lochs (lakes) and islands. Quartz tools have shown up in Islay excavations. Oronsay was home to Mesolithic fishers. Evidence from South Uist suggests early slash-and-burn of woodland for deer pasture. Rum has the earliest signs of industrial activity. Excavations there in 1986 found spores and pollen consistent with whisky production c. 4000 B.C. The islands offered security, and farming was underway in the fourth millennium B.C. Cattle and sheep were shipped across and more birch and hazel cleared to accommodate them. Hebrideans sowed oats and barley with simple stone ards (early plows), fired clay pots, and built individual dwellings surrounded by their own farmland, much in the style of later frontiers, not nucleated villages as in Orkney. In a similar vein to the Northern Isles, however the burial practices became more elaborate and tombs were painstakingly constructed beneath stone cairns. The presence of animal bones, pottery and fires points to ceremonies for the living. At Hornish Point, South Uist, signs of sacrificial rites surfaced in butchered human and animal remains.

Two-thirds of the chambered tombs identified in the Outer Hebrides are on North Uist. The best preserved is the chambered cairn of Barpa Langass near the stone circle of Phobull Finn, a sanctified area comparable with those in Orkney. It does not equate with Maes Howe in its present state but its burial chamber is intact. The Clyde islands also supported significant Neolithic populations. Bute has one surviving stone ring at Ettrick Bay while the concentration of chambered tombs and megalithic circles of varying type on Arran's Machrie Moor is one of Scotland's most studied Neolithic sites. In the Hebrides proper six chambered cairns can be traced on Islay and the cairns and standing stones of Mull invite scrutiny. Over on Lewis's wild Atlantic coast, however, is the Hebridean tour de force: the Standing Stones of Callanish (Gaelic: Callanais), as compelling a megalithic site as any left offshore. A small circle has been recovered from the peat bog, built c. 3000 B.C. before the peat had formed. The configuration looks like arms extending from a small round body with neatly aligned standing stones running outwards toward compass points. Callanish was a work in progress and a small crypt inside the stone ring evolved eventually into a chambered cairn. Callanish was not alone. It stood in a wider landscape of megaliths. At least 11 other sites in the area are registered although none are as visible. At some stage during the later Bronze Age, after perhaps a millennium of service, Callanish was abandoned, and for long stretches of its subsequent journey through time it aroused suspicion, alarm and fascination, likewise noted with the Orkney megaliths.

Enough of it was visible to excite 18th century antiquary Martin Martin, a Skye physician with an interest in his Hebridean backyard and author of *A Description of the Western Islands of Scotland* (1703). He believed Callanish to be a place of pagan Celtic festivals convened by long-gone heathen druids, an erroneous presumption noted previously. There is no shortage of modern ideas to invest Callanish with meaning. One of the most authoritative recent works is Aubrey Burl's *From Carnac to Callanish* (1993) in which he examines the mathematics of a lunar relationship to support the notion of its astronomical purpose, of Callanish as a Neolithic lunar temple. Some are skeptical but "advances are not made by negative thinking,"[1] Burl retorts reasonably. Human fascination with the night sky and celestial phenomena is a given. There must have been those in Neolithic and Bronze Age society who sought to convince the rest that they had a special hold on the future forecasting eclipses and other calendar events, wielding influence in the way that the Day of Judgment exercises the modern psyche. It is not implausible that passing Mediterranean mariners such as Pytheas of Massalia reported Callanish back home to fuel the hyperborean winged temple myths. The stones were there long before the Homeric stories. Whatever the verdict, the precision of prehistoric mathematics is something archaeology has taught us to respect. The Callanish alignments were a product of numerate minds and successful pastoral societies, not at all the wild outpost for which it is taken today.

Reformation

Climatic change as much as anything else influenced the course of Hebridean life during the later Bronze Age. Analysis of tree trunks preserved for millennia in Irish peat bog,[2] a study known as dendroclimatology or tree ring science, reports changed weather patterns impacting north and west Britain c. 1200 B.C. Reduced sunlight, lower temperatures and a higher annual precipitation thickened blanket peat moss, further accelerated by centuries of slashing woodland for domestic usage. Somewhere in this tract of time the Callanish tomb was emptied. The results of forensic analysis of two adult skeletons found in excavations of a 3,000 year old dwelling at Cladh Hallan on South Uist in 2001, part of a small terraced settlement, serves the hypothesis of profound change aided and abetted by climate. The corpses had remained aboveground for maybe five centuries after death, between c. 1500 B.C. and c. 1000 B.C., tightly wrapped and preserved somehow in a mummified form, before eventual burial in a peat bog.[3] The possibility of mummification and the fact that the final interment coincided within the period of worsening weather is of interest. The later Bronze Age period is something of an information dark age for archaeologists, all the more reason to suspect dire consequences of climatic change — namely food shortages, warfare and disease. The aggregate would have been more than enough to challenge old religious beliefs and practices, bringing on a cultural reformation of sorts, perhaps the sort that precipitated this burial.

The cultivable land was reduced by peat bog but it was not eliminated. Resettlement occurred along coasts in the last millennium B.C. where sand dune pasture known as *machair* (Gaelic for "plain") predominates, especially prominent in the Uists, Barra and South Harris. *Machair* needs heavy dressings of fertilizer to maintain productivity and is vulnerable to wind erosion, but 3,000 years ago fields were laid out on it for oats and barley. Communities sheltered nearby in enclosures of *duns* or *brochs*, lighting hearths and kilns for generations to come. The inclusion of *dun* (*dunum -= stronghold*) in island place-names is very commonplace and shows how widespread these settlements were, generally assumed to have been the habitat of a single-family unit.

The most visually impressive, however, were the *brochs*, already encountered in the Northern Isles and possibly originating there. Dun Carloway *broch*, located a few miles along the Lewis coast from Callanish, is an outstanding Hebridean example — 30 feet of double dry-wall tower still standing proud amidst Atlantic elements, its thick outer wall breached only by a low doorway. The fortress tower appearance tempts the thought of frightened folk with self-protection in mind, but *brochs* may have been as much about status as defense in their completion, heirs to the megaliths in that respect. Gerald and Margaret Ponting, who have written a mini-guide to Dun Carloway, dismiss the defense theory, questioning the absence of a well, reasoning that siege preparation demanded water supply. Excavations have not turned up war artifacts either. Some think they were the work of specialist teams, experienced builders specially hired for the task of *broch* construction, the skills involved too honed for individual communities to undertake. A University of Edinburgh archaeological team has been searching the Valtos peninsula to the west of Callanish since 1985, where it has a base and field center. At least three more *broch* sites are under investigation and a wheelhouse design has been uncovered at Cnip, akin to that described in Jarlshof, Shetland. Thus far the evidence does not indicate a *broch*-village as at Gurness or Midhowe in Orkney with economic activities more widely dispersed, yet still within the watchful eye of the *broch*. Dun Carloway has great visual command, encircled by coast, lochs and land resources. The politics of architecture was well understood.

Wool weaving was common, and cattle-hides were worked into leather for multiple applications including, importantly, sea-tight coverings for coracles, not dissimilar to ones their ancestors arrived in. There is some evidence of iron and bronze working in the Iron Age, but metal was a precious import in the Hebrides and tribal leaders must have controlled supply for tools, weapons and gifts. We can assume close-knit family and community ties in a multi-island setting and a common language born through sailing contact and interaction. We cannot, however, assume a collective awareness of living in an age now too-easily labeled Celtic, one that parallels in time the Mediterranean urban world of Greeks, Etruscans and Romans.

Celts

There are a lot of misconceptions about Celts, and given the frequent application of the term some digression is necessary to examine it. Celtic is basically a construct rationalized in modernity, though its documentary usage originates in antiquity with Hecataeus of Abdera, an Ionian Greek geographer. The author of *Periegesis* (c. 500 B.C.), he located Greek Massalia (Marseilles) by placing it near the "land of the *Keltoi*"; note the hard "K" sound, not the soft "C" of Glasgow Celtic or Boston Celtics sports teams, thus "Keltic" and not "Seltic." The Greek "father of history" Herodotus, writing in the mid–400s B.C., thought the *Keltoi* inhabited lands near the source of the Danube, and Celtic became a generic noun for any rural transalpine peoples in central and western continental Europe, though curiously not Britain and Ireland. Neither Greeks nor Romans, who substituted Gauls for Celts, applied it to the peoples of Britain or Ireland.

Two new areas of understanding have developed in recent times. Firstly archaeologists classify Iron Age military and domestic metalwork with distinctive curvilinear designs as Celtic, specifically those identified in discoveries at Hallstatt, Austria (1847–63), and La Tène, Switzerland (1857). Since these finds and others like them were in locations approximating to places alluded to as "land of the *Keltoi*," the word was adopted and an association struck. The fact that geometric shapes adorning Celtic metalwork were cleverly intricate and proportionate offered a new take on the barbarians described by unappreciative Greeks and Romans. Not only their flair for creative precision impresses but their democratic use of art, employed to beautify workaday things like chariot harnesses, linchpins and bridle bits, as well as valuable bracelets, brooches and rings. A lot of La Tène design has been identified in British and Irish metalwork, and Celtic cultural geography was expanded to include Britain and Ireland. There are other criteria, notably stonework sculptures and vernacular literature, and this is addressed in islands with significant examples of that type.

The second defining quality in our age involves language. The classical writers never cared to classify barbarians' speech, and it was not until Scottish humanist George Buchanan (1506–1582) spent 30 years learning, teaching and writing the classics that insights emerged. Buchanan recorded names of chieftains and tribes and other words and terms provided by classical writers as *Keltoi* and decided that the language of ancient Celts was the ancestor of the native Scots speech of his day. His pioneering work and that of Welsh scholar Edward Lhuyd (1660–1709) laid the basis for further research. Place-names and inscriptions on monuments, altars and coins, together with familiarity with old live languages, gathered a case for a distinct Celtic language, one that was part of the Indo-European language family, but deserving of major sub-group status as the table indicates. The continental Celtic languages are dead, overrun by Latin and Germanic speech, but in Britain, Ireland and Brittany, an insular branch survives.

Irish monks used the Latin alphabet to write down Irish speech from the seventh century. Welsh speech was transcribed later. A new orthography was necessary since Latin could not accommodate alien Celtic sounds, and modern analysis of medieval manuscripts reveals differences in spelling for the same words. Variations are taken to represent pronunciation differences, and historical linguists divide insular Celtic into q–Celtic and p–Celtic. The qu-sound associated with Ireland is called Gaelic, deriving from Gwyddel, the Old Welsh word for Ireland, and the substitute p-sound is termed Brittonic or British. The easiest example to follow is that of the Celtic word for "son," written "macus" in Gaelic ("mac" in MacDonald = son of Donald) and "ap" in Brittonic (as in the surname Mapson). The prevailing view is Irish migrants introduced Gaelic to the Hebrides in the later Roman era, as we shall see. The "q and p" subdivisions refer to the post–Roman centuries, the period when the language was written down. Pre-Roman Brittonic and Gaelic is really an unknown quantity since older word forms were lost as speech was transcribed.

Table showing the division of Celtic languages is shown on page 64.

There is a tendency in modern usage to lump all definitions into one people, but we should be wary of such homogenization. The notion of singular Celts is no more accurate than Columbus's naming of diverse American aboriginals as Indians. We don't really know whether all Britons spoke Celtic. Hordes of Celtic warriors did not sweep over Britain and Ireland. La Tène sword-bearers did not necessarily accompany the swords. In fact continuity from earlier insular cultures is no less compelling than an invasion thesis. The best-case scenario is that Britons and Irish *Celticized* during the last millennium B.C. through contact with Atlantic neighbors. It was a process of cultural accretion, an ancient version of Americanization perhaps, involving gradual adherence of disparate peoples to a common denominator of creative expression and language. The Hebrides lay at the head of a sea corridor connecting

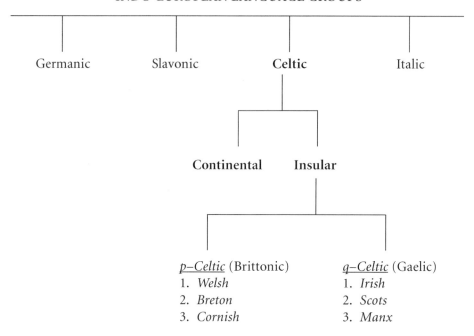

INDO-EUROPEAN LANGUAGE GROUPS

Germanic   Slavonic   **Celtic**   Italic

Continental   **Insular**

p–Celtic (Brittonic)   *q–Celtic* (Gaelic)
1. *Welsh*   1. *Irish*
2. *Breton*   2. *Scots*
3. *Cornish*   3. *Manx*

diffuse parts of Atlantic Europe with the Mediterranean (Pytheas of Massalia et.al.), enough to permit exposure to such influences.

The Scots

Roman occupation is part of the British historical psyche but not in the Hebrides. *Broch* life and Roman Britain co-existed but there is no sign of Roman presence, apart from a few coins and pottery relics, presumably from trade. Visits from legions could have caused *broch* abandonment in the second and third centuries but there is no record of it. Dun Carloway was built before Roman conquest began in A.D. 43 and abandoned before the legions' withdrawal in A.D. 410. On the other hand, as imperial authority crumbled in southern Britain in the later fourth century, raids and migratory movement did intensify and the southern Hebrides—Islay, Jura and Mull with associated small islands—experienced outside impact, the consequence of which was alignment with Ireland. Romans named Irish raiders along western British coasts *Scotti* and several hundred of these Gaelic-speakers from Dál Riata, a kingship in northeastern Ireland, sailed to the southern Hebrides in the fifth century to settle an area of mainland shore and islands now called Argyll—literally, land of the eastern Gaels/Irish. Dálriada, the satellite kingship they initiated, is the embryo of Scotland. It's hard to imagine that the Hebrides was unknown territory to the Irish (it's only 13 miles from Islay to Ulster) but only at this point can political interaction be confirmed. In reality interaction must have gone on for millennia. It is customary to emphasize the cultural influence of Ireland on Scotland but the reverse must have occurred too. At any rate these *Scotti* settlers implanted what linguists now classify as q–Celtic and Scots Gaelic was born. We do not know the prior speech of the indigenous islanders.

The northern Hebrides of Skye and the outer islands lay on the western edge of the loose Pictish confederation and there is no evidence of incursion by *Scotti*/Irish at this stage. The Clyde islands of Arran and Bute meanwhile were within Strathclyde's orbit, a p–Celtic-speaking kingdom centered in Dumbarton, covering what is now southwest Scotland. By the sixth century the cultural and political geography of the islands split three ways. Firstly there was Brittonic Arran and Bute within Strathclyde, secondly the Gaelic-speaking southern Hebrides of Islay, Jura and Mull within Scots Dálriada, and thirdly Pictish affiliated Skye and the Outer Hebrides. The rulers do not leave us their words, so we are dependent on scraps from monk-chroniclers for clues. One sixth century Brittonic monk, Gildas, probably Welsh, was not impressed with either Scots or Picts: "like dark swarms of worms that emerge from the narrow crevices of their holes when the sun is high and the weather grows warm,"[4] he wrote, adding significantly that "they differed slightly one from another." The seventh century Scots abbot Adomnán concurred on the differences, mentioning two occasions when the Scots saint Columba needed an interpreter on missions to Pictland. In one incident on the Isle of Skye Adomnán reported that "a little boat came in to land on the shore, bringing in its prow a man worn out with age. He was the chief commander of a warband."[5] The chief's vocabulary (or pronunciation) was apparently so foreign sounding to Columba's Gaelic ears that a translator had to be found. The king-lists chronicled by later monks further convey the impression of Picts and Scots as distinct realms.

Early Christianity

The unifying agent would be Christianity, and bands of Christians were in Ireland from the early fifth century. The Celtic Church, to apply its commonly given title, was monastic and autonomous. Its footloose monks often ventured seaward, many of them ascetics seeking penitence. Several Irishmen who established cells in the Hebrides are sanctified. The most venerated is Colum Cille (St. Columba), an aristocrat from the powerful Uí Néill warrior clan of Donegal. He gave up his political rank to become a monk and scholar and sailed with companions to eventually set up a monastery in 565 on Iona, an islet off southwestern Mull. It's not clear whether Iona was within the territory of Scots Dálriada or the southern extremity of Pictland, but whichever it was, Columba secured permission for his commune. Maybe his Uí Néill connections helped. Brendan, an abbot from Clonfert in Ireland, and a contemporary of Columba, sailed the Hebrides during the 560s to 570s, landing on Tiree (*Tir-iodh* = island of wheat) where he started a monastery according to repute. A later legend has it that his voyages took him as far west as North America. Another Irish missionary, St. Donnan (d. 617), is said to be the patron of the Isle of Eigg. Tangible evidence can still be seen in the form of sculptured Celtic stone ring-crosses: the one at Kidalton on Islay is the finest surviving in Scotland.

Columba's Iona is considered the fount of Celtic Christianity for northern Britons, but the Welsh (?) missionary Ninian established an earlier priory (c. 390s) at Whithorn, Galloway, in what became Brittonic Strathclyde, protector of the Clyde islands. A site on Bute is dedicated to St. Ninian but the date of origin is unknown. Ninian's influence later spread to Shetland, as we have seen, and it may have stretched through the Hebrides. There can be few better illustrations of devotional obsession than the hermit cell on North Rona, a remote islet 44 miles northwest of Lewis, furthest flung of the Outer Hebrides, named for its reclusive founder Ronan (d. 737). There are several early saints with that name but this Ronan may have been an abbot from Bute and if so it places him in Ninian's legacy.

The importance of Iona is assured nonetheless, and it is entirely possible that the tiny isle was a site of pre–Christian religious importance too. Certainly we should not think of it as isolated and remote in the sixth century. If it had received pilgrims as visitors before Christianity then from the sixth century it was in dynamic mode, sending them out to minister the faith. Columba visited Pictland as mentioned and one of his followers, Aidan, traveled overland from Iona to Northumbria, now northeastern England, to spread the word among pagan Germans in 635. His monastery on the small tidal island of Lindisfarne (a.k.a. Holy Island) was begun at the request of Northumbrian king Oswald. Earlier in his life he had been given sanctuary on Iona and was returning the favor. Aidan's teachings helped kindle conversion and a literary renaissance. Northumbria is the home of the great Benedictine monk-historian Bede (673–735), author of *Historia Ecclesiastica Anglorum* (The Ecclesiastical History of the English People), source of much about the post–Roman centuries and not least originator of the concept of the "English." By Bede's lifetime the learning and writing of letters was already a major part of Iona's work, as Adomnán demonstrates. Adomnán or 'little Adam" (c. 625–704), an Irishman educated in Donegal, homeland of Columba, reached Iona sometime before 673, becoming its ninth abbot in 679. His *Life of Columba* is the primary source on Iona's founding saint. Encouragement of the arts of calligraphy and meticulous illumination of biblical manuscripts among Iona brethren was an important facet of scholarship on Iona. Composition of the *Book of Kells* (c. A.D. 800), Ireland's greatest ecclesiastical literary and art treasure, began there. As the faith won more adherents its political stature strengthened. Consecration of union between church and crown is an important element in medieval politics, King Oswald obviously understood it, and the cemetery at Iona is claimed as the burial ground of Dálriada kings.

Tribal Confederations

A Pictish north and Gaelic-speaking south was still applicable as late as 800. Pictish law is a mystery but chronicled Pictish king lists suggest centuries-long regulatory governance by confederate means. In other words island chiefs deferred to higher over-kings when the occasion demanded it. In Scots Dálriada a clearer picture is afforded if we assume that migrant Irish imported something of Irish custom. Itinerant judges or *brehons* dispensed justice in Ireland to register the primacy of the kin, base camp in the political evolution of most peoples. Clans were held responsible for individual misbehavior with fines expressed in heads of cattle, de facto Celtic money. Acceptable forms of courtship and marriage were defined and unacceptable practices such as rape punishable. Women could divorce in specified circumstances. All were not necessarily equal before the law — rank clearly carried privileges — but judgments were to be consistent. It appears that in Dálriada the same law of royal succession applied as in the Irish kingdoms, whereby the incumbent named a *tanist* or royal successor, and the expectation was that successors were sought from wider kin. A selection confined within a nucleated bloodline militated against clan interests; sons did not succeed fathers by right. The king and his warrior retinue were at the hierarchical head but high status was given to men of the arts. Bardic poetry was a necessary part of the prelude to political acts, an improvised agitation to praise leaders, curse enemies and get the adrenalin running! In the middling ranks of society were the kinsmen who tended herds and ran the homesteads. On the lowest rung were slaves, assigned menial tasks.

Small feuding and plunder was a way of life, so when Vikings came on the scene, threatening as they must have been, Hebrideans were hardly facing hostility for the first time. Fighting was exalted among the clan elite, and the ritual of honoring the best fighter is the stuff of heroic Celtic literature. Nevertheless the Norse would be more than a match for the scattered northern Hebrides. The defeat and death of Uven, a northern Pictish king, by Vikings in 839 left them vulnerable. The more homogenous Scots Dálriada fared better, expanding with mainland gains to the east at the expense of weakened Picts. King Drust IX was beaten and killed by Scots in 843 and the Pictish royal seat of Scone in Perthshire captured. The victorious Scots king Kenneth MacAlpin is said to have brought the ceremonial stone of destiny there, on which Scots kings would be crowned until 1296. The union of Scots and Picts is heralded now as source of the Scots nation, but contemporaries may have seen it only as an extra authoritative dimension over continuing core kinship loyalties.

Enter the Norse

Irish annals report attacks on Skye in 795 and on Iona in 802 and 806 with scores of monks killed. It is not known exactly what Vikings pillaged and devastated on Skye, but somewhere in the Iona mayhem manuscripts illuminating the gospels were dispatched to Ireland for safekeeping at Kells and over a millennium later the famed *Book of Kells* is in Trinity College Museum, Dublin. The relics of St. Columba were also removed to Ireland. Within decades Norse settlers arrived, some with families and others taking Pictish or Celtic wives; as in the Northern Isles, bringing their customs with them, burying their honored dead with an array of worldly goods for Valhalla heaven. Tortoise brooches and other personal female ornaments have been uncovered at Valtos on Lewis and there is a Viking ship grave at Canna, an isle southwest of Skye. The extent of their settlement can be gauged by place-names with Scandinavian word content all over the Hebrides such as *borg* (fort), *stadir* (farm), and *uist* (from *i-vist*— an abode) among others. Arran and Bute felt the influence of the

Norse too as place-names there indicate. The greatest concentration of settlement, however, was in the northern Hebrides where Pictish traces would be eliminated. The Norse colonization of Ireland also began during this time (840s).

The Norse pursued the same economic activities as the natives, but their arrival necessitated land transfer, and they either introduced *udal* rights or expanded the practice. The former may be likely because Celts defined wealth and political authority in terms of cattle grazed rather than crops tilled and the determinants changed to an arable one, increasing the importance of acreage. The Norse too were seasoned in livestock farming. Their homeland of a few cultivable acres demanded it. Farmland was organized by run-rig, as we saw in Orkney, to serve communal interests, but it was in sea trade where the Norse opened up new possibilities and the Hebrides became useful ports of call between Norse settlements in Orkney and Ireland. An accidental discovery in a Lewis sand dune in 1831, obliged by an exceptionally high tide, suggests how widespread those contacts became. The find comprised a hoard of walnut ivory chess sets, beautifully carved pieces from the mid–12th century, thought to be the stock of a seagoing merchant. The figures are mustachioed and bearded Viking-types, apparently northern European, though the game of chess is Indian in origin, where hirsute faces were also common. Chess became known in Europe through the twin influence of Islamic Spain and Russia (where Swedish Vikings controlled Asian trade). How the Lewis Chessmen actually ended up in Hebridean waters is anybody's guess, but west had met east. They are now on permanent display in London's British Museum.

The Gaelo-Norse

Irish annals speak of a *rí innse gall* by the ninth century — a "king of the islands of the foreigners" — as if the Hebrides were so overrun that they were barely recognizable as Celtic. It's true that Norse originated place-names are everywhere in the north (nearly 80 percent of the village names on Lewis are thought to be Norse)[6] and there are 20 or so recorded pagan Norse burial sites on Colonsay, Oronsay and Islay, so the south experienced significant contact too, as the "*ay*" word endings (= Norse "isle") indicate. Yet Norse settlement no more purged the Hebrides of Celtic culture than it did Ireland. It did not prevent Gaelic-speaking expansion and movement. Not only did Gaelic survive, it became the lingua franca of the islands. Norn never rooted itself as it did in the Northern Isles. What evolved were clans of *gael-galls* or Gaelo-Norse. Clan MacNeil is a good example. It claims descent from Uí Néill, the powerful Irish clan, and is said to have arrived and begun building a castle off the Barra coast, most southerly of the Outer Hebrides, around 1050, by which time many Irish were the progeny of two centuries of Norse intermarriage. MacNeil clan sources acknowledge this ethnic mix listing the 35th chief Rory MacNeil (later 14th century) as " last of the Vikings."

The Norse named the fragmented maritime constellation of the Hebrides *Sudr-eyjar* or "Sudreys" (Southern Isles) to differentiate them from *Nordr-eyjar* ("Nordreys": Northern Isles of Orkney and Shetland) — both multiple island confederacies under Norse suzerainty. The higher ruler was named in Gaelic *ri innse gall* in the Sudreys and *jarl* (Norse) in the Nordreys, The earliest *ri innse gall* was possibly Godred mac Fergus (d. 853), a warrior of Norse and Gaelo-Irish parentage mentioned in Irish annals, who may have established himself as leader of the old Dálriada territory in the southern Hebrides.[7] By the 860s the Irish Norse settlement of Dublin was flexing its muscles (*Dubh Linn* translates as "dark pool" and dark and foreigner appear synonymous in Irish writing) with one of its kings, Anlaf Gothfrithson, marauding up Hebridean coasts winning tribute and binding islanders in some form of service to him. Alternatively the Scandinavian sagas offer up one Ketil Flatnose as an early Hebridean Norse leader, a Viking caught up in the life and times of Harald Haarfager (Harald Finehair), the ruler who unified Norway in 872. He figures as a Finehair collaborator in *Eyrbriggja Saga* but in *Laxdaela Saga* he is Finehair's enemy, a renegade who fled to Iceland and then south to the Hebrides where his descendants settled. By the 10th century the Sudreys or Hebrides were caught between rapacious Irish Sea rulers, many from Gaelo-Norse communities, and ambitious Orkney earls like Sigurd II and Thorfinn the Mighty, the Orcadian rulers discussed previously. All of them sought material tributes wherever they dropped anchor.

Kingdom of the Sudreys

Orkney's power peaked in the age of Thorfinn the Mighty (d. c. 1060) and thereafter Hebrideans became part of an Irish Sea polity based on the Isle of Man. Manx sources call it the Kingdom of Man and the Isles but in Norse terminology it remains Kingdom of the Sudreys. It began with the reign of the impressive Manx king Godred Crovan (r. 1079–1095), who organized the scattered sea realm along unitary lines for the first time. According to *The Chronicles of the Kings of Man and the Isles* his father was Harold "the Black" (Norse foreigner?) of "Ysland," probably Islay. He spent time there and maybe developed the site of Dunyveg Castle, the later MacDonald stronghold on the south coast. Only a shell survives but its masonry once spectacularly incorporated the rocky knoll on which it stood, with a sea gate through which small boats were dragged into the castle. Islay lore has it that he is buried at the Carragh Bhan (white stone), a Neolithic monolith on the Oa peninsula of the island. Crovan contrived to end *udal* custom, emulating Einar of Orkney in that regard, requiring land be held from him. Then he extended the principle northward to Lewis through a show of force, driving back the Orkney earls in the process. To institutionalize his agenda, the court of Tynwald was summoned to Man, considered more fully in the Isle of Man chapter. Suffice to state here that out of 32 summoned to it, vassals in effect, 16 represented the Hebrides. Four clan chiefs were called from each of the quadrants of Lewis, Skye, Mull and Islay. The Sudreys under Crovan was a formalized unit of territorial monarchical government, a progressive and overlooked polity, comparable in organization with other evolving European kingdoms at that time, including those in Normanized England and Scotland. He added Dublin to the kingdom later in his reign.

Godred Crovan's achievements did not, however, extend to planning a smooth succession After his death in 1095 intense strife ensued in the Sudreys. Drama included the part played by Norse king Magnus Bare-Legs Olafsson, sufficiently impressed by Celtic attire to wear it. His skald Bjorn Cripplehand recalled the ferocity of Bare-Legs' terrorizing trail through the Hebrides with people massacred and lands torched, telling of "fire in the trees" on Lewis, the "blood of foemen" on Skye, "wolves on Tiree's lonely shore," and smoke rising "heaven-high" from Islay.[8] In the face of such onslaught the Scots king, Edgar (r. 1097–1107), capitulated and made a treaty, agreeing to Bare-Legs' claim to any islands he could sail his ships around. According to one oft-told story the Norse king cheekily claimed the Kintyre peninsula as well by having horses and men drag his galley overland across its narrow neck from the Sound of Jura to Loch Fyne.

John Macleod, author of a history of the Scots Gaels, blames Bare-Legs' firestorm for the defoliated predicament of the Outer Hebrides today, compounded because it occurred in a time of cooling temperatures and more rain. The burned-off vegetation had less chance of recovery and peat bog thickened. Forests in retreat since the second millennium B.C. disappeared altogether and the landscape began to assume its bleak moorland appearance, "silent witness to that awful campaign."[9] Bare-Legs' bravado was undone when he was killed in a skirmish in Ulster in 1103. A son of Crovan Olaf Godredson got control of the Sudreys eventually to rule as Olaf I for nearly 40 years (r. 1114–1153), using his fleet and connections in the Norman-French court of England to hold sway. All of the Hebrides remained part of his realm, referred to as the Kingdom of Man and the Isles in the Isle of Man chapter. This Manx hegemony lasted until the intervention of Somerled of Argyll (c. 1105–1164).

Somerled, King of the Southern Hebrides

Although chronicles and sagas allude to Somerled's greatness among medieval warlords, he is less known in mainstream history. An Irish birth and descent through his father from earlier Dálriada kings gave him Scots Gaelic cachet but his name is a Norse epithet deriving from *somhairle* or "summer Viking." His mother was related to Sigurd II (the Stout), the powerful early 11th century Orkney earl. Somerled was Gaelo-Norse and a typical Hebridean of his day. An ambitious chieftain, he was keen to win back old Dálriada clan territory lost to Bare-Legs and Man's Olaf I, and in the 1140s married Olaf's daughter in a propitious move to further that political end. He probably was encouraged by the Scots king David I, at least until that king's death in 1153, coincidentally the same year that Olaf I died. Olaf's successor Godred II began in combative mood reasserting Manx sovereignty over Dublin but evidently he saw Somerled as a threat and prepared to subdue him. The rival fleets met in battle in 1156 off the Isle of Colonsay where Somerled's Highland galleys or in Gaelic *birlinn* (deriving from the Norse *byrdinger*, a smaller galley) proved more than a match for the Manx. His galleys were fitted with a hinged stern-rudder, an innovatory feature with the tactical advantage of tighter steerage,[10] out-maneuvering the heavier Manx ships with their side-mounted oar steerage. Somerled won the day.

His prize stretched from Mull, Islay and Jura in the southern Hebrides to Arran and Bute in the Clyde. He did not press claim for the Isle of Man, although he did briefly invade to register his supremacy. Nor did he pursue Skye and the Outer Hebrides. Somerled's ambition was recovery of old Dálriada territory (Argyll) and he had achieved that. Fertile Islay was his power base and Manx Tynwald membership shrank accordingly. The eight clansmen representing seceded Islay and Mull no longer participated but clan chiefs from the northern Hebrides of Lewis-Harris and Skye continued to maintain their presence. The unitary Sudreys of Crovan was undone, the Hebrides split north from south. Somerled was king of the southern Hebrides, a satellite of the Scots kingdom, and in 1160 the Scots king Malcolm IV acknowledged him as *rí innse gall*, some admission of his own limited influence in the islands. Yet at the very moment of Somerled's triumph, external forces were accumulating to undermine him.

The Scots kingship, with which Somerled was aligned, was in a state of flux. David I (r. 1124–1153) had earlier encouraged Norman-French knights to settle areas where he faced rebellion and nominated his son as heir on the basis of primogeniture or first-born inheritance. In fact David's son predeceased him and his young grandson succeeded as Malcolm IV. Somerled opposed it as contrary to Celtic custom, one honoring *tanists* (next-in-line) from extended kin and not first-born sons and grandsons. To his mind the wider kinship's interests was best served by avoiding a nucleated bloodline. In 1154, just two years before his great sea victory over the Manx, he had rebelled against Malcolm IV but failed to remove him. Beyond that irritation the ecclesiastical politics of the age also threatened tradition. Inspired by Pope Gregory VII's resolution to make it arbiter of "right order in this world," the Church was remodeling to continental practice. Among many changes wrought was Iona's long-held autonomy, a custom ended by the arrival of Benedictine monastic rule. To alienate Somerled further, Gaelic speech was also under threat within the Scots elite from an evolving hybrid of Norman-French, Latin and English.

Having failed to dislodge Malcolm IV by force, Somerled tried peaceful persuasion. He spent time at court trying to get the Columban Church on Iona reinstated and religious custom honored, but his efforts were futile. Malcolm IV was willing to honor his kingship of the Argyll isles but did not want unnecessary (and bigger) enemies. Suspecting the king's collusion with higher forces, Somerled and other Highlanders began to fear ultimate vassalage to Henry II (r. 1154–1189), the new Plantagenet ruler of England. In 1164 they raised a large fleet to make their feelings known, and galleys came from all over the Hebrides and Orkney in an impressive display of solidarity, sailing up the River Clyde in protest to put pressure on the Scots king. The sight of all these ships must have been quite something for Lowland Scots onlookers, but for Somerled's men the occasion turned to tragedy when he was singled out and murdered at some stage in arbitration at Renfrew, his body carried back to Iona in shock and dismay. A century earlier the real MacBeth (as distinct from the one of Shakespearean artistic license) feuded with and killed the Scots king Duncan I (1040) over violation of *tanist* custom. Somerled and MacBeth held in common to old clan ways of distributing lands and power but neither could prevent the march of centralizing forces, circumstances where kings would own people *and* territory. Somerled's protestations on behalf of the Celtic Church proved equally ineffectual. Rome tightened diocesan control and Hebridean ecclesiastical communities were gathered up under the wing of the Norwegian archbishopric of Nidaros (Tröndheim) by the end of the 12th century. St Olaf's Church at Gress, on Lewis, commemorates Olaf II, the 11th century Norse king whose death accelerated Norse conversion and submersion within wider Christendom.

Divided Sudreys

For all the homogenizing portents, it is also the case that the Sudreys remained defiantly unorthodox, secure in their insular fragmentation, for at least a few centuries yet. R. Andrew MacDonald makes the plea in *Kingdom of the Isles* that in most British historical writing the islands are ignored, "an orphan with no place in national historical writing,"[11] ruled by sea-kings whose exploits are absent from the pages of Anglo-centric British history. As intriguing as these sea-goths seem, in practice their "kingdom" was as anarchic as it ever was monarchic; even the mighty Somerled managed only six years at the helm. The political twists were as complex as Celtic curvilinear design after his assassination. With the possible exception of the Crovan reign, it was always a pluralistic entity, militated by its multi-island geography. Power after Somerled coalesced in three broad groupings—Lewis-Skye in the far north and the Isle of Man in the far south with an ill-defined area (Islay/Mull) fought over by Somerled's kin in between. The northerners of Lewis-Skye stayed aligned with the Isle of Man enabling the odd scenario of southbound galleys sailing to the annual Manx *Tynwald* by the shores of seceded Islay/Mull en voyage! To further complicate matters Somerled's successors' bid for control of Islay and Mull split into two rival factions—Clan Donald and Clan Dougall. The Clan Donald base was on Islay where Godred Cravan spent time and is buried and whose people Somerled killed, evicted or assimilated. Clan Dougall claimed Mull.

The stature of Ewen Dougall was enough to have Haakon IV (r. 1217–1263) invite him to Bergen, Norway, in 1248 and invest him as king of the Sudreys, albeit a divided Sudreys. However, Norse recognition would stretch his loyalties since he owed the Scots king for mainland Clan Dougall possessions in Argyll, and under Alexander III the Scots became a potent force. Alexander was only seven when he assumed the title in 1249, but by 1261 he was in full control and Haakon was aware of the danger. According to the *Saga of Haakon* Scots attacked Skye in 1262 putting women and children to the sword. A year later the Norse king set sail to remind all of his authority. It was not a happy expedition. The old king who previously brought Iceland, Greenland and the Faeroe Islands into line summoned Ewen (among others) to his cause but Ewen chose to surrender his Hebridean possessions into Haakon's hands rather than alienate Alexander. Haakon had more success with Clan Donald of Islay, who accepted his call-to-arms partly because they did not have mainland possessions obligating them to the Scots (yet) and partly because he threatened to sack Islay if they didn't! The Gaelo-Norse fleet proceeded around the Mull of Kintyre and made for the Clyde estuary anchoring off Arran in the Bay of Lamlash where good cover was provided by a high granite islet in the bay.

The Scots claimed the Clyde islands of Arran and Bute. Although prominent Arran place-names like Brodick (*Broad-vik*), Sannox (*Sandy-vik*) and Goat Fell (*Geita Fjell*) register Norse presence, Clyde islanders still spoke a form of Celtic (given Strathclyde antecedents and Irish influence). Both islands had fallen under the rule of their Scots-appointed stewards (the Stewarts) — a bone of local contention because it violated *tanist* succession custom. In the 1230s the Norse seized the distinctive circular fort of Rothesay Castle on Bute, but it isn't clear what their status was by 1263. To assist Haakon the Manx king sent reinforcements from across the Irish Sea, but there was to be no full-blown battle. An inconclusive skirmish was fought off the Ayrshire coast at Largs where a combination of problems — loss of a cargo ship, bad weather and lateness of the year (October) — sent Norse and allies scrambling and sailing for home. Haakon managed to get his storm-battered fleet to safety in Kirkwall, but, exhausted and fevered, he died shortly afterwards in the Orkney port. Within a year Alexander III's forces had pressed their advantage, attacking various Hebridean islands and slaying any of Haakon's bondsmen they could find. Haakon's son Magnus IV conceded that he could no longer prevail and by the Treaty of Perth in 1266 ceded the Sudreys to Alexander III for an agreed lump sum plus annual payments. It was soon in arrears. The treaty specifically excluded the Nordreys of Orkney and Shetland, "which the king of Norway has reserved specially to his domain," and added the proviso that shipwrecked Norse in the Hebrides must keep their property even if their ships were "broken and shattered,"[12] inferring that while land might be conceded Norsemen and the sea were inseparable. The benefits for the Scots were dubious. It proved no easier for their kings to master the Hebrides than it was for the Norse.

The Clans

Over the span of centuries Largs (1263) and the Treaty of Perth (1266) appear consequential. They ended the era of the Norse Sudreys. The northern and southern islands were no longer split politically. In the intermediate term, however, they changed little. Real power remained centered at clan level and control of the sea was critical to that end. The clans maintained fleets of *birlinn*, shallow-drafted enough for haulage over land where necessary. As troop transports they enforced order, collected dues, and exacted revenge, and as movers of merchandise they helped move necessities and luxuries, although the decline of the Norse empire did not help Hebrides commerce. The place of the galley in island affections is assured in poetry such as the 18th century *Birlinn of Clan Ranald* by Alisdair Macdonald (written in Gaelic) and in art with *birlinn* lovingly carved on stone slabs and gravestones, a unitary symbol. On a grave slab in the chapel ruins of Eilean Mor on Loch Finlaggan, Islay (to be discussed shortly), is a finely etched effigy of Donald MacIlaspy, who held the island in the mid–1500s. He is depicted in his Highland tunic, firmly grasping his claymore, a galley at his feet. The modern Lords of the Isles Trust maintain a replica galley, *The Aileach*.

In the absence of sustained external authority and served by their indispensable galleys, the clans increased territorial influence. Clan Leod became a force to be reckoned with in the Outer Hebrides and Skye, its rise spun out of Manx political intrigues. When Olaf II, a potential heir to the Manx kingdom, was passed over as a child by a half-brother Ragnald I (r. 1197–1226), he was given Lewis as territorial compensation (1207). Olaf won the kingship eventually (r. 1226–37) and gifted Lewis to a kinsman, Leod (derivative of the Norse *Ljot* or "ugly"). After Leod's death (c. 1280), the territory divided between Tormod, who took parts of Harris and Skye plus Glenelg in the Highlands, and Torcuil (or Thorkil in Norse), who got Lewis. The Clan Donald branch of Somerled's house grew stronger too. Alexander III honored chief Angus Mór (d. 1296) as king of the isles, better his ally than his foe. Clan Donald could pressure MacLeod interests better than he could.

Modern romance has shrouded the clans in images of daring and heroic figures in dashing tartan, men glorious and free in a state of nature, societies of "bravehearts," but the reality was less glamorous. Chiefs controlled territory by exacting dues paid in livestock, fowl, dairy and grain, and maintaining big households of bards, harpers, pipers, and warriors through the service of poorer clansfolk. Communality (Gaelic *clann*/offspring) was exalted but aristocratic rank was just as definitive — the practice of taking provisions from poorer folk without recompense was commonplace (called *sorning*), for example, the line between familial hospitality and extortion not clear to outsiders. The clans were not so far removed from Sicilian *Cosa Nostra* in some respects: both thrived in impenetrable terrain, ruled by patriarchs with life-and-death power over dependents. It must have been difficult to survive outside of one of them, and members were linked through ties both real and convenient. It has been customary to explain (celebrate) their constant feuding and cattle raiding in the politics of clan pride, but the reality may be no more thrilling than the stress effect of a deteriorating climate,[13] as food shortages, famine and disease in the 13th and 14th centuries led to ever more desperate measures for economic survival. The end of Norse influence in the Irish Sea did not help either, and sea trade growth became increasingly channeled in the North Sea on the other side of Britain.

If the Treaty of Perth changed little in the short term, Alexander III's death in a riding accident in 1286 certainly had greater effect. His sole heir was granddaughter Margaret "Maid of Norway," child of his daughter, the wife of Erik II of Norway. Scots nobles approved her as a legitimate queen and she set sail from Norway in 1290 (by then aged seven) to claim her crown only to die feverishly in Orkney, just as Haakon IV had done. Her death left the Scots crown vacant and the solution was of significance for Hebridean politics. Thirteen claimants emerged including those of two Scots-Norman knights, Robert de Brus (the Bruce) and John de Balliol. The clans divided over the claims but the fact that they took sides at all drew them into the orbit of Scots-Norman and Anglo-Norman aristocracy.

Lordship of the Isles

Clan Dougall supported Balliol while Clan Donald backed Bruce. Its chief, Angus Og the Younger, gave shelter to a fugitive Bruce in 1306 and led men from Islay in

Bruce's triumph over Edward I at Bannockburn in 1314. This important victory released Scots nobles from Plantagenet clutches, yet Clan Donald did not hurry to pledge itself further. Angus Og's successor John changed allegiances several times before swearing loyalty to the new Scots establishment, this after marriage to Robert Stewart's daughter in 1350. The Stewarts (later Stuarts) were a Norman-French originated family granted land in Arran and Bute by David I and appointed stewards, hence the name. The accession of Robert Stewart (Robert II) in 1371 began their long dynastic reign in Scotland. John Donald declared himself *dominus insularum*— lord of the isles— rather than *rex insularum* in dutiful deference to his father-in-law, but the lordship of the isles proved no less independent-minded than the kingship.

Robert Bruce is said to have endorsed the support of Angus Og at Bannockburn with the words, "My hope is constant in thee," a sentiment repeated on the arms of Clanranald, a branch of Clan Donald, but expressions of fraternity didn't last. Donald II (Lord of the Isles: 1387–1423) issued judgments and decrees independently of the Scots crown and offered allegiance to kings in England if it suited his purpose, fighting a fierce though inconclusive battle against the Stewarts at Harlaw in Aberdeenshire in 1411. His ability to incite clan resistance was always a warning to Scots pretensions in the Highlands and Hebrides. His son Alexander II, Lord of the Isles between 1423 and 1449, proved just as capable of rallying the clans, many of them on a wild rampage against James I (r. 1406–1437), because he tried to curb their autonomy with a parliament in Inverness in 1428. Clan Donald continued to hold much of Argyll and Islay/Jura, spreading their influence during the 14th and 15th centuries over the Uists, parts of Skye with adjacent Highlands coast, and smaller isles like Muck, Eigg, Rum and Canna. Fate meanwhile was less kind to Clan Dougall, who had backed Balliol. They paid after Bannockburn, losing lands including Mull to Clan Donald, and never regained equivalent stature.

Yet the clans did not hold to Celtic custom without exception. Somerled's murder in 1164 proved the beginning of the end of *tanistry*. The participation of wider kin in succession was no longer a given right and primogeniture was increasingly accommodated. The prefix "Mac" as in MacDonald and MacDougall denoted father to son passage and other clans strengthened in like manner. The MacNeills of Barra spread to Colonsay and Gigha. The Macleans of Duart ruled parts of Mull, Coll and Tiree. The Macleods consolidated their position in the Outer Hebrides. The pivotal force was the lordship of the isles with its stronghold on Loch Finlaggan in Islay, home of Clan Donald since the death of Somerled.

The genesis of Finlaggan was in prehistoric times. Five feet of a wedge-shaped standing stone exposed on the loch bank confirms ancient presence. Only the foundations of MacDonald presence survive, but excavations indicate "urban" development along the loch shore and on two *crannogs*. These man-made mini-islands are associated with the same time span as *brochs*, also found in Ireland, reminder of the longevity of that affiliation. There are probably others sunk without trace. Causeways linked the surviving two to the shore. The main *crannog* of Eilean Mor housed the lord's residence with an adjacent feasting hall, a chapel in honor of Findlugan, an Irish contemporary of St. Columba. There were other dwellings, storehouses, workshops made from stone, wood, clay and turf— some 20 buildings in all— and a jetty. The smaller *crannog* of Eilean na Comhairle (pronounced Ale-an na Cor-le) housed the clan council where 14 representatives including the Benedictine abbot of Iona convened, new lords instated upon a ceremonial inauguration stone (now lost). Excavations led by David Caldwell, Director of the Finlaggan Archaeological Project, revealed an earlier Iron Age stronghold — either a *dun* or a *broch* — with a new castle tower built over it in the 13th century. Caldwell compares its inspiration to Castle Rushen on the Isle of Man.[14] By the 15th century the lordship had converted the castle for use by the council. Defense does not seem to have been a priority. Buildings on the loch shore may conceivably have served as a garrison (or accommodation for visitors), but the loch lies within encircling higher land and is obviously not a good defensive site. In the 15th century, evidently, they did not fear attack. Finlaggan was the nearest thing to a town in the medieval Hebrides. A few artifacts, now in the National Museum of Scotland in Edinburgh, testify to its good times, a tuning pin from a harp stirring thought of an audio long gone in oblivion.

Beyond the Pale

As kings of England consumed themselves in the Hundred Years War (1337–1453) and Wars of the Roses (1455–85), Gaelic-speaking parts of Britain and Ireland remained largely undisturbed. Ireland had been affiliated to the English feudal realm since 1171, but after the reign of John (r. 1199–1216) no English monarch visited for over two centuries, leaving Celtic culture under clan patronage. Bardic poets, professionals whose skills passed from generation to generation, were still in demand. Bagpipe sounds continued to fill the air of noble households. Harpers fingered wire strung Highland *clarsach* and energetic fiddlers added to the retinue. Thousands are said to have attended a festival of arts in Athlone, Ireland, in 1458, perhaps including Hebrideans. Alexander Macleod (1455–1547), eighth chief of Harris, built the Fairy tower at Dunvegan Castle on Skye, endowed a church, and established the MacCrimmon dynasty of pipers on Skye — leading pipers and pipe teachers for generations. On the other hand, economic life was less energized. Families still huddled with livestock in low stone and sod huts, growing oats and barley by runrig, grazing clan cattle, paying their dues in kind. In Scotland burghs were emerging in a new commercial world of market towns — Aberdeen, Dunfermline, and Edinburgh — with burgesses, crafts, guilds and a money economy. Alexander III issued the first Scots coinage in 1250. The Hebrides in contrast was increasingly isolated, a cashless world where wealth was still measured in the livestock of old. The Gaelic word for cattle — *eudail* — means treasure but there was precious little of the metal currency.

Nevertheless the MacDonalds of the 14th and 15th centuries were a formidable political entity, the lordship of the isles representing a realm within a realm, and the ruling Stewarts were aware of it. In 1455 a MacDonald fleet of 5,000 men aboard 70 galleys invaded Arran, sacking Brodick Castle, registering their opposition to the title of Stewarts and successors to the island. The Stewarts for their part sought to strengthen their own feudal contracts as the Tudor dynasty began in England (1485).

The Hebrides may have been nominally Scots since 1266 but such was their "life beyond the pale" (outside the law) that the Scots Crown did not require Hebridean chiefs to hold land from it by written charter until 1493. An oath would no longer be enough; henceforth it was to be government by pen and parchment, or as one clansman succinctly put it: "whereas he previously held land on the edge of his sword he now held it on the skin of a sheep."[15] In the event it was MacDonalds put to the sword. The lordship of the isles title was abolished in the same decree and vassals of James IV (ironically the last Scots monarch on record to take the trouble to learn Scots Gaelic) attacked and razed Finlaggan c. 1500.

A rash of struggles and feuds ensued after dissolution. In 1494 the Mackenzies of Ross began a vendetta against the Macleods of Lewis and the Macleods feuded among themselves over land in Glenelg and with Macdonalds over parts of Skye and the Uists. Donald Macdonald (Donald Dubh, "the Black") rose up in 1503 against James IV in a rebellion that lasted two years, ending in his capture and phenomenally nearly 40 years' imprisonment in Edinburgh Castle. James IV then appointed two officials to try and enforce Scots law in the Hebrides, one for the north and one for the south, but he didn't live to see if it worked. He was killed in action at Flodden in Northumberland against the Tudors in 1513. A furious clan feud broke out in 1528 over the murder of a MacLean by one of Clan Campbell and the appointment of Norman-descended Hamiltons as earls of Arran led to fierce infighting in the Clyde islands.

Lewis-Skye was especially notorious for ignoring Scots law, and in 1540 James V sailed from Orkney to Lewis with 12 ships and 1,500 men to deal with it. After taking the Macleod chief prisoner he crossed to Skye to seize Macdonalds among others;[16] the harbor settlement of Portree (Gaelic: "King's Harbor") was named for his visit. However this hard line policy was tested three years later, a year after the king's death, when Donald Dubh escaped from prison and defiantly summoned a council of the isles on Islay in 1545. Nearly 200 masted galleys mustered with thousands of men-at-arms from the Hebrides and Highlands, a solidarity display reminiscent of Somerled, importantly on this occasion more loyal to a Macdonald than a Stewart. It was a last hurrah. Donald swore allegiance to England's Henry VIII to try to get English support against the Scots, but he took ill shortly after and his death ended the MacDonald bid for Scotland.

The Statutes of Iona, 1609

English government at this time was busy shoring up defenses and expanding control in Wales and Ireland following Henry VIII's break with Rome (1534). In the process of Irish conquest and resettlement, Irish customs and religious practices came under intense prejudicial attack in English propaganda. Gaels were stigmatized as primitive, uncivilized, poverty-stricken, feckless, godless and worse, barbarians undeserving of the lands they held, justification enough for relieving them of it. Such sentiments pilloried the Hebrides too. By 1600 Protestant evangelism was winning the minds of merchants and wage earners in the Scottish Lowlands, but in the

Highlands and Hebrides the clans remained resolutely Catholic (Clan Campbell was a notable exception) and a cultural schism widened within Scotland. James VI was of similar anti–Celtic persuasion to his Tudor relatives in England and for the same political ends, except in his case it was not Ireland but the Hebrides that was perceived as the Achilles heel. He recognized the Presbyterian (Calvinist Protestant) Church in 1592 to appease those in the Lowlands, where that church was strong, and went after rebellious Catholic Highlanders.

He hoped to confound with officialdom, and a Scots version of the Tudors' invasive surrender-and-re-grant land policy in Ireland, intended to disinherit the disloyal, was enacted in 1598. The Macleods of Lewis for one were unable to comply, their titles allegedly stolen by Mackenzies, themselves aligned with the Stewarts. To get the upper hand the king announced he would replace MacLeods with Scots Lowlanders and leased Lewis to 12 Fife merchants to initiate an enterprise effect. The merchant-adventurers sailed off to Stornoway with a small army in 1598 but met determined Macleod resistance. The Fifers were captured and freed only on the condition that they never return. The initiative had failed but the era of Macleod hegemony was over nevertheless. A royal compromise ended their dispute in 1613 with Kenneth Mackenzie of Kintail granted a royal charter to Lewis and the Macleods keeping Harris.

The political consolidation of Britain reached its apex when James VI of Scotland became James I of the United Kingdom in 1603, a union of crowns arranged to protect a fledgling Anglican and Protestant ascendancy and advance mutual trade interests. The anti–Celtic/anti–Catholic thrust intensified as James sanctioned colonization of Irish Ulster in 1609 by tens of thousands of Britons, mostly Presbyterians from the Scottish Lowlands. They settled lands forfeited by rebel Irish. The Hebrides did not experience this kind of demographic intrusion, but James's desire to acculturate them was far from diminished. The MacDonalds and other clans were well-known sources of mercenaries for the Irish, and after 1603 this became James's problem, all the more reason to break clan power. The Statutes of Iona (signed the same year that the Ulster plantation began, 1609) declared war on Scots Gaelic culture and society. Orkney and Shetland came under pressure too, as we have seen with a 1611 statute abolishing "foreign" (Norse) laws there.

The Iona statutes were secured in a simple act of deception. Leading clan chiefs—Macdonalds from Islay and Skye, Macleod of Harris, MacPhee of Colonsay, and Macleans of Mull and Coll—were tricked into meeting with the king's envoy (a bishop) on a galley anchored in the Sound of Mull in 1608 and promptly taken captive, freed only on the promise of reconvening on Iona in 1609. The chiefs cooperated. Paying lip service to royal orders had been done before but changed little. However the Statutes of Iona (1609) and associated acts in 1616 and 1620 went much further than they could have imagined, prohibiting a range of practices endemic to Gaelic culture and society. Some orders resembled those of Tudor Irish policy, enforcing acculturation. The chiefs' households and numbers of galleys were to be reduced in size and they were to send their sons to the Lowlands to learn English. The practice of *sorning* was condemned as thievery—those seeking food and supplies must henceforth pay for it. The bardic arts were banned, praise-songs being blamed for exciting feuds and unrest. Some interpret the statutes as a form of cultural cleansing, a premeditated Anglicization; others point to the condemnation of *sorning* as social justice reforming an exploitative clan system. The provisions were not easily enforced and in the short term did not have the desired effect, but the inference was ominous. Gaeldom was being marginalized and it was vulnerable. Clan Campbell, meanwhile, loyal supporters of the Scots Crown since Robert Bruce, consolidated and expanded their position as earls (later dukes) of Argyll, power achieved at the expense of traditionalist Macdonalds, with whom they are forever drawn in enmity in Highland lore.

Celtic Fringe

The pulse of Scots Gaelic culture beat on for a while with the writing of prose reaching its apogee in the 17th century (*Red Book of Clanranald* and *Black Book of Clanranald*) and Hebrideans dressing as they long had with woolen plaid cloaks wrapped from shoulders to knee but trousers worn too; the kilt is a modern invention. George Buchanan, the 16th century Scots scholar who did much to define Celtic as a distinct language, noted that islanders liked purple and blue dyes, and more than a century later Martin Martin (*Description of the Western Isles*, 1703) said a man's residence was told by tartan pattern. Brooches, sporrans and dirks with Celtic designs emboldened on them remained popular. Ian Macleod (d. 1693), defiant to the last, maintained a household with traditional retinue of bard, piper, harper and fiddler.

Other traditions have less appeal. Communal land tenures and run-rig farming locked generation after generation into cycles of subsistence. The cultivation of oats and barley in a cold wind blasted and sodden climate was always a challenge with crops planted in hope rather than certainty. One bad season spelled hunger and starvation. The Dutch fished Hebridean waters under license for a while in the 16th century but the commercial potential of the sea was not really explored by islanders until land clearances began to take effect in the 18th and 19th centuries. South American potatoes were planted as in Ireland, and their high yield per acre fueled unprecedented population growth, but it was an unfortunate development on such a narrow economic base. Tenants in the Outer Hebrides found opportunities in kelp production from the 1740s to the 1820s (the industry having already begun on Orkney) and it supplemented crop and animal husbandry for a few months a year, but most monetary remuneration went to the lairds who leased the rights. The underlying fuse of change would be capitalistic, but the main event of the 17th century was political, in the guise of failed attempts by Stuarts to recapture a UK throne lost in 1688.

The Bonnie Prince

A coup orchestrated by the Anglican establishment in England deposed King James II (grandson of James I) in favor of a Protestant, the Dutch king William of Orange, in 1688. James's barely concealed Catholicism had proved the last straw for an English political elite frustrated by incompatible Stuart kings. In 1715 James's son, the never-to-be James III, tried to rally loyal Jacobites (Jacobus = James) in rebellion against the newly installed Protestant monarchy of George I, but the rebellion failed. In 1745 the Jacobites tried again and on this occasion Charles Edward Stuart, the never-to-be Charles III, led Highlanders unsuccessfully against George II. The English massacred his ragged army of barefoot warriors at Culloden Moor near Inverness but there is a Hebridean postscript.

Charles evaded English capture and found his way to South Uist in the Outer Hebrides. Support for him was probably less than once claimed, with many apprehensive of reprisals, but they were not keen to just hand him over either. His savior was Flora Macdonald, one of the Clanranald of South Uist, an unlikely supporter because her father and fiancé were in the service of George II. She was persuaded to protect her island from English revenge, should the prince be found there. They sailed famously from South Uist across to Skye with clothing found to effect a gender change for the prince, his new papers describing him as Betty Burke, an Irish maidservant. The voyage is sentimentalized in the English language *Skye Boat Song*— "speed bonnie boat"—but the Gaelic songs lament those who fought and died at Culloden, mourning lost kinsmen more than the fugitive prince. Flora rode horseback while he walked, the prince replete in flowered calico gown sprigged with purple, a quilted petticoat, muslin cap, hood, and apron. She delivered him to Skye Jacobites who spirited him back to his French exile never to return. She was arrested later and imprisoned for a while before migrating in the 1770s to North Carolina, where she ended up supporting another doomed cause, that of the British in the American War of Independence.

A fresh combination of prohibition laws dismantled Gaelic culture further after Culloden with disarmament and the banning of bagpipes and wearing of tartan. Military occupation added punch to the imposition. A detailed land survey carried out by the Board of Ordinance led to military road construction through the Highlands, and new sea charts were prepared to better navigate the Hebrides, both initiatives depriving the islands of long advantageous inaccessibility. Some Jacobite estates were forfeited to open land for new lairds from the south and surviving chiefs were drawn more and more into the mainstream of commercial life, encountering a world demanding cash, one where costs mattered. The old co-dependence of chiefs and clanspeople broke down — where once chiefs needed swordsmen, now they needed money. Around a hundred clansfolk on Harris were tricked or kidnapped onto a ship to be sold as slaves in the British West Indies in 1739, though most managed to escape when the ship docked in Ireland. The terms on which land was held were changing and many found themselves surplus to new commercial requirements, marking the beginning of a mass exodus, voluntary and involuntary, what Samuel Johnson called the "epidemical fury of emigration."

Johnson and Boswell

The interest of writers in Celts peaked as the Celts themselves were dispossessed. University of Edinburgh archaeologist Stuart Piggot argued in *The Druids* (1968) that growing knowledge of American Indians kindled interest in finding equivalent "primitivism" in Britain's own backyard. As America was discovered Europeans looked for their own aboriginal tradition. It is in this context that the Hebridean visit of 18th century literati Dr. Samuel Johnson and James Boswell might be contemplated. In a century when grand tours and book reading became fashionable, the more unusual the place written about then the greater the degree of enlightenment, and the Hebrides appeared to possess enough "primal" quality to attract interest. Johnson's seminal *Dictionary of the English Language* (1755) meant his reputation preceded him, but Boswell had yet to earn plaudits. Both published accounts of their trip — Johnson in 1775 with *A Journey to the Western Isles of Scotland* and Boswell in 1786 with *The Journal of a Tour to the Hebrides.* Boswell's book came two years after Johnson's death, a prelude to his *Life of Johnson* (1791), the work that secured his place in the annals of English literature.

The Highlands were less hazardous when they set out in 1773 — military roads and forts had seen to that — but a cautious Johnson still stepped down from the London coach in Edinburgh carrying pistols and ammunition.[17] Boswell persuaded him it was unnecessary and he left them with Mrs. Boswell in Edinburgh. The anticipation of a wild frontier is not without irony since he (and Boswell) were harbingers of Anglo influences that would change forever what it was they were so curious to see. Neither was disposed to argue for solutions to the social plight they encountered but they were not indifferent, fretting over high rents, poverty and emigration. Mull in particular dismayed Johnson; he found it gloomy and desolate, feeding his preconceptions. He lamented the absence of "any collection of buildings that can make pretensions to be called a town" though he did allow that there was one reputedly on the Isle of Lewis.[18] Stornoway was by then a town of several thousand but their tour did not take in the Outer Hebrides. Boswell made the better of it, invigorated by "busy" Mull, observing ships from Hamburg, Newcastle and Glasgow at anchor in the little port of Tobermory, teasing Johnson for having imagined Highlanders used dirks to eat with; Johnson made no mention of it. Iona was the high point. Boswell recalled their emotional embrace on reaching the holy isle, though they did so "cordially," he added!

Johnson observed that plaid clothing was rarely worn, sign of compliance with the Disarming Act of 1747, and complimented books in the homes of some hosts. He was referring to books written in English, however, dismissing Scots Gaelic as "the rude speech of a barbarous people who had few thoughts to express."[19] He was a little more charitable toward Gaelic farewell songs, finding empathy with the agonies of emigration, but not the recently published *Poems of Ossian* by James Macpherson, a Scottish poet and scholar. Johnson vehemently denounced the claim that Ossian was bona fide, a character drawn from ancient Gaelic manuscripts (never produced), son of the legendary Irish warrior Fionn MacCumhaill (in Scots Gaelic Fingal). He might have been more impressed if he had journeyed south to Arran and met Scots Gaelic scholar William Shaw, author of the pioneering *Analysis of the Gaelic Language* (1778). Shaw too felt Ossian to be a fraud and was ostracized by Scottish intellectuals for his unpatriotic opinion. Johnson and Boswell found time to meet with Flora MacDonald on Skye, by then fifty-one years old; this was before her move to

America. Johnson wrote little of it but Boswell was moved to describe her as being "of genteel appearance and uncommonly mild and well bred,"[20] amused to see Johnson, a Tory, greet a woman viewed as a traitor in Tory circles. Alert to accusations of harboring any Jacobite sympathies himself, however, he adopted a suitably deferential tone toward George III.

Land Clearances

Boswell's instincts were correct. The Jacobite cause was over. The new issues would not be about dynastic claims. The new invasive thrusts were economic. Johnson and Boswell were disappointed at Sir Alexander MacDonald's hospitality on Skye; a modest affair, they thought, without the trappings of an anticipated festive clan gathering. Yet the clan chief was "a modern man, an Old Etonian with little sense of the rights and responsibilities of a Highland patriarch," as a recent Johnson biographer observed.[21] He saw his estates in business terms and either had little sentiment for customs or little time to indulge Johnson and Boswell's fancies of them.

The communal economy of commons and run-rig shares came under challenge from sheep farms, motivated by raw wool demand from later 18th century mechanization of textile production. Sale of kelp provided compensation and was a major activity in the Scottish islands during the Napoleonic War, but when tariff protection was removed in the 1820s and prices collapsed, laid-off islanders plunged into dire poverty. To survive they had to become tenant farmers, which meant paying cash rents. Clan chiefs hired factors or financial advisors to put estates on a more secure footing. The Macleods, in possession of Harris since Norse times, and Mackenzies, who held Lewis, had both sold out to outside landlords by the mid–19th century. New lairds identified productive land, clearing it of surplus settlers, dividing any remaining land into crofts, typically lots with less than 40 tillable acres. Clearance did not necessarily spell emigration. It also involved a short-hop relocation from one part of the land to another. Some moved into poorer localities to try and reestablish a livelihood. As chiefs sold out or became *rentier* lairds their poorer kinsfolk became crofters.

The potato crop failures of the 1830s and 1840s did not reach the same crisis level as in Ireland, where 800,000 perished, but official sources reported widespread malnutrition, the most wretched down to eating shellfish and seaweed. Some clan chiefs like Macdonald of Clanranald tried to alleviate suffering with handouts, but others did nothing, including the London government. The starving had no money and farmers in a capitalist age were not about to give food away for free. Colonel John Gordon of Cluny, Aberdeenshire, new laird of South Uist, Benbecula and Barra (purchased from the bankrupt Clanranald), evicted 2,000 unfortunates between 1849 and 1851, forcibly shipping them off to Canada where promises of work and land were not fulfilled.[22] The potato famine bankrupted Walter Frederick Campbell of Islay as he ran up debts at a time when stricken tenants could pay nothing in rent. He was forced to sell out in 1853. It was a cruel twist of events since his predecessors — the Campbells of Shawfield — had done much to transform Islay into the most monetary-minded island of the larger Hebrides. They introduced shorter fixed-term leases of land in the 18th century with rents payable in cash rather than in kind. In 1769 Daniel Campbell had initiated the planned village of Bowmore to house linen textile weavers, develop flax growing, and broaden Islay's economic base.

Pressured by potato crop blight, higher rents, eviction and a scarcity of waged jobs, many left to escape poverty and starvation. Australia and New Zealand as well as North America were favored destinations. MacLeod of Skye helped set up an Emigration Society in 1851 to fund overseas passages while some opted for shorter journeys and cash wages in Glasgow and other British industrial regions. Diaspora decimated island life, sapping the morale of those who stayed. Sad processions of bedraggled people with small ragged bundles trudged away from old familiar haunts for the last time. It's an emotive issue even now. Stories of people forced onto emigrant ships burn in the memory. As younger generations left and parents died, the old blackhouses, named for dark smudges on interior walls caused by peat smoke, were abandoned. The derelict shells are still there. One preserved for posterity at Arnol on the west of Lewis is owned by a historical trust and open to visitors. There are at least six abandoned settlements on Skye alone, including that of Galtrigill, home to the MacCrimmons, hereditary pipers to the Macleods. Potato subsistence had helped Skye's population double from 11,000 in 1755 to 23,000 by 1841, but land clearances, emigration and potato crop failures reduced it to 19,000 in 1861 and 13,800 by 1901. Mull lost a third of its people between 1841 and 1861 while Iona's population halved in 30 years, 1831 to 1861. The tiny archipelago of St. Kilda (from Norse *Skildir*), remote western edge of the British Isles, 55 miles west of Harris, was entirely deserted by 1930. UNESCO added it to the list of World Heritage Sites in 1986 for its colonies of seabirds. Yet not all were hard luck stories. Daniel Macmillan, great-grandfather of Harold Macmillan, UK Prime Minister 1957–63, was born on a run-rig settlement near Corrie, Isle of Arran, in 1813. The family was evicted in land clearances but his father found work as a carter in Ayrshire and Daniel became a bookseller and publisher, founder of the renowned Macmillan publishing house.

Cheaper animal feed made livestock breeding more lucrative in the later 19th century, but competitive Australian and New Zealand wool imports rendered sheep farming less viable and some of the sheep property was sold off, a perverse turnaround given the distress caused by clearance for it in the first place. The lairds turned land into sporting estates instead. Deer and grouse shooting parties for socializing gentry provided much-needed waged employment in domestic service and shooting lodges needed stalkers and ghillies. Folk memories are bitter nevertheless as harsh treatment persisted. Hated factors handed out eviction notices and when tenants failed to comply, thatch and beams were torched. When property interests are at stake, Machiavelli mused, moral obligations are forgotten.

Crofting

Some found voice in protest. The tenants on the small island of Bernera ("Bjorn's isle") in the Sound of Harris rebelled against eviction and grazing reallocation ordered by Donald Munro, notorious factor of Sir James Matheson, in 1874. The chief fired

Munro eventually to restore peace. In another *cause célèbre* at Braes, a district of Skye facing the Isle of Raasay, a pitched battle took place between angry crofters and the forces of a Macdonald clan chief. The crofters wanted to graze their animals on the slopes of Ben Lee and offered to pay a higher rent than the sitting tenant, but Lord Macdonald's factor refused the offer. The lease was due to expire in 1882 and division among crofters was not on the agenda. Provoked by what they saw as gross injustice, the crofters grazed their animals anyway, some refusing to pay any rent at all until their offer was recognized. Leading agitators were marked down for eviction but when notices were served, angry crofters burned documentation in defiance. The chief responded by whistling up the forces of law and order. Over 60 police constables arrived on the scene to a hostile reception from around a hundred men, women and children. Rounds of fisticuffs, baton wielding and stone throwing ensued between the two sides until the tide turned against the crofters. Five were arrested and imprisoned. Skye was in such a fever of discontent that warships were sent into the lochs and Prime Minister William Gladstone (Liberal) set up the Napier Commission in 1883 to look at crofters' grievances. Two years earlier he had tried to appease unrest in Ireland over not dissimilar tenancy protests with a reforming Irish Land Act and a similar solution was sought for Scotland.

The resultant Crofting Act of 1886 gave security of tenure and fixed fair rents and offered financial assistance for redevelopment but the intention was to assist those who had property and encourage improvements to it. It did not prevent evictions. Lairds could still sell up. More acreage was subsequently allocated to crofts in tacit acknowledgment that there were those who preferred subsistence on ancestral land than commercial farms, a government effort to reduce some of the bad taste of the clearances. There are still around 18,000 crofts in Scotland, most concentrated in the northern Hebrides and Shetland, in other words areas of poorer land. Around 75 percent of land in the Outer Hebrides is still in crofting tenure. Modern crofters usually have other sources of income and while it has been fashionable in recent decades for a few disenchanted urbanites to escape the "rat race" on a Scottish croft, it is typically islanders who are crofters. The incomers provide services—the post, the school, the store, the inn, the church.

Protestantism

If agrarian capitalism is one force to impinge Hebridean culture then Protestant evangelism is another. The 16th century Reformation never made much of an impact, but 18th century Protestant organizations like the Society for the Propagation of Christian Knowledge (SPCK) took notice of the islands. The initial goal was to root out Gaelic, tongue of Catholicism, but monolingual Scots Gaelic speakers presented such a barrier to evangelizing that the SPCK reversed tactics and championed the language instead. Scots Gaelic biblical translations were in hand by the 19th century. Protestant preachers angrily dismissed papal doctrine as pagan, urg-ing listeners to join their congregation on threat of eternal hellfire. In a century of calamities the Hebridean response was mixed; it must have seemed that hellfire was consuming them anyway. For those heeding the sermon it meant radical reconstruction of how they lived their lives with the old stories, songs, and dances deemed heretical and profane. Insistence on such legalities met with more success in the remote rural Hebrides, where not unlike colonial North America in the 17th and 18th centuries, the people were urged to feel gratitude for deliverance from a wicked outer world. As clan ties weakened, Protestantism filled the void to emerge as an alternative organizational imperative, co-existing with Catholicism. A sectarian demarcation developed in the Outer Hebrides to the extent that while South Uist and Barra remained resolutely Catholic, North Uist and Lewis/Harris became trenchantly Presbyterian.

Presbyterianism is the majority Protestant denomination in Scotland and like other churches has been wracked by factionalism. A third of its followers left in 1843 over lairds appointing ministers and formed the more democratic breakaway Free Church. Fifty years later, after a drift toward reconciliation, there was another change as some rejoined the main church and others split to form the Free Presbyterian Church. A small surviving rump of the older Free Church — better known as the "Wee Frees" — made their spiritual home on Lewis, consolidating their position in the community during the 20th century, living as latter day American separatists, adhering closely to Calvinist principles. The creed of Sabbatarianism has been strong amongst "Wee Frees" although the well-publicized Sunday padlocking of children's playgrounds on Lewis finally ended during the 1990s.

Victorian Enterprise

After the Macleods sold out in the mid–19th century, the new owner of the Harris estate, Lady Dunmore, began marketing tartan tweed cloth. With encouraging sales the business spread to Lewis, production based on traditional hand spinning and weaving in the home. Whisky distilled from barley malt cured with peat also came from local impetus and was helped by widening markets. A reduction of wine imports during the Napoleonic War popularized it among the gentry and the 1823 Distilling Act imposed regularities and standards to advance larger scale production and outlaw small stills. Distilling creates lucrative employment and remains one industry in which the area enjoys what economists call comparative advantage, its own resources of peat and water being integral to the product. Scotch is a synonym describing product and place.

The Northern Isles had the advantage of lying in the mainstream of the North Atlantic shipping trade between Scandinavia and North America, but it was not until the 20th century as grand tours turned into tourism that shipping integrated the Hebrides. The Clyde islands of Bute and Arran profited in the Victorian Age as middling classes from nearby Glasgow arrived by steamers to spend their wages; Arran's residency in 1901 approximated to that of 1800 as new settlement canceled out clearance depopulation. There were trade ships sailing out of the Clyde to the Hebrides and Ireland, but a new era began in 1851 when David Hutcheson and Company began a steam-ship service between Glasgow and Skye to cover in hours a voyage that previously took days by sail. Skye got closer again in 1897 when rails reached the Kyle of Lochalsh and passengers caught a short connecting ferry. The steam shipping line adopted the name of one of the original Hutcheson partners David MacBrayne, to become Caledonian MacBrayne, and a fleet of paddle and screw-driven steamers was servicing all the Hebrides by 1914 with fares to suit various incomes, third class passengers settling down with sheep, cattle, and cargo.

Demand from urban markets provided incentive for 19th century herring fishing and Stornoway on Lewis grew as a center of it. There were over 3,000 residents there by 1840 with some of the urban amenities Dr. Johnson had craved. Lewis attracted the interest of Victorian industrialist William Lever — later Lord Leverhulme — purchaser of Harris and Lewis at the close of World War I. The 67-year-old had already made millions from a soap manufacturing business in England and in the crusading spirit of the capitalist gallant saw himself as the benefactor who would drag the island into the modern age. He aimed to inculcate enterprising virtues that would make crofting, to his mind a degenerate activity, evaporate. To cut fishing costs he pioneered canning and fish cake production and converted offal into fishmeal, fertilizer, jelly and glue. He began to develop infrastructure and sought to accelerate woolen textiles' production. Hundreds became wage-earning employees for the first time through his investments. However the "wee soap man," as islanders nicknamed him, underestimated crofting's unhurried lifestyle appeal — its pastoral independence — and a contentious battle grew over land previously promised for sub-division under crofting laws. Such unanticipated intractability exasperated Lever and he quit eventually, sailing back across the Minch, the channel separating the Outer Hebrides from the mainland, never to return. In a parting philanthropic gesture he did free the island of centuries of paternalism by offering ownership of substantial property to the local district councils and the people. Some of it is administered now as part of a trust.

Battle Stations

A heavy price in fatalities was paid in both world wars. Enemy craft entered waters and air space on occasion but most died in foreign fields. The worst domestic tragedy in the first war came right at the end on New Year's Eve 1918 as hundreds of war-weary military personnel from the Outer Hebrides squeezed aboard a luxury yacht *The Iolaire* commissioned to get them home across the Minch. Fate decided otherwise and in the darkness and blustery swell the yacht crashed onto jagged rocks just outside Stornoway Harbor. It took on water so fast it sank in minutes and over 200 drowned. Waiting relatives could only watch in disbelief and anguish.

The Hebrides was a valuable haven and arsenal in the strategy of combating U-boat wolf packs preying on Atlantic convoys in World War II. The Royal Navy set up a training school in Tobermory on Mull in 1940 — HMS Western Isles — to run intensive courses in anti-submarine warfare for Royal Navy Patrol Service (RNPS) crews. The RNPS was a motley fleet of requisitioned fishing trawlers, whalers, yachts and the like manned by characters considered by navy top brass to be ill fitted for service, hence the training school. An aging RN commodore with a stentorian reputation, Vice-Admiral Sir Gilbert Stephenson, was appointed commander and is the subject of a book by British TV news personality Richard Baker, who served under him.[23] The Women's Royal Navy Service (WRNS) also had a base at Tobermory. Invasion fears and the need for anti-submarine sweeps and sorties in the Battle of the Atlantic prompted RAF airfields, radio, radar and observation units in many islands—Islay, Colonsay, Mull, Coll, Tiree, Barra, Benbecula and Lewis. The threats were real enough. Even after the D-Day landing in June 1944, six submarines were tracked and disabled in Hebridean waters. Britain's worst inshore naval disaster occurred off Arran in 1943 when *HMS Dasher,* a small aircraft carrier escorting vital North Atlantic convoys, blew up and sank with 379 lost. The cause seems to have been a fault in the carrier's aviation fuel system.

For services personnel stationed in the Hebrides, the alien speech, customs and sight of rugged crofting habitats—oil lamp lit thatched black houses with earthen floors and improvised driftwood furniture—was both intriguing and disorienting, as to feel in a foreign land. Mike Hughes recorded the encounters in photographs and memories in his *Hebrides at War* (1998). A 1943 snapshot of a B-17 Flying Fortress soaring over a Benbecula croft[24] juxtaposes new and old. If those from the outer world were surprised at what they found, islanders who had never been to the mainland were likewise exposed to new experiences, not least of which was hearing the strange sounds of English. The majority of service men and women had gone by 1946 but useful infrastructure lived on in the form of improved roads, airstrips and harbors.

Atrophy and Action

British officialdom forgot the Hebrides when the war was over. Westminster was preoccupied with nationalization, welfare state implementation, de-colonization and priority urban issues. There was some progress with an electricity grid built in fits and starts, and forestry in places like Skye improved land utilization. Cold War military presence provided a local economic boost but at best the islands stayed in a state of arrested decay. Commercial agriculture was inconsequential with the exception of Bute, *machair* vegetation notwithstanding. Land ownership remained concentrated in the hands of a few lairds (many of them absentee) and if, as Voltaire opined, "the spirit of property doubles a man's strength," then Hebridean vitality was long sapped by injustices. Few places in Europe have more unequal landownership distribution. Surprisingly little of it was put up for sale for much of the 20th century. Scots evacuated the Highlands and Hebrides in droves for 20 years after World War II, some indicator of the region's parlous health. The acclaimed American author John McPhee got to experience the negligence and intransigence of it all when he returned to Colonsay, island of his ancestors, in the 1960s. In *Crofter and the Laird* (1969) he tells of a laird, the fourth Baron Strathcona, a resident of Bath in England, who visited only in the summers, indifferent to the knowledge that he was the least popular man on his own island! His factor meantime traveled monthly from his mainland Scotland home to "collect rents, listen to complaints and tend the flame of the feudal system."[25]

A concerted effort to defeat such atrophy came in 1965 when Harold Wilson's Labor government initiated the Highlands and Islands Development Board (HIDB). It came partly in response to adverse publicity about wealth disparity between Lowlands and Highlands, partly because prescriptions to cure economic ill health at that time involved setting up a department to deal with it, and partly because Wilson's slender parliamentary majority was dependent on keeping his Scottish MPs happy. The HIDB was given executive responsibility for industry, transport and tourism but it did not find it easy — distance from markets, high freight costs and low skill levels all worked against large-scale investment and the Hebrides was in the wrong sea to benefit from the 1970s North Sea oil boom. Community cooperatives were supported in fishing, horticulture, farm machine hire, knitwear production, fish farming and so on but many had folded by the end of the 1980s. The infrastructure funding was opportune with improved telephone service and squads of labor hired for road building. Still, unemployment registered at 21 percent in the Outer Hebrides in 1984. Skye and the Inner Hebrides were also well above the Scottish national average. Admittedly 1984 was a tough year in the UK economy as a whole, but neither statistic was much of an endorsement of HIDB policy. At the same time Orkney reported 10 percent out of work and Shetland only 6 percent, both basking in the glow of North Sea oil. Communal ownership has had more success on the very small islands. The people of Eigg endured a series of negligent landlords until 1997 when the 70-strong community was able to find £1.6 million to buy it, and in 2001 Gigha's residents got funds to buy from a willing owner through a loan from National Lottery funds (£3.5 million) plus £250 of their own money.

In recent decades tourism has provided some cause for optimism on the bigger islands. The 1970s boom of packaged holidays to sunspot destinations did not augur well for revenue in the rainy windswept Hebrides, but segments of the market where the islands can compete have evolved. The coach and trailer-caravan trade is a staple, attracting those vacationers less keen on foreign holidays, and better access roads helped it develop. There is also recognition of demand from those appreciative of environmental and aesthetic attractions. The HIDB funded heritage sites and island-hopper ferry tickets. Private hostels with dormitory-style accommodations have grown. Skye leads the way in tourism; outdoor lovers have "gone over the sea" to Skye since 1851 and reforestation has given it a richer hue. Travelers now make use of a road bridge (1995) although annexation to the mainland, trumpeted by business interests, fueled local anger over high tolls (now removed) to pay back construction costs. Tourism is the biggest single constituent of Skye's GDP and islands to its south enjoy some tourism revenue too, notably Mull with 300 miles of rugged and scenic coastline and holy Iona off its coast. According to a 1997 *Arran Banner* report, around a quarter million visit Arran annually.

Highlands and Islands Enterprise

The HIDB was dissolved in 1991 as a self-help revival swept government policy to modify the old broom with a new handle — the Highlands and Islands Enterprise

(HIE). The HIE is styled as a facilitating agency rather than a governing board and does not assume the same level of responsibility for social and community development as its predecessor. It invites investment, serves as a source of business information and sets up training and retraining programs to reduce higher than average percentages of low skill manual workers in the region. Its sphere includes the Clyde islands. The Stornoway office on Lewis reported healthy new small business start-up figures for the Outer Hebrides in the later 1990s, with accountancy and financial services part of the expansion, but small-scale owner-operator businesses have limited employment needs and job creation figures were less impressive. The business activities most likely to succeed are those that do not require expensive skills, score highly on local resource utilization, and produce for dependable markets. Fish farming has filled that ticket well with salmon, shellfish and prawns recent lucrative innovations. Over 30 fish farms sprang up on Skye alone. Whisky distilling is another. A Jura distillery closed for 60 years reopened in 1963 and a new purpose-built operation started up in Arran in 1995, these in addition to Victorian distilleries on Skye, Mull and Islay still in production. Islay is positively whisky galore, boasting seven distilleries on an island 25 miles long! Meanwhile Arran sweaters are still made on Arran and Harris Tweed is still exported. The familiar name and orb logo is protected by the Harris Tweed Act of 1993, and although textiles is not the vital economic strand it was once with the total productive value percentage relatively small, it is still an important wage earner in remote areas.

The census of 2001 had mixed news on population growth with the Outer Hebrides the least encouraging. Lewis fell by 6 percent from 1991 to 20,000. The fall might have been even more marked were it not for increased life longevity. On the other hand Skye has experienced regeneration. It grew during the 1990s with Lochalsh, to which it is bridged on the neighboring mainland, the increase mostly due to English or Scots Lowland migrants. Unlike earlier English who capitalized on land clearances and never lived there, the new wave has taken up full-time residence and generate demand for services. Many live off tourism. Owner-operator bed-and-breakfast businesses are popular as are retailing and arts and crafts businesses. Skye's computer electronics companies and those on Bute demonstrate that high-tech can function offshore but both do have convenient road access in common. Arran has experienced some growth too.

Atlantic Frontier

Small-scale fishing to supplement land pickings has always been there, but, hampered first by feudal rights over shore and catch and now by prohibitive costs, commercial fishing never engaged Hebrideans to the extent that might be imagined. After disputes between Britain and Iceland over cod fishing rights were concluded in 1976 with a treaty apportioning zonal rights, Britain's northwesterly boundary was placed at Rockall. As the outer of the Outer Hebrides, some 230 miles west of North Uist, it gave the home fleets rights to tens of thousands of square miles of lucrative Atlantic fishing grounds. In 1998, however, a UN convention on sea zoning law overruled

Rockall, citing the island as uninhabitable, redrawing the western boundary to St. Kilda, some 150 miles further east, opening up a huge ocean expanse for international competitors. Factory ships from all over western and northern Europe have taken advantage and while trawlers registered in Shetland and major east coast Scottish ports fish these grounds, Hebridean fishing interests are conspicuous in their absence. The costs make it an unrealistic proposition for small businesses.

The islands may get more return from the Atlantic in other ways. A decline in North Sea oil and gas production triggered interest in finding an alternative field. Several oil companies, notably Conoco and Phillips, spent big money in the 1990s, imaging ocean floors west of the Hebrides. Preliminary reports suggested potential, but drilling operations did not commence. There has been more interest in onshore wind driven electricity turbines. Less than 3 percent of Britain's electricity was generated from wind power in 2000 and public policy favors expansion. Those Hebridean landowners who watched enviously as Orkney and Shetland grew rich from oil hope for their own windfall by cashing in on wind farm construction. Plugging wind farms into the national grid will be expensive and there will be opposition from those who fear violation of landscape aesthetics, but inevitably there will be interest in the potential monetary amount to be gained in rent. Harnessing wave power is another renewable energy innovation with trendsetting Islay home to a wave generator since the mid–1990s. This "green energy" device generates power from the energy in ocean waves as they pound the seashore.

Political Challenges

The Hebrides has no collective political identity. The last time it experienced that was 500 years ago under the lordship of the isles. One author of numerous books on the region observes that "there is nothing like having one's own people in charge of one's own affairs"[26] and at least Orkney and Shetland have a more consolidated representation. Three constituencies divide the Hebrides in UK elections and while voting histories differ, all share at one time or another a propensity for not supporting the party in power. The Western Isles constituency of the Outer Hebrides was the first seat won by the Scottish National Party (SNP) in a UK election, in 1970. The SNP hoped it would prove a wellspring for Scottish consciousness, but by the 1990s, the Outer Hebrides had joined the swing to Labor. However, in 2005 SNP won it back. Skye is caught in the gravitational pull of the Highlands and included within the large but sparsely inhabited Ross, Skye and Lochaber constituency where Liberal Democrats have generally fared well in elections. The third electoral district is a one-size-fits-all constituency called Argyll and Bute, uniting the southern Hebrides of Mull, Islay and assorted others with Arran and Bute. It has swung between three parties in recent decades. Voters chose the SNP in the 1970s, supported Margaret Thatcher's Conservative Party until 1987, and sent Liberal Democrat candidates to Westminster in the Tony Blair Labor era.

Local government is just as fragmentary. Four regional authorities out of 32 for the whole of Scotland were set up in 1996 to cover the islands, but only Comhairle nan Eilean (Western Isles Council) for the Outer Hebrides, based in Stornoway, maintains insular autonomy. The others are all offshore accessories. The Inner Hebrides from Skye to Mull is included in a Highland region based in Inverness. The threesome of Jura, Islay and Bute are part of the Argyll and Bute region quartered in Lochgilphead and lastly Arran is part of North Ayrshire.

A new overlordship, albeit a democratic one, the Scottish Parliament, also demands election and it is in this assembly that best hopes of interest reside. Members of the Scottish Parliament, or MSPs, are chosen through a mixed electoral system with half elected by simple majority vote for single electoral districts (the first-past-the-post system used in the UK and the USA) and the remainder taking seats proportionate to number of votes cast for their party. In this system Hebrideans are well represented in Edinburgh per capita, but confidence in the efficacy of it may well hinge on land reforms. According to the Scottish Landowners Association only 0.08 percent of the population owned 80 percent of Scotland at the close of the 20th century and inequity was at its most acute in the Hebrides. A Land Reform Act in 2003 sought to remedy long-standing imbalances by tilting market purchase in favor of locals and permitting access to uncultivated property. However since it gives crofters the rights to buy under some circumstances regardless of whether the owner wants to sell, critics charge that Edinburgh is more interested in fighting old class wars than serving new needs.

Scots Gaelic

There is a residual toughness about these islands and as Hebrideans of the homegrown and freshly settled variety adapt and build, the old language has displayed remarkable powers of rejuvenation. Scots Gaelic looked as if it were to be served its last rites in the 1960s but recovered lost ground in recent decades, partly due to political activism and Scots nationalism and partly because in northern Hebridean crofting communities (at least) the old ways were never extinguished. Most speakers are on Skye and in the Outer Hebrides, where around two-thirds of the population have varying degrees of command of it. A Gaelic College in Sleat on Skye, school curricula, playgroups, radio and television programs, music (one Gaelic rock group calls itself Run Rig) and road signs advance the cause of familiarity. Also the Columba Centre opened recently in Bowmore, Islay, to promote Gaelic and enhance the southern Hebrides cultural heritage. Yet it is also true that English is the majority language. If the 2001 census is accurate then the overall numbers of Gaelic speakers (islands and mainland) may have declined again despite best efforts. The challenge is to transform more speech into written language and with degrees in Gaelic being offered by the University of the Highlands and Islands in Inverness the prospects still look better than they did 40 years ago.

1. Burl, Aubrey, *From Carnac to Callanish* (Yale University Press, 1993), 17.

2. Lamb, Hubert, *Climate, History and the Modern World,* second ed. (Routledge, 1995), 99.

3. Keys, David "Europe's First Mummies," *Archaeology,* 56, no. 5 (2003): 16–17.

4. *Gildas: De Excidio et Conquestu Brittanniae,* Giles, J.A., trans. (British American Books, 1986), 19.

5. *Adomnán of Iona: Life of St. Columba,* Sharpe, Richard, trans., (Penguin Classics, 1995), Ch. I 33, p.136.

6. Graham-Campbell, James, and Batey, Colleen E., *Vikings in Scotland: An Archaeological Survey* (Edinburgh University Press, 1998), 72.

7. Ashley, Mike, *British Kings and Queens* (Carroll & Graf, 1998), 423.

8. Graham-Campbell, James, ed., *Cultural Atlas of the Viking World* (Facts on File, 2000), 219.

9. Macleod, John, *Highlanders: A History of the Gaels* (Sceptre Press, Hodder & Stoughton, 1996), 69.

10. Macleod, 73.

11. MacDonald, R. Andrew, *Kingdom of the Isles* (Tuckwell Press, 1997).

12. Donaldson, Gordon, ed., "Treaty of Perth, 1266," in *Scottish Historical Documents* (Neil Wilson Publishing, 1974), 35.

13. Lamb, 205.

14. Caldwell, David, *Islay, Jura and Colonsay: A Historical Guide* (Birlinn Books, 2001), 53.

15. Dodgson, Robert A., *From Chiefs to Landlords* (Edinburgh Univ. Press, 1998), 10.

16. Grimble, Ian, *Clans and Chiefs* (Birlinn Books, 2000), 103.

17. *Samuel Johnson & James Boswell: A Journey to the Western Islands of Scotland & The Journal of a Tour to the Hebrides,* Levi, Peter, ed. (Penguin Classics, 1984), 184.

18. *Samuel Johnson & James Boswell,* 127.

19. *Samuel Johnson & James Boswell,* 116.

20. *Samuel Johnson & James Boswell,* 265.

21. Sisman, Adam, *Boswell's Presumptious Task: The Making of the Life of Dr. Johnson* (Penguin Books, 2000), 53.

22. Macleod, 199.

23. Baker, Richard, *The Terror of Tobermory* (WH Allen Books, 1972).

24. Hughes, Mike, *The Hebrides at War* (Birlinn Books, 2001), 60.

25. McPhee, John, *The Crofter and the Laird* (The Noonday Press, 1969), 109.

26. Thompson, Francis, *The Western Isles of Scotland* (Batsford Books, 1988), 98.

4

Isle of Man: "Little Manx Nation"

"Ten times fifty, three times ten and five and two did fall; O Manx race,
beware lest future catastrophe you befall"— Rhyme lamenting the Battle of
Ronaldsway 1275, *The Chronicles of the Kings of Man and the Isles,* 1586

In Irish mythology Fionn MacCumhaill ("Finn McCool") was a colossus of mighty deeds. When on one epic day a Scottish giant invaded his land he furiously resisted and beat him back. MacCumhaill gave chase, throwing rocks at his retreating enemy, their ground impact so great that craters filled with water creating Lough Neagh, the biggest lake in Ireland. His misses meanwhile fell into the Irish Sea to form the Isle of Man and the smaller isle at its feet, Calf of Man. In time the island was settled but there were too many local rulers and no one could prevail; that is until the arrival of sea-king deity, Manannàn ap Llyr, or so legend lovingly maintains. No name is more revered in Manx lore than Manannàn, the Celtic Neptune believed to be the first to unify the island, and who, mythology insists, named the island, keeping foreigners away by engulfing it in treacherous mists: "the work of Manannàn" it was whispered.

Conception actually occurred more than 8,000 years ago as melting ice drowned the last land links between Britain and Ireland to leave it alone in mid–Irish Sea. Galloway (southwest Scotland) is the nearest landfall, some 16 miles to the north. England and Ireland are about 25 miles away with Liverpool and Dublin equidistant. On a clear day both countries are visible. Temperatures are equable thanks to the warming Gulf Stream and a predictable rainfall guarantees bubbling streams, wooded valleys and verdant meadows. Man has an abundance of natural harbors. At 33 miles long and 13 miles wide the landscape is tamer than the Hebrides although the cliff scenery can be dramatic in the south. Rolling hills cover two upland slate massifs— one northern and one southern — rising to a maximum of 2,034 ft. (620m.) at Snaefell ("Snow Hill" in Norse) where it rarely snows. The island is relatively rich in minerals, producing significant percentages of British zinc and copper in the 19th century.

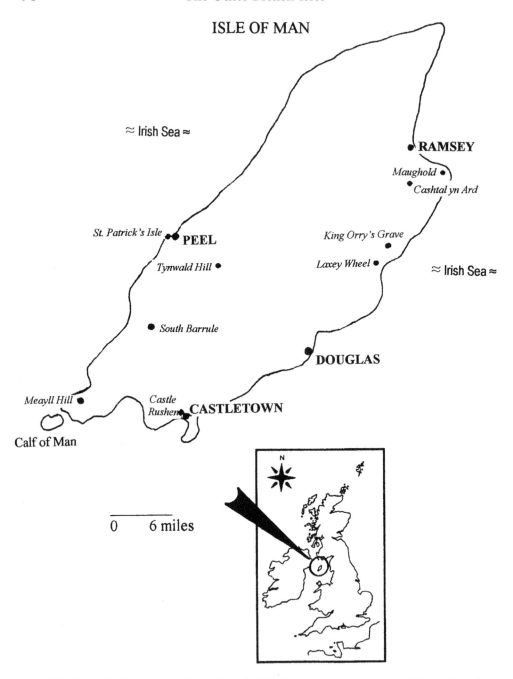

The Isle of Man is one of the British Isles but is neither a part of Great Britain nor of the United Kingdom. Its political status, like that of the Channel Islands, is idiosyncratic. Officially it is termed a Crown dependency since the primary relationship is with the British monarchy, its titular head of state, and the current queen is lord of Man. Otherwise it is one of the world's smallest self-governing regimes with a thousand year old parliament called Tynwald and no representation in Westminster.

UK administration is limited in practice to foreign relations and defense. There was no smooth inheritance of autonomy from the past, however. The modern devolved state is largely the product of a UK concession in 1958. Westminster retains intervention powers even if it does permit self-government. Man has its own laws based on English principles, its own currency backed by Bank of England sterling, its own taxes (lower than the UK), and its own language (albeit semi-extinct) called Manx, part of the q–Celtic Gaelic subdivision of Celtic languages. The 2001 census reported 76,000 living in its 227 square miles, greater than the amorphous Hebrides, which has more than twice the land area. Around half live in or near Douglas, the tidy capital town on the eastern coast. The tourist business that promoted Douglas has declined as a constituent part of revenue but the Isle of Man has successfully reinvented itself since the 1960s as a tax haven and international offshore financial center.

Megalithic Man

Geography is always a powerful determinant in history but in Man's case it seems especially so, its mid–Irish Sea position making it a good settlement proposition. Flint finds date human activities to c. 6000 B.C., and from charcoal presence in peat the burning of forest (hazel, pine, oak) to enhance hunting and gathering activities can be deduced. Although millennia of quarrying for building stone has disturbed evidence, megalithic alignments and chambered tombs were there. Enough of it survives, notably at Meayll Hill, Cashtal yn Ard, King Orry's Grave, Ballakelly and Ballaharra, to attest to settled conditions by the later Neolithic Period. The earliest farming evidence is a single grain impression on a broken piece of earthenware at Meayll ("Mull") Hill, analysis of which dates it to the fourth millennium B.C.[1] Stephen Barrow lists some 50 sites in his *Neolithic Culture of the Isle of Man* (1997), many being places where ceramics have been recovered, the pottery styles conforming to types found in southwest Scotland and northeast Ireland, indication that Man was part of a broader regional community. The Neolithic Manx knew a world bigger than their island.

Meayll Hill, a windswept knoll above Port Erin and Port St. Mary, has a most unusual megalithic configuration. Six pairs of cist graves are set in a ring with an entrance passage between each pair set at right angles to it, an arrangement referred to as "cists in a circle." Cist derives from the Latin *cista*, in this context meaning a small covered tomb. The complex developed over two phases during the third millennium B.C. with the entrance passages a later addition. Aubrey Burl explains its oddity as an insular adaptation of both Irish and British traditions[2] and it is worthy of emphasis that the Irish Sea was a link between British and Irish cultures in this age, not a divide. The old Manx name for it, *Lhiac ny Wirragh* ("stone of the meetings"), recognizes ceremonial usage, and the settlement it once served (a temple-village?) was nearby. One of the largest chambered tombs found anywhere in the British Isles is at Cashtal yn Ard or "castle on the height" near Maughold ("Mack-old"). Stone monoliths serve as a forecourt to what was originally a series of five burial chambers stretching 130 feet, almost churchlike in proportion. A similar structure known as King Orry's Grave is now cut in half by a road (King Orry was a later Norse king of Man honored in the naming but there is no connection between him and its Neolithic origins). There are others. A few megaliths survive from a simpler tomb at Ballakelly, and a damaged two-chambered tomb was found in 1971 at Ballaharra sandpit in the village of St. Johns. It is also possible that the roundhouse (later a Norse farmstead) at Braaid near Douglas was originally a stone circle. Acid levels in Manx soils do not preserve bone well so there is a scarcity of human remains at these burial sites.[3]

The quality of life by the later second millennium B.C. is hard to fathom; certainly the Manx no longer embarked on ambitious tomb building projects. We know from Irish bog oak sample analysis that Ireland experienced a darker age between 1200 and 800 B.C. due to weather deterioration, and peat formation did occur on Man, though not to the extent it did in the Hebrides or Ireland. It may have been a place of refuge and resettlement in difficult times. If the copper lode in the vicinity of Bradda in the southwest is any guide (workings suggested c. 1200 B.C.) then the island was in the expanding bronze trade. Bronze is an alloy of copper and tin and a seaway trade mixing Irish copper and Cornish tin resources flourished in the last millennium B.C. with the urbanizing Mediterranean world providing demand. The Isle of Man was probably a part of it as an additional copper source.

Celtic Man

The archaeological report by the Celtic Age is a positive one. Metalworking evidence in the form of hearths, crucibles, and molds as well as ores, slag and finished products points to an industrious agrarian society. The building was domestic rather than monumental with farmsteads of a circular Celtic type, though there is nothing to compare with the Scottish brochs. Excavations on St. Patrick's Isle at Peel unearthed postholes of timbered roundhouses dated to c. 400 B.C., and two farmsteads excavated at Ballacagen and Ballanorris, classified as Celtic roundhouses, were in usage from the third century B.C. to at least the first century A.D. An impressive nucleated settlement thrived on a hill-site (1,585 feet) at South Barrule, also known as "Manannan's Castle," where 70 small circular stonewalled dwellings perched around the summit were excavated in the 1960s. Radiocarbon dating of a hearth there produced an occupation date of 523 B.C. A double rampart surrounded the whole site. This palisade plus a series of promontory enclosures on defensible headlands, notably at Cass ny Howin, Close ny Chollagh and Cronk ny Merriu, suggests unsettled conditions, but there is no indication of serious disturbance or major immigration. The hill-site settlement (termed oppida or proto-town) is a characteristic of the last millennium B.C. in southern Britain and the European continent and South Barrule lay on the northernmost perimeter of known distribution. The intensification of settlement there certainly suggests a higher degree of organization, but whether it was because of defense considerations is not absolutely known. The same sort of discussion applied to the broch-village of Gurness in Orkney. What can be asserted is that nucleated farming villages with appreciable levels of population density thrived offshore centuries before the Roman Empire reached Britain.

The origin of the Manx language is a mystery, but philologists classify it as a relative of the q–Celtic Gaelic speech of Ireland, indicative of a close relationship with that island. It was not written down until recent centuries so conclusions about its ancient form are problematic. Some linguists point to similarities with the now extinct speech of the neighboring Galloway peninsula in southwest Scotland. It is reasonable to think of influences from the entire Irish Sea rim and maybe even Gaul. The name origin of Man is contentious rather than unknown but it likely evolved from its Roman map name of Monavia, a cognate of *Menapii* possibly, a Belgian (continental Celtic) seafaring tribe active in the Irish Sea region in the last two centuries B.C. who may have settled on Man. Caesar mentions them in *Gallic Wars* as never having surrendered to the legions. Norman Mongan has written an in-depth study about them[4] and their association with Irish Leinster and worship of the sea god Manannàn. The same stem component is in *Yns Môna* or Anglesey, the offshore Welsh island with which Man is often confused in ancient writings, both mapped by the Romans as Menavian (Menapian?) islands.

Uncovering of Roman coinage apart, the Romans appear to have ignored Man, as they did Ireland. The Manx themselves may have been curious; after all they were seafarers and would hear of developments in Britain, but the only evidence to date comes from the post–Roman period in the form of five grave markers with Irish *ogham* style memorial inscriptions, strokes carved down the edge of the stone, inspired by Roman monuments. The little documentation there is on these centuries otherwise, all of it written long after the event, points to a succession of "foreign" rulers from encircling locales— Leinster, a kingship in eastern Ireland; Rheged, a Celtic kingship in what is now northwestern England; and Gwynedd, a Welsh kingdom centered on Anglesey. All three played some part in Manx affairs. In 620 it fell for a while within the grasp of Edwin, the Anglo-Saxon king of Northumbria, conqueror of Gwynedd. How these rulers were represented on Man is not clear; little can be usefully said other than listing names of shadowy figures from chronicled king-lists. Man's political destiny was tied periodically with that of Anglesey during the seventh to ninth centuries in some form of alliance to rulers of Gwynedd. Merfyn Frych, the patriarch of the royal house that produced Welsh heroes like Owain the Great and Llewelyn the Great, is said to be a son of the Manx king Gwriad who ruled c. 800.[5] When Man was not aligned with Welsh rulers, it was involved with the Leinster Irish. The island's mid-sea position made it strategic in relations between Celtic realms on both sides of the Irish Sea and secular and ecclesiastical influence came from both.

Christianity

According to tradition, St. Patrick's Isle, a rocky islet at the mouth of the river Neb on the Irish-facing west coast, is the birthplace of Manx Christianity, St. Patrick himself allegedly stepping ashore with other missionaries from Ireland c. 450. The real Patrick, a Romano-Briton called Patricius, may not have had the power to command such a mission. Much in the life of the Irish saint is apocryphal. His seventh century Armagh biographers, bishops Tírechán and Muirchü, revered him as a Celtic hero who could out-miracle druids, and the man is hard to separate from the myth. Indeed, like a Manannàn sea fog, stories shroud early Manx Christianity. There may actually have been an early ruler called Manannàn: at any rate only Christianity could defeat him. One legend has it that he was driven out by followers of St. Patrick, who turned him miraculously into a fiery sun-wheel, curling and spinning him over the headland at Dhoon, where he changed into a whale. The symbolism is not unfamiliar in early Christian polemics— the duel of fires, the burning wheel of Celtic worship set alight by followers of Christ. In the confrontation with paganism it was the son of God who vanquished the god of the Sun.

Nevertheless it is logical to look to Ireland as a source of conversion, given its stature as an early center of Christianity. Maughold has the largest collection of early Christian crosses on the island and its name is dedicated to a fifth century Irish monk Machaoi. A 12th century church was built there over a seventh century monastery and even earlier cells. *Ogham* inscriptions at Maughold have been deciphered as dedications to Irish and Welsh tribal leaders. Since Man was within the *ogham* zone this may indicate stronger Irish influence, and the fact that Manx is a form of q–Celtic speech also strengthens the Irish connection. Yet Welsh inputs cannot be ignored. Part of the central panel of a stone altar frontal displaying a crucifixion scene found on the Calf of Man, a hermitic isle off Man's southwest tip, is thought to compare with sixth century Welsh stone sculpting. St. Trinian's Church in Marown (now a roofless ruin) was built in the early 13th century, but its dedication may derive from Ninian, the fourth century Romano-British (probably Welsh) missionary whose priory in Galloway, the nearest mainland, was one of the first anywhere in Britain.

The first chapels were cells or in Manx *keeills*— rectangular stone and timber huts with little more inside them than a simple altar. Some served as a place of retreat for ascetics and mystics while evangelists may have used others; however since the floor space was only about 15 by nine feet, any congregation remained outside for services. The whereabouts of nearly 200 *keeills* are known, though only 35 or so survive above ground. Such an extensive network suggests the island was Christianized by the seventh century.

The Norse

The Norse came to the Irish Sea region from the later 790s intent on plunder, but Man's fertile land, natural harbors and strategic position invited settlement and colonization was underway by 830. There is material evidence. Three ship burials uncovered in the 1940s at Knock y Doonee, Balladoole and Cronk yn Howe are among the first ever found in the British Isles, comprising the ninth century remains of warrior-farmers with weapons and equipment. Further discoveries on St. Patrick's Isle revealed at least seven other burials with pagan grave goods. One of the graves— that of the so-called "Pagan Lady of Peel"—contained a bead necklace, cooking spit, shears, and workbox equipped with needles, all for use in the afterlife. Since her funeral attire is not typically Scandinavian, it is thought she was native Manx, maybe the wife of a Norseman.[6] What happened to the pre–Viking population is unanswered although the plethora of Scandinavian place-names suggests that at best they became servile to a new Norse hierarchy. How many were put to the sword is anyone's guess but survival of the Manx language implies it was not a wipeout.

Christianity was already there of course and its impact on the Norse is evident by the 10th century. Thorwald's cross, a slate Christian cross slab found at Kirk Andreas, is a good example, its double-sided engraving illustrating transition from older beliefs. On one side is the battle of Ragnarök — a pagan Norse Armageddon-equivalent — while on the other a belted Viking holds a book and a cross; next to him a fish symbol informs that Christ now rules. Man boasts a rich collection of over 200 carved stone cross-slabs, grave markers usually found near *keeills*; some are on display in Douglas's Manx Museum. The runic decoration exemplifies fusion of Norse and Celtic design and some sculptors obligingly left their tag mark. The interlaced ring-chain motifs of one ends with the boast: "Gaut made this and all in Man." A clue to his identity is found on another stone: "Gaut made this, son of Bjorn from Kolli," perhaps the Hebridean isle of Col.

Their choice of habitat followed the Scottish islands pattern; in other words they chose places long habitable. At the Braaid near Douglas, Norse buildings accompany Celtic roundhouse remains. The previously mentioned Iron Age promontory enclosures were re-occupied. During the summer months Norse farmers utilized the terrain as they had at home by driving cattle to upland pastures for grazing and living up there; their *sheilings* — groups of small stone and turf built shelters — have been located and mapped. Importantly their use of the sea proved very consequential. With so many good harbors to utilize, Man became a hub of an expanding maritime empire, a reorientation that brought changes in economic life. Norse wealth-accumulating proclivities are well represented in two treasure hoards at the Manx Museum. Seventy-nine different coins from the Viking period recovered from a grave at the edge of an extension to Kirkmichael churchyard are on display, the oldest dating from the reign of Anglo-Saxon king Edmund I (r. 939–946); others are of Norman, Viking Dublin, and Gaelo-Manx vintage. All represent a valuable record of the network around Man. The second is the so-called Douglas Hoard, found by workers digging house foundations in Derby Road, Douglas, in 1894. They came by chance across a flat stone beneath which was a box filled with bracelets, necklaces, gold torque, and many coins. It is deduced from the coin dating that the deposit must have been made sometime in the later 10th century.

The first known Viking king of Man, Godred mac Fergus, ruled more than a century before the Douglas Hoard deposit. A Gaelo-Norse warrior from the north of Ireland, he established rule over the southern Hebrides and Man as *rí innse gall* c. 850, as noted in the previous chapter. Man's political affiliations then twisted and turned in the east-west political machinations of Viking York and Viking Dublin. When the Norse were forced out of their first Dublin settlement by Gaelic Irish in 902, there is a strong chance many resettled on Man. It was a base for goods-in-transit between the two and a useful refuge in troubled times. By 925 they had won Dublin back. Magnus and Godred Haraldsson, the Manx rulers in the 970s and 980s (around the time the Douglas Hoard was buried), were both kinsmen of Norse Irish kings of

Limerick and aligned with Norse kings of Dublin. Manx involvement in Irish politics then took a dramatic turn in 1013 when a war fleet of many thousands of Gaels and Norse hell-bent on an invasion of Dublin began to muster on Man, the fact of it attesting to the island's pivotal position in Irish Sea affairs. The fleet was summoned by a deposed Norse Dublin king Sitric Silkenbeard, together with Máel Mórda, the Irish king of Leinster, and Earl Sigurd II (the Stout) of Orkney. The trio planned to overthrow the ageing Brian Bóru, a Gaelic king from Munster, who had brought much of Ireland under his control by wars and alliances and had had himself crowned *imperator scottorum* by the abbot of Armagh in 1005. His reign as high king of Ireland (no one had survived that role before) had pretensions to future dynastic control and as such was a threat to Norse control of sea trade. So they plotted to remove him. The massed longships of Dubliners, Manxmen, Orcadians and Leinstermen sailed from Man to meet bloody resistance and defeat at Clontarf on the north bank of the Liffey in 1014. Many of them perished including Máel Mórda, Sigurd, and the victorious Brian Bóru, reputedly cut down in his tent by a Manxman.

The political leadership before the Norman invasion of England in 1066 is thinly documented, but thereafter a king list of sorts exists in *Cronica Regum Mannie et Insularum* or *Chronicles of the Kings of Man and the Isles*, now in the British Library in London. Compiled or copied by Cistercian monks, it covers the later 11th century through to the 14th century and like the better-known *Anglo-Saxon Chronicles* is mostly about power and how it was handed on and to whom—whether kings or bishops—but alas gives little insight into a unique Manx culture. The first ruler of stature listed is Godred Crovan, king of Man and the Isles between 1079 and 1095, the "King Orry" of Manx folklore.

Godred the Conqueror

A son of Harold "the Black" of Islay and possibly a descendant of a 10th century Norse king of Dublin Olaf Cuaran, Godred Crovan was a veteran of the epic 1066 struggle over the contested throne of Anglo-Saxon England. The epithet Crovan derives from the Gaelic *Crobhan* or White Hands, apparently the color of his battle gauntlets. He served under Norse king Harold Hardraada (Hard Ruler), who opposed the accession of the Saxon Harold Godwinson. The Scandinavian army included Anglo-Norse and Gaelo-Norse warriors already living in Britain and Ireland, and Crovan may have traveled from Islay or Man. The whereabouts of his youth is not known. He fought at Stamford Bridge near York in September 1066, sword and axe to hand no doubt, maybe witnessing Hardraada take a deadly arrow full in the chest, signal of a terrible defeat at the hands of Godwinson's Saxons. After it, the fortunes of Godwinson and Crovan took opposite turns. The victorious Saxon marched south in celebratory mood to engage Duke William of Normandy at Hastings the following month, a hasty decision that cost him his life and changed the course of English history. A beaten Godred Crovan meanwhile retreated in darker mood from York to seek refuge on Man, a destination more fortuitous for him than Hastings was for the ill-fated Harold. When he arrived the island was under Dublin's rule but impressed by what he saw he resolved to challenge for its leadership.

His first efforts ended in defeat but the chroniclers tell us that on a third attempt in 1079, he brought a war-band ashore at Ramsey, hiding 300 men in a wood to ambush defending Irish and Manx, a strategy that devastated them. His victorious men were eager to go on the rampage but Crovan's earlier sojourn had softened his attitude toward his former hosts, according to the *Chronicles*; and "moved with compassion and taking pity on their plight, since he had been reared among them for some time, he called off his army and forbade them to pursue them further."[7] His clemency did not extend to land, and those spared the sword had to accept new conditions. He may have been Gaelo-Norse in his antecedents but Godred's conquest took a leaf out of the book of William the Conqueror, who in the years since Hastings had subdued much of Anglo-Saxon Britain. New feudal elements were introduced, courtesy of Crovan, requiring all land be held from him as fiefs and not as customary kinship inheritance, an act transforming the relationships inherent in traditional clan politics. It was a revolutionary step. The king rather than the kindred represented the fulcrum of existence. Whatever the local reaction to this, his reign was remarkably successful in terms of reach. His field of conquest and alliance ultimately extended impressively over all the Sudreys, in other words Man and the Hebrides. It was he who summoned vassals from the quadrants of Lewis, Skye, Mull and Islay to Tynwald on Man, placing the island at the helm of a sea realm extending over hundreds of miles. He also overpowered Dublin and parts of Leinster for a while too, holding them from 1091 to 1094. The Isle of Man was at the peak of its political influence and in Tynwald pioneered an enduring institution of government.

Tynwald: Mother of British Parliaments

The Norse people who spread over and settled the coastlands of Atlantic Europe had an atypical penchant for populist lawmaking. The open assemblies or *things* they set up are at the root of modern representative government, forums to air the concerns of free men, review old laws, and submit new ones for approval. The Manx Tynwald — from the Old Norse *Thingvalla* meaning assembly field — is a unique offshore survivor of such gatherings. The word is maintained in other Norse founded parliaments — the Icelandic *Althing*, Danish *Folkting*, Norwegian *Storting* and the Faeroes' *Logting*. *Things* were based on the principle that free men should know the law under which they were ruled. Laws were recited, grievances heard and *deemsters* (a term equating with Domesday inferring a final judgment) ruled on law-breakers. This acknowledgment of Norse roots does not preclude other inputs and since Irish *brehons* or itinerant judges also promulgated law at periodic open-air assemblies, Tynwald may be viewed as a manifestation of Celtic practice too. The annual Tynwald took place on Midsummer's Day, accommodating a pre–Christian tradition common to Celts and Norsemen, though there is no record of the first one. It may have begun with regional *things* and progressed to a central Tynwald; it was certainly functional before Magna Carta (1215) recognized the baronial group that became the English House of Lords. The village of St. Johns, midway between Douglas and Peel, is its ancestral home. The physical features remain faithful, namely a low grassy mound on which members assemble, joined by a pathway to a courthouse set to the east. The annual ceremony is still held there every Midsummer's Day but the modern Tynwald sits in regular sessions in Douglas.

Tynwald membership was confined to members known as *keys,* and during the reign of Godred Crovan they were the vassals representing lands on Man and in the Hebrides. There is no agreement over word origin — some credit it the Old Norse *kjosa* meaning chosen, others view it as a later English corruption of the Manx *y-chiare-as-feed* or four-and-twenty, explained momentarily. Thirty-two *keys* assembled in the 11th and 12th centuries, a unilateral voice from a multilateral polity, half of them from the Sudreys, four each from the islands of Lewis/Harris, Skye, Islay and Mull. The remaining *keys* were Manxmen — four each from the four points of Man's compass, each quarter defining clan lands. As noted in the Hebrides chapter Somerled's victory over the Manx king Godred II in 1156 took Islay and Mull out of the union to reduce Tynwald membership by eight and leave a rump of 24 *keys*, in Manx *y chiare-as-feed* or the four-and-twenty.

Power Struggles

Crovan's death in 1095 after a 16-year reign brought civil war with full-blooded atrocities. A successor, Lagman, had a rival kinsman captured and his eyes gouged and genitals sliced off.[8] In 1098 Magnus Bare-Legs Olafsson arrived in the Irish Sea region with a great show of power, having bloodied and torched the Hebrides en voyage, as we have seen. The *Chronicles* report the Norse king was much taken with the Isle of Man: it was "pleasing in his sight and he chose to live in it."[9] After his devastation tactics in the Hebrides he took a constructive approach on Man and saw to improvements to defenses, mindful of enemies, ordering trees cut down and shipped from Galloway, and a timber fortress built on St. Patrick's Isle at Peel (*peel* = stockade) on the Irish-facing western coast. Peel defended the harbor of the river Neb, behind which lay the central valley route between west and east coasts. He also fortified old Iron Age hill-enclosures as coastal lookouts. As much as anything else these efforts confirm the strategic value accorded to Man at this juncture of history. The king then turned his attention to the Irish Sea perimeter, sailing off to the Isle of Anglesey off the Welsh coast to kill one Anglo-Norman earl and evict another, bringing native leaders there under his rule. His notoriety became such that an Irish Gaelic king, Muircheartach, promised to wear his shoes on his shoulders in a gesture of humble obeisance and "would eat them rather than that King Magnus [Bare-Legs] destroy a single province in Ireland."[10] When Bare-legs' envoys returned from Ireland to regale him with stories of abundant possibilities there, he prepared to go and conquer it anyway, an ill starred decision that brought him to grief. He left Man in 1103 with 16 ships but was resisted sometime soon after disembarkation on the Ulster shore. Presumably some of the defending combatants had Norse blood in their veins but there was no sentiment of brotherhood. Bare-Legs was battered to death with most of his raiding party. His Irish Sea quest had lasted five years.

Man and the Sudreys remained under Norse suzerainty despite his death, but

Man had more to do with Britain and Ireland in the 12th century. The longest reigning Crovan successor had political clout in England. Olaf I (a.k.a. Olaf the Dwarf) spent time at the court of Henry I, youngest son of William the Conqueror, and recognition there plus a powerful fleet served his long rule of 40 years from 1114 to 1153. In tacit compliance with a wider Christendom he sanctioned the Cistercian monastery at Rushen in 1134, where the *Chronicles* would be written, but his daughter Ragnhild's marriage to Hebridean sea lord Somerled unwittingly helped unhinge Manx hegemony. Olaf's successor Godred II expanded Manx influence temporarily to include Dublin, but fortune switched course when he came unstuck against a determined Somerled in sea battle in 1156. His loss of Islay, Mull and associated islands to Somerled made the Hebridean a rival sea king, honored as such by the Scots. Godred sailed to Norway to get help after Somerled's brief 1158 invasion of Man rammed home the message of new authority. The *Chronicles* blamed Ragnhild for causing the collapse of the kingdom, but it hadn't collapsed, it had only became smaller. Somerled's ambitions focused only on his native Argyll, taking Islay and Mull out of the Manx domain, not on Man itself. The northern Hebrides of Skye and Lewis remained part of the Manx polity and Tynwald continued with *y-chiare-as feed*, the four and twenty *keys*. The losses did prove permanent however. Godred Crovan's people on Islay were vanquished and power in the southern Hebrides transferred to Somerled and his successors, the MacDougall and MacDonald clans.

The news of Somerled's murder in 1164 meant that all was not lost for Godred II encouraging him to return from Norway. He regained his Manx kingship by slaying Ragnald Olafsson, king for only four days, the shortest-ever reigning British monarch.[11] His restoration was enhanced a few years later when he married Finola c. 1170, daughter of an Irish Ulster king and a descendant of Brian Bóru. The Isle of Man hung on its quasi-independence for another century, still within the Norse orbit but increasingly aware of consolidating royal power in England.

King Magnus the Last

The challenge of preserving Manx autonomy intensified in the 13th century. The last of the independent kings of Man, Magnus (r. 1252–1265), traveled on the mainland to observe developments and it made an impression. One of the most complete Norman castles surviving anywhere in the British Isles began construction during his early reign and was a lasting investment. Castle Rushen (from Old Norse *Rhos* meaning headland or woodland) is situated on the English-facing southeastern coast, and the village of Castletown that gathered around its walls became the Manx capital in the later medieval age. The test for Magnus did not come from invaders at the castle walls however, but from a standoff between Norse and Scots over the political status of the Hebrides. It was crucial for lesser kings like him to maintain a modicum of status through alliances, but he became entangled in a tripartite web that did not work out well. He was a subject of the Norse king, became recognized in the Scots court through his Scots wife, and was on oath to make ships available to Henry III of England to maintain cordial relations with the Plantagenets. It was his support for the abortive naval campaign of Norse king Haakon IV in 1263 (explained in the Hebrides chapter) that got him into trouble. The Scots king Alexander III, empowered with the news of Haakon's death in Orkney, summoned Magnus to the Scots court in 1264. He must have sailed in a mood of foreboding; after all he had opposed Alexander, but in the event came away with something. He would be recognized as king of Man until his death (it occurred a year later) but the northern Hebrides of Skye and Lewis were to be surrendered to the Scots. The kingdom of Man and the Isles was dissolved. Man's leadership of the Sudreys had lasted two centuries, no mean achievement in turbulent times.

The Treaty of Perth of 1266 ended Norwegian political influence in the Hebrides and Irish Sea, and further, the death of Magnus of Man meant that Alexander III assumed the title king of Man. The island was now within the realm of Scotland; in a few short years destiny had radically changed. The distinctive heraldic device of three legs in a perpetual sprint ("Three Legs of Man") everywhere on the island today from coins and postage stamps to road signs and government insignia may have been Alexander's idea to replace a Norse coat of arms. The same design is also found in Sicily and there is an association: Alexander's brother-in-law ruled there. Others point to pre–Christian sun symbolism as the source of it. As for Tynwald, it would henceforth be a wholly Manx institution. The "four and twenty" *keys* were maintained by substituting eight more Manxmen for the seceded northern Hebrides. These were disturbing times for the Manx elite, and some of them, unhappy with the Perth treaty, rebelled, backing Godred, son of Magnus, in a bid to restore lost independence. The uprising was a tragic failure with 537 Manxmen slaughtered by a Scots army at Ronaldsway in 1275; "Ten times fifty, three times ten and five and two did fall; O Manx race, beware lest future catastrophe you befall" went a lament of the day.[12] One story has Godred surviving the carnage and escaping to Anglesey, but if so it was to no avail. Man's fate was to become a political accessory, caught on the cusp between England and Scotland.

"Right Order in This World"

Other changes were already in progress. A new church with an Irish style tall round tower had been built on St. Patrick's Isle in the 10th century, but it would be the last representation of the traditional Celtic Church. The collection of autonomous monasteries and abbots were brought into line during Gregory VII's papacy (1073–1085) with a new orthodoxy after Rome freed itself from an investiture system where clerics and popes were lay appointees. A College of Cardinals made appointments instead. Aggressive in pursuit of an overtly political agenda, a holy war was called in 1095 against infidel Muslims in the first Crusade. Administrative changes came at parish and monastic level within Christendom as the diocesan system strengthened in areas that had resisted it (like Man). The Norman-French were agents of the transformation in mainland Britain, and the newly converted Norse likewise accepted Roman legitimacy to seek what reformers called "right order in this world." First signs of ecclesiastical change on Man came in the formation of a diocese named

Sodor, the word derived from Sodorensis, a Latinized *Sudr-eyjar* or Sudreys. There were bishops of Sodor from the time of Godred Crovan according to the *Chronicles*, placing its origins in the later 1000s, a period corresponding to Gregory VII's radical papacy. The first listed was Hrolfr, buried at St Maugholds Church.

In 1152 Sodor was brought under the archdiocese of Nidaros (Tröndheim, Norway) and centered on a new church built on St. Patrick's Isle, this one a grand cathedral in keeping with the times. The choice of location was astute, diverting focus from the old Celtic monastery at Maughold but named for an early Irish missionary, St. Germain. As Orcadian stonemasons chipped away on the pillars of St. Magnus's in Kirkwall, then, so too did Manx masons on their own cathedral. Meanwhile a parochial system with local parish churches and priests replaced the scattered *keeills* of the Celtic brethren but often based on older *keeill* sites, as noted earlier with 12th century St. Maugholds.

Continental assimilation also meant "foreign" clerics and lands were made available to accommodate them, necessitating disinheritance. What the Manx thought of that is not recorded but might be imagined. It was Olaf I who granted lands in the first instance and Rome-approved orders arrived to inhabit them. An abbey was established at Rushen in 1134, as noted earlier, on a site close to an older dispossessed Celtic monastery. At the outset it was home for monks under the French Sauvignac order, but in 1148 it became a subsidiary house of a Cistercian abbey located on the Furness peninsula in northwest England. Rushen is the final resting place of the last Crovan kings of Man — Olaf II (d. 1237), Rognvaldr II (d. 1249) and Magnus (d. 1265). Furness Abbey appropriated more and more churches in Man including that of Celtic Maughold. The loss of Maughold may have precipitated a revolt in 1299 against Mark, bishop of Sodor. The *Chronicles* mention that Bishop Mark, a native of Galloway in southwest Scotland, was deposed by Manxmen and sent into exile; this after ruling Sodor for many years. One secondary source attributes his expulsion to an order by Edward I of England[13] (by then ruler of Man) and the matter did not go unnoticed in the eternal city. The Isle of Man was put under a papal interdict for three years. To remove the sentence, Bishop Mark, said to be "kindly and blind" by sympathetic chroniclers, was recalled and the island put under a "smoke penny" tax of one penny from every house that had a fire,[14] a tax that was to last centuries. Mark died in 1302 and was buried at St. Germain's Cathedral on St. Patrick's Isle, new resting-place for venerated Manx.

When Alexander III of Scotland and king of Man died in a riding accident in 1284, Edward I of England took advantage of feudal maneuvering to claim Man. It then passed through several hands as a royal gift including that of Piers Gaveston, doomed favorite of Edward II. The tide turned again in 1315 when *gallowglasses* (Scots mercenaries) of Robert Bruce, Scots victor over Edward I at Bannockburn in 1314, seized the island in pursuit of an ambitious effort to place Robert's brother Edward in power in Ireland. The ruse failed and the collapse of a singular authority left Man vulnerable. These were particularly wretched times for the islanders, open to pirates and marauders. The last detailed entry in the *Chronicles* is for 1316, a year when "evildoers from Ireland" landed at Ronaldsway looking for tributes and money, plundering Rushen Abbey of "its furnishings and its cattle and sheep [leaving] nothing at all."[15] The short entries are intermittent thereafter and disappear altogether in 1377. The abbey community revived, but maybe not until the 15th century, and the *Chronicles* were not published until 1585.

Feudal Right

The end of the Norse-led maritime network removed Man's advantage as a service base at the center of the Irish Sea, and for the next half-millennium it drifted on the periphery. Feudal right was reasserted in 1333 when, as a byproduct of Edward III's victory over the Scots at Halidon Hill in the English/Scottish borders, suzerainty passed to an English knight, William de Montacute. The son of a Norman-French baron who had served under Edward I, he was titled king of Man as reward for service to Edward III. He had to use force to persuade suspicious Manx of his sovereignty and set about strengthening defenses, notably at Castle Rushen, but spent little time there, a portent of things to come. As the English king's vassal Montacute continued to give military service and became earl of Salisbury in 1337. His heir sold Man to a supporter of Richard II and it passed again through several English hands until 1405, when Henry IV granted it to one of his knights, Sir John Stanley.

The beleaguered Henry IV (r. 1399–1413), whose accession and reign is a good illustration of the "byzantine politics" of the day, bestowed favor to win favor and awarded Sir John Stanley the kingdom and fiefdom of Man (among other offices) with all attendant regalities, franchises and rights. The English Channel was by now at the heart of feudal politics and the Irish Sea a comparative backwater. The value (or decline) of Man's political capital can be measured by the minimal service expected of its new owners, reputedly two falcons to be presented by the Stanley family at English coronations.[16] Sir John Stanley never visited the island and neither did many of his descendants (later earls of Derby), but they held it for over three centuries nevertheless, imposing their authority through lieutenants (later governors). A notable exception was John Stanley II, king of Man 1414–1437, the first recorded as having visited since William de Montacute. He was sufficiently bothered by what he found there to order major judicial reform. The primacy of civil law over ecclesiastical law was asserted in a bid to weaken the power of the church. Church sanctuary was abolished for example. Laws were codified, judicial proceedings recorded and trial-by-jury introduced. Most Stanleys were not interested, however, and after John none visited until 1507, by which time the royal title had been dropped (1504) at the behest of Henry VII's centralizing agenda. The title lord of Man was assumed instead, a change of no consequence to islanders.

Tynwald met irregularly, summoned when needed by lieutenants and *deemsters*, less a parliament for the people than a useful vehicle for arbitrary government. The four-and-twenty *keys* remained as appointees but nominated by Stanley lieutenants and not by their kindred. This change must have impacted island elites as new *keys* came from England over time, granted lands by the Stanleys. Once the honor was in the family it was expedient to continue the privilege. Land was held from Stanley kings and lords of Man by consent with no written security of land tenure, but heritable rights were not rescinded. A de facto freehold tenure based on custom continued, not dissimilar to the *udal* custom of the Northern and Western Isles.

Events in the outside world disturbed routines from time to time. Although there seems to be no record of the 14th century Black Death on the island, it's hard to imagine how a seafaring community could have escaped it. The epidemic devastated Dublin and Drogheda on the eastern Irish seaboard and impacted northwestern England likewise. Significant change came during the reign of Henry VIII (1509–1547) with Catholic properties confiscated throughout the English realm. Cistercian Rushen Abbey was dissolved in 1540 and the new Anglican diocese of Sodor and Man came under the archbishop of York. Anglicanism may have changed things little theologically, but its devotions did not please all consciences, as Henry's efforts to impose it on the Irish would prove. Many of the country folk privately clung to the old faith, and discontent on Man would express itself at least over the payment of hated tithes to the new church.

On a different tack the sixth earl of Derby, William Stanley, lord of Man in the early 17th century, is worthy of mention if only because he is one of those proposed by anti–Shakespeare pundits as the real author of some of the immortal bard's plays. The evidence is no more than circumstantial, inspired by a mentality that finds it difficult to accept that a provincial from middling social ranks (Shakespeare senior was a glover) could write such exquisite lines. The alternatives are drawn from the aristocracy, even though an increasing number of writers and scholars came from backgrounds like Shakespeare's. William Stanley's modern admirers think he may have written *The Tempest* (and *Love's Labors Lost*) with the Calf of Man a prototype Prospero's Island. In fact, details about his life are little better documented than those of Shakespeare's.

"Illiam Dhone"

Documentation of everyday life is minimal too, but voices of protest over government, church tithes, and land law were heard in the mid–17th century, emboldened by the English Civil War of 1642 to 1649. The lord of Man at the time (1627–1651) was James Stanley, seventh earl of Derby. He was the first Stanley to actually live on the island and had taken the step of appointing a Manxman, Captain Edward Christian, a sailor and adventurer of some repute, as deputy governor in 1631. The Christians were of Gaelo-Norse origin (formerly MacCristen) and very influential with members documented as *deemsters* back to the 15th century. The infamous *HMS Bounty* mutineer Fletcher Christian came later from an English branch of the same family. Edward Christian, a populist, used his position to lobby for grievances about tithes and land tenure and to propose elections of *keys*. Clearly this was not what Lord Stanley had in mind when he appointed him and he relieved him of his duties in 1639. He returned to favor in 1642, however, when the Civil War broke out in England, appointing him sergeant major of the island militia. His time out of office had not dampened his reformist ideals. There is a reference in later trial documentation that in that same year he played "adviser, counselor and persuader" to an armed crowd at Tynwald angrily protesting church tithe payments.[17] Meanwhile as English parliamentary forces squared up against Charles I in England, Lord Stanley sailed away to assist the royalist cause.

Edward Christian saw the English conflict as a great opportunity to challenge the status quo on Man, and when a massed protest took place in Douglas in 1643, following the arrest of a man who had refused to pay tithes, the militia took control under his command. Stanley was contacted in England and he hurried back to upstage Edward at a Peel Castle meeting summoned to hear people's grievances by offering them reforms. It worked. The uprising dissolved and Edward Christian was arrested and thrown in prison. Moreover the reforms did not sit well with islanders once they understood them. Instead of the tithe reform anticipated, new land leasehold arrangements with expiration terms were introduced, a change that threatened the kindred inheritance of old. Stanley also appointed William Christian, a relative of Edward, to the important office of receiver (tax collector). It was a calculated move. William Christian, affectionately known in Manx lore as *Illiam Dhone* or "Brown-haired William," was well connected. His father was a prominent *deemster* and significantly a defender of traditional land custom. It was also a reward for compliance. William had inherited property from his father at Ronaldsway, held from the Stanleys, and in 1643 agreed to hold it on the new terms of "three lives" leasehold,[18] although it seems he had little alternative since the land would have gone to someone else otherwise.

Stanley rejoined the fray in England, but after the rout of Charles I at Marston Moor in 1644, where 4,000 royalists died and another 1,500 were taken prisoner, he returned to resist potential invasion of Man. It did not arrive at this juncture, but the report of Charles I's execution in 1649 devastated him. So when he heard two years later of a Scots plot to restore the deceased king's son, he could not resist again the call to arms. Nine months later the royalist effort collapsed in abject failure and the would-be king (future Charles II) fled to France. Fate was less kind for Stanley. His Manx militiamen were easily defeated in Lancashire and he was taken prisoner and beheaded as an English traitor.

After centuries of relative inactivity these were stirring times on Man. Shortly after the news of James Stanley's execution another revolt erupted, this time against his widow, Charlotte de la Tremouille, countess of Man. William Christian was charged with her protection but actually became involved in her removal. His motives were mixed. It is not clear that he was imbued with the same populist zeal as his relative Edward (released from prison at this time) though posthumous representations of him as *Illiam Dhone*, the Manx patriot-martyr, would have us believe that. What is clear is that a parliamentary force of 44 warships massed offshore in 1651. Christian must have heard that Oliver Cromwell himself, leader of the English parliamentary cause, had returned recently from Ireland where thousands were massacred in Drogheda and Wexford. Maybe he figured that Manx resistance might meet similar treatment. The countess was forced to abdicate, her own guard unwilling to defend her, and she surrendered the castles of Peel and Rushen and left the island. The Manx were free of Stanley rule. Exactly how premeditated the liberation was is debatable, but it had transpired nonetheless. It did not last, of course, but for the next few heady republican years the Manxman William Christian enjoyed power as governor of Man from 1656 to 1658.

Constitutional provision for Oliver Cromwell's succession was not secured in England (he died in 1558) and the Stuart monarchy was restored in 1660 for want of a better solution. Royalists sought to settle old scores in the Restoration, and the most famous Manx victim was William Christian. Accused of financial irregularities with revenues from confiscated bishopric lands in his last year as governor, he was arrested for non-payment of debts and endured a year in London's notorious Fleet prison, den of hapless debtors, before being freed on bail. He returned to Man thinking an amnesty granted by Charles II applied to the island but instead found the new lord Charles Stanley (eighth earl of Derby) determined to have revenge for usurping his command in the Cromwell years. He was promptly arrested and imprisoned in Castle Rushen. His arrest caused great uneasiness among his peers. Those members of Tynwald unwilling to condemn him were removed from office and replaced by those willing to sign a death warrant. The trial seems to have been a farce with no evidence taken on his behalf. He was sentenced without a hearing and executed by firing squad in Castletown in 1663; a last ditch appeal to Charles II arrived a week too late. The king at least placated some by ensuring that William's land was restored to his family.

Memorialized by Manx ballad (1781) as a patriot-martyr — "thy fate, Illiam Dhone, sickens my soul" — and included in one of Sir Walter Scott's romantic histories, *Peveril of the Peak* (1822), such characterizations dramatize his historical importance, but they should not detract from it. William (and Edward) Christian gave voice to the Manx. It might be a stretch to see either in the same breath as English radical movements of that age seeking overthrow of the old patriarchy such as Ranters, Diggers and Levellers, but William's decision in 1651 to support the parliamentary cause had more to do with representing islanders' interests than defending the lordship that ruled them, whatever his other motives. The notion that government is for the governed was advanced and the cause was not entirely lost with Restoration. The male Stuart dynasty was deposed in Britain in 1688, and limitations on royal powers were reestablished in the 1689 Declaration of Rights. The UK's constitutional monarchy was born. It took longer for constitutional change to reach Man, but William and Edward Christian had laid a precedent.

A British Isle

During the lordship of the 10th earl of Derby, the last of the Stanleys, the 1643 land tenure reforms were reversed under the Settlement Act of 1704. Traditional inheritance rights were reclaimed and put in statutory law. It was a triumph for Manx custom but at odds with the wider world of English land allocation. Around 50 percent of cultivable commons and open fields in England had been converted into commercially viable farms by this time, and in the process customary land rights of the type freshly enacted in Manx law were lost. The new farming techniques of crop rotations were inoperable in collectivist open field societies under communal property law. It isn't clear exactly what the first James Stanley intended by his land tenure reform (the Campbells of Shawfield used such reform to break subsistence economics on Islay in the 1700s, as noted in the previous chapter), but repeal of it didn't help. "This isle will never flourish until some trading be," Stanley wrote in 1643,[19] recognizing the ill health of his day, and with no enterprise-driven surpluses to trade, Manx economic life remained rooted in subsistence until the 19th century.

Herring fishing was a constant of that subsistence economy, fluctuating in success from season to season. Potatoes introduced in the 18th century quickly became a part of Manx diet — the ubiquitous "spuds and herring" supper brought land and sea together in the same pot — but it too was a subsistence activity. Oats and barley were grown for thousands of years, and later 18th century arable diversification brought clover and turnips, but crop rotation was irregular and cereal output unimproved. The grazing of small native black cattle was still the norm, and curious sheep unique to Man called *loghtans,* having between two and six horns, continued to provide soft brown fleece to hand spinners, their name coupling two Manx words of *lugh* (mouse) and *dhoan* (brown). Flax was cultivated for linen fiber. Cottage based spinning and weaving and boat building constituted the craft economy, but in sum the profile was similar to that of millennia. A sense of this timeless working world is conveyed at Cregneish in the south of the island where an open-air folk museum of farm and village is dedicated to the old ways. The setting was felt to be sufficiently authentic for the box office hit movie *Waking Ned Devine* (1998) to be filmed there doubling as traditional Ireland because the real thing is in retreat.

Not all were enamored with the old ways in the 18th century. Basil Quayle, a progressive farmer from Castletown, presented a report to the Board of Agriculture in London in 1794, concluding that too many practices were guided by old customs, draining and fencing needed attention, and the hoary old thorn of church tithes needed to be addressed; "a method of maintaining the clergy less unpopular than the tythe in kind would excite the farmer to improve,"[20] he argued. He recommended funding, touching a nerve that would be repeated in 19th century pleas for investment. Farmer Quayle estimated the total population to be 26,000 in the 1790s, and we can assume that the majority of them were very poor. When Thomas Wilson, Bishop of Sodor and Man (1698–1755), was given the chance of a richer diocese in England he refused, saying "I will not leave my wife [the island] in my old age [just] because she is poor."[21] Others reacted differently and emigration became a part of Manx life. Because customary inheritance was protected by law, however, the island did not experience rapid depopulation on the scale that occurred in the Hebrides; instead there was a steady exodus of native-born, attracted by opportunities elsewhere.

Those who stayed were not averse to supplements from smuggling when harvests were meager, joined by outlaws and others of questionable background who saw in Man a convenient hideaway. High demand merchandise like brandy, wine, rum, silks and tobacco were landed on the surrounding British and Irish coasts with Man in an intermediary role. Tynwald, empowered to fix Manx customs duties from 1737, took no action. Across in England, the UK Parliament, burdened with heavy war costs in Europe, North America and India by the 1760s, was vexed at the revenue loss and looked for ways to recoup it and combat further tax evasion. There was another irritant. The island provided a refuge for those seeking to avoid debtors' prison. English and Irish debts could not be recovered in the Isle of Man. A solution to both problems was sought by buying back the island.

The direct line of Stanleys ended with the 10th earl in 1736 and the lordship passed to James Murray, second duke of Atholl, whose grandfather married a Stanley. His son-in-law claimed the lordship in 1764 but sold the title (though not Atholl properties) to the Crown for £70,000 in 1765. His right to the dukedom of Atholl had yet to be confirmed by the House of Lords and this influenced his willingness to surrender the title to Man. The sovereignty of Man passed to King George III. Under the 1765 Isle of Man Purchase Act (Revesting) Act the island's customs service, post office, harbors and ports and judiciary were all taken over by the British Home Office in London. In the matter of the public purse, Man was a British isle. The Revesting Act may have suppressed the loss of British tax income but it did little for the Manx economy. Tighter trade restrictions caused merchants to move elsewhere, and any monies collected in the island went to London. It was London's prerogative to figure how much of it returned in the form of investment. In that same year (1765) Parliament approved the infamous Stamp Act with the intention of creating an alternative source of tax revenue to import duties for the North American colonies, the consequences of which led to the American War of Independence. On Man, the disenchanted voted with their feet and left the island.

The Murrays were not quite done with Man since the family retained their properties. John Murray, fourth Duke of Atholl, was made governor in 1793. The previous year he had pushed Parliament to open an inquiry into Revestment (he thought the title sale price had been too low) and his salaried appointment was part-compensation. He proved an unhappy choice, more interested in taking what little there was out of the island than raising money to develop it. His main contribution was to have a large mansion house, Castle Mona, built in 1804; it's now a Douglas hotel. A partiality for putting members of his own family into paid offices put him at odds with the House of Keys, the institutionalized four-and-twenty, and an attempt by his nephew George Murray, Bishop of Man, to raise tithes in 1825 provoked riots and protest all over the island, hastening departure of bishop and duke. John Murray sold out the remaining family interests in Man, both civil and ecclesiastical, to the Crown between 1826 and 1829 for £417,000. The feudal era was finally over but at not inconsiderable expense to British taxpayers.

Industrial Man

Fortuitously Manx slates contained the means of its restoration in copper, silver, zinc and lead. It was this mineral endowment that helped begin the process of transforming its economy. Copper had been worked in the late Bronze Age and Cistercian monks from Rushen Abbey once extracted silver from a site now occupied by Ronaldsway Airport. The Stanleys and Murrays leased out mineral rights. The new extraction incentive came from 19th century British industrial demand to galvanize steel products and as a component of several alloys. Major production centered in two areas—one in the Laxey valley and slopes of nearby Snaefell and the other in the Foxdale and Glen Rushen area. Over a hundred operations were financed, from major working mines to small trials that yielded nothing. Scores of abandoned workings testify to the extent of it. By the third quarter of the 19th century—high noon in Britain's industrial world leadership—Manx mines were producing about 20 percent of all British zinc and 5 percent of the lead. Snaefell and Laxey were particularly busy with annual zinc averages of 9,000 tons mined and exported (in 1875: 11,000 tons). Snaefell was once one of the deepest mines in the world. Hundreds found waged work there turning out 2,500 tons of lead and silver and 500 tons of copper every year. In the Foxdale and Glen Rushen mines, 4,000 tons of galena (a lead ore rich in sliver) and copper was extracted annually. Industrialization has its own folk-lore and there are plenty of tales about the dangers of the work. The worst disaster occurred in 1879 at Snaefell when 20 men died from the toxic fumes of carbon monoxide. The mining had passed its best years by 1900 as metal prices no longer justified costs and Britain felt the cold chill of international competition for its products. The Foxdale mines closed in 1910 but Laxey stayed operational until 1929. The giant Laxey Wheel (1854) that once pumped water from the mine has been restored to working order and still stands as a tourist attraction.

Some of the endeavors may have been relatively short-lived but industrialization permanently impacted Manx life. As in other mining boom regions the miners were not necessarily locals; many of them came from Cornwall and Cumberland where there were long family traditions of tin and lead mining. The foreign born represented 18 percent of the population in 1891.[22] Significantly the census reported 55,000 for that year, twice that of the 1790s, quite the reverse of the Hebrides where numbers were decimated by famines and land clearances. There was a marginal fall-off between 1891 and 1911 as laid-off miners took off for South African and Australian goldfields but working folk who stayed home could benefit from services generated by a growing tourist trade even if they competed with incomers who saw the same opportunities.

Principal among the new spinoffs were railways, quite a turnaround for a small island where packhorses had been the main conveyance and wheeled transport was not that common. The British railway mania peaked and passed before it got under way on Man. The Duke of Sutherland and Sir John Pender MP (both with connections to the lieutenant governor of the day, Henry Loch) raised funds to connect Douglas with Peel and open a coast-to-coast corridor (1873). Another track from Douglas to Port Erin via the old capital of Castletown opened up the south in the following year. As with many rural railway operations the business revenue did not match optimistic promotional rhetoric and directors were reluctant to consider further expansion to the northern port of Ramsey until existing costs were covered. The Ramsey initiative was taken by a group of Ramsay businessmen and the Manx Northern Railway was formed to connect Ramsay with the Douglas-Peel line at St. Johns. After overcoming several engineering challenges it opened for business in 1879. A third railway, the Foxdale Company, connecting Foxdale to St. Johns, hauled lead ore to the port of Ramsey. Electricity made its mark as well with several light electric railways opening before the end of the 19th century, one of which was an electric tramway to the summit of Snaefell, the first in the British Isles. It served tourists who came in growing numbers.

Tourist Isle

The Lancashire middle classes came first and then the workers with pay packets to cover a yearly holiday splash, pouring onto steamships (a Liverpool to Douglas service began 1829) to enjoy raucous promenade entertainment, dance halls, beauty contests, puppet shows and Man's version of the burlesque. With its sweeping seafront terrace of Victorian villas offering board and lodging, Douglas sought to compete with English seaside resorts like Blackpool and Morecambe on the adjacent Lancashire coast. The Isle of Man Steam Packet Company was carrying more than a million passengers annually by 1913 and this to an island with less than 100,000 permanent residents. The island had 663,000 ship arrivals in 1913 alone. An initiative to introduce motorcycle racing, tempted by revenue as well as love of a fledgling sport, raised the island's profile further. The first Tourist Trophy (TT) Race was held in 1907 on a 14 mile St. Johns–Kirkmichael–Peel circuit and big crowds still thrill to cutting edge machines as they speed down narrow twisting country lanes on island circuits. The "ton" was first topped in 1957 with an average speed of 101 mph. Television rights maintain its place in the international sports calendar but TT fatalities are a yearly inevitability, an incongruous and horrifying statistic in such a benign setting.

A decidedly less dangerous and enduring Manx innovation was the holiday camp. Cunningham's Young Men's Holiday Camp opened in Douglas 1894 and within ten years had developed the kind of organized holiday experience that defined later and very successful mainland British holiday camp chains like Butlins, Pontins, and Warners. Advertised as "the largest most popular holiday resort in the world," Cunningham's campers (men only) slept in rows of tents, dined mess hall style, and were encouraged to participate in team games, swimming and sing-along. The regimen would be too militaristic for today's tastes but lasting friendships were made and the camp remained in business until mid–20th century, playing an unanticipated part in both world wars, as we shall see.

State of Tynwald

In 1801 the Isle of Man, together with the Channel Islands, was classified as a dependency and shepherded under the wing of the British Home Office, a move prompted by disquiet in the face of Napoleonic France. As the economy diversified through the Victorian Age, pressure for constitutional reform grew. Change came, but it took most of the 19th century. Tynwald began that century as it had many others, as a bicameral parliament of medieval patricians. Its upper chamber comprised a handful of law officers (*deemsters* and an attorney general), ecclesiastical potentates and aristocrats — an ad hoc cabinet to a sequence of kings, lords and lieutenant governors of Man. The last governor was John Murray (d. 1830). Lieutenant governors were appointed thereafter to represent the British monarch. The other chamber — the medieval "four-and-twenty" *keys* of the House of Keys — gave consent to laws and judgments but did not initiate them; that was an executive privilege. The executive of lieutenant governor plus the upper chamber assumed the last word legislatively. The medieval practice of holding a Midsummer's Day *thing* at St. Johns (July 5) — the day when new laws were read aloud — lived on but the House of Keys had little effective power. The Keys was hardly *vox populi* anyway: an electorate did not choose them. They chose themselves and over the centuries nepotism ruled. John Murray knew as much, deciding "they were no more representative of the people of Man than of the people of Peru."[23] When the Whigs redrew the electoral map of British parliamentary representation in the 1830s, there was talk of Man's absorption within the English county of Cumberland. It did not materialize but its consideration is a reminder that Man's quasi-independent status could have been expropriated; island autonomy was not writ in stone.

Funding was the problem on which reform initiatives focused. Lawlessness increasingly strained policing resources as demographics changed. In the 1830s food shortage riots and gangs intent on plundering shipwrecks posed the challenge while 50 years later it was rowdy miners and the first generation of drunken tourists. In both instances the constabulary, poorly paid and undermanned, waged out of local poor rates, was stretched. Unlike the Channel Islands, with which Man is otherwise best paired, tariff revenues and tonnage duties were not the outright property of the island. All monies went to the British Treasury in the first instance, and it was up to sharp bookkeeping to ensure that the island was self-supporting and parsimony ruled the roost. One Tynwald ruse to generate income was to grant import licenses for high demand items (sugar, tea, spirits, tobacco) to those who could afford the fee, but it isn't immediately clear how the money was spent. Certainly it was a source of increasing aggravation to those who wanted to open up competition and in 1844 the licensing privilege was struck down. The reform served free trade interests but it did not solve the funding problem. The appointment of Henry Brougham Loch as governor (1863–1882) provided a turning point.

Governor Loch

Henry Loch was an able, well-traveled and unusually young administrator, only 36 when appointed. He had served in the Crimean War, held a commission with the East India Company and as a private secretary to Lord Elgin in China saw the inside of a Chinese prison and endured torture. A commentary in *The Times* [of London] rated his appointment as little more than largesse but in his defense he took the post seriously, more so than many of his predecessors. Loch was a Whig in the tradition of Lord John Russell, bent on making the old money interest accommodate the new, hardly a democrat in any modern sense (a patrician more like) but a Manx Renaissance Man for all that. Russell believed that efficient government needed the stimulus of a wider electorate, though not too wide; he stopped short of universal suffrage. Loch was in that mold.

There were two pressing needs. The first was to reverse remittance of Manx tax money to London and enable local revenue to be mobilized for island development while the other was to loosen the grip of the old boys' network and broaden the power base. Loch proposed that the House of Keys be allowed input on public expenditure decisions on the condition that they became a popularly elected body, albeit with a limited property franchise. It was agreed and the British Crown gave its assent. The first elections by ballot for the Keys took place in 1867. Most of the self-elected "old boy" incumbents were "reelected" but the die had been cast; the Keys was open to renewal in the longer term. The franchise was widened in 1903 and the first candidate to represent labor union interests was elected. These reforms complemented industrial expansion and with more control over insular customs revenue, investment and capital growth became feasible. Priority was given to improving harbors and building roads and developing Man as a resort capable of competing with those on surrounding coasts. Loch proved the right governor in the right place at the right time for commercial interests. Not everyone was convinced, of course; there was a price to be paid for becoming a playground. Man was progressively "Englished." The novelist Hall Caine (1853–1931), author of a series of stories with island settings, regretted the passing of insular rural simplicity, but ironically it was his best-selling English language books that helped draw people to the island and with them worldly influence. In 1871 the seat of government shifted to Douglas, by then the principal port and center of commerce and most "Englished" of island towns. Castletown, home of Castle Rushen and power base since the 13th century, was left to history.

During Loch's term of office, propertied women won the right to vote (1881)— the first women anywhere in Britain — but the reform was something of a false dawn. It took another half a century before a woman was elected to the Keys (Marion Shimmin of Peel took her deceased husband's seat in 1933) though in fairness this was not out of step with the wider democratic world. In an overdue measure to separate government powers the House of Keys lost its traditional judicial role to a new High Court (1882), and became a purely legislative assembly. Yet islanders were still far from home-rule.

Governor Raglan

Manx laws still required royal assent, not always a formality, and the UK Parliament could intervene legislatively. Most importantly the authority of the Crown expressed through the lieutenant governor's office was still absolute. George Fitzroy Henry, Lord Raglan, amply demonstrated the undiminished power of the office by imperiously resisting pleas for reforms during his tour of duty, 1902–1919. An attempt by the House of Keys to wrest control of budgeting from the Legislative Council, the small upper house comprising Crown appointees and governor, proved futile, though reformers did succeed in winning gubernatorial term limits. Governor Raglan, grandson of a British Crimean War commander, thought his appointment should be for life.

Nonplussed by reform agitation, Raglan set his face resolutely against calls for centralized social welfare of a type introduced in Edwardian Britain, preferring the charities and local poor relief practice of old. Social initiatives were not the only reforms he resisted. His opposition to tax breaks for Manx businesses badly impacted by World War I triggered protests and demonstrations. British funding of Manx government reached an unprecedented high because of the war and the feeling was that some of it should be shared with the population. Feelings ran high, though not as high as in Dublin where the rebellion of Easter 1916 against British rule led to executions and prison sentences. Lord Raglan's appearance on Tynwald Day in 1916 met with hostile groans and boos and he had to suffer the indignity of having a grassy sod missile thrown at him, but it got no worse than that. His nemesis, a journalist and political activist called Samuel Norris, leading light in the optimistically named Manx National Reform League, described him as a man with "a supreme contempt for change" and a "Caesar on the Isle of Man."[24] Yet Lord Raglan's resignation in 1919 changed nothing in the short term. Tynwald remained subject to the office of lieutenant governor and Man remained firmly within UK jurisdiction.

Little Manx Nation

Manx speech had long been the terra firma of "Manxness," in a changing world its definitive chord. The first known efforts at writing it down are rooted in the Reformation when a Welsh born Anglican bishop of Sodor and Man, John Phillips, translated the Elizabethan Book of Common Prayer into Manx (1610), but publication did not happen until 1894, as philologists hastily recorded Manx words in the face of an English language onslaught. Another bishop, a better-known island cleric, published various religious books in Manx. Thomas Wilson, Bishop of Sodor and Man (1698–1755), saw printing the vernacular as the best means of inculcating the faith and his *Principles and Duties of Christianity* and *Gospel of St. Matthew* were in the tradition of 16th century English Lutheran William Tyndale, who vowed famously that even the humblest plowboy should be able to read the scriptures. His work was carried on by successor Mark Hildesley, bishop 1755–72, who undertook publication of a Manx Bible and Prayer Book and encouraged their use in churches. Manx dictionaries were published in the first half of the 19th century to help preachers (by then mostly Methodist and Anglican) in their sermons. The number of Catholics, incidentally, was small, although migrants from the Irish potato famine in the 1840s provided a mini-boost.[25]

The same dictionaries were less in demand by the end of the Victorian Age, as accelerating political and economic changes advanced the English language relentlessly via government, business, and immigration. After 1850, the Manx-born were more likely to speak and write English. The formation of *Yn Cheshaght Ghailckagh* (The Manx Language Society) in 1899 would not be enough to save it. No laws specifically outlawed Manx. There was no need to; its demise was encouraged by perception of it as a rustic oddity in a modern world. Recordings of native speakers from places like Cregneish, home of the rural life museum, were made in the 1930s, when there were fewer than a thousand speakers left.

The custody of Manxness was in the hands of Manx writers in the Victorian Age, even if scripts were in English. Collections of Manx myths and legends have found a reading public from then onward and today the annual Manannàn Trophy is awarded to the person judged to have contributed the most to cultural heritage. One of its most famous recipients, Mona Douglas, was a 20th century authority on folklore and legends. The best selling English-born novelist Hall Caine wrote stories set in the Isle of Man for decades, so much so that his readers thought of it as Hall Caine's island. Among purists, the name of his friend T.E. Brown (1830–1897), a Douglas-born poet, stands out proudly; son of a clergyman, he taught at Clifton College in Bristol, England, for much of his life, returning to live only in his retirement. Brown's collected poems, published after his death, were very popular with Edwardians but you may look in vain for him in modern anthologies. In *Epistola ad Dakyns* he wrote of "three places by you must be visited" and "the next is where God keeps for me; A little island in the sea; A body for my needs, that so; I may not all unclothed go."[26] His deft weaving of Manx words into light-of-touch English rhyme catches the cadences of a passing age in *Spes Altera*, mourning the passing Manx tongue: "In dialect colloquial, retaining; The native accent pure, unchoked; With cockney balderdash. Old Manx waning; She's dying in the *tholtan* [ruin]. Lift the latch."[27] *My Garden* opens with: "A garden is a lovesome thing, God wot,"[28] a line that might serve as a metaphor for the modern isle. The vernacular found musical expression too, through Victorian collectors who wrote down scores and arrangements for old melodies and songs. W.H. Gill's *Manx National Songbook* (1896) included the lyrics of what later became the Manx national anthem:

Ry Gheddyn er ooir aalin Yee;	Oh Island so strong and so fair
Ta dt' Ardsoyl Reill Thie	Built firm as Barool
Myr Baarool er ny hoie	Thy throne of Home Rule
Dr reayll shin ayns seyrsnys	Makes us free as thy
as she	sweet mountain air

Internment, Depression and Internment

One of the less publicized facets of the home front in both world wars is that the British government, fearing internal security risks, interned thousands of British residents on Man. The foreign-born or those of foreign descent were vulnerable, irrespective of political affiliations. The island played a considerable role as a covert for these alleged "undesirables" and Westminster made it fairly clear that it had little say in the matter, though it did subsidize Tynwald. As a policy it was not new. The British initiated concentration camps in South Africa during the Boer War (1899–1902), detaining thousands of noncombatant civilians, but never in Britain itself until World War I.

Several books have been published relating internment memoirs, and in one of them edited by David Cesarini and Tony Kushner[29] the conclusions do not serve the British self-image of fair play. The authors concede that internees suffered less compared to war-front experiences but argue that that does not negate injustices

perpetrated against non-risk civilians. The targets in World War I were mostly nat-
uralized German-Britons and Austrian-Britons, about 60,000 having settled in the
UK by 1914, many of them in the bigger cities. Animosity toward them existed before
1914 — part of the xenophobic nationalism of the day — and war exacerbated it. Several camps were set up in mainland Britain but many were shipped to the Isle of Man,
seen as a perfect hideaway whether security risk or not. Czechs and Poles were thrown
in for good measure and POWs were incarcerated also. The distinction between them
and internees may have been clear to officialdom but not necessarily to islanders
who saw only prisoners.

The first site to accommodate internees was Cunningham's Holiday Camp in
Douglas, where they were secured behind unfriendly barbed-wire fences. Chronic
overcrowding and a riot, in which five internees died, led to a larger site being commissioned at Knockaloe Farm near Peel. Prefabricated huts thrown up within a three-
mile area grew into a self-sufficient "town" with its own electricity generator, butcher
and bakery. Knockaloe was a male-only affair, fueling the sense of imprisonment,
and music concerts, sports events, and lectures tried to relieve the monotony. The
numbers rose as anti–German sentiment intensified, especially after news about the
sinking of the British passenger liner *Lusitania* by a German U-boat in 1915. By the
end of the war Knockaloe housed over 23,000 civilian internees. At least for islanders
the camps provided work for local services, welcome respite from a shrunken wartime
market, since with 8,000 away as volunteers and conscripts these were lean times,
especially for hotel and catering businesses.

The unemployment malaise that afflicted northern England after the war, with
loss of markets for industrial staples, impacted Man too, dependent as it was on vaca-
tioning northerners in work. New concert halls, cinemas and theaters had opened
but visitor figures never quite reached Edwardian heights, although the TT event
built on its reputation. The Laxey mines closed in 1929 and buses undermined railway viability. Air transport arrived though it never threatened shipping. The population fell substantially for the first time — from 60,000 in 1921 to 49,000 in 1931. The
Manx-born numbers remained constant but the foreign-born fell by 50 percent. Residency recovered somewhat in the 1930s though only to a level reached back in 1911
(52,000). Farming had finally commercialized in the later 19th century but at the
price of jobs. In the interwar years a significant acreage of tilled land was turned over
to sheep grazing and imported shorthorns replaced Celtic black cattle, as farms
became more market oriented. Fishing had to adjust to new competitive realities too
with dredging for scallops beginning at Port Erin.

The UK declaration of war against Nazi Germany involved the island just as
World War I had with conscription, internment and POWs. Concern about the
"enemy within" in this war was more intense than in the earlier one, and those
interned included Jews who had fled Nazi persecution, hardly likely to be security
risks but dispatched to Man anyway. Italians who were resident in Britain were
interned as well, even if they had opposed Mussolini. Potentially dangerous British
fascists were added to the mix. When Italy entered the war in 1940, male Italian-
Britons were shipped to Man (and Orkney) to await deportation. Internment arrangements took a different form and instead of the large camp concept of 1914–18, hotels

and boarding houses were requisitioned. To maintain a semblance of economic normality, hotel owners and hosts were compensated for their "guests," but since these accommodations were contained within barbed wire compounds, any other thoughts of normality should be dismissed. Those classified as low-risk were placed in private homes in Port Erin and Port St. Mary.

Cesarini and Kushner make several revelations about the Second World War. One concerns Jewish refugees from Nazi Germany, who, together with British-born Jews with German connections, had extra incentive to support the Allied war effort, but were denied the right to participate and had to endure the frustration of incarceration. Home Office files reveal their efforts to serve in the war: 22 Jews from Peveril Camp, Peel, petitioned in December 1942 for the right to fight Nazism and although some early understanding of anti–Semitic atrocities by Nazis in Russia had reached officialdom from intelligence codebreakers their request was denied. Another troubling issue involved the woman commander at Port Erin and Port St. Mary, where an "open" camp housed 5,000 female internees. Testimonials allege that she carried a bullwhip to maintain order and treated internees, many of whom were Nazi victims, as if they were POWs. Some accused her of being a Nazi sympathizer. One of the most disturbing stories only indirectly involved the Isle of Man, in that some of the internees had been briefly held there, but again raises questions about government wartime civilian decisions. The cruise ship *Arandora Star* left Liverpool with over a thousand internees aboard in 1940, sentenced almost like 18th century convicts to transportation to Australia. Many were British-born or had British families. The ship did not get very far. It was torpedoed off Ireland by the same German submarine, the U-47, that sank the HMS *Royal Oak* in Scapa Flow, Orkney, the previous year. Of the 734 Italian internees on board, 486 lost their lives, while 175 out of 479 German internees likewise drowned. One of the Italians who died, Silvestrio d'Ambrosio, had lived in Scotland for 42 years and had a son serving in the British Army and another with the Canadian forces.

On a rejuvenating note, Cesarini and Kushner's study includes an article by Klaus Hinrichsen (*Visual Art Behind Barbed Wire*) about artists labeled degenerates by Hitler's Third Reich. For some of them (many Jews but not all) internment in the Isle of Man was a relief, protection from a hostile world. For others it was a desperate disappointment to escape to "freedom" only to find creativity stifled, living cheek-by-jowl with a thousand others. Yet adversity works in perverse ways and their presence inspired fellow inmates to deal with feelings of disillusionment and betrayal by expressing it creatively on wallpaper, window glass, wood, cigarette cartons, tent pegs, even toilet paper. Improvisational art exhibitions were held with the usual local landscapes and portraits popular subjects, but poignant dada-ist and surreal depictions, objects d'art expressing the subconscious, the irrational, the bizarre, the apolitical, are the most revealing, the very expression suppressed in Germany. The most celebrated professional internee artist was Hanover-born Kurt Schwitters, Jewish *persona non grata* in Nazi Germany and a Manx internee from 1940 to 1944. His avant-garde arrangement of everyday discarded items helped describe dada art in the first place.

Other talents of renown endured on the island. The famed Viennese concert pianists Marjan Rawicz and Walter Landauer were Douglas internees. Nikolaus Pevsner, a German Jew born in Leipzig (an art professor at the University of Göttingen before fleeing Nazi Germany), was interned on Man. After the war he became a well-published authority on British architecture and art editor of Penguin books, later knighted in recognition of his services to Britain. Other postwar success stories were publicly compensated with peerages such as Italian-born Charles Forte, founder of the global hotel and restaurant chain Trust House Forte, a Scottish immigrant before suffering the ignominy of internment, and George Weidenfeld, founder of Weidenfeld and Nicholson publishing house, an Austrian Jew who spent time in Camp Man. Unfortunately the overwhelming majority of internees have never been acknowledged. The UK government has never admitted the possibility of unfair conduct or considered compensation for property losses, as did the US government in 1988, following several lawsuits on behalf of interned Japanese-Americans.

War Maneuvers and Postwar Challenges

Three of the Chain Home radar stations stretching from Scilly to Shetland were housed on Man to monitor enemy aircraft and guide British fighter pilots to their targets by radio. There were glitches and error messages but ultimately the system was a key component in the air war victory. The island was also a major services training center. The multi-purpose Cunningham's Holiday Camp entertained Naval trainees. The Army Medical Corps ran a field hospital in Douglas. RAF aerodromes at Jurby and Andreas were used to prepare bombing flight crews. The civil airfield at Ronaldsway (the current Isle of Man Airport) functioned as RAF Ronaldsway until 1943 when it was taken over by the Admiralty for the Royal Naval Air Fleet Arm who renamed it HMS Urley from a Manx word for eagle. HMS Urley crews flew Fairey Barracuda dive-bombers, the same planes successfully used in disabling the German battleship *Tirpitz* in Norwegian waters in April 1944. *Tirpitz* was the destroyer targeted in the brave but abortive 1942 "Shetland Bus" mission. Although Man was outside the field of enemy fire, scores of military fatalities occurred from accidents in training maneuvers. At any one time, some 10,000 military personnel were on the island, a bonus at least for Manx businesses. Off-duty personnel seeking distractions from war fears and deprivations made Douglas livelier than it was 1914–1918.

There was an initial boom after the war, as a spending splurge followed wartime austerity, but it did not last. Tourism remained viable for a few decades, but its decline was in evidence by the 1970s as fast jets sped sun-starved Britons to Mediterranean hotspots at prices cheaper than a Douglas vacation. Man attracted over half a million long-stay visitors (those staying at least a week) yearly in the 1950s but 40 years later that number had fallen by 50 percent. The TT maintained its hard-core following but otherwise customized short-stay (few days) packages became the norm. Tourism accounted for only 6 percent of Manx income at the outset of the 21st century. The tourism-generated rail network is a shadow of its former self. The Manx Electric Railway was brought under public ownership in 1958 to prevent its collapse, but the three steam-traction railways were less fortunate and closed by 1965, although enthusiasts and Tynwald backing got the Douglas–St. Erin branch reopened as a holiday attraction in 1978. Fishing, farming and textile manufacturing held their place for a while after the war but their growth potential became progressively limited. The impetus for change came from a timely change in constitutional arrangements, one granting Manx government more fiscal autonomy.

Political Devolution

Home-rule was being discussed and approved by Tynwald as a laudable objective even as World War II raged, in essence a proposition to reverse the 1765 Revesting Act and win control of economic affairs without recourse to the British Treasury. The first step on this road to self-empowerment came in 1947 when Tynwald was permitted to re-purchase lands sold to the Crown in the 1820s. A bigger step came in 1958 when Parliament's Isle of Man Act permitted the transfer of control of island finances to Tynwald with the lieutenant governor accorded a treasurer role. After nearly 200 years, the control of ports and harbors lost in 1765 reverted to Manx authority. UK responsibility retreated to areas of defense and foreign policy. The British monarch remains lord of Man but domestic policy passed into the hands of the Manx government, a demonstration of devolution some 40 years before that of Wales and Scotland. The UK Parliament retains full powers to pass laws applicable to the Isle of Man, but in a nod to tradition, it defers to Tynwald. Acquiescence came after Manx compliance with UK defense fund contributions and common customs duties policy.

What remained unresolved was the balance of power within Manx government, specifically that between Tynwald and the office of lieutenant governor. The 1958 Act did nothing to remove the vote casting power of the latter. Full modernization needed further transfer of power to the elected house, the House of Keys. This came gradually. Tynwald's upper house, the Legislative Council, lost its ultimate veto power over the Keys in 1961, 50 years after a similar reform limited House of Lords power over Commons in Westminster. Most significantly the lieutenant governor lost his presidency of the Legislative Council in 1980 and with it the long-held role of head of government. Lieutenant governors now assume the role of viceroys or titular monarchical envoys on the island, submitting new laws to the UK Home Office for royal assent, while a newly created office of president of Tynwald, elected by all members of Tynwald since 1990, serves as the modern executive. All propositions come from the Keys— the "four and twenty" of old — democratically elected by registered adults for a term of five years. A cabinet of ministers and their respective departments (as in Westminster) handle policy implementation.

Man Inc.

Economic interest was a driving force of political reconstruction, and in a new era of self-determination, savvy political decisions have carved out a lucrative role for Man as a tax haven (defenders prefer the moniker offshore financial center), a veritable isle of money, inspired by the example of the Channel Islands, with which it is a competitor. A reformed Tynwald administered over a period of remarkable growth from the later 1980s with spells of double-digit percentage annual growth. The origins can be traced back to the decade after the 1958 Isle of Man Act, when Tynwald used its renewed monetary powers to full effect by initiating tax reductions. Income tax rates slid down to a base of 15 percent and with no death or estate duties, capital transfer or capital gains taxes, new residents came ashore. The population was declining in the 1950s but has grown every decade since and so has the percentage of foreign born.

Some preferred to send money instead of themselves. As inflation dogged the British economy in the later 1960s and 1970s, there was great interest in transferring savings to places like the Isle of Man, where lower taxation offset real value shrinkage, and the tax shelter advantage brought in corporate money too. Margaret Thatcher's 1979 British election victory further enhanced Man's fiscal appeal. One of her first decisions was to free movements of funds in and out of the UK from regulatory controls and end restrictions on lending for banks and building societies. Tynwald lost no time in response. In that same year Tynwald followed Jersey's 1962 example by abolishing the old practice of fixing interest rates. It was quite a revolutionary step in the evolution of Manx values: once usury was viewed as immoral, and now it was dismissed as anachronistic. Financial capital is more mobile than physical trade goods in the digital age, when investors look to avoid countries with onerous taxes and banking regulations. Customers got in line, and the number of Manx banks increased substantially.

Tynwald sought to attract the non-banking financial sector too, by offering tax breaks to insurance companies; whether services were to residents or non-residents was immaterial, the only imperative being a fee for the privilege of Manx registration. Reinsurance companies, those indemnifying insurance companies against loss, and fiduciaries, companies handling company and trust management, proliferated. The closely allied professional and scientific services of accountancy firms, legal advocates and medical staff moved in and set up house too. Ship management (merchant ships registering in the IOM) is another growth activity. Banking and non-banking white-collar enterprise together accounts for over 50 percent of the Manx economy. Manx incomes rose in real terms by a healthy 6 percent in the first half of the 1990s. What was once a dirt-poor island has turned into an international financial center, albeit one with a recently clouded reputation, to be discussed. The Isle of Man has a rich country economic profile, reporting a billion pound gross product. Manufacturing produces less than 10 percent of it, even if it has been helped by Tynwald incentives since the 1970s in the form of tax breaks, investment and training grants. The old mainstays of Manx life, agriculture and fishing, contribute only 3 percent.

The upshot of this remarkable reconstruction is a turnaround in demographic trends. Manx residency rose from 48,000 in 1961 to 76,000 in 2001, its highest ever level. The Manx-born were a minority in their own island by 1991, although at 49 percent only marginally so. There are no special residency permits or financial constraints placed on prospective residents, unlike the Channel Islands, although UK immigration policies do apply. The new Manx are predominantly migrant Britons with resources at their disposal, their presence stimulating housing and food demand. Some point to a strain on social services as a negative element, and the Isle of Man has not slashed welfare provisions to the same extent as mainland Britain at the time of writing. Some argue that economic stimulus has put the Manx government in better financial shape to afford it, and earnings from the sale of postage stamps and coins (Post Office authority, 1973), customs duties (Manx Customs and Excise Authority, 1980) and fees collected from the licensing of banks and fiduciaries help solvency. There have been expressions of local resentment over the changes. Anger was vented in arson attacks on newcomers' property in the 1970s and 1980s but the seductiveness of consumer capitalism has engineered a higher degree of acceptance. Irritants remain nonetheless and pressure for residency controls is building.

Another Man

Weighted against its own economic history, the Isle of Man is an offshore success story. The modern economy is a remarkable reversal of destiny, especially if centuries of neglect in protracted feudal servitude under the Stanleys and Murrays are taken into account. The Manx government is a prototype of political devolution, an example for the newly devolved UK assemblies in Scotland, Wales and Ulster. It has also had its share of adverse publicity, the first wave of which came in the aftermath of the "swinging sixties" when liberalized standards of British laws were not duplicated in Man.

Long after other western states ruled such treatment barbaric, an insistence on corporal punishment for law-breakers put the island in headlines in the 1970s, as did refusal to acknowledge abortion rights or legalize adult homosexuality. The image portrayed was of a reactionary and arcane society with draconian laws, out of step with modern living, and according to local accounts this was the way residents wanted it. In 1972 British newspapers reported a 15-year-old Castletown boy whipped by birch at a police station for unlawful assault, a minor misdemeanor involving another schoolboy. His case was appealed to the European Court of Human Rights. The 1978 judgment was that it amounted to degrading punishment, in breach of Article III of its articles protecting citizens against maltreatment. At a time when Britain was being hauled over the coals by the same court for ill treatment of political detainees in troubled Ulster, this case pales in importance, but the story made good copy with sensational revelations of the extent of Isle of Man birching. Sixty cases were cited for the period 1960 to 1976. The Manx hierarchy defended it as a deterrent against holiday hooligans, expressly the "mods and rockers" of that era, and remained defiant after the 1978 ruling. In 1981 a magistrate sentenced a brawling 16-year old Glasgow visitor to be birched, but his whipping was thrown out on appeal after intervention by an embarrassed UK government. There were no more cases after that, but Tynwald did not formally abolish corporal punishment until 1993. It lagged on capital punishment as well. The UK ended executions in 1965 but Tynwald not until 1992, although the Home Office reserved the right to commute Manx death sentences. The question of homosexuality between consenting adults also exercised Manx tolerance. Tynwald finally confirmed its legality in 1991, some 30 years after decriminalization in Britain. Women's rights to abortions, permissible in Britain since 1967, were not recognized until 1994.

OECD Blacklisting

A second round of unwelcome exposure came at the turn of the 21st century with rising concern about the near 2,000 banks and hundreds of insurance companies and investment funds crammed into Man's few square miles. The island complies with European Union (EU) directives in the trade of physical goods but is not subject to regulatory controls on social, financial and taxation policies. Tax haven opponents grew in the 1990s. The UK-based overseas development organization Oxfam condemned wealthy individuals and companies for using places like Man to shelter funds instead of investing in the world's poor. For the UK government it meant billions of lost tax revenue. The Paris-based Organization for Economic Development and Cooperation (OECD), representing many rich industrial nations, publicly attacked what it saw as tax evasion, sapping the competitiveness of their own economies as well as depriving governments of income. A "name and shame" OECD blacklist of 35 global tax havens was published in 2000 including those of the Isle of Man (and the Channel Islands).

The furor surrounding these blacklisted states extended beyond revenue losses to allegations of harboring drug trafficking monies and the money laundering of criminal gains. The International Monetary Fund estimates that money laundering may amount to anywhere between 2 percent and 5 percent of world GDP. In the competitive spiral of promoting its investment and company registration business, Manx authorities asked few questions of new foreign clients beyond confirmation of ability to meet licensing fees. The Manx smuggled liquor once; now was it illicit monies? FBI agents investigating international fraud in the 1990s rated the weak regulations in the Isle of Man (and Channel Islands) as conducive for criminals with cash to launder, and for some years at least it would seem that local politicians turned a blind eye. The OECD instigated a multilateral Financial Action Task Force (FATF) to tactically coerce independent financial centers to implement "know your customer" laws and exchange information. It pressured for harmonization of taxation levels at the same time. In the event the Isle of Man was not listed by the FATF for money laundering. The "know your customer" guidelines have been applied. Reforms began before the terrorist attack on New York's World Trade Center on September 11, 2001, but that ill-fated day was a powerful fillip. The US government turned from being a not unfriendly godfather, taking a libertarian view of places like Man as good for free market competition, into an angry pursuer of low tax jurisdictions everywhere, fearing that it was they who helped finance al–Qaeda (albeit unwittingly). Time and money has been spent researching accounts: a challenge since in the end knowing your customer's customers can be beyond reach.

By 2002 the Isle of Man was viewed as a cooperative jurisdiction, its name removed from the OECD tax haven blacklist, and it benefited from a flight of funds from less reputable offshore centers. Otherwise, it's business as usual. Manx taxation and corporate registration polices remain competitive. Foreign companies register as "exempt companies" if the beneficial interest belongs to non-residents; on this basis they incur no tax liabilities provided they pay an annual registration fee for the privilege of calling Man home. There are still no death or estate duties, capital transfer taxes, capital gains taxes or wealth taxes. Income tax rates remain comparatively low.

A Manx Renaissance?

Former British poet laureate John Betjeman once called the Manx "a shy, poetical people" with names that always seemed to begin with a C, K or a Q such as Caine, Christian, Crellin, Kelly, Kewley, Kermode, Quayle, to list some of them.[30] The Isle of Man has reconstructed itself so thoroughly that such a homely description no longer seems apt. There is not much of an insular atmosphere on contemporary Man — it's an urban and suburban isle, some parts Home Counties, some parts domesticated northern hill country. It does make an effort to preserve heritage, however. The "three legs" flag flaps everywhere in the sea breeze and the Manx Language Society thrives. Various Manx grammars and dictionaries are published and some literature. A Manx Celtic festival (*Yn Chruinnaght*) is held each July in Ramsay, including music, art, drama and dance. There is at least one Manx-speaking play school, newspaper articles, radio programs, a high school graduation certificate course, street names, road-signs and no doubt other manifestations, but since more than half of the rising population is not Manx-born, English-speakers may not be so easily persuaded to assure its revival.

Man is an island of immigrants and not necessarily the worse for that. It's a deceptive place. To walk the two-mile curve of Douglas's sweeping Victorian seafront is to experience out-of-season in season, passing five-level terraced villa frontage, horse trams and deckchair sellers dressed up for a seaside trade that won't come again in the old numbers. The promenade hotels have made business in recent times providing lodging for British construction workers building new bungalows, supermarkets and office blocks. A few streets back from the promenade the forlorn feeling evaporates as the island introduces itself, all three feet in the present, an enterprising place at a rural pace. Guidebooks describe it as a chunk of Pennine country in mid–Irish Sea, but money has softened the rugged contours to a gentler rolling terrain of stone walled mansions, ubiquitous English gardens, and anglers' retreats. Equestrian scenes relax the senses. There is a quiet self-satisfaction about the place, and why not with income tax pegged at 18 percent maximum. The challenge of the future will be protecting its nouveaux riches.

---

1. Burrow, Stephen, *The Neolithic Culture of the Isle of Man: A Study of the Sites and Pottery* (Archaeopress, 1997), 9.

2. Burl, Aubrey, *A Guide to the Stone Circles of Britain, Ireland and Brittany* (Yale University Press, 1995), 188.

3. Burrow, 13.

4. Mongan, Norman, *The Menapia Quest, Two Thousand Years of the Menapii* (Herodotus Press, 1995).

5. Ashley, Mike, *British Kings and Queens* (Carroll & Graf, 1998), 149.

6. Graham-Campbell, James ed., *Cultural Atlas of the Viking World* (Facts on File, 1994), 157.

7. *Cronica Regum Mannie et Insularum: Chronicles of the Kings of Man and the Isles*, Broderick, George, translator, (Manx National Heritage, 1996), f 33r.

8. *Chronicles*, f 33v.

9. *Chronicles*, f. 34v.

10. *Chronicles*, f 35 r.

11. Ashley, 5.

12. *Chronicles*, f 50r.

13. Kinvig, R.H., *The Isle of Man: A Social, Cultural and Political History* (Chas. Tuttle, Vermont, 1975), 89.

14. *Chronicles*, f 51r.

15. *Chronicles*, f 50r.

16. Manx National Heritage Library, X40–4, Atholl Papers.

17. Moore, A.W., *Manx Worthies* (Douglas, 1901), Ch. 3, 60 (http://www.isle-of-man.com/manxnotebook/fulltext/worthies/p060.htm).

18. Moore, Ch. 3, 64.

19. Kinvig, 119.

20. Quayle, Basil. "General View of the Agriculture of the Isle of Man," presented to the Board of Agriculture, February 1794 (http://www.isle-of-man.com/manxnotebook/fulltext/agricultr/index.htm).

21. Kinvig, 112.

22. Belchem, John, ed., *A New History of the Isle of Man, Vol. 5: The Modern Period 1830–1990* (Liverpool University Press, 2001), 426.

23. Kinvig, 117.

24. Norris, Samuel, *Manx Memories and* Movement (Modern Press, 1938).

25. Coakley, F., "1851 Religious and Educational Censuses" presented to Manx Methodist Historical Society, 11/7/98 (http://www.isle-of-man.com/manxnotebook/methodism/rc1851/rcu1851.htm).

26. Brown, T.E., "Epistola ad Dakyns" from *Collected Works of T.E. Brown* (Macmillan, 1909), 713.

27. Brown, 105.

28. Brown, 699.

29. Cesarini, D., and Kushner, T., eds., *The Internment of Aliens in Twentieth Century Britain* (Frank Cass, 1993).

30. Molony, Eileen, ed., *Portraits of Islands* (Denis Dobson London, 1951), 17.

5

Isle of Anglesey: "Mother of Wales"

"Along the [Anglesey] shore stood the enemy in a close-packed array of armed men interspersed with women dressed like furies in funereal black, with streaming hair and brandishing torches. Round about were the druids, their hands raised to heaven, pouring out dire curses. The Roman troops became rooted to the spot as though theirlimbs were paralyzed"—Tacitus *Annals* XIV, 29–30 (A.D. 115–120)

When Thomas Telford engineered a turnpike road to Anglesey in the early 19th century, it was heralded as if he had just broken through the frontier. Perched off the northern Welsh shore beyond the mountains of Snowdonia the island was often a hideaway—from conquering Roman centurions, Norman knights and the English language—an image given further credence as embattled Anglo-American aircrews flew in and out Anglesey's RAF Valley in World War II, airbase motto *In Adversis Perfugium* "A Refuge in Adversity." It's an unassuming place, still distant but tamer, minding its own business in mind if not in kind. The fact that it boasts Britain's longest place name[1] (a wordy creation by an enterprising Victorian tradesman to boost tourism) is uncharacteristically demonstrative. Its soft green-carpeted interior is less dramatic, a checkerboard of working farms, retirement homes, market towns and stone walled villages, with the highest point—ambitiously named Holyhead Mountain—only 700 feet above sea level. A glance at the region's topography tempts the thought that the island must have slid off nearby Snowdonia, but it was movement against Anglesey's hard igneous rocks that folded and crumpled the mountains. Insular form began some 8,000 years ago amid ice meltdown when a narrow valley flooded to form the ravine-like Menai Straits. Grandeur is reserved for the coasts where a rim of rocky headlands, sandy coves, dunes and bird sanctuaries delight naturalists. Acclaimed nature artist Charles Tunnicliffe lived on the island for several years.

Borders are writ in minds as well as on maps and once an island, always an island. Telford's road bridge may have hooked it back to the mainland, but as a haven of non–English speech Anglesey is arguably more "isleted" than the Isle of Man.

ANGLESEY

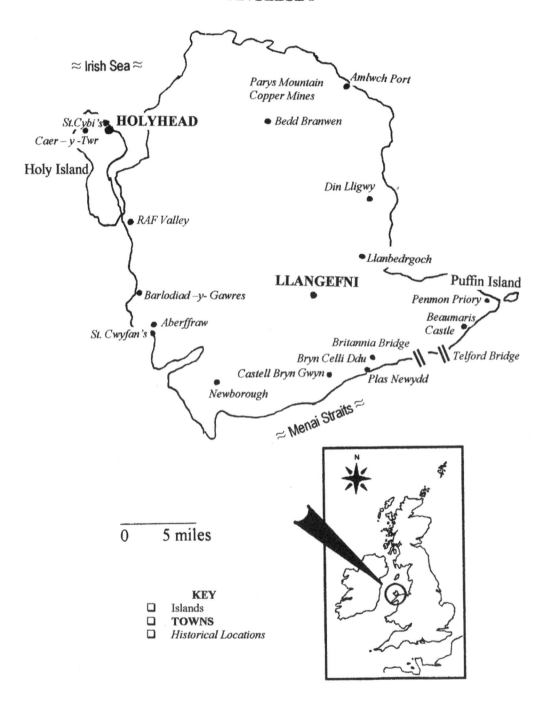

≈ Irish Sea ≈

Parys Mountain
Copper Mines

Amlwch Port

St.Cybi's **HOLYHEAD**

Bedd Branwen

Caer – y -Twr

Holy Island

Din Lligwy

RAF Valley

Llanbedrgoch

LLANGEFNI

Puffin Island

Barlodiad –y- Gawres

Penmon Priory

Beaumaris
Castle

Aberffraw

St. Cwyfan's

Britannia Bridge

Bryn Celli Ddu

Telford Bridge

Castell Bryn Gwyn

Plas Newydd

Newborough

≈ Menai Straits ≈

0   5 miles

N

KEY
☐   Islands
☐   **TOWNS**
☐   *Historical Locations*

Welsh is the most spoken of surviving Celtic languages and nowhere more so than on Anglesey. Listening to locals speak English is to hear tones and articulation coping with a less familiar tongue; there's nothing contrived about it. Yns Môn as the Welsh call Anglesey (from the Roman name *Insula Mona*) was chosen to hold the annual celebration of Welsh music and arts known as *Eisteddfod* in 1999, last of the millennium, to honor what Gerald of Wales called *Môn Mam Cymru* "Môn, Mother of Wales." The English name of Anglesey is Norse in derivation, developed from *Öngul's ey* or Ongul's isle, perhaps after a settler with reputation enough to have the place named for him or from an Old Norse word for "straits." Unlike on Man the population is in a decline mode with its current 66,829 residents (2001 census) dispersed across its 261 square miles, largest of the offshore islands. The biggest town, Holyhead, is a major seaport for Ireland.

Megaliths

Anglesey has been domesticated for at least 6,000 years, and its earliest farmers were well supplied with abundant rock and flints for axes to cut clearings among pine, alder, oak, and hazel woods. There was a productive axe factory at Graig Llwyd, east of Bangor on the mainland, although none are known of on the island. Megalithic burial and ceremonial sites survive, mostly around the perimeter, indicative of significant levels of Neolithic population. They stand at the southern end of the Boyne-Orkney axis of megalithic innovation, part of the same tradition as the Boyne Valley in Ireland and Orkney. One of the best known is Bryn Celli Ddu ("Brin Kethlee Thee") — "mound in the dark grove" — a third millennium B.C. passage grave on the Menai Straits side of the island, first excavated in 1865. Its midsummer sunrise alignment corresponds to one fixed by an earlier stone circle and henge, a display of cosmological awareness by now familiar to the reader. A short distance away two standing stones survive from the stone circle of Castell Bryn Gwyn, the same duo that fired the imagination of an 18th century Anglesey vicar, Reverend Henry Rowlands, with ideas inspiring the modern cult of druidism. In the same vicinity is the burial chamber of Bodowyr, one of the oldest sites, only its mushroom shaped capstone left for posterity. On the western coast near Aberffraw is Barclodiad y Gawres ("the giantess's apronful") where a mound protects five original decorated stones in its cruciform shaped interior. The spiral and maze-like zigzag carvings compare to those of Newgrange in the Boyne Valley, and a reconstruction of the chambered tomb can be seen at the Anglesey Heritage Center at Llangefni.

The tidal island of Ynys Gybi or Holy Island, positioned off the northwestern corner of Anglesey (now separated by mud flats and bridged by an expressway), has sacred-place associations reaching back to the Neolithic. Longevity of habitation is confirmed by excavations at the three-chambered tomb at Trefignath, dating activity to 3750 B.C. Christians would much later claim the holy isle mantle. In prehistoric Anglesey this islet was a hub, and still is in that Holyhead is here, a transit point with Ireland for thousands of years, shores busy with boats loading and discharging trade goods. It was originally thought that the 20 or so stone dwellings spread over

20 acres on the slopes of Holyhead Mountain at Caer y Twr in the north of Holy Island represented an Iron Age hill fort, but work carried out between 1978 and 1982 found occupation went back two millennia earlier. A village thrived there in the Neolithic Age with perhaps eight distinct homesteads. By the Iron Age there were Celtic roundhouses with adjoining stores and workshops, farmers laying out and plowing fields, grinding grain and grazing livestock as countless generations did before them. Excavated seashell dumps show that harvesting the seashore was another perennial life support.

Over on the eastern coast of Anglesey near Moelfre is another link in the island's megalithic rim chain — the Neolithic burial chamber of Din Lligwy. Eight uprights support a great capstone, standing forlornly now with much of its chamber submerged. The Iron Age dwellings nearby (like those at Caer y Twr) were probably also built over a Neolithic settlement. In all Anglesey was evidently populous in the third millennium B.C. with organized farming groups clustered around coasts near sacred burial and ceremonial sites, apparently in contact with other Irish Sea and North Atlantic communities.

Hidden Bronze Age

Peat bog formation did not blight Anglesey as it did Scottish and Irish islands, and farming may have been less disrupted in the later second millennium B.C. Yet there is a strange paucity of material evidence from this period. Bronze artifacts are dug up in other parts of Wales, with torcs and bracelets displayed in the National Museum of Wales in Cardiff, but Anglesey is less forthcoming. Perhaps its bronze and copper were stripped long ago, because other than some hair-rings, armlets and a shield boss (possibly Iron Age) there is a void of material. We are left with scraps from which to deduce developments. Single cairns are found, so there were leaders rich and powerful enough to warrant burial honor, the best-known being Bedd Branwen, named for Branwen, a Celtic queen from *The Mabinogion*, a medieval Welsh literary source to be discussed shortly. Analysis indicates an origin of c. 1500 B.C., long before the era designated Celtic. Amber and jet beads found at the site suggest sea trade, perhaps as far as the Baltic source of those minerals, and there are other metallurgy clues.

Copper ores outcrop in the vicinity of Parys in the north of the island, not far from Bedd Branwen, and while there is no hard evidence of Bronze Age extraction it cannot be ruled out either. Mines along the mainland coast at Great Orme near Llandudno (open to the public today) were worked c. 1500 B.C., so it is a reasonable assumption islanders took advantage of their own metal. The later second millennium B.C. witnessed widespread working of metals in Atlantic Europe, and copper was a highly valued exchange item. The working of it on Man was noted in the previous chapter. Rhys Carpenter argued for a long distance "megalithic seaway" of metals shipment in *Beyond the Pillars of Hercules* (1973), megalithic because shipping utilized sea corridors with shores where standing stones and tombs proliferate, namely the North Atlantic and Irish Sea coasts.[2] Anglesey was surely a contributor to that Bronze Age commerce.

Celtic Isle

Iron first appeared in Wales around 600 B.C., and on the basis of Hallstatt and La Tène classification, this is the start of the era termed Celtic. After the silence of the Bronze Age, it's a deafening period in Anglesey prehistory. A hoard of insights came to light quite by chance in the midst of World War II with La Tène iron goods dug out of a boggy water marsh called Llyn Cerrig Bach, once a prehistoric lake, within the boundary of the RAF Valley airbase near Holyhead. During construction work there in 1942 an iron chain suddenly appearing at hand was grabbed to help pull a stricken truck out of mud. It turned out to be a slave-gang chain, over ten feet of it, complete with neck manacles, dated to the Roman period. It is now in the National Museum of Wales in Cardiff. Whether it was for Celts enslaved by Romans or for slaves of Celtic Britons is not clear, but the chain was not all. Hopes that there could be more material were realized when almost a hundred metal objects were recovered from the marsh including iron spear heads, swords and daggers, the afore-mentioned boss (center) of a bronze shield, iron money ingots, chariot wheel hub fittings, part of an Irish-type curved bronze trumpet and a wealth of horse gear and blacksmith's tools. The whole find is broadly dated to 100s B.C. to A.D. 100. Since insular varieties of La Tène motifs appear on designs, the craftsmen were likely Britons or Irish, inspired by continental Celtic metalwork.

Anglesey folklore lauds the occult, and Miranda Green, author of *Celtic Myths* (1993), considers Llyn Cerrig Bach one of the most important sites in this context,[3] a place where gifts to appease the supernatural were deposited. She notes bronze cauldrons in the hoard, precious vessels with redemptive and deadly powers in folk-lore. Human sacrifices may have been part of ritual life at Llyn Cerrig Bach. The young man whose well-preserved remains are on permanent display in London's British Museum — "Lindow Man" — met his fate in a watery grave not so far distant in Lindow Moss, Cheshire, having suffered sacrificial execution. Yet not all agree it was a holy lake. The Roman historian Tacitus tells of a major confrontation with druids on Anglesey in A.D. 60, and another explanation is that the Roman Army sim-ply dumped a concentrated deposit after ransacking the place. The druid connection is examined shortly.

Also of interest in a Celtic context are stone-carved heads found in various island locations. Classical writers were appalled at Celtic severing and displaying of human heads. The Celts apparently considered the head the seat of the soul, and some of these artifacts have "cigarette holes" drilled around the mouth area to serve ritual purpose. The best known is the Hendy Head, found in a field at Hendy Farm, Lanfairpwll, in the 1920s, measuring some eight inches by ten inches and now on permanent display at the Anglesey Heritage Center in Llangefni. It is worth recall-ing that Anglesey's principal town is Holyhead.

The divine head features in the tale of Branwen in *The Mabinogion* or "Young Men of Old," a four-set compilation of Welsh myths emanating from two extant manuscripts — the *White Book of Rhydderch* and the *Red Book of Hergerst*. Written when Celtic traditions were under pressure in the 11th and 12th centuries, they draw on a rich source of folklore to paint an unstructured and magical Welsh past. There

are inserts of recognizable historical possibilities although the stories are not necessarily popular with historians. Anglesey features in the tale as "Talebolion" or the
land where the ridges end. Branwen was a Welsh beauty newly wed by an Irish king
Matholwch (one of her brothers is said to be Manannán, the Manx Neptune) but
mistreated by him. Her kin avenged her humiliation in battle in Ireland, but their
druid Brân the Blessed was mortally wounded and called for his own head to be severed and kept as a perpetual reminder of his divinity. The depleted war band returned
from Ireland with the precious head (very much alive until its eventual interment)
and Branwen. Mortified by the great loss of life in her name, the young queen is said
to have reached Anglesey and "heaved a great sigh, and with that broke her heart. A
four-sided grave was made for her and she was buried there on the bank of the Alaw."[4]
When antiquarians found a burial cairn on the same riverbank in the 19th century
they named it in excited tribute Bedd Branwen, though it is now understood to be
a Bronze Age grave as noted earlier. Importantly the story tells of Welsh-Irish union
and dissolution and at the least is suggestive of Irish Sea interaction in which the
island was a participant.

Roman Conquest

Modern Anglesey appears languid and quiescent with nothing more threatening than the occasional red-faced farmer irate at those crossing and re-crossing his
land to find sacred sites. Yet 2,000 years ago the Romans thought it defiant and rebellious, worthy of repeated military intervention. Julius Caesar's visits to Britain in 55
B.C. and 54 B.C. and Emperor Claudius's colonizing invasion of A.D. 43 passed without disturbing island life but *Insula Mona,* as they named it, eventually demanded
more attention than any other offshore British island. Incidentally the word stem
mon as we saw in the case of Man may emanate from an earlier presence of *Menapii,*
a Gaulish Celtic tribe well known to the Romans and active along Irish and Welsh
coasts. Such was Anglesey's reputation that in A.D. 48 the second governor of Britain, Ostorius Scupula, was preparing an assault to root out a stronghold of *Ordovices*
(a name given to the tribal confederation of northwest Wales) and was only diverted
at the last moment by an outbreak of dissension among *Brigantes* in what became
northern England. Twelve years later, in A.D. 60, another governor, Gaius Suetonius
Paulinus, determined to flush out pockets of Celtic resistance and upstage a rival commander Gnaeus Corbulo winning battles far away in distant Armenia, attacked Anglesey with two legions and auxiliaries. It cannot have been a casual decision. He
probably had enough information about the place—copper mines, granary potential, sacred sites, druidism and refuge for those fleeing the long arm of the legions—
to warrant belief it was a laudable challenge, a hotbed feeding insurrection and one
worth subduing.

Our primary source for the invasion is Cornelius Tacitus (c. A.D. 55–120): a
Roman historian highly regarded by modern scholars for his craft and insight. His
father-in-law was the prominent Roman general Julius Agricola, the subject of his
biography *Agricola* (A.D. 98), in which he first mentions the attack on Anglesey. The

greatest of his writings, *Annals of Imperial Rome* (c. A.D. 116), drew on a lifetime of reflections on the Roman Empire, and in it he writes more fully of Suetonius Paulinus and the invasion of A.D. 60, of flat-bottomed boats built to contend with the Menai Straits, infantry swimming beside horses, and a hostile island shore. Tacitus's vivid description of the Anglesey reception, used at the outset of this chapter, is one of the most oft-quoted passages on Roman Britain — painted warriors, howling druids, frantic women in black, air thick with curses screamed at centurions threatening their sanctuary, a level of fanaticism so intense that centurions were paralyzed in dismay and suffered casualties. Eventually pressed on by their commanders, they recovered ranks and "advanced with their standards, cut down all they met, and enveloped them in the flames of their own torches."[5] At some point during the conquest Paulinus was shocked to receive reports of an unexpected uprising hundreds of miles away in southeastern Britain, and he abandoned the island. The unexpected uprising was that of the Iceni, a Celtic people in Norfolk (England) angered by brutal Roman misgovernment, broken promises and humiliating treatment of their queen Boudicca and her daughters. The Iceni and allies sacked Camulodunum (Colchester) with a large force and raided Londinium and Veralamium (London and St. Albans respectively). Thousands of centurions were slaughtered before Paulinus arrived with his legions from Anglesey to put down the rebellion. Boudicca reputedly took her own life in despair, but the uprising was not in vain for the Ordovices. If her insurrection had not diverted Paulinus, then the annihilation on Anglesey might have been more emphatic.

It was Julius Agricola who tamed Anglesey. In the same year as his appointment as governor in A.D. 78, a band of Ordovices massacred a cavalry regiment somewhere on the nearby Welsh coast, and he resolved to deal with the rebellious island, presumably a base of the Ordovices, and finish the job begun by Paulinus. The fact that he gave it immediate priority is a measure of its importance. Tacitus reported that Agricola took the island by surprise, resisting the temptation of a large naval attack that might alert and excite the ferocious resistance of A.D. 60. He opted instead for a special-forces advance taskforce, crossing the straits furtively and using guerrilla-style ambush tactics to secure a beachhead, before a full invasion by centurions.

Druids and Insula Mona

The Roman annexation of Anglesey is often explained as part of a plan to flush out druids. Yet Tacitus makes no mention of them in *Agricola* (c. A.D. 98), only doing so years later in *Annals*. Why he omitted them in the first instance is unclear. The druids are not easy for document-minded historians. If we stacked all the primary evidence about them, the pile wouldn't amount to much. The word is rooted in Greek *drus* ("oak on which mistletoe grows") and Indo-European *wid* ("to know"), assigning power to those understanding the mysterious natural world, literally wisdom of the old oak. The Greek Hecateus (c. 500 B.C.) reported that Celtic religion forbade druids from putting their own thoughts in writing so their secrets remained secret, teaching recitation and memorization instead. In time druids became wrapped up in the Mediterranean mind with myths of a barbarian elite with fantastic powers. Modern scholars interpret them as a powerful priestly caste, paralleling intellectual elites found in other traditional societies.

Julius Caesar was the first Roman to mention British druids, learning of them when fighting in Gaul in the 50s B.C. He believed druidic doctrine came from Britain, novices training there, though he never saw it firsthand, and probably copied much from Poseidonius, an earlier Syrian Greek scholar, who said they were a powerful brotherhood officiating religious rituals, ordering punishments, and teachers of matters celestial and terrestrial. There is no reason to doubt their presence, and it is not difficult to imagine they made use of surviving megalithic sites for ceremonies, but it would be a big stretch to presume their corporation dated like megaliths to Neolithic times. The climatic and associated disruptions of the second millennium B.C. break the likelihood of any continuum back into that epoch. It is not inconceivable that druids emerged in the later Bronze Age, as climate change and metallurgy shifted thought and values.

Roman writers admired the druids, even while expressing horror at Celtic head-hunting and distaste for facial hair and body paint. They applauded them as communicators of values necessary for organization and order. In matters spiritual, however, their world-views digressed. The Celts held notions that sophisticated first century A.D. Romans would have dismissed as irrational superstitions. Roman religion served the state: their gods were civic gods and the focus of Stoicism, the life philosophy educated Romans embraced, was on preserving civic order in this life. They were relatively tolerant of beliefs of others provided the believers were deferential but significantly less so when those beliefs were politicized. Such may explain a determination to eliminate druid cells like that of Anglesey and eradicate supernumerary priests whose stature transcended tribal kings. Yet we must guard against overstatement. Tacitus paid them no attention in his *Agricola* account of what happened in A.D. 60.

Anglesey has played an important part in the invention of a druidic tradition. John Aubrey, a 17th century English collector of ghost stories and folklore, was possibly the first to argue for a relationship between megaliths and Julius Caesar's druids, but it was an Anglesey clergyman, Reverend Henry Rowlands (1655–1723), who took things a step further. In *Mona Antiqua Restaurata* (1723), the vicar of Llanidan, as the frontispiece announces him, postulated that Anglesey was the ancient seat of British druids. His presumptive leap was simple enough: Tacitus mentioned druids on the island in *Annals*, Aubrey and others associated them with megaliths, and he was living among megaliths. Bryn Gwyn Stones were within sight of his home. It was a combination difficult to ignore. He ascribed to druids a biblical pedigree, believing them purveyors of a pre–Christian wisdom. Another Anglican William Stukeley from Lincolnshire, taking his cue from Rowlands, developed the primal religion theme further. Stukeley reconstructed the biblical story from creation to accommodate megaliths and druids by aligning them with Jewish prophets, a development far removed from the Gallic priests of Caesar. Rowlands included a fanciful drawing of a druid in his book, replete with long gray beard, hooded cloak, staff, bare legs and sandal-clad feet, and the imagery stuck. So too has the proposition that druids are the property of North Wales; Rowlands is entitled to the credit for that, though it doesn't validate its accuracy.

The Romans administered *Insula Mona* from a fort at Segontium (Caernarfon) across the Menai Straits on the adjacent mainland. The Segonti may have been a sub-tribe of the Ordovices. The closest known road was the coastal one from Caernarfon to Chester where the nearest legion was headquartered. As for the island itself, after all the effort to take it, there was little or no Roman building, at least in the first few centuries. Daily life carried on under the scrutiny of *Segontium*. Copper was mined and smelted (probably by private lessees) while dwellings, granaries and workshops remained within the same dispersed farmsteads utilized for millennia. Several centuries passed without further disruption. By mid-fourth century however, Roman authority was in progressive disarray, and the threat of Irish attacks led to construction of a shore-fort facing Ireland. Its walls now enclose St. Cybi's churchyard in Holyhead. It didn't last long as a Roman garrison. The legions quit Britain in 410, and, released from the imperial order, Anglesey entered a twilight world of warlords and sea kings, part of a loose Irish Sea polity involving kingdoms in Irish Leinster and the Isle of Man.

Gwynedd

By the sixth century the p–Celtic kingdom of Gwynedd had emerged in North Wales. Sequestered by encircling mountains, forests, estuaries and sea, it succeeded in preserving varying levels of independence for over six centuries, an impressive feat given the experiences of small kingdoms elsewhere. Centered briefly on the mainland, the governance shifted to Anglesey. The other half of the Menavian islands, the Isle of Man, played some elusive part in it early on, but Aberffraw on the western Anglesey coast became the operational center. Shadowing this time is the story of King Arthur, the quasi-historical British king who may have organized resistance to Anglo-Saxon invaders c. 500, but there is nothing to connect him with Anglesey. On the eastern side of Red Wharf Bay is Beddwr Arthur (Arthur's Table), but banish thoughts of Camelot and the Round Table since all that is on offer is scattered slabs of pavement grazed by sheep, foundations of what was once an Iron Age farmstead built over an earlier habitat. The closest chronicled king is Maelgwyn Hir (the Tall), an early sixth century ruler thought by some to be an Arthur-type, a warrior powerful enough to set Gwynedd on its course.

These were warring times with territory disturbed by Anglo-Saxons on eastern British coasts and the Irish on the west. Cadfan, one of Maelgwyn's successors, is generously memorialized in Latin on a commemorative stone at Llangadwaladr Church near Aberffraw: "Cadfan, the king most wise, most highly esteemed, of all kings." He died in 625 and it took only a few years (629) before Edwin, Anglo-Saxon king of Northumbria, overran the island. His successor, Cadwallon ap Cadfan ("son" of Cadfan), was forced into sanctuary on a tiny monastic islet off the Penmon shore at the northern entrance to the Menai Straits, and Gwynedd Celts were forced to pay tribute. Cadwallon rallied by finding a Saxon ally in Penda, king of Mercia, a new

English kingdom north and east of Snowdonia. Their combined force pushed the Northumbrians back to the east coast, killing Edwin in battle at Hatfield Chase in Yorkshire in 632. The Northumbrian monk-historian Bede, whose *Historia Anglorum Ecclesiastica* (731) is the seminal account of these times, condemned Cadwallon for his barbarian heart and bestial cruelty, accusing him of trying to destroy the English race,[6] his patriotic sentiments probably fueled by Germanic antipathy for Celtic Christian practices discussed shortly. A new Northumbrian king, Oswald, pursued and killed Cadwallon two years later. Differences between the two cultures led to the construction in the later eighth century of a 150-mile-long earthwork known as Offa's Dyke, delineating Celtic territory in a line approximating to the modern Wales/England border. The Welsh called themselves Cymry (compatriots) but the English "Wales" from the Old English *Wealas* is construed as meaning "foreign," a perverse reversal of history given that the English were the more recent arrivals! John Davies, author of the encyclopedic *History of Wales* (1993), argues that Wales really meant "Romanized," a deft reminder that German-speakers were considered barbarians from outside the Empire while Wales lay once within its civilizing influence.[7]

Ireland's proximity raises the question of its role in the early medieval period. The sea between the islands had unified them in maritime exchange, and Irish kings had interest in Anglesey on occasion with goods swapping hands in plunder and commerce. The Leinster Irish periodically intervened. Welsh literature offers us the tale of Branwen, as we have seen, allegory of a Welsh-Irish union dying in Anglesey. Irish and Welsh speech may well have been similar enough to facilitate mutual understanding, but the work of monastic scribes to make sounds fit a Latin alphabet eventually accentuated differences. In the meantime monks were frequent travelers across the Irish Sea, as the inclusion of Welsh kings in Irish Chronicles and tales of early saints testify. The sixth century monastery of St. Cybi's at Holyhead was well positioned to send and receive such guests. Early ecclesiastical artifacts are minimal with no precious illuminated manuscripts, no costly chalices or decorated stone crosses. Little survives beyond a few hand bells and chapel foundations. What we have are the lives of saints, written down centuries later, from which involvement of Anglesey in the larger Celtic-speaking world can reasonably be deduced.

Early Christians

Several of these saints were Celtic aristocrats who chose a different calling. Cybi (early sixth century) refused the offer of kingship in his native Cornwall, in p–Celtic southwestern Britain, to pursue religious study in Ireland instead. Afterward he crossed to Anglesey to become abbot of a monastery that made use of the old Roman shore-fort, now St. Cybi's Holyhead. His contemporary Seiriol built a small monastic cell on Puffin Island (Yns Seiriol), off the Penmon shore near the northern entrance to the Menai Strait, Cadwallon's sanctuary. Gerald of Wales mentioned it as Yns Lannog or "island of priests" in his 12th century travels, finding monks there "who live in the service of God, by the labor of their hands."[8] On the other side of the island, on a rocky islet in the tidal river estuary near Aberffraw, is the island's most atmospheric church site, begun in the seventh century and rebuilt in stone 500 years later. Surrounded by water at high tide through coastal erosion with a curtain of 19th century sea wall protecting it from further encroachment, this "church in the sea" is dedicated to St. Cwyfan (St. Kevin), probably the same Kevin (Coemgen in Old Irish) who founded Glendalough monastery in Ireland, famed center of the Celtic church in Leinster. Then there is Tysilo, a relative of Asaph (another early Welsh saint), who built a cell near a red cave in the vicinity of the Menai Straits. His name is embedded in the longest place-name, credited as the place where Christianity was first preached. North Wales is rich in such associations. Thirty miles down the coast from Anglesey is little Bardsey Island (Yns Enlli), a Welsh Iona, a final resting-place of scores of Celtic monks.

Island lore also offers St. Dwynwen, the daughter of a fifth century ruler who was unable to marry the young man she loved. Instructed through prayer to live a secluded life in prayer, she chose a finger isle at the southern entrance to the Menai Strait — Yns Llanddwyn — as her retreat, and it became a place of pilgrimage for angst-torn lovers. Fidelity or treachery was divined at its holy well by watching the movement of eels in the water. Offerings to her cult were made until the 16th century Reformation. The chapel ruins can still be seen.

According to Bede the Celtic Church was increasingly at odds with Rome by the seventh century. One source of discord was a difference over the dating of Easter with a Celtic deference to abbots rather than bishops and unorthodox tonsure shapes among testy others. It is possible that Edwin's assault on Anglesey in 629 was premeditated by a desire to fight nonconforming Celts. The Northumbrian king had recently been baptized in the Roman order. The divisive issues were decided in favor of Rome at the Synod of Whitby in 664 although not necessarily with immediate effect. It has long been conjectured that the Celtic Church was different because it evolved from the bottom up, families of monks integrating themselves within clan societies, while Rome was more of a top down organization, a patriarchy reigning over a hierarchy of bishops. John Davies finds these differences exaggerated (without denying the importance of the Easter controversy), dismissing them as claims to serve later nonconformist Protestant agendas of historical interpretation. He prefers a definition of Celtic Church as simply that of congregations within the universal church who happened to speak Celtic.[9]

Royal Aberffraw

The modern working village of Aberffraw, set off the main west coast road, is an unexceptional sort of place. It has a post office, general store, pub and small village square, its street names those of any Welsh village, Llewelyn Street, Bridge Street, Chapel Street. It is hard to imagine the town a thousand years ago as the fortified seat of Gwynedd kings, one of three key power bases listed by Gerald of Wales in his 12th century *Journey through Wales*. Nothing remains, its timbers looted, burned and rotted long since, yet Aberffraw was once for Welshness what Islay's Finlaggan was for Scots Gaels — an offshore anchor, centrifugal politically and culturally. A suggestion of earthworks shaping its outer boundary recently came to light, but appearance can only be speculated. The location, however, is not so hard to figure. Bede rated Anglesey's cultivable acres three times greater than that of the Isle of Man, and a thousand years ago Aberffraw was an accessible river port with its *aber* (estuary where two rivers joined) still navigable for sea-going vessels. It is silted with grassy sand dunes now and the seaport is hard to visualize, but communities made a home there for millennia and the Romans probably used it.

Kings shared government with prominent kinsmen at Aberffraw, maintaining control through fear and favor. As in other Welsh kingdoms power centered on the *maerdref* or royal estate with outer subdivisions or *cantrefi* as local government units, the arrangement likely a Roman inheritance. Homesteads were either nucleated or dispersed within each *cantref* (both patterns are found) and the occupants either bonded as unfree labor and slaves or free. Economic problems in the later Roman Empire raised the numbers of unfree, tying tenants to the land, and free and unfree distinctions persisted. Kings or their stewards periodically rode through the *cantrefi* to demand tributes, paid in produce and labor. The royal court or *llys* ("leese") was itinerant, but one base was on Anglesey. In the mid–1990s excavations by the Gwynedd Archaeological Trust at Rhosyr, about four miles from Aberffraw, found dry stone foundations of at least three timbered buildings buried deep in the sand of a field named *cae llys* ("field of the court").[10] One of the buildings housed a grand hall with adjoining rooms. A spur and ring brooches were dug up with pottery, and the presence of coins points to a court treasury. This was the court of royal Aberffraw.

Royal law co-existed with clan custom and local *commote* courts served kindred needs within the individual *cantrefi*. Land claims of king and kin had to accommodate the religious, too, and grants to monks were made at least as early as Cadfan. The plaque honoring him in Llangadwaladr Church (to the immediate south) probably acknowledges his benefaction, and seventh century St. Cwyfans confirms early presence. Whatever autonomy early monks enjoyed, it was over by the ninth century. The efforts of a Gwynedd bishop Elfoddw (768–809) was instrumental in persuading clannish Welsh religious to accept Roman authority and when Gerald of Wales visited in the 12th century, the island was in the diocese of Bangor, centered across the Menai Straits.

Aberffraw was more than a citadel and court of law. It was a sociable hive (as was Finlaggan, the later MacDonald stronghold on Islay) alive with music and revelry. Cerebral life had its place too. Scribes must have frequented it, among them perhaps the mysterious Welsh scholar and monk Nennius, author of *Historia Britonnum* (History of the Britons). The book was not collated and titled until c. 1150, long after his death, and since Nennius admits in the preface to compiling information of dubious veracity, making as he says "a heap of all that I could find," it's tempting to dismiss it. Yet whatever its flaws it is a surviving effort to report on Welsh ancestry and may represent scholarship at Aberffraw. We do not know Nennius's life dates, but he tells us his task was undertaken during the rule of "Mervin, king of the Britons," adding he was a follower of St. Elbotus, conceivably Elfoddw, the bishop credited for getting the Welsh Church to conform. Since his royal genealogies end in the later 700s it is not unreasonable to time his life with the rule of Merfyn Frych

(r. 825–844), a powerful king who strengthened Aberffraw's reputation. The Bible included genealogy to register legitimacy, and such scholarship would have lent credibility to Aberffraw although Nennius humbly insisted he wrote only to benefit his "inferiors." He does not acknowledge Anglesey (not yet known by that name), but in a list of "thirty three British cities" his third is "*Cair gurcoc,*" identified in at least one English translation[11] as being on Anglesey. Nennius admits to a deficient education and being "rude in speech," and *Cair gurcoc* does read like a phrase of Welshified Latin but it is taken to mean (without certainty) an encampment (*cair*) by the flood or river eddy. This might place it in an Aberffraw location (or alternatively the Menai shore).

Öngul's Ey

Merfyn ruled expansively. The son of a Manx king Gwriad (c. 800),[12] reminder of a relationship stretching back to Roman coupling of Man and Anglesey, he may have ruled both islands. His son Rhodri Mawr (d. 878) was less fortunate. The arrival of Vikings as an accessory third party force reoriented political life. Anglesey is thought to derive from *Öngul's ey*—Öngul's isle—but while Öngul is an unknown quantity, Viking presence is not. Chroniclers tell us that in 855 Rhodri Mawr repulsed vicious hit-and-run Vikings, active in the Irish Sea region since the 790s, slaying their Danish leader Gorm. As John Davies points out Rhodri Mawr must have made a powerful impression, because claiming descent from him became a new qualification for subsequent Welsh rulers. He was undone nevertheless in 878 by an onslaught from Saxons, aided and abetted by Danish Vikings, dying as he had lived, in battle. Recent archaeological discoveries at Llanbedrgoch on the eastern coast tell a different tale, however, indicating Viking settlement from the 850s, at a time when Rhodri still ruled. In short, he did not drive them out. They came ashore and stayed. Dublin Vikings were strengthening their control over Man and the Hebrides at this time, exacting tribute and establishing settlements, and Vikings from the Danelaw, headquartered in *Jorvik* (York) in northeastern England, were likewise engaged in mainland Britain. Gwynedd lay midway on an axis between Dublin and York, and *Öngul's ey* probably saw plenty of Vikings, welcome or not.

By now it hardly warrants repeat that the notion of the Viking wrecker is at odds with scientific evidence. Archaeology does not eliminate the wrecking crew, but findings point to ways of interaction other than destruction. There is nothing visible above ground at Llanbedrgoch. It was metal detectors combing a barley field that alerted suspicions, and excavations began in the 1990s. Painstaking efforts have pieced together a picture of domicile remodeling: one begun at the time of the first chronicled incursions, when Rhodri Mawr was king. The Norse modifications were in the form of rectangular and square timbered structures with stone footings, changes reminiscent of realignments in other offshore pre–Viking settlements. Viking burial finds in nearby Red Wharf Bay add to the picture of colonization. Archaeomagnetic dating of hearth clays and analysis of back-fill soil at Llanbedrgoch suggests habitation from the 850s through to c. 1000.[13] The village was not another Dublin, but it may have been in the making.

Britain's political boundaries were in further flux by the early 900s as the Saxon kingdom of Wessex successfully reduced the Viking Danelaw, and reluctance at Aberffraw to toe the Saxon line led to more struggles in the 930s. Control of Gwynedd passed to Hywel Dda (Hywel the Good), king of neighboring Deheubarth in mid and southwest Wales. His government is seen as a defining moment in Welsh consciousness, a time when laws were written down for the first time, inspired by other patrons of codification like Alfred of Wessex and Offa of Mercia. It is from this source that Welsh social stratification and landholding is understood. Hywel's death in 950 set in motion another phase of political instability with successive rulers striving for power. Into this turmoil sailed more Scandinavian longships, coming ashore not only in Anglesey but right down the coast into south Wales.

The Isle of Man was playing a more central role in Irish Sea politics by the later 10th century, and Magnus Haraldsson, member of a powerful Norse Dublin and York dynasty, king of Man and the Isles, is chronicled as having attacked Anglesey from Man. Aberffraw was again wracked with infighting, and it is possible that the Norse were useful as a third party tiebreaker. Rulers made alliances whenever expedient, and the Norse were valuable allies in war. Distinctions between Norwegians and Danes (all Norse Vikings) can be problematic, but west coast raids are usually assigned as Norwegian. Assuming it followed form, then, these Norse got lands as reward and *Öngul's ey* continued to nurture a hybrid Celto-Norse population. This perspective breaks Anglesey out of its usually inseparable Welsh context to present its inclusion or co-existence in a culturally pluralistic Irish Sea rim. The Isle of Man was at the heart of it but Anglesey was not excluded. Medieval Irish genealogies such as the *Book of Glendalough* and *Book of Leinster* list the famed Welsh dynasty of the Llewelyns (ruling Gwynedd from 1005) as having Irish Viking antecedents.

Gwynedd stabilized under Irish-born Gruffydd ap Cynan (r. 1081–1137). The longest reigning of all Welsh rulers, he was the son of a former Gwynedd king who fled to Ireland in exile, and he had to retreat there too for a while. William II, son of William the Conqueror, sent two vassals, Hugh de Montgomery (Earl of Shrewsbury) and Hugh de Avranches (Earl of Chester), to oust him in 1098. The Norman earls are credited with building the first castle on the island, a timbered keep affair at Aberlleniog near Penmon priory, but their rule did not last long. Two years later Magnus Bare-Legs arrived in the Menai Straits with his warband, mentioned already with reference to the Hebrides and Man, landing to fight hand-to-hand with defending Norman forces. This was the battle that alarmed conscientious objector St. Magnus-to-be of Orkney. Montgomery was among the fatalities. Bare-Legs' victory brought Gruffydd home from exile in Ireland and Gwynedd recovered its identity.

The Mother of Wales

A half-century after Gruffydd's death in 1137, Giraldus Cambrensis (c. 1146–1223), better known as Gerald of Wales, visited Anglesey and wrote about it. He claimed not to know Welsh speech well, admitting only to the French and Latin of the elite, although he was Welsh-born with French antecedents on his mother's side (Fitzgerald) and managed to comment on Welsh pronunciation nevertheless! A strong-willed career cleric, he served in Henry II's court (1180s) and aspired to but never achieved his goal of a Welsh archbishopric centered on St. David's in southwest Wales. Stubbornly refusing other assignments, he remained an archdeacon, traveling widely and writing extensively. His 1188 visit was recalled from diary notes in *Journey through Wales*, part of a mission undertaken with Baldwin, Archbishop of Canterbury. The prelate made an ironic companion since Gerald dreamed of liberating St. David's from Canterbury control. The Anglesey visit was brief—an overnight and a day—but his commentary was enough to glean some impressions.

After spending the night in Bangor and crossing in a small boat with an archdeacon of Bangor and a Cistercian abbot, the party met with Rhodri ap Owain, king of Gwynedd. They did not travel to Aberffraw, or at least Gerald made no mention of it. His Aberffraw references were past tense, about it having been one of three great Welsh palaces, but *llyseod* were widely dispersed and those on the mainland such as Aber (between Bangor and Penmaenmawr) may have been better favored in his time. At any rate it was a church visit and they came to visit Penmon, the monastery at the northeastern entrance to the Menai Straits. The old timber church was torched by Vikings in 971 but rebuilt in stone, and masons had only just finished the priory transepts and tower when they arrived. Gerald thought Anglesey "rough and unattractive" yet advised it had long been called *Môn mam Cymru*—"Mona, Mother of Wales;" "when crops have failed in all other regions," he wrote, "this island, from the richness of its soil and its abundant produce, has been able to supply all Wales."[14] Of copper he had nothing to say, and while the megalithic antiquities interested him, the inference is of an island that had seen better times. On a revealing note about Welsh custom generally, Gerald grumbled about kinship inheritance censuring fosterage, a common practice to strengthen kindred ties; "You will find that friendships are much warmer between foster-brothers than they are between true brothers,"[15] he warned, blaming endemic strife on fratricide. He tells us nothing of island arts, though he was not deaf to music elsewhere on his travels, generally complimenting the singing and harp playing of his countrymen. If Anglesey bards and poets traveled to southwest Wales in 1176 at the behest of Rhys ap Gruffydd, Irish-born lord of Deheubarth, for the first *eisteddfod* or "session of music, arts and conviviality," Gerald neglected to mention it.

Edward I

In the wider world the Plantagenets, French-speaking dukes of Anjou, were kings of England and increasingly powerful. Successive Gwynedd kings contrived to keep their community in a state of abeyance, hidden behind the mountain wall of Snowdonia, through spells of altercation and concord. Llewelyn Fawr ap Iorwerth ("the Great"), Gwynedd's ruler from 1195 to 1240, benefited from opportunities afforded by the politicking of England's King John and Norman-French lords in the Marches, the powerbrokers on the margins between England and Wales. His grandson Llewelyn II (r. 1246–1282) won back mid–Wales from Marcher lords in 1267 and had the satisfaction of Henry III acknowledging him as a prince in his own right. It was the accession of the fifth Plantagenet king in 1272 that fatally wounded Gwynedd. Edward I ("Longshanks") proved resourceful and bellicose, more than a match for Llewelyn II. It took only ten years.

Edward's reign began inauspiciously for Llewelyn II. An effort to overthrow him by his own kin was aborted but an ill omen. His principality had grown impressively large with over two-thirds of Welsh territory under his rule, but maintaining control over people, especially regional rulers, was another matter. History was against him. None of his predecessors had cemented a national loyalty. John Davies interprets this as less indicative of "weakness in political instincts" and more absence of an external unifying agent, comparing it with an England unified by invading Anglo-Saxon *conquistadors.* The Anglo-Saxons did not manage to sustain an English nation for long either; it was Norman-French feudalism that provided the adhesive, enforcing contractual political relationships under a national king. Llewelyn came unstuck by ignoring Edward's summons to pay fealty, preferring to see how tenable the new king's position would be; it was a costly miscalculation. As Edward's vassal he may have engineered a stay of execution; as an enemy he accelerated it. Edward mobilized an army of 16,000 against him in 1276: the pretext a planned marriage by Llewelyn to a Plantagenet foe. The king turned Welsh factionalism to his advantage with about half of his victorious force Welsh-speaking archers and weakened resistance by intercepting Anglesey grain shipments. Llewelyn was defeated and humiliated but not deposed. He had to pay reparations by the Treaty of Aberconwy of 1277, including an annual payment specifically for Anglesey, reminder of its granary potential. His fiefdom was shrunk back to the old Gwynedd heartland west of the River Conway, namely Snowdonia, the Lleyn peninsula and Anglesey. A consolation was permission to marry his betrothed.

For the next five years (1277–1282) Edward rigorously enforced his rule, so much so that historians suspect his intention was to incite Welsh uprising and justify total conquest, but Llewelyn II appeared resigned to his status and the king had no immediate reason to eliminate him. It was brother Dafydd who lit the fuse, attacking Marcher lords in northeastern Wales in 1282, putting Llewelyn under great pressure. He dithered over it before joining the insurrection. Edward's rage was palpable, though the systematic way in which forces were marshaled and deployed suggests he was ready. The Church tried to arbitrate but the matter was beyond reconciliation. There was a short respite as an attempt to invade via a pontoon bridge of boats in late 1282 failed. Less than a month later Llewelyn II lost his life in mid–Wales, dying not in battle but in an ambush in the wooded Wye valley, his whereabouts suggesting a betrayal. His severed head was delivered as trophy evidence to Edward I. Dafydd assumed the kingship of Gwynedd and fought on for a few months, but by spring 1283 he was beaten, captured and beheaded for treason.

In his iconoclastic *The Isles: A History* (1999) Norman Davies describes the invasion episodes of 1277 and 1282–1283 as "exterminatory,"[16] citing the logistics of armored knights on horseback, infantry, archers, ships financed by Italian bankers and (tellingly) a construction gang–at-arms with shovels, picks, hammers and chisels. It was a formidable force. Nothing like it had been seen in Anglesey since Julius

Agricola. In the aftermath, an impressive chain of *motte-and-bailey* castles would tower above the north Welsh coast complete with turrets, portcullises and moats, including adjacent Caernarfon and Bangor castles. The imposition of Norman-French primogeniture and the new order was further announced when Edward I made his eldest son the Prince of Wales, a practice that persists. A Welsh viceroyalty was established at Caernarfon Castle to face Anglesey across the straits (as Roman *Segontium* once did), and in a further act of dénouement, Aberffraw timbers were put to use in the castle construction work.

The County

As for the island, Edward I traveled there in 1283 to pick out the fishing settlement of Llanfaes on the Menai shore as a suitable castle site and sheriff's seat for the new county of Anglesey. Not all went to plan. The following year another uprising erupted, this one led by Madog ap Llewelyn, not actually Llewelyn's son but a kinsman. Caernarfon (its castle unfinished) was put to the sword and Llanfaes was torched to prevent Edward from using it. The new sheriff of Anglesey, Roger Puleston, was killed. A tax increase to pay for war in Gascony (such was the "international" web of the Plantagenet empire) provoked the rebellion, but recovery of the principality was also on the agenda. Edward I suspended his Gascon operations and suppressed the revolt by March 1295, his army of 35,000 slaughtering all the ringleaders. The work on the Anglesey castle began only weeks after Madog's death, in a saltwater marsh area near Llanfaes named in Norman-French patois *Beau Marais* (fair marsh) or Beaumaris.

Norman-French castles had progressed beyond timbered keeps by this time, and stone fortresses as formidable as those of the Byzantine and Muslim world were sought. The majestic (and magnificently preserved) Caernarfon Castle provided just that, and thousands of workers were hired to achieve the same level of military architecture at Beaumaris— quarrymen, woodcutters, ditch diggers, carters, smiths, carpenters, brick and tile-makers, masons and others. The architect was a master mason credited with two-thirds of Edward's Welsh castles, summoned for the task by the king from France, where he had built the fortress of St. George d'Esperanche in Savoy, hence his name Master James of St. George. In the 1290s Master James was in his sixties, and Beaumaris would be his last castle; he did not disappoint. As a bow-and-arrow castle it is a masterpiece, best appreciated from outside amid the half-timbered houses and Victorian terraces of the modern town. An adjacent green with picnic tables and swans in the moat is deceptive. Somnolence was far from the castle's original intent. It was there to awe the Welsh, not sooth them, and unwelcome visitors were tested by a gauntlet of defenses— sea-fed moat, intimidating rotund guard towers, sets of portcullises, stout wooden doors and non-aligned gatehouses (a Moorish disorienting design tactic) with aggressors vulnerable to small "murder hole" windows from which arrows and fire could rain down. A "boxes within boxes" concentric design maximized security for castle occupants with high inner walls protecting the bailey and lookouts to enhance surveillance.

Islanders found work on the construction project, but other colonization experiences evoked intense bitterness. High and low born faced disinheritance. The *maerdref* and *cantrefi* were reorganized into manors consistent with English land arrangements. The manor of Plas Newydd or New Hall on the Menai banks has been called "New" since the 14th century! Llanfaes was purged of its native population. Survivors were relocated to the southwest of the island near the former Aberffraw *llys* of Rhosyr in a new settlement called Newborough. Another borough (deriving from Anglo-Saxon *burhs* or defensive centers) formed around Beaumaris Castle. The king's justiciar or viceroy was at the apex of the new guard, but the office was based in Caernarfon Castle. Beaumaris was of secondary importance. Contrary to perception, the first incumbent was not an Englishman (neither were most others in the Norman-French elite) but a Savoyard knight named Otto de Grandison. He was rewarded with lands and title after fighting against Llewelyn II and served from 1283 to 1295; thereafter his administrative career progressed to include that of warden (in absentia) of the Channel Islands. Edward I did not repress all Welsh customs. The Statute of Rhuddlan (1284) brought Wales "into a dominion of our ownership" but *commote* courts continued, as did partible land inheritance based on division among siblings, the practice that Gerald of Wales had roundly criticized. Further, widows were entitled to a third of their husband's land, a concession not permitted under Welsh custom.

A few island highborn survived the revolution by joining it. Tudur ap Ednyfed Fychan of Penmynydd is a case in point. Tudur (translation = territorial king) showed no inclination to support Llewelyn II as his father had done and swore allegiance to Edward I. His kinsman, Gruffydd ap Llwyd, served as a sheriff for 15 years, including a spell as sheriff of Anglesey (1305–06), a position placing him in Beaumaris Castle residence. His descendants, the Griffiths (from Gruffydd), garnered much local civil and ecclesiastical power. Sheriffs were crown appointees responsible for county tax collection and court supervision, an office to which noble Welsh could aspire, and willingly granted by kings who recognized the value of incorporating them in the power structure. Church reorganization meanwhile affected Anglesey as it did elsewhere with new churches built (or rebuilt) in the 12th and 13th centuries. The island did not get a cathedral, a privilege that stayed with Bangor, in whose diocese subject Anglesey remained, its bell peals heard tellingly across the Menai Straits.

Manorial Life

A manorial peasantry evolved holding a variety of tenancies, owing labor and dues to lords whose feudal superiors were kings of England. Daily routines were unaltered. Land and livestock continued to be utilized communally and cultivable land remained in strips supporting homesteads or *trefi*, just as run-rig did in the Hebrides. Arterial tracks covered the island as they always had with dwellings clustered at meeting-points, although an increase in churches provided new impetus for nucleated settlement. Geographical isolation still spelled sea-trade dependence, and insularity militated against innovation; too much improvement raised rents or dues anyway, disincentive enough. The pace of change was slow but these were changing times. The use of horse harnesses improved draft animal efficiency, and waterwheels and windmills improved milling processes, and Anglesey had great tillage potential. The clearance of woodland intensified, and over 60 mills are recorded for the island in the 14th century, although ownership was confined to a privileged few.

Beaumaris Castle was more than a garrison. Ships docked in the moat and a small town gathered beneath the walls, alive as markets and fairs brought animals and people into the streets. A borough charter was approved to attract craftsmen and merchants, exempt from tolls and dues, but the first burgesses did not stay long, competition from Caernarfon probably a factor. The mainland borough enjoyed the nodal advantage of island proximity and a larger hinterland. Those who took estates in the island shire were more likely to commit since land was an investment not so easily given up. Life was disrupted by a lethal combination of worsening weather and plagues in the 14th century, reducing British populations by as much as 60 percent, a catalyst force with its own velocity. It is doubtful if Anglesey's population was larger in 1400 than it was in 1200. Lands emptied and communities were decimated, rich and poor afflicted. The boroughs were hard hit too although the prospects of Newborough were not good anyway. Its exposure to wind-driven sand deposition limited expansion and buried the *llys* in the process. Episodes of storm blown sand plagued North Atlantic and North Sea coasts for several hundred years from the 13th century,[17] increasing dune growth, and any comments about Anglesey's agricultural productivity must be tempered by this development.

Edward I would surely not have invested so much in Beaumaris Castle had he been able to see the future, for the fortress saw little in the way of action. The age of the Llewelyns was over. The folly of the castle became a metaphor for the island's anonymity, and until the 18th century when it played a new role in British economic growth, Anglesey was obscure and provincial. This book focuses on the provincial fringe of course, so there is nothing exceptional in that, but in Anglesey's case it was calamitous. After heady centuries at the helm of a medieval kingdom, it shrank into a backwater, unimportant except to its inhabitants.

A Tale of Three Owains

Two attempts within decades of each other to turn back the clock and restore Welsh-led rule deserve a mention. Neither involved Anglesey directly, but they summoned memory of Aberffraw. The first involved the grandson of Llewelyn II's brother, Owain Lawgoch ("of the red hand"), an exile whom the French knew as Yvain de Galles or Owain of Wales. He plotted on several occasions, and in 1372, during the Hundred Years' War, the French king funded him for anti–Plantagenet reasons of his own. Owain sailed the Normandy coast from Harfleur intent on crossing the Channel to round Scilly and sail to Anglesey (perhaps?) but he never made it past Guernsey in the Channel Islands. He had sympathizers on Anglesey, and John Davies mentions one "condemned in 1370 for being in correspondence with him."[18]

The death of one Owain (1378) saw the embrace of another. Owain Glyndŵr

(Glendower) is a Welsh braveheart beloved in Welsh history. His links with Aberffraw are tenuous, his ancestry closer to the last rulers in Powys and Deheubarth, but he was a genuine Welsh-born contender nonetheless. His rebellion took off in 1400, helped by aristocratic sentiment against Henry IV, winning for a few heady years a chunk of Wales including Anglesey. He planned a centralized government and entered into an alliance with the French in 1404, fortunes declining thereafter. He was defeated by Henry V and forced into mountain retreats and oblivion by 1415, his disappearance the stuff of legend. The bid for independence did not go unpunished. Henry IV's government had retaliated in 1402 with a Penal Code prohibiting the Welsh from settling in boroughs or becoming burgesses, and it was reissued several times during the 15th century and not repealed until 1624, by which time Beaumaris was long since re-Englished.

Anglesey's best claim to national fame in the later medieval age was to breed Tudors, royal architects of the English nation-state, an irony compounded by a Tudor law (Act of Union, 1536) that redefined Welsh status in ways more profoundly anti-Welsh than their Plantagenet predecessors. Anglesey-born Owain ap Maredudd ap Tudur (c. 1400–1461) was the family member whose progeny changed the course of English history. This Owain was a child at the time of Glyndŵr but held positions at Henry V's court, and during the early 1430s married the king's widow Catherine of Valois, in defiance of a parliamentary remarriage law. One of their sons, Edmund Tudor, married into the Lancastrian branch of the feuding Plantagenet dynasty, and it was this step that paved the way for the royal claim of Henry Tudor, Owain's grandson. The Anglesey Tudors supported the Lancastrian cause in the so-called Wars of the Roses, an English Civil War of nobility, and when Henry Tudor won a famous victory over the Yorkist Richard III at the Battle of Bosworth Field in 1485 he became Henry VII, first of the Tudor kings. The fact that he had little interest in Wales is a mark of the dilution of Owain Glyndŵr intensity in just a few generations.

The Bulkeleys

Henry VII granted land and position in Anglesey to Sir Roland de Veleville, a knight of Breton descent and probably his illegitimate son. Veleville (d. 1535) was appointed constable in 1509 and resided in Beaumaris Castle. As constable he *was* the county government of Anglesey: absolute power lay with gentry like him. Henry VIII awarded another Beaumaris resident Richard Bulkeley a knighthood in 1533, the start of a long power relationship between family and island. The Bulkeleys were Anglesey landlords prior to his knighthood but with it they moved up the lengthening ladder of social rank. French in origin — a Richard de Bulkelegh held part of Cheadle manor in Cheshire in 1326 — the Anglesey interest evolved through marriage by William Bulkeley (d. 1484) into the influential Griffith family of Penrhyn Castle, near Bangor, themselves a branch of the Anglesey Tudurs (from Gruffydd ap Tudur). Sir Richard enhanced his stature by marrying the daughter of Sir William Griffith, then chamberlain of North Wales, and when Henry VIII dissolved the Catholic monasteries, the Penmon monastic lands passed into Bulkeley hands (1537) and were used for deer hunting. His descendants rooted themselves in island life through inter-marriage, endowment and high office and were referred to as the Bulkeleys of Angle-sey, as if they were sole proprietors.

Henry VIII had no sentiment about Welsh uniqueness, carrying on what his father had begun, driving a unifying agenda, namely imposition of English law, gov-ernment, language and church. Some of it was calculated and some of it convenient, most famously after papal excommunication over his divorce and remarriage issues in 1533. Fear of Catholic invasion through a western (Celtic) backdoor grew, and Acts of Union between 1536 and 1543 incorporated Wales into England. County reorgan-ization in the case of Anglesey involved the appointment of eight justices of the peace to manage local government and keep order, meeting in quarter sessions, mostly in Beaumaris Castle. The Acts gave the island representation in the English House of Commons with a knight elected for the shire and a burgess for the borough, but the franchise was limited and candidacy restricted to leading families. The Bulkeleys of Beaumaris had the borough seat by the 1550s, but the shire was contested with the Owens (from Owain's) from the Newborough area, where families with longer island antecedents settled in the aftermath of 1283.

The Bulkeleys added Irish lands to their Welsh and Cheshire properties in the 17th century, and elevation to the peerage and House of Lords came in 1643 when Thomas Bulkeley was made Viscount Cashel of Ireland, after declaring for Charles I in the English Civil War. Although Wales generally did not embrace Cromwell's dissenting force of parliamentarians, the garrison at Beaumaris did not resist it and surrendered in 1646, after hearing news of a royalist defeat at Chester. Whatever was lost under the republic of Cromwell was recovered. The Bulkeleys held the shire and borough seats in the Commons from the later 17th century into the Georgian age. George III made Viscount Thomas James Bulkeley of Beaumaris a baron in 1784, an honor trumpeted in the grandeur of nearby Baron's Hall.

In Transition

The Georgian century saw land enclosure, crop rotations, seed drills and selec-tive stockbreeding advance commercial agriculture in Britain's lowlands. The Angle-sey farming report is mixed. Anglesey vicar savant Reverend Henry Rowlands was a pioneering propagandist for the "new farming" revolution before he took up mega-liths and druids, and he urged improved farming practices in his *Idea Agriculture* (1704). Daniel Defoe of *Robinson Crusoe* fame thought Anglesey pleasanter than other parts of North Wales, productive in oats and cattle, in his *Tour through the Whole Island of Great Britain* (1724–26), but he never saw all the places he claimed to visit. Waterwheels and windmills dotted the land, and Newborough, Aberffraw, Llangefni, and Pentraeth held markets, but the lack of a bridge over the Menai Straits plainly restricted business. Arthur Aitkin described the perils of getting cattle across the straits to Abergele market near Conway in his *Journal of a Tour through North Wales and Part of Shropshire* (1797). Other commentators acknowledged the potential but remarked on the lack of cultivation, seeing emaciated poor grubbing a living from scattered strips across the deforested landscape, their dwellings unimproved in a millennium. Henry Skrine, who visited in the 1790s, found that "it bore that rugged and ill cultivated aspect which rises from poverty ... the few houses which appeared matched the wretchedness of their tenants."[19] New roots like potatoes and turnips helped, and herring was the staple it was on the Isle of Man, but choices were meager. Epidemics of typhus ("famine fever"), typhoid and smallpox periodically plagued the population, the undernourished especially vulnerable. Yet despite deprivation and distress, people indulged the old pastimes of cockfighting, football, harp music, and dancing when opportunities presented.

Wrecking and smuggling thrived, a sure sign of un-reconstruction. A Rhosneigr-based wrecking gang was found guilty in 1715 of plundering a sloop called *The Charming Jenny*,[20] but there is no record of their punishment. The worst shipwreck off Anglesey, that of *The Royal Charter*, came later in 1859 with over 400 lost, but by this time waged opportunities assuaged the more desperate. Duties on high demand goods such as tea, tobacco, liquor and soap made smuggling worthwhile in the 18th century, and until UK authorities challenged Manx smuggling rackets in 1765, contraband was an important source of income. Irish "wherries" (rowing boats) brought in Manx cargoes with locals serving as lookouts and carters, mostly destined for the British mainland but some of it consumed on the island. Brandy was a favorite. Most social ranks were complicit as producers or consumers; "them that ask no questions isn't told a lie" is how Kipling put it in *A Smuggler's Song*.

Anglesey copper interested Elizabethan alchemists, but after ages of inactivity 18th century war demand for ships' bolts, plates and ordnance created new incentive for copper extraction. The island was in the right place at the right time. Once the extent of ore was appreciated in the vicinity of Parys, a struggle for mining rights ensued. Thomas Williams of Llansadwrn, a local lawyer instructed to arbitrate, not only untangled it, he bought into it. Williams managed Parys mine (1774) and Mona mine (1785) for the lessee, building the business by applying close attention to costs. Rival Cornish copper sales were bought out and the Amlwch Shipping Company set up to import coal and other necessary raw materials, all in a manner befitting later corporate capitalism. A copper boom raged for the last third of the 18th century with 80,000 tons produced annually. Parys alone produced 40 percent of British copper in the 1780s and 1790s, employing 1,500 men, women, and children. The metal was shipped from the busy little harbor at Port Amlwch to industrial regions in northwestern England and southern Wales, where the company owned smelting works. When British coinage was in short supply during 1787–1793, the company paid its workers with a trade token copper penny. On one side was the company logo with the words "we promise to pay the bearer one penny on demand in London, Liverpool or Anglesea," on the other side a druid's head was surrounded by a wreath of oak leaves and acorns. Setting aside the iniquitous enslaving "truck payment" system (already encountered in the kelp-producing Scottish isles) the choice of a druid was apt. This was the age that revisited them.

Welsh Enlightenment

As geology dragged the island back into a position of some national importance, a cultural lobby worked to counteract such affiliation. In an enlightened age Welsh literati sought to resist the homogenizing effect of English hegemony and language by promoting the ideal of Welsh exclusivity, drawing on inspiration provided by an earlier Welsh scholar, Edward Lhuyd (1660–1709), whose work on the Welsh language helped to define medieval Celtic culture. Invasion of things English had taken several routes into Wales. On one hand the Welsh gentry assumed the private family lifestyles of English gentry, living in landscaped mansion houses removed from the populace, no longer with the bards, harpists and poets of Celtic grandees. On another track 18th century hellfire preachers like Hwel Harris helped introduce Calvinistic Methodism from South Wales (the island was hitherto conformist in religion) and while nonconformist churches were not averse to Welsh speech and Welsh advocates were not necessarily averse to Methodism, the message to congregations was culturally invasive. The Sunday markets, fortune tellers, "folk tales," bonfire rituals, gambling sports, drinking, dancing and singing to the harp and other behavioral habits considered immoral and ignorant were condemned wholesale from the Methodist pulpit. The new message began a process of realigning allegiances and values among the lower social echelons. The Baptists opened 16 new chapels in Anglesey between 1791 and 1826. One prominent evangelist leader, Christmas Evans (1766–1838), was popularly referred to as *Esgob Môn*, the "bishop of Anglesey." The loose-living isle of repute had met its nemesis.

Welshness advocates were predominantly middle-class, secular in spirit, and eager to enlighten anglicized Welsh in positions of power and influence. Reverend Henry Rowlands had made a start by appropriating druids as symbols of lost Welshness. Druidism gave the Welsh a British pedigree older than that of the English, and for that reason alone it was potent. A generation later, three Anglesey brothers— Lewis, Richard and William Morris— used the image of a druid on the title page of the publication of a society to promote a Welsh enlightenment, the Honorable Society of the Cymmrodorion (1751). The Morris brothers collected, corresponded, authored, organized and propagandized Welshness through the mid–18th century, and among those they patronized was Goronwy Owen, one of the great Welsh poets, born in 1722 in Llanfair Mathafarn Eithaf on Anglesey.

The Morrises funded his formal education at Beaumaris and Jesus College, Oxford, but Owen's talents were in emulating the free thinking poetry of the bardic age. He considered his bardic title of *Goronwy Ddhu o Môn*—"Black Gornowy of Anglesey"—his greatest achievement, and apparently the English translation does not do justice to his masterpiece: *Cywydd y Farn* or "Day of Judgment." His professional life was never a success, and sometimes disastrous. He had a brief career as a curate in his native parish but was banished. He still pursued clerical positions, though none proved fulfilling. In 1755 he tried a teaching post in colonial Virginia (William and Mary College) but was charged with public drunkenness. Away from Anglesey, Owen pined for it. In *Y Gofuned* ("A Wish") he wrote nostalgically of its serenity (prose translation): "the well-regulated parish, a house at the foot of the sunlit hill, a herd of cattle and a fold where my sparklingly genial wife could milk them." He added longingly, "The pope loves Rome with its graceful battlements, the Frenchman Paris, of the graceful turrets, the Englishman, London rich in man's splendor. But give me Anglesey."[21]

The dedication to the cause and the patronage of the Morris brothers and the poetry of Gornowy Owen turned Anglesey into a hotbed of ethnic revivalism and generally gave higher profile to Welsh poetic, literary and musical arts. It led to revival of national *Eisteddfodau* in 1789. The enlightenment engendered renaissance — the numbers of books published in Welsh increased throughout the 18th century with historical works strongly featured. At the 1832 Beaumaris *Eisteddfod*, Angharad Llwyd won a prize for her *History of the Island of Anglesey*. It was a poignant moment. The island's resurrection in Welsh consciousness had been lauded and applauded.

Mining, Money and Mansions

Copper mining peaked in the later 18th century, but production lasted through the Victorian Age. Amlwch's population registered 5,000 in 1800 with boatyards, sawmills, a windmill (tallest on Anglesey), and limekilns crowding the narrow rocky inlet. Seventy pubs served the port. Although more investment arrived in the form of Cornish labor to deep shaft mine as open cast resources were exhausted, business was declining after 1850. The operations at Parys and Mona mines shut down progressively through the 1870s and 1880s, and by 1900 it was all in terminal decline. Nevertheless over a century of development left its mark on the island in the form of new wealth and improved infrastructure. Other enterprises utilizing island mineral resources remained viable such as salt, clay, limestone and marble. The English cathedrals of Bristol, Worcester and Peterborough were customers of Anglesey marble, and stone quarries continued to produce millstones and grindstones, as they had done for centuries.

Land enclosures accelerated as demand for food and wool grew in the populous 19th century, to the extent of reclaiming salt marsh and sand dune in the west and southwest for grazing. Food prices remained high after the French wars (with price control) until 1846, and even for 25 years after that in a free trade atmosphere they were favorable for cereals, meat, dairy and wool to the benefit of those owning land. A slump came in the 1870s as floods of cheaper cereals, refrigerated meats and Australian wool hit British shores. Farm contraction coincided with the collapse of local copper. Laboring wages were best found off the island, the closest being at Penrhyn slate quarries near Bethesda, which employed thousands, peaking in the 1880s.

Meanwhile Anglesey society was affected by the new commerce, and new skills were increasingly represented with managers, surveyors, engineers, bookkeepers, and clerks. Mining and quarrying rights were still leased by the landowning gentry, however, and they profited. Their indulgence was mansion houses. Copper profits helped Sir Henry Paget, owner of Parys copper mine, to afford the remodeling of Plas Newydd manor house. His architect, James Wyatt, designed Gothic exteriors and Neo-Classical interiors fit for a Medici. Meanwhile Samuel Wyatt (the Wyatts became an architectural dynasty) rebuilt Baron Hall for Lord Bulkeley. Thomas Williams may have risen from Anglesey's professional middle-class (the Morrises too were of similar background) but such upward mobility did not yet disturb the status quo. Wealth was beginning to be displayed by those profiting in the emergent market society, as newly built houses in Beaumaris, Holyhead and Pentraeth testify, but the highest prestige was still defined in the feudal language of old: in duty, honor and title. Such language was exemplified in the life of William Henry Paget, Marquis of Anglesey, son of Sir Henry Paget and the last of the Marcher lords.

The title of Marquis was given for his service at the Battle of Waterloo in 1815, where stories of his command as colonel of the Seventh Hussars are now legend. In the one that made him a national figure, he was astride his horse beside the Duke of Wellington, surveying the end of the day's fighting, when a random cannon ball hit him full in the right knee. Paget cried out in agony, "By God, sir, I've lost my leg!" and the Iron Duke, dragging his gaze from the battle for a moment to appraise the situation, said shortly, "By God, sir, so you have," and turned his spyglass back to the retreating French. Or so the popular story has it. In fact Wellington aided the stricken man in his saddle until help arrived. Paget minus his limb still came home to great fanfare, his carriage drawn triumphantly through London streets and a 100-foot obelisk stands in his honor at Plas Newydd, topped by a 12-foot bronze statue of him in the uniform of the Seventh Hussars. Success in business had yet to win that level of approbation.

The Bridges

Trade's voracious appetite did succeed in bridging the Menai Straits, and a road bridge and a railway bridge were built within 25 years of each other. The road bridge (1826) was at least partly Irish induced with Dublin the second biggest city in the UK at the outset of the 19th century and Anglesey well placed to handle its commerce. The shortest sea link was between Kingstown (now Dun Laoghaire) and Holyhead, but poor connections frustrated trade. Interested Irish merchants were petitioning for improvements on the British side from the 1780s, specifically a bridge across the Menai Straits. In order to embark from Holyhead, Irish-bound travelers and goods had to negotiate the treacherous currents of Menai Straits. Over 50 ferry passengers were swept to their deaths in one 1785 incident. In addition the mountainous challenge of Snowdonia meant that London mail coaches could journey no further west than Shrewsbury, an English city 70 miles to the east. The Act of Union of 1800 was a spur to action, bringing Ireland under direct London rule in the midst of the French wars. National security was a government priority, and a Scottish civil engineer, Thomas Telford, a road, bridge and canal builder of repute, was contracted to speed up the London to Dublin mail service with a turnpike road from Shrewsbury to Holyhead. Bridging the Menai Straits became part of the project.

Turnpike road building was the first concerted effort to improve infrastructure since the Romans, and although there is no evidence that they ever had done so in Anglesey, it seems appropriate, given Roman interest in Anglesey, that the island should be part of it. Bridge opposition came from ferry owners and the borough of Beaumaris, fearing loss of business to Holyhead, but it was to no avail. Telford built what some claim to be the first major suspension bridge in the world—16 massive chains holding up a 579-foot length of road slung between two towers. It opened in 1826 to great expectations, but the travel time between London and Holyhead only fell from 36 hours to 27 hours, hardly a breathtaking reduction, speed still being restrained by horse-drawn conveyance. Before ten years was out, a parliamentary committee reported on disappointing growth in Holyhead. High fares, poor ship accommodation, sailing vessels in an age of paddle steamers, and rival packets to Dublin from Liverpool and Fishguard were all cited as causes. Port management was transferred to the Admiralty in 1837 in a bid to improve shipping service, but it was railway connection that solved the problem.

Railway venture capitalists proposed a route to Holyhead from the English city of Chester in the early 1840s with Dublin and London connections at either end. It would be a cash cow, the prospectus declared, and the investing public was urged to buy up shares. Anglesey dignitaries helped promote the project, but it found itself in competition with others and won only narrowly in 1844 before the House of Commons Select Committee that decided such matters. The engineer was Robert Stephenson, son of the Newcastle-born railway pioneer George Stephenson, well accomplished in his own right. He contoured a rail track bed around the cliffs, headlands and bays of the North Welsh coast before rails crossed the Menai Straits on the Britannia Railway Bridge (opened 1850, destroyed by fire 1970). Victorian locomotives steamed through two rectangular iron-tube tunnels assembled on the Menai banks, supported by stone towers of Penmon limestone. As corporate mergers and buy-outs swept the railway board nationally, the original minnow company was absorbed within the giant London and North Western Railway (LNWR) in 1859. This time, growth did ensue. The harbor and facilities at Holyhead expanded, causing the population to triple in 40 years, from 4,000 in 1841 to over 12,000 by the 1880s. Island branch lines opened to Amlwch and Red Wharf Bay/Benllech.

Outside of Holyhead, however, benefits were mixed. Heavy and bulky minerals were moved efficiently and farmers found markets for dairy and meat produce with refrigerated rail cargo services, as did fishing enterprises. Alternatively rails brought cheap cereal imports, and waged farm work declined as Anglesey farmers committed less acreage to crops. Manchester and Liverpool were within reach to supply goods once considered rare luxuries but local rural crafts had to deal with competition from mass production. The old ways of making a living came under challenge. The management of the Amlwch and Red Wharf Bay branch lines hoped for seaside traffickers, but the island never caught public imagination or attracted the investment of Welsh coastal resorts like Prestatyn, Rhyl, Colwyn Bay and Llandudno, all en route to Anglesey. The impression is that most trippers had alighted before trains crossed the Britannia Bridge.

Modernity

The wider world came closer in the years after the bridges opened. Outlaws had to contend with a police force (1856) and the ruling gentry became accountable to a voting public as county council officials had to seek election for the first time following the Local Government Act of 1888. Social and political disestablishment was furthered after World War I when the old guard found their landed estates too costly and sold out to smaller freeholders. In the meantime rural job loss, the squalor of cramped, overcrowded cottages with few amenities, and the dire specter of Poor Law workhouse life helped make up the minds of poorer people to leave. To counter migratory losses, fresh settlers arrived in an age of newly found mobility, many of them English and Welsh-born commercial and professional middle classes, those with the means to pursue opportunities. The bridges worked as something of a revolving door in that regard, but the balance was in deficit mode. Residency rose in the first half of the 19th century to 57,000, but as rural depopulation gathered pace it had fallen back to 50,000 by 1911.

Uniformed personnel crossed the Menai Straits in both directions with regularity in the first half of the 20th century. The opening of an airship base in 1915 in the southwest of the island (now RAF Mona), one of 12 Royal Naval Air Service (RNAS) bases, was an economic bonus at a much-needed time, though it was powerless to prevent the sinking of a British submarine (H5) in collision with an unidentified vessel in offshore waters in March 1918. All lives were lost including one Lt. Childs of the US Navy, first American submariner to die in European conflicts.[22] Anglesey-born soldiers paid the ultimate price themselves, coughing, choking and dying in chemical and trench warfare. Anglesey's flat land was again put to use for an air base in World War II, this time at RAF Valley near Holyhead. It opened in February 1941 as a motley collection of dispersed billets and hangars for fighter pilots engaged in the Battle of Britain. United States Air Force detachments arrived in 1943 to set up a facility for trans–Atlantic patrols and from this frontline position RAF Valley gained its motto—*In Adversis Perfugium* ("A Refuge in Adversity")—apropos Anglesey history. Island air space has rarely been quiet since. Valley became one of the busiest flying stations in the air force, training and running fast jet aircrews, air-to-air missile operations and helicopter land-and-sea rescue units.

Reform and Conflict

Aristocratic Anglesey is largely passé. The baronial hall of the Bulkeleys was abandoned after 1921 (apart from some brief use in World War II) and Plas Newydd was acquired as a National Trust property in 1976, though the Pagets maintain a low-profile presence. The Menai shore country still has an illustrious air about it however. The Barons Hill Golf Club and Royal Anglesey Yacht Club have that whiff of prestige (Sir Richard William Bulkeley was a founding Victorian patron of both) and £1 million homes in the vicinity preserve the social gulf, though this one is one maintained by bank balances rather than primogeniture.

The *ancien regime* may have abdicated in the inter-war decades, but rural deprivation did not, and premature deaths from diseases persisted, particularly tuberculosis. Anglesey's mortality levels were higher in the 1930s than those in industrial Lancashire and Yorkshire, counties of "dark satanic mills" renown. Poor housing standards were blamed for exacerbating health problems. Many of the island's rural dwellings had no damp course, no fireplace, no bedrooms, no kitchens, no water supply, no toilet, no plumbing. Solutions cost rent money, and in a time of impoverishment by low investment and over-dependence on a traditional agricultural economy, the prospects looked gloomy. Funding rural distress was a low priority in an urban age. Anglesey's MP during these years was Welsh-born Megan Lloyd-George, daughter of Liberal Prime Minister David Lloyd George. She represented the island in Westminster twice between 1929 and 1951, the first woman to represent a Welsh constituency. Her father promised "homes fit for heroes" after World War I, but political will was slow to turn into action. Anglesey did get some council houses (public housing) during these years, one of the first rural areas to do so, but not enough to defeat tuberculosis. Public health standards improved in the post-war years as Aneurin Bevan, Welsh-born health minister of the Labor Government of 1945–51, initiated the National Health Service and revitalization of national housing stock began.

Government-sponsored initiatives have played a hefty role in postwar life. Anglesey Education Committee pioneered egalitarian "comprehensive" secondary education under its director E.O. Humphreys (1946–48), and in 1957 Anglesey became the first county to scrap the discriminatory pre-secondary school examination known as "11-plus." The Agriculture Act of 1947 offered farmers support mechanisms for modernization in an effort to maintain competitiveness, but it encouraged capital and not labor-dependent farming. Investment in new machines did not help labor demand. In the absence of alternative job creation, unemployment stalked the island at levels higher than the national average. Farmers are even more at the behest of government in the modern era of EU Common Agricultural Policy, and enhancing the rural economy remains a major challenge. Anglesey County Council gave support for measures to form cooperatives for locally grown and reared produce but these did not resolve private sector job shortages.

Anglesey was able to catch some tourist trade of the caravan-and-camping, bed-and-breakfast variety in the motoring age of the 1950s and 1960s and the nature-loving outdoors' business is still a viable specialty. The Anglesey Sea Zoo at Brynsiencyn grew to attract 100,000 visitors annually in the 1990s and employ locals in season. Meanwhile around 17 percent of the workforce still lives off the island's natural resources, a combination of minerals, quarries, forestry, fishing, reservoirs and farms. The arrival of the Rio Tinto Company in 1970, a global consortium begun a century earlier to work copper mines in Spain, was a catch. Its Holyhead aluminum smelter employs in the hundreds, a significant enterprise on an island where small businesses proliferate. Land room has been found for light engineering and pharmaceutical factories, food processing and fish farming, but overall the prognosis could be healthier. The public sector remains the biggest single employer with its county council workers and military services personnel. Unemployment is still among the highest in Wales, and depopulation is again a reality with residency falling from 72,000 in 1991 to 67,000 in 2001.

The port of Holyhead has held its own, processing half a million vehicles and two and a half million passengers annually as the 21st century began. Servicing Anglo-Irish through routes has brought benefits, but functioning as a corridor has drawbacks. The island was struggling to cope with road volume by the later 1960s, and the Britannia Railway Bridge disaster compounded the problem by forced closure in 1970 (teenagers looking for bats in the dark tube tunnels accidentally torched the structure!). A new two-level road-and-rail bridge was built to replace Stephenson's original, but Telford's bridge is still there — modified, reconstructed and strengthened many times over. Congestion fueled environmental protest at the end of the 20th century ("Too Menai lorries" was one slogan of protest) and the response was to widen the permanent way and complete a £104 million road project across Anglesey, linking it to the mainland motorway network. A London to Holyhead road journey should take in the region of seven hours, traffic permitting.

The changing demographics pose vexing new questions. An influx of retiree migrants and pre-retirement second homes has ruffled island feathers. Anglesey is a marketable retreat. Leafy lanes and ancient sites, natural history, coastal hiking trails, and on a practical note improved communications invite those seeking to escape urban life. The average age is higher than it was, pressuring health care provision. People wait longer for treatment. At the same time property prices have risen, by 20 percent in 1999. Land Registry figures for 2001 reported that median house prices were higher than the neighboring mainland county of Gwynedd, although they were lower than the British average and appreciably lower than the Isle of Wight, though that may trigger more purchase interest! More to the point the property boom pushed prices beyond the reach of locals, creating resentment against government for not intervening. The new demographics present conflicts in life quality expectations also. Young islanders need job creation enterprise, but older retirees and pre-retirees with comfortable bank balances want the opposite. They want peace and quiet. Feelings can get heated. The much-publicized closure of Wylfa Nuclear Power Station (opened 1971) due to a faulty reactor in 2000 was a case in point. Big business feared increased energy costs and locals feared layoffs, particularly at the Holyhead aluminum smelter. Those with environmental priorities and assorted others, for whom there is no such thing as a safe nuclear power station, were joyous. The reopening in 2001 reversed the emotions.

Welshness

Such conundrums are found elsewhere offshore, especially on Wight, as we shall see, but a strong ethnic identity compounds the Anglesey predicament. No other offshore island houses a greater percentage of non–English speakers. The 2001 Census reported about 39,000 people (60 percent of the island population) having ability in speaking, reading and writing Welsh. County reorganization restored its 700-year-old island county status in 1994, and it is entirely appropriate that

Eisteddfodd organizers chose it — the "Mother of Wales"— to host the last celebration of Welshness of the millennium in 1999. Yns Môn is still a womb of Welshness.

Anglesey MPs have long been elected as much for their Welsh-leaning demeanor as their party affiliation, characteristics that embrace religious nonconformity (chapels are havens of Welshness), commitment to social justice, a desire for Welsh self-determination and (not least) an island association. Since World War I there has been only one notable exception, Keith Best, a young English barrister from Brighton, elected in Margaret Thatcher's 1979 landslide Conservative Party victory. Newly arrived English-born voters, those heeding the anti–Labor call, probably helped swing the vote. The archetype was his predecessor, Holyhead-born Cledwyn Hughes. The son of a Protestant minister, Hughes went into politics against the advice of his father, defeating Megan Lloyd-George in the 1951 election. He proceeded to represent Anglesey in the House of Commons for 28 years. A passionate supporter of Welsh exceptionalism, he lived long enough to witness realization of the devolution cause in 1999. However his Labor politics and Welsh patriotism did not prevent him from accepting that English aristocratic oddity of a peerage, becoming Lord Cledwyn of Penrhos, grandee of the House of Lords to his death. There is less compromise at the grassroots on Anglesey. Homebuyers are urged to learn Welsh if they wish to be accepted by the community. Voters have opted for solidly Welsh candidates since the aberration of 1979. The Welsh nationalist party *Plaid Cymru* has a strong base on the island, as might be expected, and candidate Ieuan Wyn Jones won the Westminster seat in 1987 and later became party leader. He also won election to the new Welsh parliament in Cardiff in 1999, standing down from Westminster to focus on his Cardiff mandate. A native-born islander Albert Owen (Labor) replaced him in the 2001 election.

The "fit" between Welsh language and Welsh culture is easily assumed, but the so-called "mass culture" is as conspicuous on Anglesey as it is anywhere else. Any expression of hostility to Englishness remains just that, an expression of hostility; it does not necessarily translate into political action. In the referendum on devolution Welsh voters were surprisingly less motivated than Scots by the prospect of having their own national assembly. The pro–Welsh activists must have been privately disappointed in the 1997 vote; even the non-native constituency of Anglesey cannot entirely explain the low turnout and sliver of a winning margin. The referendum recorded 15,649 "yes" votes in Anglesey against 15,095 "no's," and the 50.9 percent victory margin was little better than the 50.3 percent in all of Wales. What pulses is residual pride in a non–English identity, pride in the feat of having kept Welsh alive, and determination to resist further dilution of it. There is no reason for immediate alarm. Welsh speech has thrived. Schools' curricula require Welsh understanding. Media and entertainment broadcast in Welsh and more books are written in Welsh than ever before. Welshness stands a much better chance of recognition and acceptance in the multilingual atmosphere of the European Union than the Anglo-Britain of 50 years ago. English retirees may have sought residence on Anglesey hitherto, but in the fullness of EU time the continental Europeans may make migration homes there too; at the very least it would dissipate the old fear of being *Englished*!

1. Llanfairpwllgwyngllgogoerychwyrndrobwillanttysiliogogogoch — "St. Mary's Church in the hollow of white hazel near a rapid whirlpool and the Church of St. Tysilio near the red cave."

2. Carpenter, Rhys, *Beyond the Pillars of Hercules: The Classical World through the Eyes of Its Discoverers* (Tandem Books edition, 1973), 165–166.

3. Green, Miranda, *Celtic Myths* (University of Texas Press edition, 1995), 52.

4. *The Mabinogion,* Jones, Gwyn, and Jones, Thomas, trans., (Everyman Library paper, new revised ed. reprinted 1996), 32.

5. *Tacitus: Annals* Grant, Michael, translator (Penguin Classic, 1971), XIV, 29–30

6. *Bede: The Ecclesiastical History of the English People* (Oxford University Press, McClure, Judith & Collins, Roger, ed., World's Classics Series, 1994), II, 20

7. Davies, John, *A History of Wales* (Allen Lane: The Penguin Press, 1993), 71

8. *Gerald of Wales: The Journey through Wales and the Description of Wales,* Thorpe, Lewis, trans., (Penguin Classics edition, 1978), Journey, Bk. II, 7, 190.

9. Davies, John, 242.

10. Mersey, Daniel, "Welsh royal court found in sand," in *British Archaeology, 18,* October 1996 (http://www.britarch.ac.uk/ba/ba18/ba18news.html).

11. *Nennius: Historia Brittonum,* Giles, J.A., trans., (British American Books, 1986), 8.

12. Ashley, Mike, *British Kings and Queens* (Carroll & Graf, 1999), 149.

13. Redknap, Mark, project director, "Vikings at Llanbedrgoch," in National Museums & Galleries of Wales, Archaeology and Numismatics section, report on 2001 excavations. (http://www.nmgw.ac.uk/archaeology/2001/anglesey/backa.en.shtml).

14. *Gerald of Wales,* Journey, Bk. II, 7, 187.

15. *Gerald Of Wales,* Description, Bk. II, 4, 261.

16. Davies, Norman, *The Isles: A History* (Oxford University Press, 1999), 369.

17. Lamb, Hubert, *Climate, History and the Modern World,* second ed. (Routledge, 1995), 194.

18. Davies, John, 193.

19. Skrine, Henry, *Two Successive Tours throughout the whole of Wales with several of the adjacent English counties* (London, 1798), 206.

20. Hughes, Wendy, *Anglesey: Past and Present* (Carreg Gwalch, 1999), 134.

21. Ramage, Helen, *Portrait of an Island: 18 Century Anglesey* (Anglesey Antiquarian Society, 1987), 56.

22. University of Wolverhampton, "First American Submariner to Die in War Commemorated," press release, March 2002 (http://asp.wlv.ac.uk/Level5.asp).

6

The Isles of Scilly: "Last Port of Call"

"We pray thee, Oh Lord, not that shipwrecks should happen, but
if that wrecks do happen Thou wilt guide them into the Scilly
Isles for the benefit of the poor inhabitants" — Island prayer[1]

Clustered in the Atlantic swell some 25 miles off southwest Britain, the Isles of Scilly enjoyed their 15 minutes of fame when the late Labor Prime Minister Harold Wilson made a getaway home there in the 1960s, slipping back into grateful seclusion thereafter. Radio weather forecasts of advancing Atlantic storms may raise faint smiles from schoolchildren hearing them pronounced "Silly" for the first time but in the national conscience Scilly is out of sight and out of mind, beyond Land's End literally and metaphorically. Mariners have had less reason for indifference. The local sea is a minefield of unforgiving rocks, a vicious claimant of lives, and watery grave of countless vessels, with a trove of wrecks for modern divers. Over 600 sites are charted. The etymology of Scilly is conjectural and considered later in the context of its first usage (1st century A.D.) but whatever the verdict Scillonians prefer the unitary Scilly to "Scillies."

Fifty small low-lying islands plus nearly a hundred more rocks total Scilly's land area of little more than six square miles, akin to that of central London but without the crowds. The biggest five are inhabited — St. Mary's, Tresco, Bryher, St. Martin's and St. Agnes. Residency in 2001 numbered 2,153, most of them on St. Mary's, the hub of which is the small port of Hugh Town. The rest is a natural habitat of breezy treeless vistas, rugged granite cliffs, rare seabirds, caves, empty beaches and incessant sea. Visitors without sea legs can take air services, but the real way to experience Scilly is to brave the briny exuberance in the company of shrieking seagulls. The Victorian author Walter Besant, whose undistinguished romance *Armorel of Lyonesse* (1890) is partly set in Scilly, thought the plowing seas perfect for "taking the conceit out of a young man." Atlantic storms are endemic but there is a silver lining. A sun-kissed Gulf Stream effect means that winter temperatures are rarely below 50°F and summer sunshine hours are often longer than elsewhere in Britain. It's

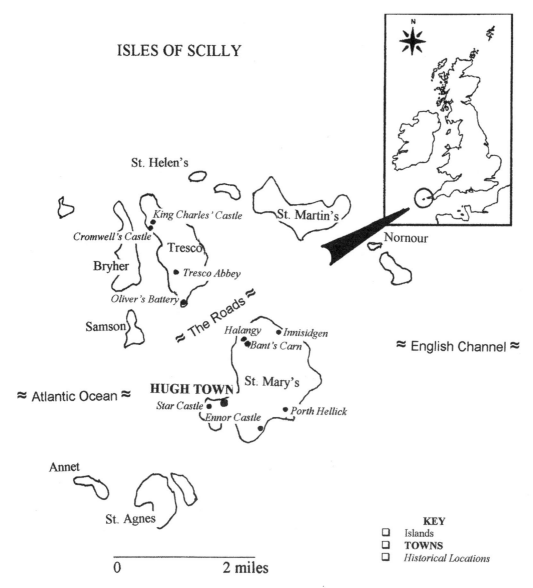

ISLES OF SCILLY

St. Helen's

King Charles' Castle

Cromwell's Castle

St. Martin's

Nornour

Tresco

Bryher

Tresco Abbey

Oliver's Battery

The Roads

Samson

Halangy · Innisidgen

·Bant's Carn

≈ English Channel ≈

≈ Atlantic Ocean ≈

HUGH TOWN St. Mary's

Star Castle

Ennor Castle

Porth Hellick

Annet

St. Agnes

KEY
☐ Islands
☐ **TOWNS**
☐ *Historical Locations*

0   2 miles

enough to nurture subtropical flora, particularly on Tresco, where Victorian horticultural enterprise began winter cultivation of bulbs, flowers and vegetables for urban markets.

Each island defends its own identity, and nicknames draw on historical caricatures: "bulldogs" for the men of St. Mary's, long the garrison of British bulldog authority, "ginnicks" for those from St. Martin's, understood only in some local context, and "Turks" for St. Agnes. The latter may derive from the time of Muslim corsairs erroneously known as "Turks" or allude to anyone there who looked foreign, plausible since it is the nearest shelter for sailors coming to grief on the perilous Western Rocks.

Lost Geography and Early Settlers

The islands are a continuation of the same granite landmass as the English south-west, splinters of drowned Cornwall, surviving summits of an even longer Cornish peninsula before post-glacial melting. They figure in Cornish folklore as peaks of the vanished Arthurian kingdom of Lyonesse and there are kernels of truth to it, at least as far as geological involvement with Cornwall is concerned. The sea covering has been a prolonged affair. Scholarly opinion differs over the pace of inundation, but Admiralty charts of shallow water channels, visible underwater stumpy oaks and stone built dwellings with field boundaries, and the ability to walk between some islands at spring low tides register the fact of it. A team of divers found a submarine village of seven huts between St. Martin's and St. Mary's in 1961. The valley between St. Mary's and Tresco probably flooded in the 11th century, but Professor Charles Thomas, a Cornish archaeologist, has presented figures on tidal heights and sea levels to argue that while the sea was rising at the time of earliest occupation it did not reach its current level until about 1500,[2] meaning that Scilly assumed its present geography only 500 years ago. In his opinion one large island dominated until a rising sea formed the archipelago of St. Mary's, St. Martin's, Tresco, Bryher and Samson. Thomas applies the name Ennor to this lost mainland island, using an old Cornish/Celtic name "En-Neor" from 12th century church records, estimating its former size as roughly comparable to Yell (Shetland), Hoy (Orkney), Barra (Hebrides) and Guernsey (Channel Islands).[3] The isles of St. Agnes (originally Eknes—there never was a saint) and neighboring Annet had already separated.

The first known settlers were farmers and fishers, probably crossing during the third millennium B.C. in skin-covered wicker craft from nearby Cornwall, at a time when the population there was growing. Earlier visits when it was part of the greater landmass cannot be discounted. The Ennor islanders found woodlands of oak, elm, ash and a red deer population. They also found dolphins, seals, porpoises and stranded whales for blubber and bone. A wealth of conger eel, cod, sea bream and bass improved supper. Archaeological surface observations indicate early field agriculture with barley cultivation and livestock grazing. Burial sites confirm the sedentary settlement, most with tomb entrances set in an easterly orientation to acknowledge the rising sun. St. Mary's has three of the best known chambered sites: one on Porth Hellick Downs (down = hill) near the curious rock shape known as the "Loaded Camel," a pair on Innisidgen Down, and lastly one on Halangy Down at Bant's Carn. All probably functioned as temples for the living but have long since been stripped of contents. Bant's Carn is now close to St. Mary's northwestern shore but 4,000 years ago stood on a valley slope between St. Mary's and Tresco. Other megaliths survive in the form of simple stone pillars, and with nearby Cornwall, Brittany and Ireland all major megalithic centers we must deduce that the Scillonians of 4,000–5,000 years ago were firmly within that wider cultural community.

After centuries of clearing woods, cooling temperatures and increased rain from around 1200 B.C. led to peat bogs and moorland, and with reduced cultivable land population declined. Professor Thomas points to what he suspects was a rise and fall scenario in the last three millennia B.C. with habitation at a higher level in the earlier

Bronze Age. It is known that climatic degeneration in the last millennium B.C. forced depopulation of moorland areas in Devon, not so far away, resulting in an economy dependent on pasture rather than cultivation, and the same process probably occurred on Scilly. Promontory forts or fortified farmsteads of a type not dissimilar to those on Man and in the Channel Islands have been identified, enclosures to protect livestock rearing activities. Immediately below Bant's Carn is Halangy "village," where the stone foundations of 11 interconnected dwellings, animal enclosures and field walls—a Celtic Iron Age village (c. 200 B.C.) in effect—can clearly be seen. The area experienced continuous settlement over millennia, it would seem, and excavations of fields with blown sand in the vicinity provide a clue to its depopulation and abandonment. Hut dwelling circles with continuous occupation from the Bronze Age through the Iron Age were excavated on the small island of Nornour in the 1960s and 1970s and since then a similar settlement has been discovered on Tresco. Doubtless there are more undiscovered farmsteads out there beneath the waves.

There are about 35 Iron Age *cist* graves on the islands, some with grave goods such as brooches and pins. The Nornour dig uncovered some 300 bronze brooches (A.D. 50–270), many of which are on display in the Scilly Museum in Hugh Town, expertly enameled with delicate colorings and Celtic design. Further confirmation of inclusion within the Celtic world came in 1999 when a La Téne sword, lying in the dirt for 2,000 years, was found by accident in a potato field on Bryher, together with the remains of a shield, a bronze mirror and bronze ring: votive offerings of a warrior-king's burial (?). The sword and mirror are showcased in the museum.

Isles of Discovery?

Although Scilly's early megalithic expression and farm settlement generally follows the offshore experience elsewhere, it may deserve a special distinction. Britain is usually cast as a dynamic agent of discovery rather than a passive object of it, but perhaps Scilly is to British history what the Caribbean island of San Salvador is to American — namely a first in new land sighted by voyagers. Archaeology has established through excavation of "foreign" artifacts that migrations and overseas trade brought cross-cultural interaction, but who first wrote about the British Isles? When was it first written down for posterity and where was the sighting? The oldest alphabetic writing is that of seventh century B.C. Mediterranean Greeks and there are oblique references to North Atlantic Europe in that literature by the fifth century B.C. "About the far northwest of Europe I have no definite information," Herodotus remarked, "nor do I know anything of the existence of islands called the *Cassiterides* [Tin Islands] whence we get our tin,"[4] thereby confirming knowledge of them. It was Mediterranean sailors who sailed to North Atlantic shores for tin, copper and amber and the *Cassiterides* gained publicity. In modern times the French have claimed them as islets in the Loire estuary, where there are traces of tin working, the Spanish as isles off northwest Spain, used as trading centers for imported tin, and since tin (and copper) is found in Cornish granite a case might be made for Scilly too, if only as a place en route to the metal.

We have already discussed Pytheas of Massalia's voyage in Shetland's latitudes, and it is the reported *periplus* (sailing log) of that same voyage that warrants attention in this hypothesis. The gist of his *Peri Tou Okeanu* ("On the Ocean") was communicated through secondhand transcribers like Polybius (c. 200–118 B.C.), a Greek historian of some repute. He got his information from Dicaearchus, a student of Aristotle and probably a fourth century B.C. contemporary of Pytheas. Modern scholars think that Pytheas's voyage took place in that century, and the head of Alexander the Great on a silver coin (c. 326 B.C.) found at Holm Chase in neighboring Devon adds weight to the later 300s B.C.[5] About 18 writers had cited Pytheas as an information source on the North Atlantic by the sixth century A.D., the most quoted being Strabo (c. 64 B.C.–A.D. 24), an Asiatic Greek geographer and historian whose *Geography* is still in print. Another two, Poseidonius (135–50 B.C.) and Diodorus Siculus (100–20 B.C.), probably made use of Pytheas, although he is not credited in their surviving work. Nothing is known of Pytheas's life except that he was not an aristocrat; it is a reasonable guess that he was from a commercial background with seagoing experience.

Pytheas sailed from Massalia (Marseilles), a Greek colony, through the straits of Gibralter and along the Iberian coasts to the Bay of Biscay. Assuming commitment to a northerly route (rather than following the French coast east along the Channel) and allowing for the capricious nature of pre-compass navigation, it is not inconceivable his first British Isles sighting was Scilly. Diodorus Siculus told of landfall near Belerion (Lands End) and in a recent study of the voyage the Oxford archaeologist Barry Cunliffe supposed a northward voyage past Lands End toward the Irish Sea,[6] a course with Scilly in its path. Diodorus added that natives had a clever way of extracting tin from its bed, and although this is understandably taken to mean Cornwall, where tin mining has a long pedigree, Scilly does have tin. There were several tin mining ventures in the 17th and 18th centuries, and although they proved commercial disappointments, it does not discount placer prospecting in times B.C. Boring through hard granite for tin was beyond the technological know-how of the fourth century B.C., but prospectors could pan for crystal tin-stone pebbles in alluvial gravel beds of streams. How much of it was present on Scilly is hard to say since some of the lower land is now submarine. Pliny the Elder mentioned an adjoining island named Ictis as a distribution point for the tin trade, and Scilly cannot be ruled out of an entrepôt role. There are other British candidates. Many favor St. Michael's Mount, a tiny tidal isle off the south Cornish coast, or even the Isle of Wight (called Vectis by the Romans), nearly 200 miles to the east, but until either location is proven the prospect of Ictis is open.

There is another window on discovery in a piece of Latin verse titled *Ora Maritima*. Admittedly more controversial as evidence, it is dismissed outright by some but merits scrutiny because it presents the possibility of a voyage at least 150 years before that of Pytheas, one containing what may be speculatively interpreted as a reference to Scilly. The author was an obscure Roman official called Rufus Festus Avienus, a resident of the Roman province of Africa Proconsularis (modern Tunisia). He wrote nearly a thousand years after the implied voyage took place and this is only the first problem with veracity. He claimed to have gathered his historical information from a collection of old documents available to him, principally a *periplus* known as the *Massiolote Periplus*, deriving from its port of embarkation Massalia. After describing a voyage north from the Pillars of Hercules (Straits of Gibraltar) toward islands inhabited by the Hiberni (Irish) and Albiones (British), Avienus throws in the name of Himilco: "Himilco of Carthage reported that he himself had investigated the matter on a voyage."[7] Avienus does not tell us how far north Himilco sailed up the Atlantic coast, but he adds that "a lot of seaweed floats in the water ... the depth of water does not extend much and the bottom is covered over with a little water."[8] Was he was in the shallows of formative Scilly, allowing for the lower sea levels and other tidal phenomena of that age? Such a conclusion is a leap, and other shallows could suffice — perhaps he had encountered the floating Sargasso Sea — but Scilly is no less a contender. Avienus reported that Himilco was not the first to sail in this direction. *Tartessians* (Iron Age Andalusians from southern Spain) were already trading with tin and lead-rich islands called the *Oestrymnides*, two days' sailing from Ireland,[9] usually taken to mean islands off Brittany, meaning that Mediterranean sailors had come within reach of Scilly.

Ora Maritima does contain information that looks suspiciously like Pytheas references, and it may simply be *Peri Tou Okeanu* revisited. The *Massiolote Periplus* itself does not survive, and Avienus doesn't tell us who wrote it; he may have just regurgitated common knowledge. In this train of thought the *Massiolote Periplus* is just the old Pytheas tale repeated and there never was another document. On the other hand *Ora Maritima* never mentions Pytheas by name and includes several unique lines involving the navigator Himilco of Carthage, a sailor not mentioned by Pythean redactors. Carthage was once a great Mediterranean power, the greatest of the Phoenician colonies, named from the Phoenician *Kurt-Hadasht* ("New City"). It was by all accounts a very rich place in the sixth century B.C. It was also aggressively expansionist. Pliny the Elder remarked in his encyclopedic *Natural History* (c. A.D. 77) that when the famous Hanno of Carthage navigated the West African coast c. 500 B.C. and published an account of it, a contemporary Himilco was sent at the same time to explore "the outer coasts of Europe."[10] Carthage had an important bronze industry and, like its Greek rival Massalia, was interested in finding tin. If Himilco did reach Scilly, having followed the *Tartessians* at least to the Breton islands, then he did so more than a century before Pytheas.

Unfortunately no Carthaginian account of Himilco's voyage survives. Avienus claimed in *Ora Maritima* to have access to ancient Carthaginian records, and he was posted for some time in Bulla Regia, a town located in the same North African province as Carthage, so he may have spoken the truth. At the end of the Punic Wars (146 B.C.) the Roman army razed Carthage, but it was colonized under Julius Caesar and Augustus, and, by the time of Avienus (c. A.D. 400), had revived with a reputation as a place of learning. His contemporary Augustine of Hippo (St. Augustine) trained there in the later fourth century A.D. Writing that is lost to us now may still have been around at the time of Avienus. Pytheas's presence in the Cornish region is now widely accepted but the possibility that the Greek was pre-empted in documentation by a Carthaginian is not yet out of the picture. There is some circumstantial corroboration. Pottery ware shards identified as sixth century B.C. Mediterranean/North African have been found in Scilly and Cornwall.

Sacred Isles

The ancient sources offer up another proposition on Scilly's ancient vocation, that of a pre–Christian sacred place. Charles Thomas examined nomenclature for British headlands and capes used by Alexandrian Greek astronomer Ptolemy in *Geography* (c. A.D. 150) and noted that Pytheas's Belerion (Land's End) was contained in a longer phrase *Antivestaeum sive Bolerium promontorium*—"the temple (*vestaeum* from the Greek *hestiaion*: temple) opposite (*anti-*) to the *Belerion* promontory."[11] The temple opposite, he reasons, must have been on Scilly since there wasn't any other land "opposite" to Lands End. As for the naming of Scilly, the first known usage was by Pliny the Elder who referred to it as Silumnis,[12] so it was common knowledge by the time Ptolemy wrote. But what does it mean? Thomas thinks that Silumnis may derive from Sulis, a Celtic Iron Age goddess admitted into the Roman pantheon and the focus of worship at Aqua Sulis (Roman Bath) in southwest England. The "y" suffix of Scilly is a later Norse amendment, as in Sulis' isle (*ey* = island). There is no unanimity of agreement. Others point to Skylla, the deathly sea-monster in *The Odyssey*, her six heads devouring luckless sailors, as the source, but this would not refute the temple isle. Nor would the argument that Scilly connotes with the German word *selig* meaning "blessed."

There is some material evidence to strengthen the holy temple isle contention, though not necessarily to prove worship of Sulis. A small granite altar without inscription from the Roman period was recovered on St. Mary's, and a Celtic (?) stone head was found in the 1940s by a local antiquarian vicar the Rev. H.A. Lewis. The altar now stands in the Abbey Gardens on Tresco and a replica cast of the head is in the Isles of Scilly Museum. The facial features are eroded unlike Anglesey's Henty Head (it may just be a weathered monolith), but shoulders are distinguishable. There is more. After a fierce gale in 1962, unfriendly to all but archaeologists, the aforementioned remains of a small settlement came to light on tiny Nornour in the Eastern Isles of Scilly with a significant deposit of coins, glass fragments, small clay pots, clay figurine pieces and the hoard of brooches discovered near the settlement, dated to the pre–Roman and Roman period. The collection, as stated earlier, is in Hugh Town's museum. Professor Thomas argues that such a large deposit in such a remote place must represent votive offerings, speculating that it may have involved a beacon-shrine to guide mariners in dangerous waters,[13] a credible basis for Ptolemy's temple. The fact that Scilly was chosen later by Christians as a monastic site does favor the notion of Scilly's sacred renown. It was common practice for Christians to commandeer existing pagan shrines.

There is no indication that the Romans found any use for Scilly until the late fourth century, when it was used to exile heretics. During the spell when renegade army commander Magnus Maximus assumed imperial authority in Britain, Gaul and Spain (383–388), a theological controversy erupted over Spanish originated Priscillianism. It taught an unorthodox monophysite doctrine that Jesus differed from God only in name, a creed that flew in the face of the Holy Trinity agreed by the Council of Nicea of 325. Priscillianism was deemed blasphemous, and Magnus Maximus, seizing an opportunity to win support among the Christian mainstream, sentenced Priscillian to death for sorcery and heresy. Sulpicius Severus, a Gaulish ascetic who wrote of these matters in *Chronicles* (c. 402–404), tells us that Maximus also banished two leading Spanish Priscillians, Bishop Instantius and Bishop Tiberianus, to Silia Insula (the Isle of Scilly).[14] Why Scilly was chosen is for conjecture. Were Christians already there? There is no archaeological evidence until the sixth century. Perhaps it was still a center of paganism and therefore punishment enough for heretics? Worthy of note is the Latin use of the singular expression Silia Insula, the one main island of antiquity.

Saints, Saxons and Sagas

Analysis of broken lettering on a memorial stone lying flat near the south doorway of the ruins of the later Benedictine priory in Tresco, located now within the 19th century Abbey Gardens, confirms Christian presence in the sixth century. Excavations reveal an enclosed cemetery on St. Helen's by 700. The earliest churches or oratories were small simple cells, often without ornamentation, as noted in the case of the Manx *keeills*, and Scilly seems to have had several of these by the sixth century. The best known is a stone oratory on St. Helen's, between St. Martin's and Tresco, excavated in the 1960s. At Tean, now a small island next to St. Helens, investigation found a smaller and earlier timber-made version. The old version of these times was hermitic but understanding of pre-submergence geography changes that perception. It places the oratories of St. Helen's and Tean on the greater island of Ennor serving a pastoral and fishing community, committed and curious gathering outside for sermons and offerings, the building reserved for the holy man.

How it began is unclear. The most prominent of Scilly place-names endowed with a saint, St. Mary's, doesn't help much since it was a continental import, introduced by 12th century Normans. St. Martin's might reasonably derive from St. Martin of Tours, the fourth century French bishop who opposed death sentences for Priscillians, good enough reason for those on Scilly to venerate him. In most places saints were local worthies, people whose devotion or deeds earned them immortal recognition, worship of them personalizing the new faith for folk long accustomed to deifying their environs. Catholic sources point to Lide (Celtic) or Elidius (Latin) as the one who founded and named St. Helen's. He may or may not have been a Scillonian; some writers identify him as one and the same as Elliau, a sixth century Welsh-born bishop of Llandaff, a center of Celtic Christianity. When plague ravaged Wales in 547, he crossed to Brittany to find hospitality with another prominent Celtic missionary, Samson (c. 390–565). The latter was a British Celtic noble who spent instructional years as a monk on tiny Caldey Island off the south Welsh coast before traveling throughout the southwest and sailing off to Brittany to build monastic communities. Britons looking for land in post–Roman Gaul settled and named Brittany during the sixth century, and Samson was part of that migration. He is acknowledged as an evangelist in the Channel Islands, and the Scilly island of Samson is surely dedicated to the same man.

There is nothing to indicate that Romans imposed any meaningful authority over their lives, and economic life was little different from before, determined by the whims of nature. Scilly's destiny hovered between the two opposite shores of Cornwall and Brittany in post–Roman centuries. Scillonians spoke Cornish, a p–Celtic tongue within the same Brittonic family as Breton and Welsh, so presumably they were at home on either mainland coast. As Germanic immigrants settled chunks of eastern Britain (the future England) change would come, but later rather than sooner. In southwestern Britain, the land west of the river Tamar remained Celtic-speaking in the sixth through ninth centuries. Roman sources point confusingly to three different places in Britain as the home of the Celtic Cornovii[15] but the name stuck only in the extreme southwest as Cornwall. The Saxons came up with *Kern-wealhas*, the "wall" suffix comparable in inference to "wales": a place of foreigners to them. The Cornovii were likely part of the larger confederation of Dumnonii (origin of County Devon), the dominant Celtic group in the area.

Only a small population can be imagined on Scilly, measured in fluctuating hundreds, kindred centered in organization, settled according to tradition and disturbed periodically by refugees. Scilly's association with the Cornovii and tribal Dumnonia is unclear, as is its relationship with the satellite kingdom across in Brittany. Probably it was a law to itself—a rude enclave of survivors and seafarers, and since isolation encouraged it, also a haven for questionable characters and activities. The first authoritative intrusion came in 938 when Athelstan, a successful Germanic Wessex king who imposed his will over the southwest, sent monks to what is now Tresco. Their arrival was testament to the emerging political marriage between church and crown, one cemented in Wessex, where his predecessor Alfred had either been anointed by the church or gone on a pilgrimage to Rome. The accommodation of Saxon religious must have impacted Scilly, and presumably this was part of Athelstan's intention.

Saxons were not the only arrivals in the southwest in the 10th century. Athelstan held off Norse incursions during his reign (925–939) but Scandinavians came ashore eventually. The most famed in saga (*Heimskringla Saga*) was Olaf Tryggvasson, who landed on Scilly c. 988, having heard of a holy seer there who "could tell things beforehand not yet done." The fulfilled prophecy proved to be his succession to the Norse kingship (he was great grandson of Harold Finehair) and Olaf repented his sins and accepted baptism, presumably at the Tresco abbey. Eight years later he became king. Christian saga writers understood the power of providence! Other Norse longships periodically arrived in Scilly waters through the 12th century. *Orkneyinga Saga* tells of a great battle in Mariuhofu or "Port St. Mary" involving the great Orcadian Viking Svein Asleifarson, where "they shared a massive share of plunder,"[16] though it is difficult to imagine that much wealth present on Scilly. On another occasion, again involving Svein, together with a Hebridean comrade-in-arms Holdbodi Hundason, a ship belonging to the monks of Scilly (Tresco?) was relieved of its merchandise. Both incidents might be dated to the 1140s. One thing seems sure; Scilly was a regular port of call. It was a source for fresh water, a source for provisions, a place of shelter, and if the Olaf Tryggvason story is to be accepted, possessed still of a mystical aura.

Frontier Isles

William the Conqueror's invasion of 1066 and subsequent conquest of England did not involve Scilly immediately, even though Cornwall is listed in the Domesday Book inventory of 1086. Scilly was not included. The Domesday Book impression of Cornwall is one of a poor land with sparsely populated small manors. We can only conclude that Scilly was even more so. The first documented mention of Norman intervention came in 1114 when Henry I, youngest son of William the Conqueror, ordered church and lands transferred into Norman-French hands for ecclesiastical and military purpose, part of a wider process to strengthen religious ties with Rome. The Tresco lands were given to the Benedictine order under the authority of the abbey at Tavistock in Devon. The new church was called Ste. Marie de Heumor (read Ennor), the origin of St. Mary's, the same ecclesiastical community that felt Svein Asleifarson's presence.

By 1176 some land had passed into the hands of a Norman vassal, Richard de Wyke, whose forefathers are recorded in Domesday as holding the hamlet of Week St. Mary in northeast Cornwall. Wyke built a small garrison on the south coast (what is now the south coast of St. Mary's) to register his governance, and it became Ennor Castle. A small settlement gathered nearby at Porthenor (Port of Ennor), now Old Town. This is the place *Orkneyinga Saga* called Mariuhofu or Port St. Mary's. There is little left to remind of its medieval past, only the castle shell hidden on a wooded knoll overlooking the small boats harbor. Part of a 12th century Norman church survives (in the sheltered cemetery of which is the grave of the late Harold Wilson, prime minister and island resident). A mile away to the west Hugh Town developed later as an alternative port. At the end of the 12th century Scilly's status was that of a frontier colony, and while native Scillonians may have remained Celts, their church and castle overlords were outsiders, feudal stakeholders in the Norman-French Empire. For the next several centuries there is little in the historical record other than a list of feudal proprietors. Successive Plantagenet kings thought Scilly strategically important enough to appoint governors. Henry III appointed Dreux de Barrentine in 1248 and Edward I appointed Ranulph Blancminister in 1306. His family held fiefs in Cornwall and Yorkshire and was given Scilly on the understanding he would settle 12 armed men to preserve the peace, a body that became part militia and part manorial court. It would be the island council for the next 500 years. Ennor Castle was his residence, though it is difficult to imagine he stayed there much, if indeed at all. Over time Scilly passed to Tresillians, Coleshills and Arundells among others.

Duchy of Cornwall

Scilly was formally associated with Cornwall in 1337, when it was included in the newly created duchy of Cornwall, a gift by Edward III to his eldest son Edward "The Black Prince," famous for his later campaigns in the Hundred Years' War. It was (and still is) a source of independent income for the English royal heir apparent. The title of duke of Cornwall is reserved for the oldest surviving son of the monarch, and when there is no male heir it reverts to the monarch. Cornish tin mining gave the duchy added value. The metal was in great demand for bronze church bells (later for cannon) and Cornish production grew. The working of metals was a royal interest and the Crown levied an annual tax on production from 1156. It also earned dispensations. Edward I gave Cornish tin miners special privileges in 1305, placing them under the separate jurisdiction of *stannary* (tin mine) courts, where they could bring civil suits. It's difficult to know how much of this applied to Scillonians since there is no proof of tin mining there at this time, but the *stannaries* at least indicate that the duchy in which they lived permitted retention of some customs. Scilly's exports were said to be dried fish and seabirds, of which puffins were a valued delicacy. Blancminster paid his annual rent to the Crown either in shillings and pence or puffins.

Daily labors to subsist and monastic prayer routines described the norm, but it is hard to avoid the thought of a clandestine economy involving loot from piracy, smuggling and wrecking; such is the omnipresence of the sea and isolation of Scilly. These activities must have gone on for centuries, whenever there were cargoes of value. Scillonians did not need lessons from Orcadians in that regard. Benedictines in the priory of St. Nicholas's on Tresco told of it, complaining of furtive maritime operations with all the attendant vices. Local lore has it that the monks hanged 112 pirates on one day in 1209! The islands were good havens for pickings from ships in distress whether the ships were in trouble because of treacherous waters or because of some pre-meditated deadly maneuver. Wrecks were so anticipated that they were included in feudal grants to lords as a form of property, a unifying legality offshore.

An Apocalyptic Age

Episodes of storms, floods and coastal inundations were at work everywhere from the 13th century.[17] The sea swallowed the English North Sea ports of Ravensburgh (Yorkshire) and Dunwich (Suffolk). Kent's "Cinque Ports" silted up from deposition, as did the Aberffraw area on Anglesey. In Scilly's case rising sea levels had drowned landscape to form the current island geography by c. 1500, according to Professor Thomas. The loss of terra firma to salt sea was a protracted process and its disruptive effect is hard to gauge, but increasing wetness from the 13th century and concomitant blight and sickness point to the likelihood of difficult times for Scillonians. Desertion of farming settlements in the face of crop failure and pestilence is a general feature of this age. Ennor Castle was in a ruinous state, probably sacked, its collapse either a cause or effect of Scilly as a pirate hangout. The Benedictine community had dwindled, many of them gone because "they dared not stay there."[18] The monastery was not listed in the Tavistock possessions when Henry VIII dissolved the property in the later 1530s.

The portents for revival in 1500 were not good either. Scilly was on the wrong side of Britain to benefit from growing Anglo-Dutch business. When the Tudor dynasty began its rule in 1485, England (and Britain at large) was still little more than an economic satellite of continental Europe, exporting raw wool to cities in Flanders and Brabant and shipping out other natural resources. Henry VII and Henry VIII shifted the emphasis on trade, legislating to prioritize English interests, and a national economy began to emerge, based on the market demand of an expanding London and its environs and reciprocal trade with neighboring continental states. The population of the southeast rose substantially, its vitality well evident from the 16th century, but the Celtic-speaking southwest was less well placed to benefit from Channel and North Sea trade, its lands less productive, excepting tin, and it suffered comparatively. Statesmanship rather than economics impacted Scilly. In the aftermath of excommunication by Pope Clement VII for divorce and remarriage decisions (1533), Henry VIII and his advisors radically reoriented the English state by dissolving Catholic monasteries, seizing their wealth, and unseating abbots and bishops in the House of Lords. Tavistock was one of those to go and with it the Tresco priory. The ecclesiastical lands were annexed to that of the duchy of Cornwall, and by 1550 Scilly was under the direct rule of the Tudors.

Henry VIII centralized power to a degree not seen since the Romans. Wales disappeared as a separate political entity in 1536 with English common law, county administration and land law overriding Celtic custom. English became the official language of its courts. Traditional landholding based on kinship rights, permissible within Norman-French feudal arrangements, was replaced with individual landowners under Crown patronage, usually English. The Council of the West was set up in 1537 to point the duchy of Cornwall in the same direction as Wales, judicially and militarily. It was short-lived, its work apparently done by 1547. Within two years, however, two rebellions erupted, precipitated by several factors. One was outrage at overrule of local power and another was the Act of Uniformity (1549) making the Anglican Book of Common Prayer compulsory in all churches. The dissent was suppressed, but it is not insignificant that Celtic Cornwall should feel aggrieved. A close bond existed between its kinship based culture and Catholicism, one comparable to Irish society where unprecedented pressure from Tudor interference was also felt. The old religion was not given up so readily. Yet the Celtic culture of the British southwest was fated despite the protest. Translation of biblical texts into Cornish does not seem to have developed or survived, a way to preserve the status and currency of a vernacular tongue, and the Cornish language began its descent into oblivion. In Cornish history the 16th century was an apocalyptic age, and Scilly felt some or all of it.

A different threat grew on the Scilly horizon in the dread form of corsair ships—pirates from the Barbary ports of Algiers, Tripoli, and Tunis—looking to seize cargoes, ships and crew (in some cases shipping the latter off to North African slave markets). A recent publication on the subject[19] includes a description of an attack on a Cornish village by scimitar wielding Islamic warriors who seized villagers to carry them off to Morocco for sale. The corsairs probably used Scilly as a haven, but whether there was collusion with the islanders is unknown; the population was probably very small, estimated at around 250 in 1550, reason enough to look for safe anchorage there. What is verifiable is that Scilly attracted Tudor attention in a short conflict with the French in 1549–50 during the short reign of Edward VI. The war was fought at Boulogne in the eastern Channel, but it prompted orders to shore up all vulnerable points of entry. Around 150 men were transferred from a new garrison at Falmouth in Cornwall to St. Mary's and Tresco, where new fortifications were built. It marked the beginning of a new life for Scilly, as royal watchdog of the western Channel, to be a lookout post for enemy ships including corsairs. The role might be interpreted as recognition of its own lawlessness; it takes a thief to catch one! Certainly Sir Francis Godolphin, appointed governor by Elizabeth I in 1571, was shocked by it. He reported only gorse bushes and pirates and praised Edward VI for having fortified the place. The Godolphins (formerly Godolghan) held a Cornish lineage back to 1100 and were highly influential through lands and marriage alliances to other prominent families, having made a fortune from rich alluvial tin streams in south Cornwall. The mansion of Godolphin House, seven miles northwest of Helston, bears witness to their prominence in Cornwall. The family would hold the Scilly lease for over 200 years with judicial powers over life and death.

Spanish Invasion Fears

The reigns of Henry VIII and Elizabeth I witnessed enforcement of a harsh surrender-and-regrant land policy to secure loyalty in vulnerable regions, usually associated with the setting up of English-run plantations in Celtic Ireland, but applicable to the British southwest. Scilly was re-peopled just as surely as were parts of Ireland. The earlier depopulation likely made it less disruptive but new settlers changed the composition nevertheless, some from as far away as Shropshire, families with English names like Banfield, Mumford and Edwards. English Scilly began under the Tudors.

The port of Hugh Town (taking its name from an old word for garrison: *hue*) exemplified the fresh start, its position on a sandbar giving it northern and southern shores, preferable to the medieval anchorage of Porthenor, now truly Old Town. The new garrison did not have to wait long for excitement. News in 1588 of a Spanish flotilla sailing into the Channel in tight formation with 24,000 sailors and soldiers on board must have filtered through from local seafarers. This was no social visit. The 130-ship armada was under orders from Philip II to mobilize Catholic support in England and overthrow Elizabeth I. Its failure is one of the great stories in naval history. What is often not appreciated is that for a decade afterward rumors of other armadas proliferated, some with good cause. In autumn 1590 the Duke of Parma, a key figure in the Spanish Armada expedition of 1588, invaded France with 30,000 Spanish troops and took up position in Brittany. There was great fear in the southwest, not least in Hugh Town, of imminent attack. Scilly was a convenient launching pad for any invading force. The garrison had been reduced since Edward's time with the numbers down to fewer than 30 soldiers and gunners. The harbor was well regarded (sea captains' reports to the Admiralty claimed it could anchor over a hundred sail) but if those ships were Spanish, they would not be easily driven out.

The famed Elizabethan courtier Sir Walter Raleigh, in his new capacity as Captain of the Guard, arranged for a hundred men to be on alert on the mainland, ready to go to Scilly's defense upon warning from fire beacons on the islands. There were reports of a score or more vessels out at sea, although it is unclear whether the ships were friend or foe. These were worrying times for Sir Francis Godolphin. However, the Spanish force hit the Penzance coast instead, retreating only when ships arrived from Plymouth, sent by another celebrated sea dog, Sir Francis Drake. The threat was over, but a sum of £400 was allocated out of Cornish customs revenue nonetheless to build a stronger fort on Scilly, one that might better defend the harbor. Scillonians were given the task of building it, on the west-facing rocky promontory reached by the isthmus of Hugh Town. The fort became the octagonal shaped Star Castle.

Star Castle

Scilly missed the action but was left with a tangible asset in Star Castle, its best surviving historic building (now a fine hotel). The later Charles II, then Prince Charles, stayed there in flight from Cromwell's army. The English Civil War had begun in 1642, and in June 1645 parliamentary forces routed 7,500 royalists at the Battle of Naseby. The 15-year old prince spent that autumn and winter in Launceston and Truro, where as Duke of Cornwall he could demand hospitality. His Cornish respite was shattered early in 1646, however, by news of the approaching forces of Cromwell's able general, Thomas Fairfax. He found an escape route through the aid of Scilly's governor, Sir Francis Godolphin III. The Godolphins, like the Stanleys of Man and Carterets of Jersey, were not yet prepared to bite the royal hand that fed them. The young prince sailed from Pendennis Castle with around 300 royalist refugees to take hospitality at Star Castle. The party was not altogether the object of sympathy: there is a story of belongings stolen en voyage. He stayed with his entourage for six weeks before retreating further to Jersey in the Channel Islands, as we shall see in that chapter.

With the prince gone, Scilly came under the command of Colonel Anthony Buller of the parliamentary forces, but local royalists did not concede so readily. A recapture in 1648–49 was organized with the assistance of the governor, still at large, under the command of Sir John Grenville, a prominent Cornish noble (his father was killed in action 1643). The newly established parliamentary garrison in Star Castle was overthrown, a victory that ran contrary to the grain elsewhere, since this was the time when Charles I was tried and executed. Rebellious Scilly went back to pirating ways, this time serving as a base for so-called "sea tories," royalist privateers who sought to attack parliamentary ships. Privateers were privately owned vessels commissioned by European governments to capture enemy commerce; a ship-owner obtained a *letter of marque* from the Crown (in the islands this could be the governor) to permit the privateer to share booty with crew and Crown. It is a trifle ironic that the same nefarious practices condemned by the first Godolphin were now encouraged by the third.

The presence of a hostile Dutch fleet spurred Parliament into action in 1651, friction caused by passage of the first Navigation Act, a measure detrimental to Dutch shipping interests since it gave a monopoly in English ports to English shipping. A Somerset-born naval commander, Admiral Robert Blake, was sent to secure the islands, and he set up a base on the southern tip of Tresco at Carn Near (now named Oliver's Battery) to bombard any ships in "The Roads," the sea channel between Tresco and St. Mary's, trying to enter Hugh Town. Blake's occupying force of 2,500 dwarfed the island community numerically. The defending royalist strength under Sir John Grenville was only around 50. Such show of force was a sort of backhanded commendation of Scilly, a bane of insurrection but a place worth taking. How welcome it was among Scillonians is not known. At any rate Blake's strategy worked and the royalists surrendered. A round tower on the western Tresco shore called Cromwell's Castle marks the return of parliamentary control with the older garrison above it built by Edward VI in 1550 (renamed King Charles' Castle to register royalist sympathies) overthrown. The surrender of the Channel Islands a few months later ended any lingering royalist hopes of landing troops in Cornwall to revive the exiled king's cause. Another native of the southwest, the Cornish Lieutenant-Colonel Joseph Hunkin of Cromwell's New Model Army, arrived to govern Scilly, putting to death or flight hostile royalists.

Déjà Vu

Restitution came after Cromwell's death and the Stuart Restoration. Charles II was installed in 1660 and royal favors were quickly bestowed. The fiefdom of Scilly was born again with Sir Francis Godolphin III returning as governor for a second time and Sir John Grenville, imprisoned during Cromwell's Protectorate, elevated in the ranks. He became earl of Bath and governor of the garrison at Plymouth, part of his watch being the waters of Scilly. The islands never again entertained British leaders in flight, the 1960s premier Harold Wilson's choice of it as a holiday getaway notwithstanding. Godolphin interest in the Scilly estate evaporated as their military obligations declined in a post-feudal age, and management of the islands was typically left to their stewards and the part militia/part council initiated under Ranulph Blancminister in the early 14th century.

The Reformation and anti–Catholic sentiment weakened (though not eliminated) Cornish ties with Celtic-speaking Brittany, and so too did the influx of English speakers to work expanding tin and copper mines in the southwest. The digging of subterranean veins and smelting of ore advanced, and a new lease signed between Sidney First Earl of Godolphin (1645–1712) and the Crown in 1698 for the yearly rental of £40, payable to the duchy of Cornwall, gave him sole rights to profits and control of tin mining and any other minerals on Scilly. There is good reason why he might have felt bullish about prospects. In that same year, a Devonshire man, Thomas Savery, successfully demonstrated his "Miner's Friend," a steam powered vacuum pump to reduce mine flooding. Annual Cornish tin production had peaked at around 600 tons in the 14th century, but by 1700 it reached 100,000 tons. Copper output was even greater. The business potential of southwestern metal appeared rosy. The anticipation and realization of profits on Scilly did not equate, however, and the tin leases were fairly short-lived. William Borlace (*A Natural History of Cornwall*, 1758) visited in 1752 and was surprised not to find more extensive tin mining traces. He looked at two workings on Tresco, both dating back to the 1640s, but apparently neither was commercially successful. Forty years later Governor Francis Osborne, the fifth Duke of Leeds, also attempted to mine tin on Scilly (1791–1792) but made nothing. Another abortive attempt followed in the early 19th century with prospective investors advised of a tin mining tradition stretching back to the Phoenicians (read Carthaginians!). Whether the failure was to do with production costs, transportation costs, mainland competition or just a plain lack of quality veins is not clear; it seems the historic tin treasures were more reputation than fact. Scilly's primary asset remained the sea.

Sea-Girt Scilly

Scilly was a port of call for ships leaving and entering the Channel from prehistory, whether legitimate or pirate, an anchorage demanding payments in one form or another. Scillonians could pilot local waters and supply provisions, shelter and freshwater. Certain island families must have been well known to the crews who visited regularly. However the concentration of warships begun with Henry VIII's Royal Navy made piracy an increasingly risky occupation in the Channel by the 17th century, and pirate action shifted to the Atlantic and Caribbean. Shipwrecks were always a lucrative alternative income source, if similarly unpredictable. Dangerous rocky waters replete with reefs and shoals helped out in the demolition work. A coal-burning lighthouse was operational on St. Agnes in 1680 though the governor had been against it because it would lead to a loss of revenue from wrecks![20] Sidney Godolphin's lease renewal in 1698 reasserted the proprietor rights of old, "the moiety of all Ship-wreck to be divided between the said Sidney, Lord Godolphin, and the King," but preventing scavenging was another matter: what the sea cast up belonged to those that found it, unless someone informed on them.

The church did not necessarily discourage these actions. The fruits of the sea were the fruits of the sea, however they were discharged, God's will to aid the poor and needy. One oft-told Scilly story has a parson in St. Agnes' church begin his sermon with the words, "Brethren, I have a sad duty to perform, there has been a wreck..." his church emptying before he finished! The moral consensus was better the rocks of Scilly than the rocks of anywhere else. Perhaps the parson joined his flock, clerical stipends being small and parsons probably not being averse to sharing in any little pickings providence might send their way. Tales of wreckers deliberately shining lamps to mislead and lure ships into danger, of wreckers killing the survivors to claim booty, are chilling enough, but they cede first place to the murderous elements themselves. Howling gales and boiling white water washing over unseen jagged rocks could serve up ships to the slaughter readily enough without onshore assistance.

A good percentage of the little that has been written about the history of Scilly reflects on these terrible shipwrecks, as do exhibits in Hugh Town's Scilly Museum. Scilly's waters did not discriminate. In October 1707, four ships of the fleet of Rear Admiral Sir Cloudesley Shovell, a national hero of the day, sailing from Toulon, struck the Western Rocks, four miles southwest of Star Castle. The vessels did not stand a chance in hostile pounding surf, and 1,600 crew and officers went down including the admiral. A popular but unproven island story has it that locals found his body (or murdered him) and having pulled an emerald ring from his finger, stripped him and buried him in the sand.[21] A granite monument on Porth Hellick beach on St. Mary's marks the spot. The body was recovered later and reburied in Westminster Abbey. It appears that the admiral set a wrong course, and his miscalculation is claimed as a precipitating spark in the search for a means of determining longitude. The rocks continued to be unforgiving. In 1798 *HMS Colossus*, a 74-gun frigate returning to England from Admiral Horatio Nelson's victory over the French at the Battle of the Nile, came to grief on a shallow reef off Samson. There was only one casualty on this occasion, but a fine collection of Etruscan funerary vases belonging to Sir William Hamilton, ambassador to the Kingdom of the Two Sicilies in Naples, was lost. His other claim to fame was to be the husband of Nelson's mistress. On this occasion neither landlord nor tenants got the prize; divers salvaged it from dense underwater weed in 1975 and the contents are in the British Museum.

Bishop Rock Lighthouse has been the first and last sight of Britain for seafarers in the modern era. A gray tower balanced on a small rock, it was constructed with some difficulty in 1858. Yet despite the presence of lighthouses, ships have still come to grief. In 1875 the German transatlantic liner *Schiller,* sailing from Hamburg to New York via Plymouth, was driven by heavy seas onto rocks at Retarrier Ledges, the Western Rocks again. It went down in minutes with over 300 lives lost. A merchant ship, *The Cita,* sank off Porth Hellick, St. Mary's, in March 1997 en route from Southampton to Belfast. Some of its cargo of miscellaneous consumer goods is in the local museum. Some reputedly found a way into islanders' homes, old habits dying hard!

If wrecking was one diversion then smuggling was another. Smuggling was a mainstay of Cornish economic life for centuries. A demand for duty-free luxuries, a need for fishing communities to supplement paltry incomes, and a geography of secreted coves on inaccessible coastlines all helped make it so. It may have been unlawful but it was too important economically for wholesale prosecutions. Officialdom benefited too. Prior to the 16th century, smuggling efforts concentrated on getting goods like tin out of the region, to evade a 12th century export duty. When Tudor and Stuart mercantilist policies sought duty protection from foreign imports, the illicit trafficking switched to shipping goods onshore. A Customs House was set up in Hugh Town in 1682, but they had their work cut out. The penalty for smuggling was death but local law enforcement, sometimes complicit, was capable of turning a blind eye. Aided by swift sailing cutters, a complex cross–Channel smuggling network grew with strongholds in the Channel Islands, Brittany, Cornwall and Scilly. It reached its peak in the 18th century with wines, spirits, tobacco, silks, laces, tea — anything taxable — all fair game and in transit. The consequence was a reduction in customs revenue and legitimate business profits, obviously a matter of concern in London. In the 1780s, after the American War of Independence, Prime Minister William Pitt (the Younger) lowered duties to undermine reasons for smuggling, but the French Revolution in 1789 and the Napoleonic War delayed further trade reforms. From the 1820s a new legislative wave to reduce tariffs got underway with efforts stepped up to ensure collection of surviving duties. The net result was to place smuggling on the wane, good news for government and legitimate business but hardship for those who had become dependent on it.

Poverty Isles

The principal arbiter of economic security was the sea, and while it unloaded a ship's cargo from time to time, its generosity could not be relied upon. To seek its cooperation, Scillonians had always taken to boats themselves, supplementing land crofts with inshore catches of lobster, shellfish, crabs, conger eel, mackerel, plaice, cod, and so on. Porpoises, dolphins and seals visited the shore, as did whales from time to time. It all helped but was never enough. Baptist and Methodist missionaries, visiting during the later 18th century, some of them staying, were shocked by the poverty, though it helped them appreciate the temptations of smuggling while opposing it in principle. If the experience of founding Methodist John Wesley (1703–1791) was representative then there was a desperate side to life on the islands. He preached in a Hugh Town street on his evangelist travels in 1743, the Anglican minister having refused him the church, and he recalled the wildness of the people in his journal: "They were ready to tear both them [his tracts] and me to pieces," he wrote, happy to be departing the following day from what he called this "barren dreary place."[22]

As we saw previously in the Scottish islands, there was money in burnt seaweed or kelp. Production began on Scilly in 1684 (the first place in the UK) and grew during the 18th century with the alkali of value to makers of glass and soap. It thrived until the post–Napoleonic era. The shutting down of kilns in the second quarter of the 19th century cleared the air of putrid seaweed stench but compounded the social distress, already impacted by the demise of smuggling and poor potato harvests. The Isles of Scilly Museum displays part of a letter written in 1818 appealing for aid after the collapse of kelp prices. With few viable alternatives poverty persisted. An archaeological team excavating on Samson in 1977 found a dwelling measuring 12 feet by 23 feet, little different in construction or dimension from those of two millennia earlier. The last two families on the island, the Woodcocks and Webbers, had lived there between 1837 and 1855. The Woodcocks had been in Scilly since the 17th century but according to local lore were involved in a long-running feud with Banfields and Mumfords, influential families on the medieval council since Elizabeth I and often deputies of the ruling Godolphins. The feud probably explains the Woodcocks' isolation on Samson. The team found pottery fragments, brass buttons, gunflints and a daily diet writ in middens of limpet shells. If potatoes or oats failed then boiled limpets—so-called sea-beef—were always a last resort. Hunger was a fact of life. This does not seem to have bothered Walter Besant, a Portsmouth-born writer, who found enchantment in such simplicity by weaving a romance about a Samson heroine, Armorel Rosevean, in his *Armorel of Lyonesse* (1890). She leaves the island to find experience in the outer world, only to return eventually to her beloved Samson. A century later, Michael Morpurgo, a writer of children's books, found use for the same island in *Why the Whales Came* (1985), recasting it as cursed, domain of the mad Birdman, and the book became a movie. The 1861 census showed the real Samson as uninhabited.

Augustus Smith

By the 1820s the Godolphins had ruled Scilly for two and a half centuries, though in practice they delegated authority to leading families like the Banfields and Mumfords and the medieval council, by now called the Select Vestry. It met periodically to rule on local complaints and misdemeanors. Change came from an outside source. Although Scillonians still supplemented incomes by supplying visiting ships (most successfully during the Napoleonic War, when thousands of bushels of potatoes were grown for British troop ships) the economy had not progressed much beyond subsistence. As much as anything one person changed that, a law-abiding, non-aristocratic and fiercely ideological individual named Augustus Smith. He has been variously portrayed as an altruistic Victorian entrepreneur, in keeping with how the rest of Britain was reinventing itself, or a self-seeking imperialistic autocrat. Whatever else, he was a radical break with the past.

The foundation of Scilly's new lease on life was the 15 or so years following the Napoleonic War, tough ones in many parts of rural Britain with high bread prices, land enclosures, and the threat to traditional rhythms of work posed by new industrial machines. By 1830, bands of agricultural laborers throughout southern and southwestern England were in protest: the era of "Captain Swing" and the so-called "Last Laborers' Revolt." In Scilly's case, the declining kelp business, a series of poor harvests, and isolation persuaded the lessee, George Osborne, fifth Duke of Leeds, representing the Godolphin family, that Scilly was a liability he did not need (John Murray of the Isle of Man reached the same conclusion at a similar time and sold out to the Crown). In 1831 Osborne surrendered tenure back into the hands of those who gave it in the first place, the duchy of Cornwall. Three years later the duchy granted a 99-year lease to one Augustus Smith. Born in 1804 to a Hertfordshire family, its money derived from London banking, Smith was educated at Harrow and Christchurch Oxford. Years before the famous apologist of Victorian entrepreneurship Samuel Smiles wrote *Self-Help* (1859), Augustus Smith was as eager as an evangelist to prove similar convictions—the belief that self-improvement was the best salvation for the poor. He paid £20,000 for the lease in 1834 (it included an undertaking to pay the local clergy) and promptly moved in. He would be no absentee landlord, arriving in 1834 and living there until his death in 1872, a tenure of some 38 years. Not unlike his Roman emperor namesake, this Augustus was also a moralist and benevolent despot. He knew what was right for others and was going to make sure that they got it whether they wanted it or not. One of his first actions was to make a new ruling on sub-letting.

Before Smith secured the lease, surveyors Edward and George Driver had been ordered by the duchy of Cornwall to report on Scilly's leaseholds. They found a plethora of sub-let smallholdings held on verbal agreements, a product of centuries of administrative neglect by the Godolphins. Sub-letting guaranteed everyone a piece of land, however small, and was customary inheritance practice. It served community needs but was not conducive to agribusiness. Smith announced that any tenant who sub-let land without his permission would have his tenancy terminated. Sub-letting is one reason why the potato famine hit western and southern Ireland with such devastating consequences in the 1840s, as more and more people became dependent on less and less land (most in the hardest hit areas lived on five acres and less) and a crop fungus left them vulnerable to hunger and starvation. Although population density never came close to the level it did in rural Ireland, Scilly's population had risen substantially. For centuries it fluctuated in the hundreds (250 in 1551; 500 in 1720) and then Scillonians too grew potatoes. The high yield per acre made it possible to support a family with a few acres, and by the Napoleonic War there were close to 2,000 residents. The census of 1841 reported an unprecedented 2,788, some 600 more than today.

Smith's order on sub-letting assumes a poignant urgency in light of the Irish experience. He made possible viable productive land units, even allowing for the smallness of the islands, preventing one-crop subsistence dependency from further growth. In the fullness of time, his land reforms appear wise, engineering the foundations necessary for change into a monetary economy. The average landholdings are about 20 acres now, four times greater than the "at-risk" land units of Ireland's potato famine. Malthusian fears of Scillonians outstripping resources were allayed. By 1901 the population had steadied at 2,288. On the other hand as sub-letting disappeared, a familiar way of life disappeared too. Adjustments for the dispossessed were not easy. His land rationalization and evictions met with virulent local opposition on occasion. On Samson the Woodcocks and Webbers did not leave of their own volition, but were evicted under protest. Dirt poor and bedraggled they may have been, but the individuality of small island life fed a sense of personal independence that was not easily given up, whatever the material privations.

Smith represented the Cornish constituency of Truro in the House of Commons, but there is not much to suggest that he was a parliamentarian in his own backyard. As democratic rights unfolded in Britain, he chose to rule Scilly as an autocrat, despite the fact that voting rights were extended twice during his lifetime (1832 and 1867). All that might be said in his defense is that some ruthlessness was necessary to roll back centuries of deteriorating conditions. The Select Vestry was the nominal local government, but, like its medieval predecessor, it was not much of a check on the governor's power. Smith dominated it and was called variously "The

Governor," "My Lord," and "The Emperor of Scilly." Not all of his decisions were in the spirit of capitalism. A requirement of primogeniture in land inheritance, for example, was a throwback to medieval times. His social decrees were draconian. Young people were forbidden to marry until they had a house to live in and if they did not become self-supporting they were banished to the mainland. Meanwhile Smith lived as an aristocrat, having a house built on Tresco, close to the ruins of the old Benedictine priory, calling it, with a nod to the medieval past, "The Abbey."

Pretensions apart, Smith was a Victorian with an appreciation of the possibilities of his times, convinced for example that education was a way to correct bad habits (smuggling et al.). He made schooling compulsory before it was on the mainland. Parents had to pay a penny a week or two pennies if their children stayed at home. An HM Inspector of Schools Report in 1848 was favorable on the result, commenting on basic literacy and number skills plus knowledge of some English history. Ten years later the nationwide Newcastle Commission (1858) found that the vast majority of British children left elementary day schools without attaining even that minimum standard. Smith set in motion infrastructure improvements with road construction and a quayside extension at Hugh Town (1836). A boat-building industry had grown up in the 18th century to service kelp exports, and despite the decline of kelp production it boomed in Smith's time. St. Mary's had four boatyards by 1850, in what was really a market response to shipping orders boosted by new free trade laws. However, the wooden hulled sailboats were unable to compete with the materials science and motive force of technological revolution in the later 19th century. Smith did not live to see it, but the yards had closed by the 1880s. To add insult to injury, in a new maritime age of steel-hulled turbine driven ships Scilly would no longer be used as a port of call.

Augustus Smith's greatest legacy came out of his own garden. Taking advantage of the mild frost-free climate, he began a sub-tropical garden in the south of Tresco, triggering a remarkable economic metamorphosis. Some of the plants he introduced came from the botanical gardens at Kew in London while sailors brought others from places around the world. Equable year-round temperatures, the construction of sheltering high walls, and dedicated attention of garden workers combined to make Tresco a commercial success. When Smith arrived, it was a treeless windswept island covered in bramble and broom. At his death there was a seven-acre garden with over 100 species, many of them specimens never cultivated before in the UK. Smugglers had become market gardeners! After the railway reached Cornish Penzance in 1859, adventurous trippers took ferryboats out to Tresco from the mainland to admire the gardens.

Flower Power

Smith's successor was his nephew Algernon Dorrien Smith, who took up residence in 1874, aged 26. A father to six children, the second Smith extended Tresco Abbey with a great square tower, but more importantly for Scillonians, he encouraged the cut-flower industry. Impetus came from growers in Guernsey in the Channel Islands, where an experimental consignment of daffodils had been sent to London's Covent Garden market in the 1860s. Scilly responded competitively when Augustus Smith was still alive (the Scilly Museum credits a St. Mary's farmer, William Trevellick, as among the first) and under Algernon Dorrien Smith the enterprise took off. What Augustus had begun, Algernon and successors turned into a lucrative Scilly specialty. In a vote of confidence, the duchy extended the lease by 31 years in 1884, affording further incentive.

As town took over from country in Britain, flower growers found demand from new urban dwellers, specifically those craving the nostalgia of fragrance and color in a smoky, indelicate age, whether on window ledges, shelves or tabletops. The fresh flower business boomed with year round activity of planting, picking and packing. Monterey pines were introduced from California to better shield the plants from Atlantic gales. Arthur Dorrien Smith, Algernon's son, carried on the horticultural enterprise in 1918. Thousands of tons of boxed bulbs and blooms made their way to London — daffodils, lilies and the famed *Soleil d'Or* (Tazetta Aurea) or "Sol" as it is more familiarly known, a rich yellow narcissus with several flowers on each stalk and a rich sweet scent. Edwardian Scilly was a different proposition than the one John Wesley encountered, the temper of the place radically altered with a new *raison d'être* in flowers. J.G. Uren, a Penzance postmaster who knew Scilly well and wrote about it in *Scilly and the Scillonians* (1907), found the islanders to be a mostly God-fearing and law-abiding lot, more given to propriety than excess, not at all the wild bunch of old. The islanders recovered some long lost political autonomy in 1891, benefiting from democratizing local government reforms to get their own representative council and the possibility of electing and being elected, although the Dorrien-Smiths continued to dominate the leadership of it.

Battle Stations

The onset of world wars evoked Scilly's past for a while as gunboats, garrisons and ordnance surfaced. Algernon Dorrien-Smith and his son both held military officer rank. In the first war a seaplane base was established at Porthmellon on St. Mary's, and after the creation of the Royal Naval Air Service (RNAS), a station was set up on Tresco to keep an eye open for U-boat activity. Following the fall of France and the Channel Islands (1940) in World War II, Scilly assumed a greater role. Two air-sea rescue launches were stationed on St. Mary's, Hurricane fighter planes used the airstrip in the Battle of Britain and Scilly was again a center of anti-submarine activity. The hostile marine environment played its part too — the infamous Western Rocks and Wolf Rock taking out enemy submarines — but it was in covert operations that Scilly was able to play a special role, revisiting its clandestine past.

In the same year (1942) that the "Shetland Bus" sought to ease beleaguered Norway, Special Forces sailed out of New Grimsby Sound, Tresco, in trawlers refitted and painted to look like Breton ships, bound for Nazi occupied French beaches. The mission was to maintain lines of communication with Confrèrie-Nôtre-Dame (CND), largest of the French underground intelligence networks, by dropping and collecting agents and mail and rendering aid in whatever way feasible. RAF planes escorted the vessels halfway across the Channel, but it was in the third quarter of the crossing that crews faced the gravest danger since they were in waters ruled *verboten* to fishing craft. Closer to the Breton shore they looked for anonymity of association with other home trawlers. Most sought to rendezvous with the boat of the prominent French Resistance leader Colonel Gilbert Renault (alias "Remy") off the west Breton coast near the fishing port of Concarneau. In one notable operation Remy was liberated from the menace of Gestapo by a trawler under RN command but crewed mostly by fishermen.

Modern Realignment

Military presence brought welcome economic stimulus, but two swallows did not make a summer. The Dorrien Smith flower enterprise was only beneficial to those involved, and material life otherwise (compared to the mainland) remained less than auspicious after World War II. The 25 miles or so separating Scilly from Cornwall was (and still is) isolating. Helicopter service arrived before electricity did, at least for the inhabited off-islands (St. Mary's having a generator in 1931). An undersea cable from St. Mary's finally gave the off-islanders in 1985 what other Britons had had for over 50 years, with mainland grid connection following by means of a 36-mile undersea cable from St. Just in Cornwall (1989). Emigration had by then already depleted Scilly of many native sons and daughters as surely as it did other offshore islands, the push and the pull forces of such movement doing battle with emotional ties felt for their island-world. The numbers have held up despite exodus because of newcomers attracted by marketing promise of mild temperatures and two seasons, spring and summer! The population hovered just above 2,000 for most of the 20th century.

The political patriarchy of the lessees finally ended after World War II. The oligarchic Select Vestry was abolished in 1891, but the Dorrien-Smiths served as hereditary chairmen of the new council until elections for that office were finally introduced in 1955. In a twist of fate, George Woodcock, of the same lineage as the evicted Samson family who ran foul of Augustus Smith, became chairman of the new council. It now functions within the Cornish District of Penwith. Scilly is part of the St. Ives (Cornwall) electoral constituency for British parliamentary elections. Although the feudal past is not all past — the duchy still owns virtually all of the freehold land (only Hugh Town is excepted) and maintains a land steward's office there — Scilly has responded to changing circumstance, and the circumstances have changed. Commercial fishing employs only a small number. Its Cornish market is Newlyn near Penzance, but competition and EU constraints render significant growth unlikely. Agricultural land now represents less than 40 percent of the inhabited islands' land area. The salt-laden winds and high soil acidity do not help productivity for commercial gain, despite hedged enclosures. The horticultural prospects are not as rosy as they once were either, with EU and international competition plus high freight costs unfavorable. By 2002 flower farming was less than 15 percent of Scilly's income. Since it has become more expensive to take Scilly to market, a new thrust has been to bring a market to Scilly.

The Friendly Isles

In that vein the islands have found a new niche in natural history tourism. The annual night-stay and day visitors are counted now in six digits, numbers not equaled over entire centuries in the past. In a gesture to Scilly's unique natural habitat, the duchy leased the uninhabited islands to the Environmental Trust for a hundred years at a peppercorn rent. Visitors outnumber residents in the summer, especially on St. Mary's where 70 percent of them arrive. Star Castle, opened as a hotel by the future Edward VIII in 1933, is transformed into a five-star resort with a powerful launch for the exclusive use of guests. Robert A. Dorrien Smith (grandson of Arthur), lessee of Tresco, opened a garden heliport in 1983 to bring in tourist helicopter trade to the Abbey Gardens. Scheduled ferries and air services, yachts and cruise ships help support shops and services. Tourism is now the mainstay of the economy, accounting for about 85 percent of income. Available bed spaces registered with the Isles of Scilly Council rose by 50 percent from 1974 to 1991, but traffic is variable from year to year and any downturn can have far-reaching effects. Employment patterns have seen an increase in part-time work but not full-time jobs.[23]

If demography is destiny, as Auguste Comte once asserted, then the majority of Scillonians will be in the senior citizen category by the mid–21st century. Savvy property development marketing as the "Fortunate Isles" or "Isles of the Blest"—hardly appropriate monikers historically—have brought longer-term stays ashore with an annual increase in retirees and the number of second homes. The holiday-retreat of the late Harold Wilson (Labor Prime Minister, 1964–1970 and 1974–1976) got Scilly national attention as somewhere pleasant to spend the autumn years. His bungalow on St. Mary's named "Lowenva" is a very modest affair, at least judged from the curbside. The same cannot be said for more recent housing development with prices well above the national average. Around one-third of all housing stock was second homes in 2000. For Scilly-born residents access to affordable housing is a critical ongoing issue as rises in home prices and local wages are not in equilibrium, a contentious offshore question all the way to Shetland.

---

1. Vyvyan, C.C., *The Scilly Isles* (Robert Hale, 1953), 90.

2. Thomas, Charles, *Exploration of a Drowned Landscape: Archaeology and History of the Isles of Scilly* (Batsford Books, 1985), 22–31.

3. Thomas, 48.

4. Blakeney, E.H., ed., *Herodotus: Histories* (Everyman's Library, 1997), Bk. II, 125.

5. Hawkes, C.F.C., "Pytheas, Europe and the Greek Empire," print of the JL Myers Memorial Lecture, New College, University of Oxford, May 20, 1975, 45.

6. Cunliffe, Barry, *Pytheas the Greek: The Man Who Discovered Britain* (Penguin Books, 2001), 97.

7. *Rufus Festus Avienus: Ora Maritima*, Murphy, J.P., trans., (Ares Publishing, 1977), lines 117–121.

8. *Avienus*, lines 121–129.

9. *Avienus,* lines 113–115.

10. *Pliny the Elder: Natural History*, Healy, John F., trans., (Penguin Classics, 1991), Bk. II. 169, 33.

11. Thomas, 153.

12. *Pliny the Elder*, Bk. IV.103, 52.

13. Thomas, 172.

14. Ashbee, Paul, *Ancient Scilly: From the First Farmers to the Early Christians* (David & Charles, 1974), 223.

15. Snyder, Christopher A., *The Britons* (Blackwell Publishing, 2003), 160.

16. *Orkneyinga Saga* Pálsson, Hermann, and Edwards, Paul, trans., (Penguin Classics, 1981), Ch. 100, 207.

17. Lamb, Hubert, *Climate, History and the Modern World*, second ed., (Routledge, 1995), 191.

18. Vyvyan, 26.

19. Milton, Giles, *White Gold* (Hodder and Stoughton), 2004.

20. Harris, Simon, *Sir Cloudesley Shovell: Stuart Admiral* (Spellmount Press, 2001), 337.

21. Harris, 360.

22. Singleton, John, "Wesley's Perilous Voyage," Worldwide Faith News Archive, 8 Jan 1998 (www.wfn.org).

23. Cornwall County Council, "Socio-Economic Profile: Isles of Scilly," 2003 (http://www.cornwall.gov.uk/Facts/Socio-ec/SE003.htm).

7

Isle of Wight:
"John Bull's Other Island"

"She thinks of nothing but the Isle of Wight and she calls it the Island, as if there were no other island in the world"— Jane Austen, *Mansfield Park* (1816), vol. I, ch. II

If there is a corner of some foreign field that is forever England, then home field must be the Isle of Wight. Thatched cottages, manors, old mills, venerable churches and wooded lanes personify a John Bull fancy, neatly tucked into gentle hill folds. Add the small pleasures of its seaside, a healthy sunshine-hours record by meager British standards and an easy reach from the metropolises, and you have the ingredients of an England in miniature, a coffee-table picture book Englishness. It has been the idyll of pre-industrial England since the 19th century, so much so it suffers from nostalgia excess. Paul McCartney sang of Wight summer vacations in "When I'm Sixty-Four." In 1969 visiting American folk-rock luminary Bob Dylan was asked by a BBC TV journalist why he had wanted to come and retorted dryly, "Because I want to see the home of Alfred, Lord Tennyson." The poker-faced singer-songwriter characteristically declined to acknowledge what the reporter knew anyway — namely a three-day open-air rock festival at which Dylan starred — but his instincts were correct. The works of the Victorian poet laureate described an ordered Englishness as well as any, and he kept a home on the island at Freshwater.

The diamond-shaped isle has assumed different hues in different times but in all there is a kinship with avuncular England; it is John Bull's other isle. Queen Victoria loved it so much that she bought an estate, Osborne House. Charles Dickens and Lewis Carroll took working holidays to find material for *David Copperfield* and *Alice in Wonderland* respectively. J.M.W. Turner sketched there. John Keats stayed awhile. Tennyson supposedly composed "Charge of the Light Brigade" (1854 on an island ramble. Longfellow visited Tennyson and Karl Marx took the train down from London for health reasons, calling it a "little paradise." A few years later (1888) communism's implacable foe Winston Churchill spent a summer as a 14-year-old. Not all stayed voluntarily; for King Charles I, imprisoned at Carisbrooke Castle prior to

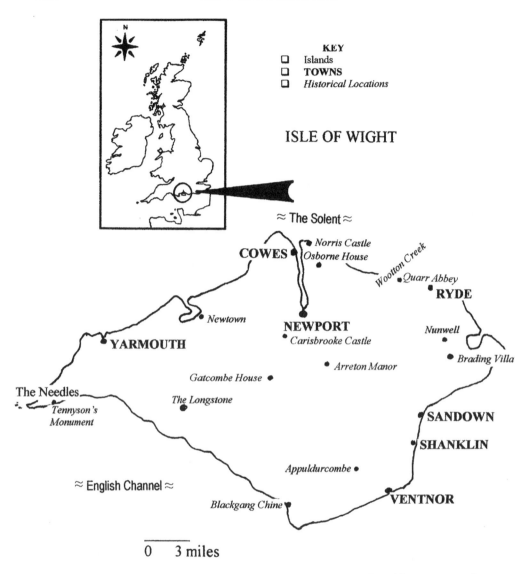

his 1649 execution in London, it was purgatory. Inmates of Parkhurst, one of Britain's maximum-security prisons, only two miles from Carisbrooke, serve out life sentences at the Queen's pleasure. The recent prison roster reads like a chamber of horrors–child-killer Ian Brady, serial murderer Stuart Sutcliffe (a.k.a. "Yorkshire Ripper") and the Kray brothers, notorious London gangsters.

A buckling of rock strata some 40 million years ago pushed up Wight's chalk hills or "downs" to straddle it east to west and make two mini-regions, today lazy rivers and quiet meadows in the north and busy holiday resorts and smuggler coves in the south. An equable climate and fertile lowlands support various forms of farming, but most of the 132,000 residents (2001 census) live in an urban or suburban environment. The island measures 36 miles across and 21 miles from north to south, and there are several sizeable service towns—Newport the administrative center,

Cowes the home of the famous yacht regatta, and resorts of Ryde, Sandown, Shanklin, Ventnor and Yarmouth.

Genesis

Human presence stretches back before it was an island to the impossibly long Paleolithic Period. Notice of activity in Wight's vicinity was served with a 1993 discovery of shinbone fragments and two teeth in a gravel pit 20 miles away at Boxgrove, Sussex, belonging to a tall muscular 20-year-old hominid, his life lived out half a million years ago. Wight has been an island a mere 9,000 years. Post-glacial flooding repositioned it first of all as a coastal contour on the base of a new British island, separate from the Eurasian continental landmass; later the ribbon channel of the Solent formed between Wight and Britain, turning Wight into a peninsula arm connected by a chalk ridge to the west. A final phase was under way by 6000 A.D. as an expansive English Channel submerged the westbound ridge until Wight was alone and free, a diamond shaped stopper guarding the River Test estuary. Not all the evidence is under water; photogenic pointed chalk stacks known as The Needles pierce the waves still, last survivors of the western ridge. The name Wight is likely a corruption of Celtic *gwyth* or "channel," as in channel isle.

Families were putting down roots in the fourth millennium A.D., clearing dense thickets with knapped flint axes, grazing livestock, plowing and harvesting with picks and sickles. Wight has had greater levels of population density than other offshore islands and after all that domesticity megalithic evidence is minimal. There are no known stone circles but in western Wight stands the forlorn Longstone, an upright sandstone monolith, some 20 feet of it above ground. A fallen companion is close by, all that remains of a chambered tomb and once vibrant farming community. A 1990s archaeological survey of the coast between Ryde and Wootton Creek revealed maritime activities from the tomb-builders' time with three Neolithic track ways running seaward at Quarr, visible at a very low tide. They are thought to be access for fish traps, fowling, and reed collection when this coastal stretch was a salt marsh.[1] Ceramic pieces as old as the third millennium A.D. have been found elsewhere on the island, confirming of domesticity in later Neolithic and early Bronze Ages.

If the numbers of Bronze Age round barrows or earthen topped burial sites are any guide (over 240 have been reported) then farming did not deteriorate in the second millennium A.D., at least not to the extent it did in more northerly isles. Grave robbers relieved the barrows of their contents over centuries, but enough has been recovered along the traverse of the chalk ridge — arrowheads, axes and bracelets — from Arreton Down, Moon's Hill, and Chessell Down to suggest a thriving aristocratic culture. The epicenter was only 40 miles away in Wiltshire at Avebury and Stonehenge, famed complex of barrows and stone circles. Toward the end of the second millennium A.D., another change in burial practice grew across Europe, one evident on Wight, described by a preference for cremation over inhumation. Cemetery areas where burial urns were deposited, known as urnfields, have been identified on Afton Down in the west of Wight, near Freshwater. Urnfield presence points to a reformation of values, a metaphysical appreciation of a soul independent of body matter perhaps, although practical considerations (an unwillingness to build elaborate graves for example) cannot be discounted. The change was not comprehensive. Inhumation still continued. Cremation was extensive enough, however, for scholars to characterize "Urnfield Europe" as a cultural departure from the past, precursor of a new age in European prehistory, that of the Celts.

Celtic Wight

Wight continued to be industrious in the last millennium A.D., but alas, there is very little to see. There were settlements at Yafford and Sud Moor in the same southern vicinity as the Barnes urnfield and a farmstead enclosure at Chillerton Down (c. 100 A.D.). Celtic sword and shield fragments have been found. Field surveys in mainland Britain show that Celts plowed their land twice over, with the second plow line set at right angles to the first, and these Celtic Fields have shown up in aerial photography, south of the chalk ridge, where lighter soils were easier to turn over. Given the favorable conditions, residency was probably measured in four digits before the Romans arrived.

The island was engaged in cross–Channel trade and may even have been an entrepôt depot for Cornish tin. Pliny the Elder, citing the fourth century A.D. historian Timaeus, wrote of tin being taken to an island named Ictis for onward shipment, said to be "six days sail up–Channel."[2] Since the Romans named Wight Insula Vectis and the word resembles Ictis, a case is made. There was safe warehouse, mart and distribution potential for the ore, and it is less than a mile across the Solent from Cowes. On the mainland shore is Stansore Point (Latin for tin is *stannum*) where tin may have been ferried across. Some Wight guidebooks talk up a "Tin Trail," an ancient southbound track traversing the island chalk ridge down to Niton, for ore shipment to the continent. It could be argued, however, that for Pliny the Elder, who lived far away near Mount Vesuvius in the Bay of Naples, a journey six days up the Channel might mean anywhere, conceivably Ushant off the Brittany coast or St. Michael's Mount, the tiny tidal Cornish isle, if six days is taken as an exaggeration for a journey from Land's End. There is little more to tell on this. Every island is entitled to its secrets.

Roman Vectis

Fortunately Roman occupation is less concealed. Indeed of all Britain's offshore islands, the Isle of Wight was the one most thoroughly settled by them. The commander credited with taking it was future emperor Vespasian, Roman sources conveying the impression that he battled heroically to win it (c. A.D. 44) in an expedition that was part of the Claudian conquest begun the previous year. Suetonius reports in *The 12 Caesars* that he fought many battles before taking 'the entire isle of Vectis."[3] Some excavated store-buildings at Fishbourne, near Chichester, have been proposed as base camp for the invasion. The sight of his Legion II Augusta armed, helmeted, kilted and drilled in formations must have been formidable, but their appearance was hardly a bolt from the blue. Wight was on the western edge of an area feeding off trade with Roman Gaul since Julius Caesar subdued Gallic Celts a century before. Not all Britons were averse to inclusion within an expanding rich empire, and those who saw benefits may have included Wight's tribal rulers. A peaceful capitulation cannot be ruled out. Wight was not Anglesey. It was already involved in cross–Channel trade, and domestication rather than fortification was all that was needed.

Evidently the Romans liked the island. They built at least seven villas on it — a lot of estates for one island — most of them south of the chalk ridge and founded on existing farmsteads. Native islanders were coerced to provide the labor. Army officer veterans may have settled there, or the villas may have functioned as second homes for the wealthy Romano-British class. Two of them are open to the public: Newport with its bathhouse and hypocaust (under-floor central heating) and Brading, which has arguably the finest set of mosaics of any surviving Romano-British villa. It began modestly (c. A.D. 50) as a timbered farmhouse but by the fourth century had become a great stone and timber frame villa with some 40 rooms set around a garden courtyard. The design and grandeur would not have disgraced Tuscany. Barns, byres and stables added to the prosperous look of the place, and it was situated near a natural harbor (Brading Haven) although land reclamation has left its ruins two miles inland. At one time or another governors of Vectis called Brading home. Interior walls were finished with brightly painted plaster and surviving pieces of which portray floral and woodland scenes. The fourth century mosaics catch the eye. An intact Medusa is recognizable and Orpheus playing his lute, but it is the depiction of Roman deity Iao, his presence indicative of mysteries' cults, that fuels speculation about happenings at the villa.

Iao was exalted in eastern Mediterranean cultures and imported by Romans following conquests there, to be accommodated within the Bacchus cult. Bacchus, the god of wine and good times, was counterpart to Greek fertility and pleasure god Dionysus. He was popular with the Roman upper class and worshipped through festivities of great excess at no little expense. By the second century A.D. the Bacchanalian cult had assumed monotheistic traits with a resurrection promise. Plutarch described Bacchus as "the god who is destroyed, who disappears, who relinquishes life and then is born again." Hedonistic enjoyment was integral; wine drinking, singing, sexual abandon, with a climax reached in some kind of bloodletting, usually ritual slaying of animals. Iao's depiction at Brading may reveal no more than the aesthetic tastes of the owners, but when a well shaft was found to contain assortments of animal and human remains plus some expensive looking ceramic ware from the Roman period,[4] imaginations ran overtime. We are left to wonder.

In the meantime wheeled traffic hauled produce, minerals (tin?), stone, and finished goods from villa to port and vice versa, trundling along roads leaving their mark on maps and creating a new intensity of commerce. Several place-names stem from roads the Romans built, including Havenstreet near Ryde, Rewstreet near Cowes and Streetplace near Calbourne. The population grew, but instability crept in during the later third century as Germanic pirates, sailing along southeastern British coasts, raided settlements and farmland at will, thieving anything of value they could find. The entire stretch from East Anglia to the Isle of Wight came to be at risk, and to compound imperial problems, threats to order materialized within the ranks also. Marcus Carausius, a Menapii native and a sailor of some repute, was commander of the British fleet. According to Roman sources he had craftily developed the ploy of allowing pirate ships to invade Gallic and British shores first, attacking them only when they were laden with booty, so as to requisition it for himself and his crew. As a Menapian Celt under Roman yoke he no doubt saw it differently. The new emperor Diocletian (r. 284–305) sought to deal with such liberties (and insurrection else-where) by reorganizing imperial government. Rome was no longer at the heart of its empire (Diocletian never visited until 303) and the western region was ruled from Ravenna. He delegated power to a co-emperor (Maximian) and two deputies, one of whom, Constantius Chlorus, governor of Transalpine Gaul, marched north to deal with Carausius in 293.

The admiral was by then behaving as if he too were co-emperor, having set up base on his native Belgian coast. It seems that there were those on the Isle of Wight who were happy to help him. Roman sources record that Carausius regularly hid out there "as look-out and in ambush."[5] It was not to last. Constantius Chlorus flushed him out of the Gallic port of Gesoriacum (Boulogne) first and then an obliging mist gave his fleet the cover to pursue him across the Channel to Britain and torch his ships. The Celtic imperial pretender suffered the mortal indignity of murder by a lieutenant disenchanted with the dire turn in events.

In the fourth century Vectis found itself at the western end of a long line of coastal forts stretching from East Anglia. The nearest was at Portchester across the Solent under the unified command of a *comes litoris Saxonici* or "count of the Saxon shore." The post was created during the rule of Constantine I (r. 306–337) to mobi-lize defensive units, but it sounds more impressive than it proved. A much greater military investment was needed to defend Roman Britain as Picti burst through Hadrian's Wall in the north in the 360s and *Scotti* (Irish) raided the western coasts. In the southeast the count of the Saxon shore was killed in action by Germans. Roman authority in northwestern Europe was disintegrating, and when Emperor Honorius told Britons to defend themselves in 410, without help from Rome, trans-ferring the last of the British legions to the Rhine, the last pretenses of a unitary Roman Britain fell apart.

Germanic Wight

The name Vectis dropped out of currency after Roman withdrawal, and the island re-acquired its former name of Wight, but its vulnerability intensified with more Germanic coastal incursions. The productive soils and Roman infrastructure made it an attractive place for settlement. Bede reported three powerful Germanic tribes—Angles, Saxons, and Jutes—coming to eastern and southeastern Britain in the fifth century, getting some of his information from Gildas Bandonicus, a sixth century Romano-British monk. Gildas made no bones about his dislike of them, writing in *De Excidio Britanniae* (c. 540) of "fierce and impious Saxons, a race hateful to both God and man." The "hateful" Saxons (i.e. pagans) were as much invited as they ever were invaders, coming as mercenaries to secure one warlord's defenses against another, as Celt fought Celt in the aftermath of Roman withdrawal. It was like inviting wolves into the sheepfold in Gildas's mind, but this was not tidal-wave immigration. The numbers were probably quite small initially. It was plague epidemics in the sixth century, Gildas's own time, emanating from trade contacts with Gaul perhaps, that transformed demographics and left Celtic Britons stricken. The German Britons emerged from the plague stronger in relative numbers.

The Germanic people who settled on the Isle of Wight were Jutes, according to Bede, migrants from Jutland, the Danish peninsula. Some historians are skeptical about Bede's groupings, arguing that his Germanic subdivisions have more to do with the demographics of his own day, early eighth century, than that of the fifth century. Archaeology might support Bede. Jewelry and decorated gold discs found in graves in Kent (another Jute settled area) are evidently comparable to items uncovered on Wight and in Jutland. As for specific names, the *Anglo-Saxon Chronicle*, a retrospective Germanic king list completed in Norman times, credits Cerdic and his son Cynric, the founders of Wessex (kingdom of the West Saxons), with conquering of Wight c. 500, massacring its inhabitants. This is misleading on two counts. Firstly Cerdic and Cynric are not German-sounding names, and secondly it is doubtful that there were enough Jutes (or Saxons) in the pre-plague era to massacre the islanders all at once. Historians have steadfastly divided Celtic and Germanic realms as resolutely distinct, but it may be more realistic to visualize some form of fusion. If we assume some assimilation rather than absolute ethnic repopulation then Cerdic and Cynric become leaders of bands of Celto-Germans, less the pedigree Germans of repute. Over two centuries later, by Bede's time, Germanic speech (Old English) and culture was ascendant and modern maps reveal the extent of dispossession. Carisbrooke seems to be the lone Celtic place-name (from Welsh *carreg* or rock), but there is an abundance of Germanic name endings such as *combe* (valley), *ham* (homestead), *ing* (land of), *ton* (township), and *bury* (fortified place). Nearly 40 places end in *field* (cultivated place), a useful reminder of work routines amid all the gore and mayhem summoned by chroniclers as history.

From Pagan to Christian Wight

The kingdom of Wessex consolidated its position during the sixth and seventh centuries. Wight as its constituent was ensnared whenever predator kings took a fancy to Wessex territories. Wulfhere, the ambitious king of Mercia, seized Wight in 661, for example, gifting it to the kingdom of Sussex (South Saxons) as a christening present for the newly converted king, a shift in politics of hitherto non–Christian rulers. According to Bede the islanders were "entirely given up to idolatry."[6] Early German settlers found no reason to convert and kings typically hitched their own ancestry to that of the Germanic pantheon to enhance personal prestige, the god of war Woden being particularly popular. If Christianity existed on Wight at one time it was not strong, and surviving pagan practices fused with that of the German-speakers. Paganism (deriving from Latin *pagani*: country people) never evolved into an organized religion in the way Christianity did, and differences were worked out at community level. The effort to convince German-Briton warlords that Christ was a better protector than Woden was spearheaded through two separate missions. Celtic monks from Iona traveled to Anglo-Saxon Northumbria in the early 600s, and in a separate initiative Pope Gregory I sent Augustine in 597 (not to be confused with St. Augustine) to proselytize for the Roman Church in southern Britain. Many kings had converted by the later seventh century. Insulated Wight may well have been one of the last places to accept the new message.

In 686 the situation changed in a dramatic manner, according to Bede. The force was Caedwalla, pagan king of Wessex, a Germanic warlord with a Celtic name, hellbent on recovering what had been lost earlier to Wulfhere. Appearing like some Beowulf, or at least a dark force out of that heroic world, he "endeavored to wipe out all the natives by merciless slaughter and replace them with inhabitants of his own kingdom."[7] Caedwalla came from a dispossessed lineage of Wessex rulers and had been in exile (probably in Wales) before returning to seize power in 685. He quickly established overlordship of Essex (East Saxons), had his brother rule Kent, and attacked Wight. Victory on the island was registered by killing Arwald, the last ruler during 25 years of annexation to Sussex. He hammered home his authority by burning homes and crops and terrorizing anyone who resisted him, the fighting so fierce he too was hurt in combat. Two brothers of Arwald were put to death and the spoils of victory parceled out to Caedwalla's own warriors and kinsfolk. Then, either in a genuine show of repentance or posturing to win approbation, he vowed to gift land to the church of the Christian God. Bede tells us that Caedwalla met with Bishop Wilfrid no less, an eminent British monk credited with introducing Benedictine rule to British monasteries. He offered him 300 hides of land in humble tribute, a generous chunk of island territory. The island's spiritual journey turned on that gesture. Through a heady mix of terrorism and contrition, Wight's destiny as a Christian island was secured. Caedwalla set off to Rome in 689 to win recognition from Pope Sergius I, dying, it is said, a few days later, still clad in his white baptismal robe.

There is a paucity of local saints. The best known is St. Boniface, but even he had only a fleeting relationship with the island. Baptized Wynfrith, c. 675, in southwest Wessex (modern Devon), he may have visited the island at some stage before missions earning him his sainthood took him off to heathen continental Germans. The village of Bonchurch near Ventnor and St. Boniface Down, the highest point on the island, are both named for him. Nonetheless during the eighth century Wight was thoroughly Anglicized, in the sense that the language of Germanic settlers prevailed, and Christianized, as the diocese of Wight was gathered up under the episcopal wing of the bishopric of Winchester. Some churches still bear the marks. All Saints Church in Freshwater has some Saxon masonry, as does St. George's Church at Arreton.

Manorial Saxon Life

A few artifacts survive from the early medieval period in the form of weapons, coins and even skulls, and we know that limestone was quarried at Quarr-Binstead between Ryde and Wootton, near the coast where Neolithic folks once fished. The stone was ferried across the Solent for sale in Wessex. Brading Haven continued to function although it was not as busy as in Roman times. A fortified settlement existed where Carisbrooke Castle was later built, and the *tuns* (townships) around Freshwater in the west of Wight suggest density of settlement with names circling the compass— Norton, Easton, Weston and Middleton. Sutton has been renamed Freshwater Gate.

Agricultural work altered little in terms of its technology in the immediate post–Roman centuries, but the land organization in which that work was carried out did change. The names of manors are found all over the island — King's Manor (near Yarmouth), Ningwood Manor (near Shalfleet), Great Budbridge Manor (near Godshill), Landguard Manor (near Shanklin), Barton Manor (near East Cowes)— and some discussion of manorialism is appropriate at this juncture. It can be traced back to a sixth century reversal to localized non-monetary economies. Manors or estates of land emerged out of Roman villas with lords providing protection and various categories of serfs (bonded unfree tenants) serving as labor. The fields were open, not enclosed as in modern farms, patterned by cultivable strips, and apportioned haphazardly among households, similar to practices already encountered on other islands. The usable land was typically designated in tripartite division — lord's demesne, villagers' arable strips, and the meadows, commons and woodland for pasture and resources. Plows and oxen were shared communally but the lord determined rights to grazing and woodland. The demesne of the Church added a fourth division. Caedwalla's ecclesiastical allocation made the Church a major landowner on Wight. A solvent Church was politically desirable, and Christian kings of Wessex enforced payment of tithes (one tenth of incomes) to it.

It is a moot point, but while Wight was generously endowed in land and climate, its manorial serfs were more coerced and under a heavier weight of supervision than their Celto-Norse counterparts. Wessex became an increasingly aristocratic, hierarchical and militaristic kingdom, more so than the multi-island constellations functioning in the Irish Sea and Atlantic. It was richer, too, and we can point to better soil, land utilization, and watermills by the 11th century among reasons for it. Productivity was helped by well-organized bonded labor, and Wessex serfs were very much bound to the soil they cultivated. Slavery, a part of Roman Wight, disappeared, but the numbers with free status declined too, as more people were drawn into the ranks of servility. Only the free were permitted arms. In Celtic Britain cattle were prized more than tillage whereas wealth on the Saxon manor meant acreage. Free men (*thegns*) holding more than five hides of land (a hide roughly equivalent to 100–120 aces) dominated manorial councils with kindred less important as a source of power. Landownership became the prime determinant. In its defense the manorial system maintained stability, a condition absent in the anarchic fourth and fifth centuries, and it supported a growing population at tolerable levels of living. The redundant monetary economy revived, and a coin found in Bonchurch dating from the reign of Aethelwulf, king of Wessex (839–56), may suggest inclusion of Wight in that recovery.

Danes

Wessex proved strong enough to counter the ninth century shock of Scandinavian incursions and immigration. Norwegians were coming ashore to the north and west of Britain by the 830s, as we have seen. Danes meanwhile raided eastern and southern coasts. The Norwegians took to settling and farming quickly, with less cultivable land in fjorded Norway than in lowland Denmark, and the Danes would follow suit, but not before they made a terrifying nuisance of themselves in Germanic Britain. Kent was humbled in 865 by having to make the first recorded protection payment, *Danegeld*; this after Vikings used the Isle of Thanet (then separated from the mainland by the rivers Stour and Wantsum) as an offshore base. The Danish onslaught defined England (albeit inadvertently) by uniting resistant Germanic kingdoms in opposition, and the formative agent was Wessex or more specifically its late ninth century king, Alfred (r. 871–899). A Christian ruler who codified law and encouraged writing (ordering the start of the *Anglo-Saxon Chronicle*), he achieved as much in negotiation as he did in fighting. After a successful siege in 878 Alfred persuaded the Danish leader Guthrum to withdraw from Wessex by the Treaty of Wedmore. It did not stop attacks immediately — six Danish ships raided Wight the following year — but a standoff developed that redefined Germanic Britain. Alfred kept Wessex and its subject kingdoms of Mercia, Sussex and Kent independent of Danish Britain, laying the prospect of an English state. Danish Britain (a.k.a. The Danelaw) functioned separately. Its looser polity encompassed the former Anglo-Saxon kingdoms of Northumbria, East Anglia and Essex. The Isle of Wight, subject to Wessex since 686, appears to have been a satellite of English Britain. Or was it?

The Danes favored use of the island as a bridgehead against Wessex. In the late 10th century Wessex kings were finding it harder and harder to sustain their overlordship against a reviving Danish threat, even though Aethelstan had earlier defeated Danes in the Danelaw. At the start of the 11th century, Danish raiding intensified. The Isle of Wight is mentioned several times by the *Anglo-Saxon Chronicle* in this context. It seems to have been a place where Danes enjoyed safe refuge. There is no record of who ruled the island, but islanders plainly chose discretion over valor and accommodated rather than resisted. It may be a bit far-fetched to say it was an Achilles heel, but Wight did partly host the restoration of Danish Britain, whether by intent or not. After a Danish fleet "burned and slew" along the southern coast in 1006, the Danes wintered on Wight, finding everything they needed there, the Wessex chroniclers inform. Ten years later, victory was assured. The Wessex king of the time, Aethelred the Unready (from *unrede*: lacked advice), infamous for having paid more *Danegeld* than anyone else, spent the Christmas of 1013 on the island, but was at the mercy of the Danes when he died in 1016. The Danish ruler Knut (Canute), leader of the strongest naval force of the day, became king of the English in 1017. Knut was also the king of Norway, and English Britain expanded his maritime empire. He paid Wight a visit in 1022, anchoring his ships in wait for the outlawed Viking leader Thorkell the Tall, who, he feared, might make trouble for him. In the event nothing transpired and the two were later reconciled.

Norman Conquest

After Knut's death in 1035 and the collapse of his Danish empire through dynastic failure, England's political future was progressively influenced by Normandy. Knut's eventual successor Edward the Confessor (so-called because of his piety), a Wessex king who ruled 1043 to 1066, was a Saxon on his father's side, but his mother was Norman and it was Normandy where he grew up. Normandy took its name from Northmen or Norse who settled northern France from the ninth century. Edward appointed Norman political advisors and clerics, and the language of his court was Norman-French. His death in January 1066 brought cross–Channel relationships even closer with profound consequences for Wight.

The epic struggle for the English crown in 1066 was in causation a family affair. The childless Edward favored a successor from the House of Rollo, the ducal dynasty of Normandy sheltering him during Knut's reign, and the sitting duke in 1066 William (conqueror-to-be) was determined to claim it. The Wessex nobility preferred its own and crowned Harold Godwinson instead, son of Edward's father-in-law. Fearing that William would challenge him, King Harold gathered his forces on the Isle of Wight during the summer of 1066 in readiness, informants advising that William planned to attack through the island. When the news arrived in September of a Norse invasion hundreds of miles away on the Yorkshire coast, where a force led by Harald Hardraada, king of Norway, aimed to return England to its Scandinavian fold, Godwinson promptly marched north to fight. He won a great victory at the Battle of Stamford Bridge and Hardraada was killed in combat. Yet fortune proved fickle. Less than three weeks later, triumph turned to tragedy for Godwinson, when he failed to halt the invasion of Duke William on the south coast at Hastings. He had rushed there in too much haste, and England's political future turned on his impulse and death in battle.

Lords of Wight and Domesday

The Norman duke's march of conquest led to an upheaval of magnitude not seen since Emperor Claudius. A massive land transfer to the Norman-French ensued, not necessarily intended in the first instance but occurring because of resistance to him as new king of England. The Isle of Wight was obviously valued because William gave it, together with the earldom of Hereford on the Welsh borders, to a prominent Norman lord, William FitzOsbern, a close confidant and key figure in the logistical planning of the 1066 invasion. FitzOsbern became the first lord of Wight in 1067 and the feudal title would survive for over four centuries. To announce his presence, he had a timber-framed great hall built on the foundations of an older Saxon/Celtic fort, the site that became Carisbrooke Castle. Nothing of the hall remains. It is probably the predecessor of the 13th century great hall occupied now by the castle museum, and it's the place where William the Conqueror arrested half-brother Odo of Blois, Bishop of Bayeux (for whom the famous Bayeux tapestry was commissioned), for treachery in 1082.[8] William's appeal to the pope for support in his war against Harold Godwinson had made his invasion a crusade against infidels and the church came out well from the conquest. The first beneficiary on Wight was the abbey of Lyre in Normandy, which FitzOsbern had founded in 1045. The new lord of Wight generously endowed it with extensive lands and resources, tithe income and rents. His lordship turned out to be brief, however, as he was killed in battle in Flanders in 1071, and William lost one of his most powerful supporters. His son Roger de Breteuil succeeded him but fell foul of the king, accused of conspiracy in 1075, and lands and title passed back to the Crown.

FitzOsbern had not arrived alone. Manors changed hands all over the island as Norman knights were rewarded for services rendered. For this information we have the rare luxury of Domesday Book evidence. Wight is the only offshore island reported in this unique inventory. The Domesday Book was presented to William I in 1086 listing land, people, animals, resources and tax values, not just a tax survey but a feudal data base, an official record listing identities of tenants-in-chief holding lands from the Crown and their tenants and under-tenants. The king needed armies to maintain authority, and conquered lands were divided into fiefs, frequently based on Anglo-Saxon manors, granted to vassals or tenants-in-chief in return for military service. When the project was initiated William feared a Danish invasion, and knowing which vassals owed him liege was of great interest, but like the biblical Day of Judgment the decisions of the Domesday Book (a later name) came to seem eternal, with no more appeal against them than against God.

The Domesday Book separated Wight from the neighboring county of Hampshire on the mainland, though for some reason more than half of the island holdings appear in the Hampshire section. Almost 40 manors are listed as being in direct possession of the Crown, three of them ecclesiastical — the bishopric of Winchester, the chapel of Carisbrooke Castle and the abbey of Wilton (Wiltshire). The abbey of Lyre lost properties with the disgrace of Roger de Breteuil but still kept six churches,[9] two mills and a salt house. Sitting tenants with Germanic names such as Aelfric of Yarmouth, Wufsi of Chale, Godric of Huffingford, Alric of Nettlestone, Estan of Bonchurch and Dunn of Alvington were dispossessed and in their place came just a handful of Norman-French vassals — principally William FitzStur and the brothers Jocelyn and William FitzAzor.[10] The last named held 16 manors alone, all but one of them on the eastern side of the island, their name changing later to Lisle or de L'Isle — "of the island." Land distribution was shaken top to bottom within 20 years and society and power was entirely reconstructed; details on the conduct of it can only be imagined. It is worthy of note that 24 watermills are listed in the return (windmills are not recorded before the 13th century), strong evidence of a developed agriculture.

The Redvers Dynasty

Henry I granted the lordship in 1102 to Richard de Redvers, a Norman-French knight from Reviers, in the vicinity of Bayeux and Caen, and his dynasty held sway for the next 200 years. The greatest achievement of his successor Baldwin de Redvers (c. 1100–1154) was to begin transforming Carisbrooke from a timbered structure into the impressive stonework castle seen today, one of the best known island landmarks. The imposing tower-gateway is its best surviving feature. The stone keep experienced its first assault in 1136, during a civil war over succession to Henry I (d. 1135) when Stephen count of Blois, a grandson of William I, besieged and took the castle. Baldwin was forced to flee the island (he supported Henry's daughter Matilda) but was reinstated later when Stephen and Matilda settled their differences. Carisbrooke, like many other Norman-French *motte-and-bailey* castles, was not just a fortress, it was a seat of local government: a garrison, prison, arsenal, town hall and law court combined, command center of Wight for centuries.

If land transfer was one element of Norman capture then the church was another. An Anglo-Saxon held only one out of 16 English bishoprics in 1090. The others were all imported appointments. Romanesque cathedrals, monasteries, and churches dotted the English landscape by 1200, and while the old Wessex capital of Winchester got the cathedral, the island was not excluded from new construction or French monasticism. Several orders set up house before and during the Redvers lordship — a Cluny congregation began an abbey at St. Helens (c. 1090) and monks from the Norman abbey of Monteburg established a priory at Appuldurcombe (c. 1100). Cistercians from the abbey of Savigny in Normandy set up a monastery at Quarr early in the 12th century, and the abbot of Lyre had a priory built at Carisbrooke in 1156, under the protective watch of the new castle.

Outside intervention does not appear to have held back material progress. Indeed the impression is that the industrious monks were a dynamo in the medieval economy: their granaries and mills productive, freshwater carp bred in monastic ponds, and Wootton Creek near Quarr abbey alive with maritime traffic. The island exported flour and woolen cloth, and limestone quarries were worked under license from the Crown. Importantly several Wight towns grew up under the Redvers. Newport grew on a Roman grid across a road leading down from Carisbrooke Castle to the Medina estuary, its borough charter granted c. 1130, allowing a degree of self-government through election of magistrates. Yarmouth was granted a similar charter in 1135, likewise developing along a grid with roads crossing a high street at right angles. Along the northern Solent coast between the two boroughs was Frencheville, already in existence, a vibrant port crowding around a busy quay. The whole stretch from the Medina to Yarmouth was alive in commercial endeavor. The taxation lists for 1377 report an island population of 4,733 excluding paupers and children.[11] At least three languages were in regular use — the Norman-French of the ruling class, an English (or Old English) dialect spoken by commoners, and the Latin of the religious community.

The last of the Redvers' lords of Wight was Isabella de Fortibus (1237–1292). Born Redvers, she married William de Fortibus Count of Albemarle when 12 years old. Widowed at 23, she assumed the lordship two years later in 1262 on her brother's death as sole heir. Since the Redvers also had the earldom of Devon, her inheritance was handsome. In an age when church and monarchy conspired to reduce the likelihood of female inheritance she survived remarkably against the grain for 30 years as "the lady of the isle," living and ruling from Carisbrooke Castle. She had a new great hall built and added a private chapel (now part of the museum). Accounts of the economic health of the manors compiled by her constable Hugh de Manneby (equivalent post to sheriff) survive and from them we learn of significant production of wheat, oats, barley (mostly for ale), peas and beans. Income supplements from wool, poultry, dairy, cider, woodland resources and shipwreck sales kept the island exchequer solvent.[12] At the end of her life she entered into negotiations to sell the eastern portion of her estate, namely Hampshire, Dorset and the Isle of Wight, to the king Edward I. Conveyance was apparently sealed on her deathbed in 1292 but its validity was challenged in the House of Commons. The king eventually paid a sum of 6,000 silver marks (£4,000) to end the Redvers' proprietorship, a sign again of the high value placed on the island.

Diamond in the Rough

Nevertheless Wight was particularly prone to instability and disruption during the 1300s and 1400s, deriving from external afflictions rather than proprietor change. A defensive unease was signaled in 1324 when warning beacons were set up, and it was not long before they were regularly lit. In the mid–1330s a cross–Channel war broke out, one lasting intermittently for more than a century, the Hundred Years' War. It began as a struggle between competing aristocratic factions over feudal land claims and extended to commercial rivalries and bids by Plantagenet kings of England for the French throne. It finished up as a war between two fledgling nations, France and England, defined by mutual antagonisms. The opening salvo for Wight was fired in 1338 when the French burned nearby Portsmouth to the ground. Sir John de Langford, titled warden of Wight, ordered militia and priesthood to be on the alert, but the threat diminished and fears were further allayed by Edward III's victory at Crecy in 1346 with his son "The Black Prince."

There was no respite from calamity because any relief of invasion anxiety was overshadowed by the curse of deadly diseases. Wetter and cooler weather made for unhealthy times, and in the mid–14th century a series of European epidemics spread like wildfire among combustibles, wreaking devastation on body and senses, a plague conveyed in its morbid name. One part of the "Black Death" was a highly contagious bubonic plague attacking the lymph nodes of its victims, a contagion traceable to the Italian seaport of Messina in 1348. The other was an equally deadly pneumonic plague eliciting hacking and spitting death coughs from infected lungs. The plagues(s) reached southern England within months. Seaports were especially vulnerable and chroniclers report an early outbreak in Southampton with 1349–1350 an especially critical time on adjacent Wight. The "dreadful pestilence" killed half or more of the population in some parts of Europe in a matter of decades. A chronic labor shortage resulting from it helped loosen feudal rigidity, an advantageous supply and demand situation for survivors as historians frequently point out, but scant solace for those who actually endured the horrific maladies.

Fear of backwash from the Hundred Years' War revived in 1369 as the French renewed hostilities, and the next few years were troubled ones with invasion expected daily. Wight was an easy target, its river estuaries offering direct access to the innards of the island. The only significant defense was Carisbrooke Castle and it was not ideally located. The Crown threatened to seize the land of any tenants-in-chief fleeing the island. There is a charge that some had done that in the 1330s, after all knights held land on the understanding it would be defended. Invasion fears were realized in 1377 when a combined French and Spanish fleet sailed into the Solent to drop anchor off Yarmouth. A Wight militia offered token resistance, but forces stormed ashore and Yarmouth, Newport and Frencheville were all put to the sword. Carisbrooke Castle came under siege but it was called off after a ransom was paid up. In another version of events a skillful archer, Peter Heynoe, saved the day, having spied over several days the French commander's movements from high ramparts, killing him with a well-flighted arrow. A slit on the west wall is designated "Heynoe's loope."[13]

Richard II's murder in 1399 and accession of Henry of Lancaster to the English throne (Henry IV) brought fresh attacks. French nobles condemned the coup in England, charging that Princess Isabel of France, the late king's child-bride, was the rightful monarch. Over a thousand French landed in 1402–1403 to burn cottages and villages. The French priories were closed down in a move to close security leaks and war weary islanders must have been heartened by news of the capture of the French port of Harfleur by Henry V and his subsequent victory at Agincourt in 1415. Agincourt did not prevent the French from attacking Wight again, but it did lead to a cessation of hostilities in 1420.

Unlike the Isle of Man, ruled by one dynasty for over three centuries, Wight never again became the sole property of one family after the Redvers. Richard II had revived the lordship in 1386, bestowing the title on William Montecute earl of Salisbury, the same family given the kingship of Man by Edward III in 1333. Dynastic succession did not follow on Wight and a series of nobles served as lords of Wight during the first half of the 15th century — the earl of Kent, the duke and duchess of York, the duke of Gloucester — until Henry VI departed from form in 1445 and personally crowned Henry de Beauchamp, duke of Warwick, as "king of the Wight." For this particular king to be anointing another is not without irony. Henry VI was the Lancastrian who inherited two crowns and lost both. He claimed French title through the death of his maternal grandfather, the Valois French king Charles VI, and assumed full control of the English kingdom as a 16-year-old. Finding it hard to deal with influential and wealthy vassals, his Wight coronation gift to Henry de Beauchamp, son of his tutor and a peer, can be read as a gesture to friend and foe alike. Another view is that it was influenced by his well-documented health afflictions. The king of Wight's reign was short-lived at any rate, barely a blip in the narrative of Wight government. Beauchamp died in 1446 and the kingship expired with him. For his part Henry VI lost the Hundred Years' War in 1453 and with it his claim to the French crown. To compound his problems he had to endure bouts of insanity, a domineering wife and the inevitable loss of his English crown: he was murdered in 1471.

Tudor Reforms

Henry VII, first of the Tudor dynasty, abolished the old feudal lordship in 1490 and appointed Sir Edward Wydeville as captain (later governor) of Wight. The lords of Wight had been agents of the crown since William Montecute anyway, hardly autonomous rulers, but the change in terminology is worthy of emphasis because it spoke the language of a new national administration. It wasn't long before Wydeville had to give national service. In a prudent move to gain a powerful ally, the king arranged by the Treaty of Medina del Campo in 1489 for his eldest son Arthur to marry Catherine of Aragon, daughter of Ferdinand of Aragon and Isabella of Castile. The marriage did not happen until 1501, but England agreed in the meantime to support the two Spanish monarchs in their war with France. Months after being appointed captain of Wight, Wydeville sailed across the Channel with over 400 islanders to fight and die with the forces of the duke of Brittany against the French. Henry VII acknowledged the island by visiting it in 1499, but it seems that an accumulation of plague and endless war had taken its toll, depleting and displacing communities. These were not happy times. Regeneration lay in the two centuries ahead.

The excommunication of Henry VIII in 1533 has already been referred to several times in previous chapters. Excommunication of English monarchs was not in itself new, but the 1534 resolution confirming the king as spiritual head, releasing the church in England of any loyalty to Rome, was a firecracker, worthy of repeated emphasis, shelling a half-millennium old balance of power in Christian Europe. The Church of England differed little theologically from Catholicism, but such a conspicuous bid for autonomy greatly strained international relations and for those living along the southern coasts an edgy fear of papal retribution grew. The Isle of Wight felt the fire of French attack in 1524, even before Henry's break with Rome during a war between Spain and France over papal politics. Lord Chancellor Thomas Wolsey had pledged English support for Spain. After the break with Rome it felt the force of Henrician Reformation, as the king lost no time in making forfeit the lands of the Catholic abbeys and priories on Wight. Continental monastic orders had held property on Wight since the 11th century, and this constituted cultural revolution. Henry VIII has not had the last word, however. Benedictines from the French abbey of Solesmes recovered some of the Quarr property in the early 20th century and a monastic community reconvened with a distinctive new abbey church built in 1912, winning musical acclaim for restoration of Gregorian chant.

HMS Mary Rose

Henry VIII's snub to the continental establishment intensified defense concerns, and it was in that nervous atmosphere that the king was forced to witness a naval disaster of some proportion in the waters off Wight in July 1545. The south coast was being harried in retaliatory French attacks for English seizure of Boulogne and the king traveled to Portsmouth to review his fleet and oversee operations. The Royal Navy, though not yet a match for the likes of the Spanish, was progressing, and it was to be a proud occasion. On July 19, 1545, he prepared to view proceedings from Southsea Castle's ramparts, but with 200 French sail massing off Bembridge, the eastern tip of Wight, there was menace in the air. As the Royal Navy moved into the Solent to confront the enemy the Tudor flagship *Mary Rose,* one of the first ships capable of firing a broadside and the toast of the Tudor fleet, began to keel over suddenly and sink. The aging king could only watch in horrified disbelief, pacing up and down helplessly as it went down in a matter of moments. In *Westward Ho!* (1855) Charles Kingsley would write: "And the king he screeched out like any maid, 'Oh my Gentlemen. Oh my gallant men' ... drowned like rats, drowned like rats." A thousand French troops seized advantage of the catastrophe to land on Wight but the island militia responded and Henry's fleet recovered to drive them back.

The *Mary Rose* disaster drew attention to the island's vulnerability and the governor, by this time an islander, Richard Worsley of Appuldurcombe, was commanded to upgrade defenses. Every parish was ordered to provide and maintain a gun (cannon). Fortifications were improved at Yarmouth where the castle survives (and at Sandown and Norton), and two forts were built on either side of the mouth of the Medina estuary–East and West Cowes— to protect Newport and the island interior. In fact there would be no more French raids on Wight. In 1982, over 400 years after the sinking of *Mary Rose,* a giant floating crane called *Tog Mor* eased the shell of the Tudor ship from the encasing mud and silt of the Solent into the light and scrutiny of the 20th century, watched by a TV audience of millions. Henry VIII's distressing day was finally put to rest. Whether the ship sank because it was overloaded or because it suffered a hit from the French is still not clear. Discovery of the missing front section in 2003 may yet provide the answer.

Spain posed the next serious threat and in the epic year of 1588, islanders came close to experiencing the leviathan-like Armada, sent by the king of Spain to overthrow the "heretical" Elizabeth I. Wight's governor George Carey is credited with keeping the island in a state of readiness. The militia did not see action because by the time the crescent-shaped flotilla reached Wight, it was already in a running battle with English ships and never entered the Solent. Its failure, specifically a failure to coordinate naval and army forces, has long been seen as a defining moment in English history, and during Elizabeth's long reign, English power gathered momentum within the orbits of Britain and Ireland. By 1600 both population and economy were in growth mode as England reached 4 million people, around 9,000 of them settled on the Isle of Wight.

"Gentrification and Commonality"

Most of Wight's governors are invisible in the national story, but Henry Wriothesley, third earl of Southampton, deserves mention as an interesting exception. His notoriety derives least of all from his governorship (a role given him later in life) and most from a controversial Shakespeare connection and excused capital offense. He has attracted conjecture as the alleged "fair youth" of Shakespeare's love sonnets: the young man of exceptional beauty who was object of an impassioned but not necessarily sexual affection. The young earl impressed Elizabeth I's court and was a known patron of Shakespeare. The sonnets written between 1594 and 1597 urge a young man to marry and father children, a rather unusual request, and Wriothesley did marry aged 25 in 1598, but beyond that circumstance the evidence is flimsy. Shakespeare had recently suffered the death of his only son and at least part of the sonnets are autobiographical. What is known is that Wriothesley was an accessory in an abortive plot against some of the queen's closest advisors in 1601 and he was fortunate to escape execution. Elizabeth I's death two years later and accession of James I brought him an early release from prison and a royal pardon. Wriothesley lived a charmed life. His title, land and money were restored and the office of governor of Wight thrown in for good measure.

The period is an interesting mix of court intrigues and a new profit-seeking mentality, a fusion of medievalism and fledgling capitalism. A patrician he may have been, but Wriothesley was not averse to the new commercialism. He was a stockholder in the East India Company and took an active role in the London Company of Virginia, corporate promoters of the first English-speaking colony to survive in North America (Jamestown 1607). He eventually lost favor with James I but remained governor until his death in 1624. A newly laid-out and finely manicured bowling lawn at Carisbrooke Castle seems to have been the main legacy of his residence.

Wight's knights and squires lived comfortably off landed inheritance in the 17th century: Oglanders, Lisles, Chekes, Urrys, Worsleys, Leighs and others, some with lineage stretching to the Norman Conquest. Improved defenses and a growing money economy afforded a better quality of life and there were social and sporting distractions. The forests still had deer and wild boar and there was plenty of small game. Yet it was a testing time for the gentry. A growing friction between Parliament and Charles I over financial matters and the royal prerogative turned into military confrontation in the 1640s, otherwise known as the English Civil War. The island did not escape the ferment. It exercised Sir John Oglander (1585–1655) of Nunwell House, Brading descendant of Richard d'Oglandres, a knight-in-arms who had come ashore with FitzOsbern in the 11th century. A diarist before Samuel Pepys elevated the genre, he saw it as "a time when the gentry were made slaves to the commonalty."[14]

The hand that would shake the tree was already expressing itself in the form of Calvinist Protestantism, a firebrand religious fundamentalism that defied popes and kings as sources of moral authority, spreading a form of republican populism under God. It was a potent message and one not lost on those in the middling ranks of society. It had won followers on the island. Newport was a nonconformist hotbed, declaring against the king at the outbreak of Civil War in 1642. One prominent minister, together with the mayor, led the common folk against the royalist governor and drove him out. For Sir John Oglander, these were galling years, as first the king was defeated and then executed. Wight itself played a role in the king's fate.

After Oliver Cromwell's army again outwitted and crushed royalist forces at Naseby in 1645, Charles I came under house arrest in Hampton Court, London (1647).

In that same year, he was forced to flee London to seek refuge on the Isle of Wight following murderous threats by republican Levellers, a radical political movement that sought the leveling or end of social rank and abolition of monarchy. Sir John Oglander was vociferous in his support for the beleaguered monarch, but it says something about grassroots anti-royalist sentiment on the island that while he was delighted at his surprise arrival in November 1647, he "could do nothing but sigh and weep for two nights and a day" at the prospect. He believed him to be among enemies. The fugitive king stayed at Carisbrooke Castle where he was treated at first as a guest. After coded messages appealing for Scots support were intercepted on the mainland and brought to Oliver Cromwell's attention, the parliamentarian governor Colonel Robert Hammond was obliged to put him under house arrest. Charles made escape attempts, famously getting stuck in the bars of a window, until orders came for his removal to London for trial, where, having refused to govern with Parliament, he suffered the ignominy of a death sentence by them. His daughter Elizabeth saw the inner walls of Carisbrooke too, after the drama of Charles's execution, catching a fever and dying there.

"Where Wealth Accumulates and Men Decay"

By the 17th century the English economy was responding to a rising demand for food and raw materials through enclosure of manorial land into privately owned farms, a process achieved initially by agreement or purchase but increasingly by forcible eviction. It was underway on Wight before 1700. The island's wool product was competitive as were its stone quarries. Grain mills ground out healthy flour output, and oysters and rabbit meat found their way to rich London tables. Rabbits were so prevalent (introduced by the Normans) that they were mentioned in 15th century land lease agreements.[15] By 1800 Wight's farms had developed a greater emphasis on livestock. Sheep were reared for their meat as well as fleece, and by the 1830s around 8,000 lambs were sent to London per season.

Wight's gentry prospered in this atmosphere of agrarian enterprise. Architects, masons, sculptors, artists, landscape gardeners, upholsterers and a host of crafts were hired to create palatial mansions out of older manor houses such as those at Swainston, Nunwell and Gatcombe. The Worsley family began remodeling at Appuldurcombe House in 1710, hiring the great Lancelot "Capability" Brown to landscape its estate in 1768. A much-sought-out landscape gardener, his nickname reputedly came from his sales pitch: "I see great capability of improvement here." Lord Henry Seymour, second son of the Marquis of Hertford, not to be outdone, had an entire mock–Norman castle built overlooking the Solent at East Cowes. Called Norris Castle, it was where the young princess Victoria enjoyed her first taste of the island. John Nash, the celebrated architect who designed much of Regency London, had a Gothic revival palace built at East Cowes and spent his retirement years there (it no longer exists). Garden parks, lawns, sham nymphs, artificial lakes and follies were fashionable; whims and fancies were indulged with no expense spared. Roman opulence had returned to Wight after a lapse of over 1,300 years.

As appreciation of business potential increased, prospects of communal rights to land, grazing and fuel deteriorated; "Where wealth accumulates and men decay" is how playwright Oliver Goldsmith put it in his protest poem *Deserted Village* (1770). In the longer run transferring agricultural labor to other economic sectors would prove beneficial in raising incomes, but in the 18th century population growth and waged opportunities were not in tandem and rural distress rose. Rural poverty is insidious. Austerity does not leave its traces as conspicuously as wealth does; yet it was no less real. Amid Wight's rolling greenery of backcountry tracks and high hedgerows, small stone churches, landscaped mansion houses and sniff of salt air lurked a plethora of low dank dwellings, unsanitary smells, grinding hunger and a harsh under life. For the destitute the workhouse beckoned, paid for out of local parish taxes. Niton had one in 1756 and Parkhurst in 1770. Workhouses originally intended to house "impotent poor" (incapacitated, elderly and orphaned) increasingly accommodated "able-bodied poor," those unable to find waged farm work at a level sufficient to survive. Newport workhouse was built to accommodate 700.

As we have seen repeatedly offshore, there were alternative ways of making ends meet. The evocatively named Blackgang Chine, hidden away on Chale Bay on the south coast, tempted 20th century tourists down a twisting pathway lit with colored lights and swaying lanterns into a damp ravine lined with gaudy plastic smuggler figures. Smuggling was real enough once. Maybe two in every three were involved in some capacity or another. Steep cliff coves like Blackgang Chine on the "back of the Wight" facing France were ideal for illicit cargo imports of brandy, tea, tobacco, silk and other high-end luxury items. It was not new. In the Tudor age, when laws made it illegal to export valued raw materials, English wool was smuggled out. The fact that the gentry were often complicit made it practical. The Irish-born buccaneer Sir Robert Holmes, who led the English force that captured the Dutch colony of New Amsterdam in 1664 (renaming it New York), was allegedly involved. He was governor of Wight between 1667 and 1692.[16] Free trade laws in the 19th century eventually undermined smuggling, but by that time the island was developing lucrative legal pursuits.

Industrial enterprise did not overlook Wight. Stone-quarries, brick-works and salt-works ensured that muck and grime was part of development too. The colored sand cliffs of Alum Bay attracted the interest of famed pottery manufacturer Josiah Wedgwood. He experimented with sand from there in the 1760s for his pottery kilns in Staffordshire. The sands became a major source for the glass industry. The northern port of East Cowes was an industrial town with boatyards, sail and rope-making works. Village crafts thrived but waged opportunities for the unskilled were limited. Most of the non-farm economy comprised small family fishing and boat building concerns, insufficient to absorb surplus labor. A lace factory set up in the 1820s near Newport employed hundreds of women and children and lasted 40 years until closure in 1868, but it was an exception. It was the advent of recreational travel and tourism that worked to benefit Wight.

"*Fresh Green Tints of Yonder Shore*"

Ryde began outgrowing its fishing hamlet origins in the 18th century after a Hampshire brewer, Henry Player, purchased the manor of Ryde from the Dillington family in 1705. Its development was slow, but by the early 1800s there were seaside accommodations and a scene lively enough to attract wealthier visitors on short sail trips, even allowing for the Napoleonic War. Ryde pier, the first promenade pier in Britain, opened in 1815, the same year that hostilities against Napoleon intensified. Richard Ayton and William Daniell circumnavigated Britain between 1813 and 1823 and wrote about it, rating West Cowes "the most pleasant and safe station of any on the British coast for persons fond of aquatic amusements."[17] By 1821 around 3,000 people called Ryde home. The spa of Ventnor, tucked snugly under the cliff of St. Boniface Down, was not far behind. Sales pitches about its medicinal airs made it popular with those choked by the ailments of urban mainland life. J. Redding Ware's 1869 visitor guide (one of many published in the Victorian Age) began with the words: "The Isle of Wight is the paradise of bees, flowers and invalids." There were only 350 people living in Ventnor in 1838, but by the time of Ware's guide there were over 5,000.

Idealization of the English countryside was not new, as Oliver Goldsmiths's *Deserted Village* illustrates, but ruralism assumed a new urgency in the Victorian Age. A craving for nature spread among those with enough money to buy it: a nostalgic hunger for rustic landscapes, the "homeliness" of country life, sea-air and not least green space. The very sound of the name "Wight" was cleansing and its powers to heal and refresh were propagated. Getting there became less and less of a problem. George Ward and William Fitzhugh of Cowes formed the Isle of Wight Royal Mail Steam Packet Company in 1820 to provide regular year-round steamship connection with Southampton. Competitor routes between Lymington and Yarmouth and Portsmouth to Ryde followed. Queen Victoria's decision to purchase the Osborne estate in 1845, based on happy childhood memories of nearby Norris Castle, gave the island its stamp of fashionable approval. What was good enough for a queen was good enough for her subjects. The first island railway got up steam between Cowes and Newport in 1862. Over the next 20 years other lines would be promoted and constructed, linking all the major settlements. The twin seaside resorts of Sandown and Shanklin, evenly spaced between Ryde and Ventnor, were thriving by the 1870s. After a week of the dirt and smoke of Victorian London such places had understandable appeal. Readers of the *Whitehall Review* of September 14, 1874, were urged to buy a weekend railway ticket and enjoy a change of air on the island: "The scene is indeed passing fair, and has a soft beauty which in truth is far lovelier than any foreign lake, for neither Como nor Lucerne can show you the fresh green tints of yonder shores." Wight's utilities were up to date, too, with telephones and electricity cables by the turn of the 20th century putting it at the forefront of offshore infrastructure.

Middle class patronage helped to grow the service economy, but the aristocracy was not done with the island. Nor was it with them. The London Yacht Club (the Prince Regent was its patron) moved its headquarters to Cowes in 1825. As the Royal Yacht Club it became one of the world's most exclusive sailing clubs, with members permitted to fly the St. George's Ensign for free entry to foreign ports. The RYC invited the New York Yacht Club to compete in a race for a special Challenge Cup in 1851, and the rest of the tale as they say is history. Not only did the 170-ton *America* win (though it should be noted that the skipper and many crew were English) but subsequent attempts to win it back, all of them futile, changed the name to the America's Cup. The America's Cup — the World Cup of boat races — is now more at home in New Zealand or California than long-forgotten Wight, but the island does not do at all badly. An international yachting and powerboat festival held every August known as "Cowes Week" has been an established fixture in the social calendar for over a hundred years.

Constituency

As manors gave way to commerce, political arrangements remained comparatively inert. Only with national parliamentary reform in 1832 was Wight aligned with the new industrial demographics. It enjoyed a more than generous allocation of parliamentary seats for centuries with two each for Yarmouth, Newport and Newtown. The medieval port of Newtown, once Norman Frencheville and now a sleepy silted up bird sanctuary, had virtually no residents at the end of the 18th century. It still returned two politicians to Westminster, a classic example of the so-called "rotten borough" (i.e. wholly undemocratic) and therefore a contributor to calls for reform. In the 1820s when industrial cities like Birmingham and Manchester had no MPs at all, the island maintained its return of six gentry. This aberration was finally overturned in 1832 and representation pared back from six to two seats. It was reduced further to just one seat in 1885, which is how it still stands. Democratization was advanced with new local government regulations creating the elective IOW Council in 1890, its administrative center in Newport. The old office of governor became an honorary title in 1841.

There was much for the new local council to contemplate. During Victoria's reign (1837–1901) the population practically doubled, as new settlement more than compensated for the émigrés. By 1921 it had climbed to 94,000. More to the point, beyond the colored sands of Alum Bay and hoopla of pier amusements, poverty persisted. Reports of public health and housing conditions in Cowes (in 1850, 1,000 were said to be living in courts and alleys)[18] show a deeply divided town with overcrowding and public squalor on one corner and the exclusive Royal Yacht Club on the other. Council (or public) administered housing did not make its island debut until the 1920s. At least part of the problem was shrinkage of farm work opportunities and contraction grew as North American grain imports drove down European prices in the 1870s, taking their toll on arable farmers. Long distance refrigerated meat imports did not help livestock breeders either. In the tourist business islanders faced competition from seasonal workers or *overners* (from "over the water") as locals called them, not necessarily with enthusiasm. Meanwhile islanders sought wages in Portsmouth and Southampton and some of them hired to caulk or weatherproof ship's hulls in shipyards were nicknamed *caulkheads*, originally a mildly derogatory term given the semi-skilled nature of the work, but celebrated later as a badge of island birth.

Air Maneuvers

The Isle of Wight assumed important roles in both world wars; its proximity to the continent saw to that. Three trans–Atlantic liners requisitioned by the Admiralty to house internees and POWs lay off Ryde early in World War I, but the War Office moved them in 1915, deciding they were too close to the action for comfort. A safer offshore location, the Isle of Man, was given the job, as we have seen. Wight became an arms chest and early warning center instead and, auspiciously for its economy, designed and built seaplanes for marine patrols and antisubmarine tasks.

Two Cowes boat-building companies, S.E. Saunders Ltd. and J. Samuel White Company, had already diversified into the infant world of aviation before 1914. The island seems to have had people with design and test flight experience from the outset of this new technology, or at least a willingness to acquire it, a scarcely acknowledged aspect of its contribution to 20th century progress. These early flying machines were so flimsy in construction (plywood and calico) that it is hard to imagine how they got into the air and stayed there, but the war revolutionized aircraft construction, not least by creating military air forces. A number of Wight-built land planes and flying boats saw service for the Royal Naval Air Service and British Army Air Corps, the latter with floats and boat-shaped hulls for water-based flights. A converted Wight seaplane successfully bombed a German submarine, UB 32, in August 1917, an early demonstration of air-sea strikes to come. Wight's aircraft business was given further impetus after the war when famed British pioneer aviator Alliot Vernon Roe bought out S.E Saunders. The new company of Saunders-Roe (1928) built monoplanes and flying boats at East Cowes and the RAF (formed in 1918) flew their flying boats across the world to Australia in the later 1930s. The company also moved into passenger-carrying aircraft. A subsidiary Spartan Airways was set up in 1933. Several island airfields were active in the 1930s with Ryde the busiest. Spartan Airways is one of a group of small airlines nationally that merged into what eventually became British Airways.

Front-Line in World War II

Wight filled a tough spot in a tough neighborhood in medieval times, on the front line soaking up cross–Channel plunderers and pillagers, mustering whatever defenses it could. Yet the prospects could hardly have seemed direr than in 1940, as news of Nazi occupation of France and Britain's Channel Islands filtered through. When tired and subdued evacuees from the Channel Islands began to arrive in the Solent in June 1940 huddled in cargo transports, fear of the enemy not far behind grew. The island was beefed up defensively and made a restricted area, but German assault took the form of air bombardment instead and the Battle of Britain ensued.

The skies raged for a year until RAF fighter command, enabled by code breakers at Bletchley Park, cracked flight path attack plans and pushed back the *Luftwaffe*. German surface invasion was postponed and when Hitler decided out of the blue, to his ultimate cost, to open up an eastern front in 1941 and invade the USSR, Wight breathed easier. The island played an important supportive role for the rest of the war. The banks of the Medina were alive with the sounds of warship repair and construction, Saunders-Roe busy building seaplanes and J. Samuel White manufacturing parts for Spitfires and Lancaster bombers, although shipbuilding remained its main business. Wight was also the base of an innovative plan to pump fuel from Britain to France to supply the D-Day landing in 1944.

A beachhead in Nazi-occupied France would need vast quantities of petroleum, and a logistics think tank named Combined Operations Experimental Establishment (COXE) came up with Operation Pluto or "Pipeline under the Ocean." If Napoleon thought that an army marches on its stomach then COXE understood it also lived on fuel supply. The question was how to span the width of the English Channel. The solution was the brainchild of A.C Hartley, a chief engineer for Anglo-Iranian Petroleum (a predecessor of BP), who proposed a three-inch diameter steel pipe, manufactured in one continuously coiled length of 30-plus miles, swathed in insulation and coated in tar. It was a first in offshore pipeline construction, a remarkable idea that would work. *HMS Holdfast*, a coastal freighter, was refitted to lay it, replete with a great floating drum in which the line was coiled, deployed aft in the manner of laying submarine telegraph cables. The operation was carried out under a cloak of secrecy with the RAF flying constant supervisory patrols. A 1,000-mile land pipeline system was already in place in Britain and a pumping station at Thorness (west of Cowes) brought the oil onshore via a pipeline under the Solent. It was then piped across the center of the island to a 620,000-gallon storage tank at Shanklin on the south coast where a battery of pumps went day and night. Some 20 pipelines were laid across to France in all, most from Wight to Cherbourg. Operation Pluto had the capability of delivering a million gallons a day to the D-Day invasion, and Dwight D. Eisenhower, US commander of the offense, applauded it as a daring and vital contributor to what became the greatest sea-borne invasion in history.

Jet Propulsion Lab

Wight has been a prospector in speed dynamics ever since famed wireless telegrapher Guglielmo Marconi conducted experiments on the island. Flying boats, jet aircraft, space rockets, hovercraft, racing yachts, powerboats and jet cars have come off drawing boards and out of shipyards, hangars and workshops (much of it in East Cowes) for a century, beginning with Marconi's determination to compete with the speed of sound. Drenched with sea spray, in a tugboat amid stormy seas near The Needles, the Italian successfully transmitted messages over a span of 18 miles in 1897. Two years later he did it again, this time from 70 miles out at sea, making contact with a telegraph mast aloft in the grounds of the Royal Needles Hotel at Alum Bay. A half century later the island was home to supersonic exploration in Britain's largely forgotten space program as Saunders-Roe diversified into rocket engine technology. The launching pad was Woomera in Australia (the Isle of Wight was not quite Cape Canaveral) but rockets were built and tested on the island with 22 single-stage rockets known as *Black Knights* assembled between 1958 and 1965. A three-stage rocket, *Black Arrow,* was built at the site of J. Samuel White's old shipyard in East Cowes in 1966, the centuries-old business having gone into liquidation the previous year. It was a *Black Arrow* that put the all–British made satellite *Prospero* into orbit in 1971, high noon of Britain's space program. There was to be no more. The government stopped financing launches in the same year. The last of the *Black Arrows* can be seen at rest in the space gallery of London's Science Museum.

Aviation enterprise preceded World War I, and after 1945 important contributions to aerodynamics continued on a variety of fronts. Saunders-Roe carried on building flying boats after World War II. A jet engine fighter flying boat, the *SR-A1,* the fastest-ever flying boat, commissioned by the Admiralty, made its maiden flight in 1947. The future was in land-based flights, however, and the company moved progressively into other marine transports, registering impressive successes in a new generation of high-speed passenger craft. A hydrofoil was launched in 1954, the *Bras d'Or,* its hull supported on ski-like wings. The bulk of it was above water so it moved at faster speeds than conventional boats. The principle had been explored before in other places, but from the 1950s hydrofoils found successful application in passenger-only sea services. Red Funnel's hydrofoil covers the Southampton to Cowes journey in 20 minutes; the conventional ferry takes an hour. Saunders-Roe built the world's first hovercraft in 1959 from a design by Norfolk radio engineer and boat builder Christopher Cockerill. A land-and-sea vehicle riding an air cushion in close proximity to the surface, the hovercraft concept was so promising that Saunders-Roe became British Hovercraft Corporation. For the next 25 years the rapidity of hovercraft attracted passengers on England to France crossings, with Hoverlloyd and Seaspeed the principal operators. Completion of the Channel Tunnel rail link in 1994 changed travel plans again, but the hovercraft is still proven for short sea crossings. It holds its own on the Solent. The Southsea to Ryde trip has become the world's longest running service, having begun in 1965. The time taken to cross is about the same as it takes to walk along Ryde Pier, and first-time passengers arrive pleasantly disoriented, still adjusting to the land change.

The island has also been a player in several water and land speed record attempts. Sir Malcolm Campbell's *Bluebird* spent some of its formative years inside an East Cowes boatyard, before it broke the water speed record in 1938 at 131 mph. The twin-engine jet cars *Thrust 2* and *Thrust SSC* set land speed records in the USA in 1983 (650 mph) and 1997 (714 mph) after workshops in East Cowes and Wootton Creek contributed in construction and assembly. Driver Richard Noble, a British fighter pilot, set up an aircraft company at Sandown Airport in 1985, one of several to carry on the tradition of small aircraft construction on the island. In the ever-evolving transportation industry British Hovercraft became Westland Aerospace in 1984 to focus on the flight business. Its contracts for helicopter structures and aircraft systems sustained the local economy, but the 2001 decision by GKN Westland to sell its East Cowes plant ended that endeavor. The property is to be converted into a residential development.

Semi-Detached Wight

Wight supported a six-digit population for much of the 20th century, doing so right next door to a major onshore metropolis. Just across the Solent lies the Southampton and Portsmouth conurbation with around half a million people. Wight consequently is a mixture of island suburb and garden park retreat for the comfortably retired, in the latter role akin to that of Roman times although far more are housed this time around. When Paul McCartney sang of "a cottage on the Isle of Wight" in the Beatles song *When I'm 64*, he was only ten years out in lifestyle anticipations. The median age on the island was around 54, according to figures released by the IOW County Council in 2002, with nearly half of the 132,000 residents over 50. This age group largely accounts for the 12 percent leap in residency between 1981 and 2001, a rate three times higher than that of the nation.

The population swells further with vacation visitors and day-trippers in season. By the 1950s and 1960s "bucket-and-spade" seaside holidays were big business. Holiday camp chains and eastern coast resorts boomed — so much so that many English have a childhood memory of a trip there and take their own children. Cheap overseas package holidays may have impacted the trade from the 1970s but nostalgia is now its specialty, selling "ye olde England." Short-break visitors still arrive in appreciable numbers and Wight's bed-and-breakfast businesses, traditional amusement arcades, ice cream stands, deck chair rentals, pleasure parks and sundry cultural distractions remain more viable than those of any of the other offshore islands. There are seven regular services to the island from Portsmouth, Southampton and Lymington, up to 350 crossings per day. Passengers choose between car ferry, catamaran, hydrofoil and hovercraft. Tourism currently generates about 25 percent of GDP and employs about 20 percent of the workforce. Wight has diversified its visitor profile to become a popular venue for gatherings of the artistically inclined, too. An international jazz festival was held in 2002, although there have been no repeats of the monster "summer of love" weekend rock festivals of 1969 (Bob Dylan) and 1970 (Jimi Hendrix), when hundreds of thousands descended on the island, the biggest single invasions in its history by far.

The semi-detached status has its advantages. Accessible inshore position brings benefits in frequent visitor revenue. No other island is closer to the major centers of Britain's population. There is a debit side, however, as costs of ferry imports have fueled local inflation. The nightly neon of Portsmouth and Gosport may shimmer across the water after dusk from Ryde pier, the Solent dark and invisible, but the daily reality of ferry fares and schedules is a running sore for commuting islanders. A Solent tunnel has been talked about since the 1880s and more recently a bridge. It is an ambitious thought. A single span would double the length of the Humber Bridge, Britain's longest.

Conundrums

Construction projects for new tourist amenities and retirement homes attract investment and create jobs, but what is good for property developers is not necessarily good for residents. Summer traffic congestion is a worry. The sheer volume of vehicular movement down narrow high streets and country lanes disturbs the folksy idyll and defeats the product on offer. Retirees and short getaway vacationers want peace and quiet. There are other issues. Seasonal labor influx competing for jobs and wealthy residents able to pay higher prices both work to the detriment of wage and price structure. IOW County Council statistics reported that hourly real wage rates fell short of national and regional growth in the 1990s while unemployment was marginally higher. Employment in hotel and catering is competitive and alternatives outside a bloated public sector are not always easy to find, especially without education or special skills. Food preparation and service rank highest of the unemployed primary skills.[19] On the plus side, inflation has been checked by the market effect of prominent chain stores opening up on the island in recent years (an "out-of-town" retail complex in Newport is one conspicuous example) and by internet "e-tailing."

The Isle of Wight is 100 percent UK; that is, there are none of the tax breaks customary in quasi-independent Man or the Channel Islands. There are no juicy EU subsidies either (as yet). Shipping costs are a disincentive for businesses with large markets and there is a low concentration of them. New business start-up rates have been lower than in the Southeast region generally. As in other offshore economies, small low cost enterprises proliferate, but they tend not to alleviate unemployment. Over half of Wight's land is under environmental protection designation, and while conservation is fine for aesthetics, part of the island's marketable appeal, it is a frustration to those who would like to attract more investment. Trying to balance the interests of those who want babbling brooks and bucolic lifestyles with entrepreneurs looking to service a rising population with economic needs remains the pressing political issue.

Political representation is another anomaly. The population pendulum has swung to its proportional disadvantage at Westminster. In the UK general election of 2001, the Isle of Wight was the most populous electoral constituency in the nation. Once it was the most over-represented, now it's the least in per capita terms. To add to the numerical burden, the MP has to deal with a higher percentage of retirees, senior voters with time on their hands and grumbles in mind (traffic, ferry schedules and car ferry fares). Liberal and then Liberal Democrat politicians represented the island for 30 years, but in 2001 a Conservative won the seat. It was held in 2005. The UK Independence Party candidate (anti–EU) increased support from previous attempts. The vote share was only 3.5 percent but an increase is some indication of EU disenchantment. The island is even less conspicuous in the EU Parliament. As just one part of the densely populated South East England electoral district, its lobby is easily lost. Island issues find a more direct expression in the IOW County Council headquartered in Newport, but its powers and resources are limited. More than half of the 48 councilors elected to serve represent the amorphous "Island First" party. The question persists—whose island?

All's Well That Ends Well

There is no shortage of whimsy on the Isle of Wight. Local history books, Wight Radio talk-ins, and columnists in the popular weekly *Isle of Wight County Press* reminisce over halcyon days of yore in an inevitable pandering to the aging audience. Times when water came from a well, gas lamps lit dark streets, and trains from Ventnor West Station (closed in 1952) slowed down for passengers to pick wildflowers from the track side are fondly recalled. Incidentally the only rail stretch left operating is from Ryde Pier to Shanklin and it uses re-painted decommissioned London Underground trains. "Praising what is lost makes remembrance dear," said Shakespeare, but all is not quite lost, at least not yet. Reassuring certainties of the kind that made Wight popular do live on. Few English rural scenes can match that seen from the upstairs of a double-decker Southern Vectis bus winding its way along country lanes of a type Thomas Hardy would recognize, with glimpses here and there of gentrification in restored manor houses.

---

1. English Heritage Archaeological Review 1996/97, #4.20.10, "The Wootton-Quarr, the Isle of Wight survey" (http://www.eng-h.gov.uk/archrev/rev96_97/wquar.htm).

2. *Pliny the Elder: Natural History* Healy, John F., trans., (Penguin Classics, 1991), Bk. IV, 104.

3. *Suetonius: The 12 Caesars* Graves, Robert, trans., (Penguin Classics, 1979), 280.

4. Brading Town Council, "Brading Roman Villa," 2004 (http://www.brading.gov.uk/villa.html).

5. Ireland, S., ed., "Panegyric on Constantius Caesar, delivered A.D. 297," in *Roman Britain: A Sourcebook* (Routledge, 1986), 133.

6. *Bede: The Ecclesiastical History of the English People,* McClure, Judith, and Collins, Roger, eds. (Oxford University Press, World's Classics Series, 1994), IV, 197.

7. Ibid.

8. Chamberlin, Russell, "Carisbrooke Castle," (English Heritage Series, 2002 ed), 2.

9. Arreton, Freshwater, Godshill, Newchurch, Niton and Whippingham.

10. Hinde, Thomas, ed., *The Domesday Book* (USA edition published by CLB, 1977), 125–126.

11. Hockey, S.F., *Insula Vecta: The Isle of Wight in the Middle Ages* (Phillimore, 1982), 85.

12. Hockey, 124–135.

13. Chamberlin, 5.

14. Oglander, Sir John, *A Royalists Notebook, 1585–1655* (First published London 1936, reissued Bloom, New York, 1971).

15. Hockey, 205–212.

16. Isle of Wight History Centre, hosted by IOW Archaeological Society, "The Life of Sir Robert Holmes" (http://frespace.virgin.net/ric.martin/vectis/hookeweb.rob.htm).

17. Ayton, Richard, and Daniell, William, *Voyage around Great Britain, 1814–1825, vol. II* (Tate Gallery and Scolar Press, reprinted 1978).

18. Isle of Wight History Centre, "Timeline of History" (http://freespace.virgin.net/roger.hewitt/iwias/history.htm).

19. Isle of Wight County Council online statistics report 2002 "Primary Skills of Unemployed" (http://www.iwight.gov.uk/library/statistics/unemployment.asp).

8

The Channel Islands: "Morceaux de France"

"Iles Anglo-Normandes et morceaux de France tombles a la mer et ramasses par L'Angleterre" [The Channel Islands are pieces of France which fell into the sea to be picked up by England]—Victor Hugo, *L'Archipel de la Manche* (1883)

An archipelago lying off the northern French coast does not invite inclusion in a book on the British Isles, yet the Channel Islands have been Crown dependencies for nearly a thousand years. The relationship began with the feudal Norman-French Empire and although the old Norman duchy is now obsolete this is of no concern to islanders, as the past is present and the toast persists: "The Queen. Le Duc!" The Channel Islands, like the Isle of Man, are self-governing jurisdictions for internal affairs, *of* Britain but not in it. The UK Parliament funds defense but they are not constituents. Those defending this anachronism argue that *Les Iles Anglo-Normandes*, as the French call them, sought an English Crown association rather than a French one precisely because they wanted to be left alone!

The four main islands of Jersey, Guernsey, Alderney and Sark plus the tiny isles of Herm, Jethou, Brecqhou and Lihou lie off Normandy's Cotentin peninsula. The total population approached 150,000 at the 2001 census, mostly English-speaking but of French descent. A local patois survives, strains of a Norman-French dialect once the speech of kings of England, lending an authenticity of heritage lost on Wight and Scilly. The islands divide politically into the two bailiwicks of Jersey and Guernsey. Jersey is the more populous with 87,000 residents, about one-third living in the capital, St. Helier. The Guernsey bailiwick includes Alderney and Sark. Victor Hugo lived in Jersey and Guernsey between 1852 and 1870 and found "a fraternization between the islands but also a gentle mocking banter."[1] Each has an unflattering epithet for the other: the Frenchified *crapauds* (toads) of Jersey and stubborn *ânes* (donkeys) of Guernsey. Most aspects of modern life are thoroughly commercial as a stroll past department stores, jewelry and cosmetics shops in St. Helier or the palatial walled homes of the rich in Guernsey's St. Peter Port communicates. Expensive cars wriggle

THE CHANNEL ISLANDS

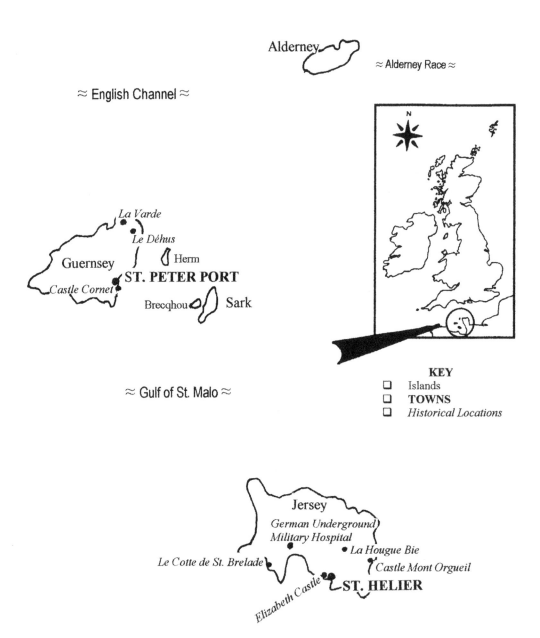

≈ Alderney Race ≈

≈ English Channel ≈

La Varde

Le Déhus

Guernsey

Herm

ST. PETER PORT

Castle Cornet

Brecqhou

Sark

≈ Gulf of St. Malo ≈

KEY

☐ Islands

☐ **TOWNS**

☐ *Historical Locations*

Jersey

*German Underground
Military Hospital*

La Hougue Bie

Le Cotte de St. Brelade

Castle Mont Orgueil

Elizabeth Castle **ST. HELIER**

0   10 miles

for space on narrow lanes and from the back of Jersey buses grins a suntanned John Nettles— the British actor who starred in *Bergerac*, a 1980s British TV series about a Jersey cop who tracks down British villains in exile and fights off drug traffickers and other undesirables. Memorabilia and coach tours still cash in from those who remember it.

The green clad island interiors undulate. Jersey slopes gradually from its higher north coast while the deep-water anchorage of St. Peter Port on Guernsey's south coast is the best natural harbor in the islands. The 300 feet high plateau of Sark is the most dramatic, daunting at close sight with wave-lacerated cliffs on every side; settlers had to tunnel through them to establish the small port. Alderney's wind blasted perimeter protects a bleak plateau rising several hundred feet, and to its east lie the treacherous Casquet Rocks, as in caskets or coffins, a self-explanatory reference to the dangers therein. The warning light from a coal-fired lighthouse could not prevent a British flagship wrecking there in a gale in 1744 with hundreds lost. Tidal currents can reach ten knots in a rolling and pitching torrent known as "The Alderney Race," effect of a fault line between island and mainland. Victor Hugo declared the fury of these seas in *La Travailleurs de la Mer* (1866) as "like an ambush — a trumpet announcing an invisible warfare."[2]

Paleolithic Finds

Tens of thousands of years ago the English Channel or *La Manche* ("The Sleeve") to the French was a dry forested valley inhabited by wandering Neanderthals and woolly mammoth. Flints and heaps of animal bone in granite headland caves on Jersey's southwest coast, particularly La Cotte de St. Brelade, testify to economic life there c. 120,000 B.C. What is now a cave was then a rocky escarpment. Nomadic bands corralled rhino herds and mammoth, pushing them to their deaths over the scarp edge and butchering them with stone tools. Elk, deer and smaller animals and birds provided alternative sustenance. Thirteen Neanderthal teeth plus the fragments of a child's skull from a later phase of activity at the site, between 50,000 and 100,000 years ago, are neatly laid out in a museum case at La Hougue Bie, Jersey. The caves are sealed off now, but a two-story-high cliff facsimile in St. Helier's Jersey Museum helps visualization of the Paleolithic habitat.

After the last ice age, a rising Atlantic gradually pushed the pre–Channel valley people uphill in an easterly direction toward a chalk embankment between the Dover and Calais of today. This land bridge, joining Britain to the continent, was breached around 7000 B.C., as melt waters from the North Sea flowed over it to meet a rising Atlantic and the English Channel began its formation. It was not a dam burst. People had time to adapt. Channel dwellers waded in places where they had paddled and then boated where they had waded. The chalk headland butts of the old land bridge live on as the white cliffs of Dover and the "isleting" of peninsula headland was still going in the later Neolithic Period; evidence is seen between Grosnez and L'Etacq on Jersey's far northwest coast, where long low tides reveal a sunken forest.

Megaliths

Grain cultivation and domesticated livestock were the mainstay of subsistence by 4000 B.C., supplemented by a marine life rich in shellfish, bass, mullet and conger eel. These farmers too erected megaliths, attesting to the wider Atlantic culture that we have followed south from Shetland. Barry Cunliffe places the islands within the influence of the neighboring Brittany field of megalithic innovation.[3] Axe finds also place them within a wider world. Information in the first instance can be credited to Frederick Corbin Lukis of Guernsey, whose investigations in the second quarter of the 19th century uncovered material now in the Guernsey Museum in St. Peter Port, much of it from the vicinity of chambered tombs such as Les Fouaillages, Le Déhus and La Varde in the north of the island. The four-sided Le Déhus is a gem. Its survival is due to one John de Havilland, who paid cash to save it from local quarrymen in 1775. A narrow entrance now fitted with a door opens into a broad chamber with side alcoves. La Varde (c. 3250 B.C.) at 40 feet long is the biggest on Guernsey with a main capstone weighing over 10 tons. In use through the Bronze Age, it is tucked away among the grassy bunkers of a popular golf course on L'Ancresse Common.

The grandest tomb is Jersey's La Hougue Bie in Grouville parish. A huge grassy mound covers a Neolithic chamber dated to 3000 B.C. Topped by a 12th century church, it was not fully excavated until 1924, and the original sunrise aligned entrance was found only after radar studies in the 1990s suggested other passageways. Visitors must squat low to get inside and crouch along a low granite-block passageway to the central chamber, where it is possible to stand upright. Three sepulchral alcoves are set off to the sides but all is stonily bare now, information boards outside imagining an interior once warmed with woven wall hangings and icons illuminated by fish oil lamps. The La Hougue Bie site includes a reconstructed rectangular Neolithic house (no houses have been uncovered) with wattle and daub walls of hazel rods and clay and a thatched roof, testimony of how it was for the living and a useful reminder that without community vitality these tombs would never have been built in the first place. The stone quarried to build La Hougue Bie came from the eastern half of the island. The heaviest block weighs at least 20 tons. Coordination of the removal effort required authority, but whether it was as coercive as the forced labor used by Nazis during their occupation of the island is not known — a subterranean German World War II command bunker sits beside the Neolithic mound.

There are no stone circles to compare with those on Lewis or Orkney, but two oval-shaped enclosures on Jersey — La Hougue des Platons and La Ville ès Nouaux — attract expert interest, compared in type to Brittany and to southwestern Ireland. Both are "cists-in-circle" formations (encountered at Meayll Hill, Isle of Man), active in the third millennium B.C., easier in the making than time and resource consuming passage graves. The passage grave of La Pouquelaye de Faldouet (origins c. 3300 B.C.), two miles east of La Hougue Bie, is unusual in that its main chamber appears to have been left uncovered, though this may have to do with the fact that evidence is lost. Elsewhere on Jersey at least eight *menhirs* have been identified and another four in Guernsey.[4] Recent studies focused on the possibility of perimeter fortifications during this time with evidence buried under later Iron Age and medieval defensive structures.

The early to mid Bronze Age is something of a mystery, a period of crisis perhaps when megalithic tombs were sealed and abandoned, earlier than the climatic change impacting the Atlantic islands. By the later Bronze Age or early Iron Age a metals trade in copper, tin, gold and silver emerged between Britain and France; probably wine and other prestige goods were part of it too, the islands being well positioned to participate. A beautifully crafted gold torque found in house foundations in St. Helier in 1889 is much prized by La Société Jersiaise. Beakers found in an *urnfield* near La Ville ès Nouaux were of a type suggesting cross–Channel contact, and if the tin emporium role of the Isle of Wight is accepted then participation in the tin trade routes can be added.

Gallic, Frankish and Breton Isles

Modern Jersey has an international reputation in offshore banking, and it would be astonishing to find it served a similar role 2,000 years ago. The evidence is not very diverse but the discovery of substantial coin hoards may variously support participation in a vibrant Romano-Celtic commerce, a war chest, or a just a convenient offshore deposit account location! One hoard alone found at La Marquanderie in Brelade, Jersey, contained a remarkable 12,000 coins, attributable to the Gallic (continental Celtic) *Coriosolites* people of nearby Brittany, Jersey, possibly a part of their tribal territory. When Julius Caesar invaded rebellious Gallic Armorica in 56 B.C. (now Brittany and Normandy) some fled his advancing forces by retreating to the Channel Islands, though he did not go there and the date of conquest is unknown. The hoard contains coins minted in the 20s B.C.,[5] defeating the argument that the entire sum was secreted by those fleeing Caesar. It is possible of course that coins were added to an existing refugee hoard, but the point is that Jersey was a treasury for some purpose. It is a reasonable assumption that the islands were utilized for their nodal advantage in cross–Channel trade, but proving their use for the Romans is another matter. Excavations at La Plaiderie, Guernsey, found what may have been Roman warehouses and a team of local divers in St. Peter Port harbor in 1985 salvaged the hull of a boat dated to A.D. 190. Nicknamed *Asterix*, it is said to resemble the vessels of the *Veneti*, a Celtic tribe from what became Brittany. It was carrying a cargo of pitch, a caulking resin made from tar, when a fire aboard sank it. However it must be conceded that beyond some Italian pottery there is little other remnant of Roman occupation. No major settlement has been found. In the imperial twilight of the fourth century when Roman authority was being tested, a fort was built at the Nunnery in Longis Bay, Alderney, presumably to protect the harbor for Channel crossings.

If Roman impact is meager in terms of physical evidence, the legacy in language is not. Islanders spoke a dialect form of Gallic, the now extinct Celtic tongue of Gaul, but this changed with the rise of Frankish Nuestria. The Germanic Franks were tribal heirs to Roman Gaul. Their warrior leader Clovis I laid the base of France by dividing conquered lands among his kin and Nuestria (later Normandy) was the name given to the northwestern portion with the Channel Islands offshore. The Franks were so intent on fighting each other over inheritance claims that the islands were probably places of refuge. The spread of Christianity gradually Latinized Frankish speech and values, and a new hybrid emerged, *Langue d'Oïl* or "Old French," a fusion of Gallic, Germanic and Latin. In the islands p–Celtic Breton must be added to the post–Roman lingual mix since Brittany was settled by émigré Britons from the fifth century and contact was inevitable through proximity, fishing and trading.

Early Saints

It is customary to credit the introduction of monasticism in northwest France to Martin of Tours (c. 316–c. 397), a Roman soldier's son who fought his good fight against *pagani*. There is no report of him in the Channel Islands, but folklore is rich about later holy men who brought the faith ashore. The conversion of Jersey is said to begin with Helier (his name given to the Jersey capital of St. Helier), an ascetic who was either the follower of a sixth century abbot from the Cotentin peninsula called Marcouf, or an inspiration to him. The association is unclear. Marcouf lived his later life as a hermit and Les Iles de St. Marcouf, off the Norman coast, are named for him. Helier was killed in mid-sixth century by those unsympathetic to the new teachings. A small oratory on L'Islet, a tidal island in St. Helier harbor where Elizabeth Castle now stands, is dedicated to his martyrdom, but it dates from the 12th century when Christianity's status was secure. Guernsey's early Christianity has a Breton source. The Welsh-born monk Samson (see also chapter on Scilly) spent his later years in Brittany, having followed migrant Celtic Britons there, and is believed to have led a missionary expedition to Guernsey (c. 525), landing at the harbor now named after him. His memory is enshrined in tales of ecclesiastical war waged on druid inspired Celtic sun worshippers; in one he gave gifts to children to stay away from bonfire rituals. The new message took root but still had to co-exist with the old ways; bonfire dances persisted for centuries.[6] Samson's successor was Maglorius (St. Magloire), possibly a kinsman, founder of a monastery on Sark. He imposed a severe regime under which reputedly even a cough during chanting or prayer earned six strokes of the lash. One of his brethren, St. Vignalis, is recognized for introducing Christianity to Alderney c. 575.

These autonomous religious communes came within the diocese of Coutances on the Cotentin peninsula by the time of Charlemagne. A Frankish warrior with Latin pretensions (*Carolus Magnus*: Charles the Great), Charlemagne consolidated territories into a larger French realm and had himself crowned by the pope in Rome on Christmas Day 800. Jersey was divided into 12 parishes and Guernsey into 10 by this time, many of them bearing saints' names, though the origins are not necessarily ecclesiastical, likely representing ancient kinship settlements. It is tempting to date assimilation within the Latin Frankish world from Charlemagne, but the islands were still outlying pieces. Charlemagne never ruled them directly. A coalition of Breton tribes under the leadership of Nomenöe rebelled against Charlemagne's grandson in 846 to release Brittany from Carolingian control, and given Breton influence on the islands, it seems more likely they were within that sphere on the eve of Norman annexation.

The Duchy of Normandy

Lightning up-river raids by fleets of Norsemen devastated Carolingian Nuestria in the later ninth century. The ruler of the western Franks, Charles III, dealt with them by accommodating them, granting lands as a fief to their leader Rollo. It was a clever gamble to enlist one Viking as a watchdog against the rest (and the Bretons). Rollo became his vassal by the Treaty of St. Clair sur Epte in 911 and wed his daughter, taking the title duke of Normandy. The following year he accepted Christian baptism. The depth of Rollo's religious conviction is uncertain but the efficacy of the arrangement was not: Nuestria had become Normandy, a land fit for Norse settlement, albeit a feudal Frankish one. The incomers needed little persuasion to domesticate the fertile farmland and river network of the lower Seine valley. As Norsemen married Frankish women the *Langue d'Oïl* of their children diluted Nordic speech and the new strain became Norman-French. La Société Jersiaise lists 76 modern Jèrriais (Jersey-French) words of Old Norse origin and many (not surprisingly) are maritime nouns like *heune* from the Old Norse word *hunn* for topsail and *vraic* (rhymes with rack) from Old Norse *wraec* or seaweed. Norse input is unquestionable; the unknown is whether it originated with Norse settlers or came from later immersion within Normandy.

Monk chroniclers recorded the Viking raids on Nuestria, and one of them, a Jersey-born cleric, writer and teacher named Maistre Wace (c. 1100–1174), the first Channel Islander beyond the saints we can name, has left us his own words. He was Norman-French, his name having a Teutonic ring to it, and he wrote in that vernacular. He came from either a seigneurial family or a monastery and was educated from a young age in Latin in Caen, Normandy, becoming a *clerc lisant,* an ecclesiastical position with a range of duties including writing, composing and teaching, hence the prefix Maistre.[7] Among his earlier writings are a rhyme about King Arthur's Round Table and a translation of Geoffrey of Monmouth's Latin text on British kings. Curiously Wace was interested in Celtic and British culture, an indication of its lingering influence in his age perhaps. Henry II commissioned his last work, *Roman de Rou,* in 1160, a heroic account of Rollo the first duke of Normandy and his descendants. Unfortunately Wace gives us precious little on the islands beyond listing island names under Norse attack, the *ey* endings originating with them.

Brittany came under vassalage to dukes of Normandy in the 10th century, and Rollo's son Duke William I (William "Longsword") probably added the islands to the duchy in 933, since chroniclers refer to annexation of the land of the Bretons on the coast. Whatever the landholding pattern and social structure prior to annexation, feudalism became the new order, families given fiefs in return for liege to Norman dukes. A Norman-French-speaking aristocracy of seigneurs emerged. It isn't clear whether dukes visited much or at all (Duke Robert is said to have been forced ashore on Jersey by a storm in the mid–1030s) but ducal benefaction did bring new monastic orders to the islands. Land tenure was granted first to Benedictines from Mont St. Michel on the nearby Breton coast, an island rock citadel and focus of Christian pilgrimages since the eighth century. Augustinians arrived from Cherbourg in the 11th century to develop a religious community on Herm, given an endowment there by Duke William II (a.k.a. William the Conqueror). Many small granite churches still seen on the islands have their origins in this time.

After William the Conqueror was crowned William I of England in 1066, the Channel Islands became part of an expanded cross–Channel feudal state. The islands are associated to the English Crown through William. Life proceeded as it had since 933. The new ruling English class spoke Norman-French as they did, the division of the islands into fiefs was in progress, and the home of the duchy remained Rouen in Normandy. A greater upheaval would come a century later during the reign of John, third in line of the Plantagenet kings, successors of the Norman dynasty from 1154.

Good King John?

John (r. 1199–1216) has not enjoyed a good press in English historical writing, having been unfavorably compared to dashing Crusader brother Richard *Coeur de Lion* (Lionhearted). He alienated Rome and lost enough lands in the French home-lands to earn his barons' scorn and enmity. Perversely his reputation in the Channel Islands is more assured; he is heralded there as a guarantor of ancient liberties and source of allegiance to the English Crown. His French problems began when his authority was challenged in his native Anjou, a duchy to the south of Normandy and home of the Plantagenets, where his young nephew Arthur duke of Brittany was pre-ferred. Strengthened by his mother Eleanor of Aquitaine, a formidable powerbroker herself, he sought resolution through war, but infatuation with and then marriage to a young and apparently very beautiful French girl, Isabella of Angoulème, com-plicated the issue. It was not an ideal liaison. She had been betrothed to one of his French vassals, Hugh de Lusignan, who promptly sought and won the support of Philippe II, king of France. Phillippe was a Capet and as dukes of Paris this dynasty filled the power vacuum created by the collapse of the Carolingians. Capetian kings ruled the Norman fiefs, and by feudal law Philippe was John's suzerain. John held Anjou, Normandy and the Channel Islands from him. Philippe summoned John to answer the infidelity case against him but John refused and war began.

The conflict opened on two fronts with Philippe attacking Normandy from the east as John struggled with his Breton nephew. He belied his nickname "Softsword" initially, an insult writ for all time through the eventual outcome, capturing the cas-tle of Mirebeau in the marches of Anjou in a dawn raid in 1202. It was a bold strike, not only releasing his mother from custody but also involving capture of nephew Arthur along with Hugh de Lusignan. He squandered this advantage by releasing Lusignan and his men, having earlier sent them in chains to England, in return for promises of liege that would be broken, and probably (though not proven) murder-ing the 12-year-old Arthur. Arthur's disappearance increased John's unpopularity among French vassals and strengthened Philippe II's cause. By mid–1204 mainland Normandy was in Capetian hands. It got worse. John antagonized Pope Innocent III over clerical appointments in a row he would lose, succeeding only in arousing eccle-siastical opposition and incurring papal taxes. Then in an effort to get the resources he needed to keep fighting, he upset barons by arbitrarily levying *scutage*, a feudal tax imposed on vassals who declined military service. His confiscation of properties ignored judicial procedures instituted by his father Henry II. To cap it all he had the temerity to lose a decisive battle at Bouvines in 1214 to Philippe and by this defeat (he was not present) the loss of Anjou and Normandy, a calamity for Norman-French barons in Britain whose ancestral homelands were there.

Although mainland Normandy was in Capetian hands from 1204, the Channel Islands were not. Nominally under charter to Piers des Préaulx (titled lord of the isles, 1200–1204), John maintained a hold through force and mollification. A colorful mercenary named Eustace le Moine (Eustace the Monk) was hired to sack the islands for him. A lapsed Benedictine who had renounced vows to avenge his father's murder, Eustace seized Sark and organized raids from there. Hostages from pro–Capetian families were shipped in chains to England on John's orders and by 1206 the islands were subdued, although Préaulx's capitulation in battle in Rouen (some suspect defection) cost him his lordship. In 1207 the king sent Hasculf de Suligny to be warden of the isles (an alternate term for lord of the isles), empowering him to raise a militia. John may have lost Normandy, but he had not given up his claim to be called duke of Normandy, and those willing to swear allegiance were promised that customs would be honored. His navy numbered over 50 oared galleys by 1206, persuasive for islanders mindful of sea-raids, many doubtless unrecorded. The process severing the islands from their French connections was underway, in Victor Hugo's memorable phrase "pieces of France picked up by England."[8]

Les Iles Anglo-Normandes

The Church was exempt from this transfer of allegiance, remaining part of the diocese of Coutances until 1569, but the islanders were no longer subject to Rouen. *Les Iles Normandes* had become *Les Iles Anglo-Normandes*, outposts strategically and economically important to the evolving English fiefdom. Warden Suligny initiated the building of two ultimately impressive castles, Mont Orgueil on Jersey and Castle Cornet on Guernsey. Both experienced repeated action. An early test arrived in 1212 when Eustace le Moine and his gang of freebooters sailed into the Gulf of St. Malo, this time under the pay of Philippe II. Repelled in Jersey and Guernsey, where newly raised militia and royal troops did their job, they took Sark and left a force of men. Warden Philippe d'Aubigny drove them out two years later and took prisoners but not Eustace. D'Aubigny caught up with him eventually off England's Kent coast (1217) and had him hanged from the masthead.

The annexed islands developed a unique system of government recognizing indigenous practice and English Crown presence. Jersey and Guernsey had been administered separately under two Norman deputies since 1177, and John permitted continuation of judicial tradition through locally appointed bailiffs (one each for the two bailiwicks) presiding over existing assizes and together with 12 *jurats* forming two royal courts. The office of *jurat* (Latin *jurare*: to swear) went back at least to Charlemagne, when jurors of free men were appointed to interrogate prisoners, a Frankish practice paralleling Anglo-Saxon oath-helpers, though their duties related more to the prosecution than delivering a verdict. It is also feasible that *jurats* institutionalized Norse principles about community involvement in legal judgments, as we saw in the case of the Manx Tynwald. Old Norse concepts of individuality and justice are frequently understated because there is no paper trail to evaluate their contribution. The wardens meanwhile functioned like sheriffs in Norman-French Britain. They were Crown-appointees responsible for supervision of royal courts and assizes. There was no attempt otherwise to introduce English laws, military service, weights, measures or currency. Island customs prevailed and these principles were supported by John's successors. Henry III sent a message to Philippe d'Aubigny in 1218 assuring him that local assizes could continue and granted the islands to his son in 1254, the future Edward I, insisting they were never to be separated from the Crown. Edward's appointment of a Savoyard knight Otto de Grandison as warden in the 1280s, however, severely strained relationships.

Appointed first as justiciar of North Wales, as we saw with reference to Anglesey, Grandison never lived in the Channel Islands. He fought in the Crusades, served as emissary to Rome, and was sénéschal of Gascony, visiting the islands once toward the end of his life. His vassals organized defenses and collected dues, but they violated tradition by making themselves bailiffs and jurats and a great outcry erupted. Allegations of extortion, murder and abuse of custom were made in petitions, protests, and delegations. The rancor did not subside until Grandison's death in 1328. Edward III had succeeded to the throne by this time and after Edward II's disastrous reign wanted to protect sovereignty over French Aquitaine and keep links open with that wine-producing region. Since the Channel Islands were in the sea path and the French threatened those interests, he thought it important to win back loyalty. A new warden, John de Roches, succeeded in restoring confidence, and it was timely because there would be repeated raids on the islands for the rest of the 14th century, as forces sought to wrest them from Plantagenet grasp.

Invasions

The protracted cross-channel feud of the Hundred Years' War began in earnest for Channel Islanders during 1338 as a French force led by Admiral Nicolas Béhuchet occupied Jersey and burned St. Peter Port, having just laid waste to Portsmouth across the Channel. Relief came within two years, after a great naval victory for Edward III's fleet at Sluys (Flanders), where Béhuchet suffered the same fate as Eustace le Moine, executed at sea. Needing a safe anchorage, the king reaffirmed customs in 1341, but the decree sought only to reassure as to the status quo, to keep seigneurs loyal (privileges were not codified), and it worked. Channel Islands' parish records report dominant families associated with one island or another for centuries, notably the Carterets of Jersey and the Saumarez of Guernsey, but in the hell of war to ensue all ranks came under threat from attacks.

Yvain de Galles or Owain of Wales, last of the male line of Aberffraw and pretender to Gwynedd rule, mentioned in respect to Anglesey, paid an unfriendly visit in 1372. His French-backed force of 600 men overpowered Guernsey's militia and inflicted heavy casualties. It took ransom payment to get rid of him. As French needs in the Hundred Years' War escalated, Owain was deprived of much needed manpower to continue his Welsh expedition and was assassinated six years later, probably under orders from Plantagenet authorities. The French came again in 1373 and 1380. On both occasions the islands were occupied until English reinforcements showed up. In 1406 a combined Breton and Castilian force was driven back only after 10,000 crowns was paid out, probably from melting church plate into coinage. Sark was hard hit during these times. Monks who endured there quit after French forces terrorized it and brigands possessed the island. During Henry V's reign (1413–1422) all properties of the Benedictine orders were confiscated (as was the case on the Isle of Wight) to prevent a drain of money into enemy hands, and there was a mini-migration to repopulate decimated Alderney and make sure it stayed in the English fold.

Deliverance

Although the English fleet kept the Channel Islands' base secure, land forces had to concede ground to the rejuvenated French in the 1430s and 1440s (Jeanne d'Arc et al.), and by 1453 the Hundred Years' War was a lost cause. Only Calais and the Channel Islands remained in English hands. In the matter of Plantagenets vs. Capetians the English Channel was the final arbiter, in retrospect a reasonable outcome since a cross–Channel state was clearly difficult to sustain. England and France emerged as national monarchies, north and south of the Channel, each with a new sense of its own uniqueness, fuel for a mutual antipathy stretching to the 20th century! The islands' future was by no means assured. After decades of hard won defense, Jersey was ceded to the French in 1461, as part of arrangements to secure the English succession of Edward IV (his mother was French-born). The island did not rise up in protest, either because Louis XI of France promised the same immunities as the English Crown or because islanders anticipated the habitual English recapture. If this were so, then so it proved. A Yorkist vice-admiral, Sir Richard Harliston (the Plantagenets were now divided into Lancastrian and Yorkist branches), sailed in 1468 from Guernsey to rendezvous with Jersey militia and forced the French out of Castle Mont Orgueil after a 19-weeks siege. He was made governor of all of the islands in 1470.

In 1450 there were 15,000 Channel Islanders (two-thirds living on Jersey) but plague epidemics and repeated attacks meant fluctuating population levels. Daily life remained rude and crude for the majority, centered on humble stone dwellings, eking out survival, a favored few earning the right to run grain mills. Seigneurs were entitled to the content of shipwrecks, a custom common to all the offshore islands, while wardens appointed receivers to look after the collection and accountancy of revenue. Economic life was largely conditioned by the vicissitudes of war but some progress is evident. The islands had always been ports of call for passing ships rather than the home of a merchant navy, but from the 14th century the number of local ships and shipmasters grew, especially in Guernsey. Conger-eel lamp oil and knitted woolens were exported with a lot of trade transacted through Southampton. Silver plate, chalices and ewers crafted by local smiths from imported silver met church demand. However the need to make tithe payments to the church, pay off invaders, and the iconoclastic fury of the Reformation means that precious little of it survives.

The protracted cross–Channel strife and pirate raids led Edward IV and Louis XI to agree in 1483 that the islands should be considered neutral territory, safe havens for mutual commercial benefit even in war. A papal bull issued by Sixtus IV validated their agreement (this pope had earlier censured Louis XI for ignoring the authority of papal mandates over royal decrees and the bull may be viewed as reconciliatory). The pronouncement did not mince words warning of "a sentence of anathema and eternal damnation with confiscation of goods on all who shall land in the islands to burn, plunder and murder the inhabitants."[9] In the century that followed, a time of frequent Anglo-French conflict, business did prosper and with it life in the islands. Wharves, warehouses and attendant services in St. Peter Port expanded and the Jersey port of St. Aubin grew as wine and cloth merchants made new homes there. The papacy was the great supernumerary power of this age, a reason why the Channel Islands had remained long within the French diocese of Coutances while politically affiliated with the English Crown. In 1499 Henry VII tried to end this anomaly when he secured a papal bull to transfer the islands to the diocese of Winchester, but at nearly a hundred miles distant over sea and land, it would take the ferment of Reformation to really separate the islands' conscience from Roman roots.

Twin Governance

The centralizing of government was a hallmark of Henry VII's reign (r. 1485–1509) and several constitutional changes were implemented with reference to the islands. The judiciary was brought more firmly under the Crown with bailiffs to be royal (not gubernatorial) appointments and rules for the election and duties of *jurats* laid down. Disputes were to be referred to the Privy Council in London, a cabinet evolving out of the old King's Council. As to the executive, Governor Harliston was an early casualty of the new Tudor regime, forced into exile for his Yorkist sympathies. Two governors were appointed to replace him, one each for the two bailiwicks. They could demand a day's work a year from islanders on defenses, but by an order issued in 1494 they did not have the right to interfere in judicial procedure. The office was no more than a sinecure with a resident lieutenant-governor fulfilling duties in absentia. Most were absent. A notorious early exception was Sir Hugh Vaughan, appointed by Henry VII to govern Jersey. He behaved as if it were his own private kingdom, seizing property, dismissing a bailiff without prerogative, and abusing local women.[10] Heavy petitioning from outraged officials and a royal investigation in 1529 finally dislodged him, but his long term of office showed that while judicial procedure was documented, guaranteeing it was another matter.

The legislatures in the bailiwicks evolved out of the royal courts in much the way that the House of Commons emerged from the House of Lords, through experience rather than design. Constables and rectors from each of the parishes came to sit as legislators with *jurats* (it is useful to note that this office involved a duality of roles: legislator and juror) in *L'Etats* or "The States," a composite term for a parliament of all the parishes and one still in use. The constables enforced civil law and the rectors represented ecclesiastical interests. The States of Jersey assembly and Guernsey's States of Deliberation both emerged in the later 15th century.

Twin Faiths

In 1500 most western Europeans were baptized, married and buried as Catholic Christians, unified by the Latin Mass under papal custody. A century later this social order had been dramatically broken in a cultural revolution sprung from Martin Luther's protest of 1517; even he could hardly have anticipated the repercussions of his call for theological debate. Protestantism broke the mold. It fractured political relationships, expanding an intrinsic meaning of "church" from *the* building in the community to that of a congregation of believers at large under God, no longer obligated to one church. The Channel Islands were substantially impacted, more so perhaps than any of the other offshore islands. Their Protestantism unsurprisingly was French-originated, coming as much as anything from the pen of Noyon-born and Paris-educated Jean Cauvin (John Calvin). His lifework *The Institutes of the Christian Religion*, written between 1536 and 1559, enunciated a radical doctrine, one revolutionizing Christian society, at the core of which were Lutheran principles of readable scriptures and personal bible reading as the test of faith. French translations of the New Testament inspired by reformer Jacques Le Févre were in the islands by mid–16th century.

Calvinism spawned a growing number of sects, each intense in its own interpretation of translated biblical text, resolute in its defiance of papal authority, and holding social behavior to rigorous Old Testament standards. The most prominent in France were Huguenots, a Protestant coalition that may have included about 25 percent of the French population by the 1550s. The Catholic establishment was not idle in response, animated by a Counter-Reformation to actively resist the heresy. Catholic France became a bloodbath with eight bitter conflicts fought between 1562 and 1598. A 1568 edict made Protestantism punishable by death in France and the first Huguenots began to arrive in the islands from that time. They did not radically impact customs at first, their presence conditioned by extraneous factors of which commerce was one. The 1483 bull of neutrality was unacceptable to Huguenots because of its implications of papal authority, but criticism of it jeopardized lucrative business and there was a lot of that with Catholic France. What really set matters in motion was the other reformation in the 16th century church, the one begun by Henry VIII with his Church of England (1534).

More than a century before Henry V had weakened the priories and abbeys' wealth. Edward Seymour, brother of Henry VIII's third and much-loved wife Jane Seymour, also Jersey's governor 1537 to 1550, helped destroy what was left. As regent in 1547 for the nine-year-old Edward VI, his attempt to cement the new Anglicanism included wholesale destruction of anything redolent of popery. Fonts, statuary, stained glass, chalices and crosses were stolen and smashed in a fever of iconoclasm. A piece of a 14th century wayside cross from St. Ouen survives in the Jersey Museum. After Mary I's brief return to Catholicism all of the islands were shepherded within the new Anglican diocese of Winchester. Leading families accepted it, particularly in Jersey where the Carterets and Lemprières were readily accommodating. Anglicanism was a logical progression for seigneurs, their status derived from allegiance to monarchs whose powers now happened to include the church. Queen Elizabeth I's reassertion of this fact in her Acts of Supremacy and Uniformity (1559) was accepted with equanimity in Jersey but feelings on Guernsey were tense, as Calvinist doctrine there was in combative mode.

Henry VIII never intended theological reformation, but his defiance of Rome helped those who did. The extent of Guernsey's cultural revolution is evident by 1576 with religious articles drawn up and agreed by civil authorities. Church attendance was made compulsory as was use of the Huguenot Prayer Book, and laws regulating social behavior along the lines of daily godliness and sobriety were enacted. Anything threatening this new orthodoxy was deemed delusional and wicked. Cruel injustices perpetrated by officials in the name of religion were an unhappy feature of Tudor times. Women especially were vulnerable and countless numbers paid a dreadful price. Guernsey records show that between 1550 and 1649 at least 100 were accused of sorcery and witchcraft, a significant number hanged, strangled and burnt at the stake. John Foxe's *Book of Martyrs* (1563) tells of a 1556 case during the reign of Mary I in which Catherine Cauches and her daughters were burnt at the stake in St. Peter Port. One daughter had just given birth, but the bailiff ordered the child thrown on the pyre anyway.[11] In another case in 1617 Colette Dumont "confessed" to the Guernsey Royal Court that the devil had appeared before her in diabolical form, that he was her companion, and that she had promised to do his devilish work for him. She was executed with two others, hands tied behind backs, hoisted upwards so as to tear arms from sockets, cut down, strangled slowly and burnt alive at the stake.[12]

Defenses, Dissent, Discord and Rebellion

English Channel defenses became a matter of priority after Henry VIII's break with Rome, and Castle Cornet fortifications in St. Peter Port were strengthened and the bow-and-arrow castle of Jersey's Mont Orgueil (by now vulnerable to cannon shot over a 13th century ditch on its land-facing side) turned into a gunpowder fortress. A huge tower was built onto the old Norman keep in the 1540s. A new fort was constructed on an islet off the busy Jersey port of St. Aubins in 1542, and work began to better defend Longis Bay, Alderney, where the Romans had once fortified. Elizabeth I granted the pirate hideout of Sark to Helier de Carteret of Jersey in 1565 with instructions to resettle it. Though Sark was never feudal in the heyday of feudalism, Carteret was given it as a fief in perpetuity, on condition that at least 40 households (or *ténéments*) settle on the island, with each tenant obligated to guard a section of coast. The queen gifted a brass cannon in 1570, still to be seen in the grounds of La Seigneurie, home of the current seigneur; as a fiefdom it has so remained. The most impressive Tudor defense improvement was Jersey's Elizabeth Castle, built on the same islet chosen by sixth century hermit Helier, better positioned to protect Jersey's riches and richest from cannon fire than venerable Mont Orgueil. Work on it began in 1590. Sir Walter Raleigh named it *Fort Isabella Bellissima*. Among his lesser-known titles was that of governor of Jersey 1600–1603.

Oxford study fellowships were founded in the 17th century to provide the Channel Islands with a loyal Anglican clergy, but while the Church of England gained acceptance among the upper echelons, Calvin-inspired Presbyterianism with its anti-monarchical inclinations gained many followers among the middling ranks. It did not take long for these denominations to find issue with each other. The anti-royal sentiment that wrought havoc in the English Civil War of 1642–1649 played out in the Channel Islands too, if for different reasons. There were plenty of disaffected folk. Opposition to royalist lieutenant-governors was expressed with enough antagonism to force both inside their respective strongholds, Jersey's Sir Philip de Carteret into Elizabeth Castle and Guernsey's Sir Peter Osborne into Castle Cornet. Carteret faced the resentment of other prominent Jersey families led by the Lemprières and the Dumaresqs, opposed to the Carteret domination of island offices. Charles I had agreed that other Carterets could inherit the bailiff position, an unwelcome concentration of absolute power. Opponents tried to remove Sir Philip in 1643, as Oliver Cromwell fought Charles I in England, but he sidestepped the coup by retreating into Elizabeth Castle (fortuitously he had enlarged it in 1636), insisting that Parliament had nothing to do with island government, a position that did not negate his own autocratic designs.

The atmosphere was even more charged on Guernsey. The island had fewer royalists than Jersey, and its lieutenant governor Sir Peter Osborne, an Englishman from an old Essex landowning family, had little in common with those he governed. As an Anglican and monarchist governing an avowedly nonconformist community, instinctively republican in its rejection of papal-like royal authority, his presence invited trouble. A merchant and landowner Pierre de Beauvoir led a coup against him in 1643 and he retreated inside Castle Cornet. Castle gunners pounded the town across the compact harbor with cannon balls, but the barrage did not prevent the Guernsey States from announcing itself a parliamentary republic with Beauvoir as president (Alderney and Sark included).

Sir Philip Carteret did not last long in his Elizabeth Castle confinement, dying within two months. A nephew and royalist naval officer, Captain George Carteret, took up the cause and ran ammunition and provisions from St. Malo to royalists within the islands, aiding Osborne in Castle Cornet, too at some risk. Jean Chevalier's *Chronicles of Events in Jersey, 1643–51,* a personal diary comparable to that of his Isle of Wight contemporary Sir John Oglander, listed bacon, salted fish, beer, wine, biscuits, tobacco, wheat and clothing among replenishments. It was effective. The anti–Carteret contingent on Jersey weakened as farmers with families to provide for balked at serving a conflict that might go on and on for years. The rebellion there was over by the end of 1643 and some rebel leaders thrown into Mont Orgueil's dungeons. Since Cromwell's parliamentary army was faring well in the Civil War in

England, their lives were spared. Three years later, Sir George Carteret, knighted in 1644, was again called to action, this time to play host to the beleaguered king's heir. The 16-year-old Prince of Wales (later Charles II) and his brother the Duke of York (later James II) arrived in three ships from Star Castle on St. Mary's, Scilly where they had spent six weeks in refuge. The entourage of several hundred nobles and artisans stayed two and a half months at a princely cost before moving on to France. A few stayed on, notably Edward Hyde, first earl of Clarendon, who began drafting his seminal *The True Historical Narrative of the Rebellion* in Elizabeth Castle, a well-known primary source on the Civil War (published 1704).

Oliver Cromwell's triumph and the execution of Charles I in 1649 exercised the Channel Islands in several ways. In London a republican House of Commons legislated against proclamation of another monarch, but it did not stop Jersey from doing just that. The Channel Islands of course were affiliated historically to the Crown, not Parliament, and Jersey's rulers publicly rejected the new English government by announcing the reign of Charles II just 19 days after his father's execution. It hardly changed the course of history but it is worthy of reminder that English monarchy enjoyed firm support among offshore gentry — James Stanley, Lord of Man; Francis Godolphin, Governor of Scilly; and Sir John Oglander of the Isle of Wight were all active in its cause. Within months Jersey once again played host to the king's sons. The prince heard of his father's death at The Hague where his sister Mary was married to William of Orange. The would-be Charles II returned to Jersey in September 1649 to prepare for English invasion and restoration via Ireland, wearing violet mourning clothes Chevalier tells us. Cromwell pre-empted him, however, and began crushing Irish opposition before the king-in-waiting had settled into his Elizabeth Castle quarters. The 20-year-old prince idled on the island for five months shooting partridge, performing faith healing rites for tuberculosis sufferers, dancing his evenings away, and running up Sir George Carteret a handsome bill. He finally sailed away in February 1650 to what turned out to be a disaster. Superior parliamentary forces had beaten his cavaliers before the end of 1651. Not even the offshore islands could offer him hospitality and the Channel Islands could not avoid Cromwell's reach either.

Republican Islands, 1651–1660

Cromwell dispatched Colonel James Heane and 2,600 troops of the New Model Army plus the escorting warships of Admiral Robert Blake to end Jersey's royal resistance, the same sea commander who recaptured Scilly for Parliament. The tables turned on Jersey as Michel Lemprière, the pro-parliamentary bailiff ousted in 1643, was restored to office. Sir George Carteret fled to France where he served in the French navy. His Jersey lands were not forfeit though; Parliament was lenient toward royalists in that regard. Guernsey's Castle Cornet surrendered in December 1651.

Cromwell's republican commonwealth excited feeling according to social rank and church affiliation. Islanders who supported the parliamentary cause were rewarded with administrative positions, but these reforms were undone, at least in

Jersey, by new governor Colonel Robert Gibbon and his deputy Captain Richard Yeardly. They are roundly accused in local histories as scoundrels who used their position to extort money, force billeting of soldiers on civilians, draft local sailors to naval service in violation of island custom, ignore court decisions, and desecrate Anglican church property. Feelings at the time were also stirred by imprisonment of well-known English Puritan and social reformer John Lilburne (a.k.a. "Free-Born John"), a radical who managed to be imprisoned by Charles I *and* Oliver Cromwell! A former lieutenant colonel in Cromwell's New Model Army and a leader of the Levellers (a democratic faction intent on abolishing rank and monarchy: leveling classes), he became frustrated at the absence of liberating progress under Cromwell and dissented with the dissenters. His opposition earned him prison sentences, the longest of which came after leadership of public demonstrations in 1653. A year of his sentence was spent locked up in Jersey. Colonel Gibbon reputedly complained that Lilburne gave him more trouble than ten royalists, and his presence must have sent Jersey tongues wagging.

Republican Guernsey fared better since the nonconformist pro-parliamentary sentiment was stronger there, but it was undone by the Restoration. Charles II was restored in 1660 because the English elite could not face any more erratic rule under republicanism and could not visualize an alternative executive. In the Channel Islands the wheel of politics turned yet again. Bailiff Lemprière quickly left Jersey and Sir George Carteret returned triumphantly from exile. Dejected leaders on Guernsey prepared for resumption of royal authority by petitioning the king for a pardon, which was granted.

American Connections

Sir George Carteret's support of the royal cause earned him great rewards, granted title to manors in Cornwall and Devon and great chunks of territory in the Americas, specifically one-6th of the Bahamas, one-eighth of newly chartered Carolina, and in 1664, half of what would become New Jersey, named in his honor. He died there in 1680. North American royal benefaction did not end with him. Sir Edmund Andros, from a prominent Guernsey family, had grown up as a page in the royal household and won colonial appointments. His first, in 1674 as governor of New York, led him into conflict with Philip Carteret, brother of George and governor of neighboring New Jersey. Andros disputed the legitimacy of the Jerseyman's authority and at one point had him arrested and imprisoned in New York, but a jury could find no case and he was released. Charles II recalled Andros in 1681 but when his brother James succeeded in 1685, Andros again found favor.

James II was more despotic than his brother and determined to tighten the reins of government in colonial America. Andros returned to impose royal will over Puritan colonies from New Jersey to New Hampshire, the so-called Dominion of New England. Ironically violation of local laws and privileges was the very thing Channel Islands seigneurs long resisted themselves, and fortunately for New Englanders the suppression of theirs did not last long. Andros was thoroughly detested and when the English coup ousting James II in 1688 became known, Bostonians rose up and jailed him. He was released later and returned to England. Andros's last appointment was as governor of Guernsey. He delegated authority in Alderney to another Guernseyman, Thomas le Mesurier, whose family operated as hereditary rulers over the few hundred who lived there until the early 19th century.

Enterprise and Commerce in the 17th & 18th Centuries

The religious upheaval was not over; Louis XIV of France saw to that in 1685 when he revoked the Edict of Nantes, a legal agreement protecting Huguenots since 1598, effectively declaring war on his non–Catholic subjects. Thousands of Huguenots fled France, many passing through the Channel Islands for more distant destinations, but some choosing to stay. Their brethren went back several generations in Guernsey. The fresh influx fed Christian pluralism in the islands, but if removal of James II to exile (with Louis XIV) excited hopes of reform among nonconformists they were to be disappointed. The signing of the English Bill of Rights in 1689, asserting parliamentary sovereignty in the UK, did not extend to the Channel Islands. Its medieval contract with the Crown remained in effect and the families dominating the offices of bailiff and lieutenant governor (distinctions between them constitutionally ambiguous) were happy to keep it so. The Royal Courts continued, as did the combination of *jurats*, parish constables and rectors in *L'Etats*. *Centeniers* and *vingteniers*, voluntary constabulary chosen from well-established families, policed the parishes.

If the royal coup of 1688 did not alter much constitutionally in the islands, the UK decision to end the 1483 papal bull of neutrality certainly benefited some purses. Repeal recognized what was already long apparent, namely that its trade policy of procuring gold and silver at the expense of competitor nations through tariffs was incompatible with trade cooperation, especially with the French. The effect was to intensify privateering and with it the curtain of sail visible in island harbors and waters. Scores of English privateers operated out of Jersey and Guernsey, some profiting and others ending up rotting in French jails or worse. It reached its zenith in the Anglo-French conflicts of the mid–18th century, wars fought in part over pursuit of world trade advantage, a daunting or enticing thought for Channel Islanders who tried to live off both.

Swelled by the new wave of refugee Huguenots, the population numbered around 30,000 by 1690. A few were silversmiths and their arrival was opportune with nouveaux riches merchants desiring fine goods. Domestic silverware was in great demand as was fine furniture carved from imported American mahogany. While subsistence farming remained the norm for most and the numbers of *les pauvres* (landless poor) rose, Parliament allowed Channel Islanders tax-free access to British markets in the 18th century, even in the midst of protective restrictions and duties. Those engaged in export businesses benefited, and cider production was one of those businesses, its growth diversifying the farm economy. Similar in method and product to the better-known hard ciders of Brittany and Normandy, it was so profitable by 1800 that

Jersey cider apple orchards accounted for about 20 percent of all arable land. The industry reached its peak in 1832 when half a million gallons were exported. Woolens was the first manufacturing activity of note to emerge with imported wool worked in response to markets for knitted stockings, waistcoats and gloves. English clergyman William Lee invented a "stocking frame" knitting machine in 1589 but hand knitting was preferred in the islands where whole families could participate. It became so popular that authorities in the early 17th century, worried by neglect of the fields, banned it during harvesting. At one stage Jersey was producing 6,000 pairs of stockings a week. The business was in decline through competition by the 18th century but revived as export markets expanded for heavy-duty fishermen's sweaters — universally known as *jerseys* and *guernseys*, almost a pre–consumer age designer product!

Commercial fishing developed from the 17th century after North Atlantic voyagers such as John Cabot (1497) and Jacques Cartier (1534) sailed back with stories of Newfoundland seas (Grand Banks) where cod could be caught by just lowering baskets overboard. Navigating the distance became practicable with new compasses, sextants, chronometers and charts, although still dangerous. Nearby St. Malo was a pioneer port. As Guernsey shipping prospered from European sea trade, this was an opportunity for Jersey fishermen, and many joined up to profit from the cod bounty in the 17th century, returning with their catches to plow home waters in the fall. Voyages became more ambitious as America-bound vessels loaded textiles, hardware and alcohol to trade on the American coasts for animal pelts. Beaver hats were fashionable in Europe and American furs worth their weight in gold. As European nations used Caribbean islands to grow sugar and other cash crops on plantations, an assortment of triangular-shaped trades between Europe, Africa and America developed. Channel Islands merchants, ship-owners and sailors worked their own version, supplying and crewing outbound vessels with cheap cargoes to trade in North America and, having fished cod off the Grand Banks, sold it dried to slave plantations in southern American colonies and the West Indies. The remuneration paid for homebound cargoes of sugar, tobacco, hardwood, and other sundries. Some preferred what they saw in the Americas and never came back. By the 18th century Jerseymen were settling in French-speaking fishing communities on the Gaspè peninsula in the mouth of the St. Lawrence River. Jersey place-names and family names can be found in modern Newfoundland. All the while, back in the Gulf of St. Malo, oyster banks were worked to supplement conger, mackerel and lobster exports.

There was plenty of legitimate business with the UK, but as noted almost everywhere else offshore, the profitable illicit trades were tempting too. Channel Islands smuggling operations stored and shipped French wines and brandies and Cuban tobacco. St. Peter Port was a principal clearing-house of *La Fraude* as it was appropriately called and singled out in Parliament's war against smuggling. A Customs House was set up there in 1767 with an armed schooner and cutter, but when the French declared Roscoff a free port to provoke the English, Guernsey smugglers transferred their contraband business there to Guernsey's detriment. Smuggling was killed off in the 19th century by improved UK customs supervision and a policy shift toward free trade.

Threats to Normalcy

The political establishment did not have it all its own way in the 18th century, and outrage at injustices ruffled feathers on occasion. There was a revolt in St. Ouens parish (Jersey) in 1701 against collection of seigneurial dues, and in 1730 riots broke out over devaluation of French copper *liards* against local silver, a mercantilist measure designed to prevent outflow of silver to the French. When angry islanders stormed the Jersey bailiff's house threatening to hang him, devaluation was hastily retracted. Some islanders alleged wheat price fixing by vested interests in the 1760s and a "charter" of grievances and radical demands was drawn up in 1769, including abolition of the seigneurs. The protest was in step with calls for an end to feudal arrangements in France, but it made little progress in Jersey or in France (yet). However the establishment was concerned enough in 1771 to introduce a formal separation of judiciary and legislature in Jersey. The Royal Court was relieved of its ancient right to legislate, leaving the States Assembly to make laws, but since *jurats* and bailiffs still sat in both the reform was more cosmetic than corrective. They were still both auditors and legislators of law, having what we would now term a conflict of interest. It was hardly the separation of powers envisaged by 18th century enlightened *philosophes*. Guernsey's States of Deliberation emerged out of the Royal Court as a legislative body with an assortment of parish and judicial representatives.

It was an old diplomatic enmity rather than protest that threatened normalcy toward the end of the 18th century, a reminder that Anglo-French hostilities could still disrupt life in a heartbeat. The year 1778 was not a good one for the Crown. George III smarted over defeat at Saratoga in the American War of Independence and news of a Franco-American alliance against him. To darken his mood Spain supported the French. Local privateers were not slow to seize the opportunity of prize money: John Le Mesurier of Alderney brought in £135,000 alone in 1779 and one Guernseyman, John Tupper, claimed £60,000 with his three ships.[13] Long irritated by such piracy, the French attacked Jersey in 1779. They had to withdraw under heavy fire from round *martello* towers dotted around the coasts, but those defensive batteries were broken two years later when a crafty mercenary, Baron de Rullecourt, came ashore at La Rocque with 700 men. He had spied out the island on an earlier visit. Marching before daylight, he and his men caught the small community and garrison of St. Helier napping, dragging lieutenant governor Moyse Corbet from his bed. Corbet believed the whole island to be under occupation and gave orders for surrender. However Major Francis Peirson, a British regular, refused to comply and a short and hard fought battle ensued in the marketplace (today's Royal Square). The 24-year-old major won a great victory at the head of the local militia, although along with de Rullecourt he lost his life. News of the Battle of Jersey (1781) was applauded in England and for the moment peace was restored. Within ten years the insecurity fears returned as the bankrupt Bourbon monarchy was toppled in the French Revolution of 1789.

There was a groundswell of pro-revolutionary fervor in the islands at first and some incitement of commoners to rebel. The establishment was in no mood to make concessions, and strengthened by British military presence, ruling families closed ranks, shelving political differences to maintain the status quo. The arrival of émi-gré aristocrats and Catholic clergy fleeing French prison and the guillotine fueled anti–French Revolution feeling in the States' assemblies, mostly because of a resentment of outside intrusion. Lawmakers sought house building restrictions, a policy echoed today. Nonetheless Castle Mont Orgueil was used as an operations center to supply arms and money to royalist resistance, and defenses were beefed up after 1792 when republican France declared war on all powers opposed to its revolution-in-progress. A 1797 Jersey law (still on the books) forbade "riotous" assembly in a reactionary response similar to laws in England where freedoms were curtailed. Napoleon, who assumed power in 1799, was alert to the privateer threat, liking it no more than his royal predecessors, and in fear of retaliatory action by him, stronger defenses were called for on the islands. The forts were slow in completion. Guernsey finally got its new garrison of Fort George in 1812. Fort Regent replaced Elizabeth Castle on Jersey, but it was not completed until 1814 at a colossal cost of £1 million, by which time Napoleon was in retreat and less than a year from total defeat. The French never attacked again. Fort Regent was to be reborn as a sports and entertainment complex, and the Fort George site is now a millionaires' housing enclave.

The Laurel and the Rose

War with Napoleon precipitated a full review of offshore security in London, and in 1801 the islands were placed under Home Office jurisdiction and recognized as dependencies (as opposed to colonies) together with the Isle of Man. Interpretation of this re-categorization language was left to the Channel Islands' rulers and to attrition. Importantly in the decades following conclusion of the war in 1815, populist ideals of government fueled by American and French revolutions did not go unnoticed. Progressives in Jersey adopted the rose as their emblem, combining against their seigneurial antagonists, the conservative "laurels." The extension of voting rights to the rising British middle class in 1832 in the UK toughened "rose" resolve and Guernsey, too, had similar polarization, as the old guard faced new money.

The office of governor was abolished in Guernsey (1835) and Jersey (1854) with duties assumed by lieutenant governors, but this was the way it had been anyway. Bailiffs became quasi-presidents of the States' legislative assemblies as well as chief magistrates, but since they were drawn from the establishment, this was arguably no change either. States' deputies were elected by limited franchise in Jersey in 1856 and later in Guernsey, but they supplemented rather than replaced the nepotistic system of *jurats* and rectors chosen by parishes. Collective representation was still the organizing principle on which island governments were founded, collective in the sense that the parishes, bailiffs and lieutenant-governors acted on behalf of all islanders' interests. In the wider English-speaking world the drive of constitutional reform was toward individual representation — one man, one vote — but it would take the Channel Islands longer to reach that point. Meanwhile the offspring of the nouveaux riches intermarried with old seigneurial families and a tight oligarchy based on commercial wealth and land held sway.

Victor Hugo and "The Toilers of the Sea"

St. Peter Port had been the best deep anchorage and busiest port, but in the 19th century it had a serious rival in St. Helier, where a new harbor built in the lee of Elizabeth Castle supplanted St. Aubin and Gorey to become Jersey's main port. St. Peter Port had the more appealing aspect visually; "a delightful disorder of gullies and hills gathered around the Old Harbor just as if they had been grasped in a giant's fist" is how resident Victor Hugo saw it in the 1850s. The impressionist Renoir liked it enough to stay and paint in 1883. Few waxed lyrical about St. Helier's appearance, but as a commercial hub its importance was undeniable, an offshore Victorian boom-town comparable to Ryde on the Isle of Wight or Douglas, Isle of Man.

Victor Hugo took up residence in Jersey between 1852 and 1855. A life-long political dissident, he was frequently at odds with the sequence of French republican and royalist regimes through which he lived, a state of mind that led him to the islands. In 1845 he accepted a post in the constitutional government of citizen-king Louis Philippe and was elected to the *Assemblée legislative* in 1848 when Napoleon's nephew Louis-Napoleon Bonaparte became president of the Second Republic. Hugo developed a dislike for him and when the *Assemblée* was dissolved and Louis-Napoleon anointed himself Emperor Napoleon III in 1851, he published the tract *Napoleon le petit* in which he famously described the Second Empire as "an odious, repulsive, infamous crime." Deemed persona non grata in France, he retreated with other exiles to Jersey the following year. In 1855 some of them denounced a state visit by Queen Victoria to the "sawdust corporal" in the expatriate newspaper *L'Homme*, a criticism that infuriated the conservative Jersey elite. The paper was closed down and editors deported. When Hugo decried this violation of free speech, he too was deported. He did not go far, crossing only to Guernsey, a "rock of hospitality and liberty" as he called it, making it his home for the next 15 years (1855–1870). His house on Hauteville, overlooking St. Peter Port harbor, is now French government property and open to the public. In a room there, overlooking the sea, he finally finished his epic *Les Miserables* in 1862. The lesser-known *Les Traivailleurs de La Mer* ("The Toilers of the Sea") was published in 1866. Hugo dedicated it to Channel Islanders, dwellers of this "corner of ancient Norman soil."

The story is set in the Channel Islands of the 1820s, its long-suffering hero a misfit called Gilliatt whose relationship with Guernsey's sea-faring community is tempered by his mysterious outsider origins. Hugo drew the novel's characters from islanders. One of them, Mess Lethierry, a crusty old mariner, he describes as a Guernseyman of type — "that is [also] a Norman, an Englishman, a Frenchman. These lands, united in him, [are] ruled by his native element, the Ocean."[14] Lethierry was a cabin boy, fisherman, sailor, and latterly a proud ship owner, yet when he planned to set up a steam ferry service between Guernsey and St. Malo, he faced hostility. Hugo noted the real-life docking of the first steamer *The Medina* at St. Helier in 1823, as he set about fictionalizing encroaching modernity. Lethierry's paddle steamer is caught on treacherous rocks in the novel's finale and only the outcast Gilliatt has the temerity to try and save it, toiling and enduring in a titanic struggle with the relentless sea, before delivering engine, boiler and paddle wheels intact to Mess Lethierry. In saving the future, he brought meaning to his own life. Hugo's own exile ended with Napoleon III's humiliation in the Franco-Prussian War of 1870–71, and he returned to Paris after proclamation of the Third Republic.

The Competitive Islands

Seagoing businesses continued to be competitive in the 19th century while new efforts to explore alternatives on land found potential in unlikely places. Copper and silver veins were discovered on Sark in 1836. Sir Charles de Carteret sold the island in the early 18th century to pay off debt, and it changed hands regularly on the same terms agreed by Elizabeth I until Pierre le Pelley, seigneur in the 1830s, became a shareholder in the newly formed Guernsey and Sark Mining Company. Promoters promised great dividends to investors. Ernest le Pelley, who succeeded his brother as seigneur, took out a £4,000 mortgage on the Sark fief from a Jersey privateer, John Allaire, to buy more stock. By the early 1840s there were several hundred miners laboring in galleries out under the seabed, their makeshift pub a nuisance for sober Sarkees. Disaster struck in 1845 when a roof caved in and ten miners drowned. The tragedy finished the venture and le Pelley's seigneurial dynasty with it. The mortgage could not be repaid and the fief passed to Allaire's daughter and descendants. Some old mine-workings are still there on Little Sark, proof of its brush with industrialization. Elsewhere granite had been quarried since the megaliths, but in the 19th century new companies crushed ever-increasing quantities of it for export to England for road paving and ornamental masonry. Quarrying provided much needed jobs and Guernsey and nearby Herm were particularly productive. Alderney exported stone too, but its economy was revived by UK expenditure on defense installations, an outlay prompted by French construction of large naval harbors at Cherbourg and St. Malo in the 1840s. Alderney's population, once measured in hundreds, had risen to 5,000 by 1860.

The cross–Channel economy expanded in the 1820s as steamer-services, à la Mess Lethierry, began to ply for passenger trade, and the first hotels were in business by the start of the Victorian Age. As was the case on Wight, visitors returned as permanent residents, a fashion begun by retired British naval and army personnel after the Napoleonic war. There were some 15,000 English-speakers in Jersey by 1840 and street names in St. Helier point to the linguistic shift. The language of money remained French with local *livres tournois* (originally minted in Tours) fixed in exchange against the world-dominant British currency. 24 *livres* bought £1 sterling. Jersey adopted British currency in 1836, but French money remained legal tender in Guernsey until 1921, both islands minting their own copper coinage. In the meantime the developing rail network in England offered connections and "railway-steamers" opened up market opportunities. The presence of island products such as knitwear, fishing equipment, printing machines and granite samples at London's "Great Exhibition" in 1851 announced a new competitiveness. Progress was further demonstrated in 1871 with a Channels Islands Exhibition at Victoria College in St. Helier. It attracted 30,000 over its three weeks' duration, the first visitors to come in such concentrated numbers and intend no harm.

The island farmers saw their opportunities in livestock. Cattle were exported to Britain in the 18th century, so many in fact that English breeders complained, but attitudes had changed by mid–19th century. Island stockbreeders won plaudits and recognition from Britain's Royal Agricultural Society with the Jersey and Guernsey breeds highly valued for their rich buttermilk. Other agricultural specialties emerged after 1850, also with urban consumers in mind. Enclosure reorganized land into small productive units, well suited for potato and greenhouse production. One enterprising Jersey farmer, Hugh de la Haye, successfully marketed his small tasty Jersey Royal potato variety in 1880 and these "new jerseys," as they were called, quickly found their niche in UK vegetable markets. Seasonal migrant workers have sown and dug seed potatoes in terraced hillside fields annually since, Firstly Bretons and since the 1960s the Portuguese. The potato season is a part of Jersey life. In the same time period, greenhouse horticulture became a Guernsey specialty. The first was built as early as 1782 to grow dessert grapes for London's greenmarkets, but in the 1870s tomato cultivation under glass proved successful, taking its place alongside Jersey potatoes in exports. The first daffodil consignment left Guernsey for London in the 1860s, before a similar business grew in Scilly.

Despite the enterprising drive for bigger markets there were still plenty whose hold on economic survival remained at best tenuous. The success of livestock breeding reduced arable land and with it job opportunities; wages were low, frequently insufficient to support growing families; and protests vented frustrations in the 1840s in line with events in England. Real wages rose eventually as free trade developed, but not in time to encourage all; Jersey's population fell from 57,020 to 52,445 between 1851 and 1901.[15]

In Flux

The shift to agrarian capitalism had been less traumatic than in some of the Scottish islands, and rural distress notwithstanding, the outlook at the close of the Victorian Age was positive with the total population reaching 95,000 (1901). English was the fastest growing language but its speakers were trenchantly monolingual, and this, together with the need to speak English for tourism and trade, pressured usage of Jèrriais (Jersey-French) and Dgernesiais (Guernsey-French). French too had changed, having been codified and standardized during the 17th and 18th centuries, relegating old varieties of Norman-French. In recognition of the threat (as occurred with Norn and Manx) vernacular dictionaries appeared in the 1800s, but they did not prevent the states' assemblies from adopting English as their official language in the first half of the 20th century, though members may speak in the old language if they so wish.

If language was in flux then so was society. Commercial growth had created a parallel society of super-rich, a small group of wealthy islanders who sought worldly diversions. No longer succored by land rents alone but rich from investments, trade and corporate profits, they enjoyed their own version of a Victorian summer with stylized homes, concerts, garden parties, open carriages, blazers, plumes and parasols.

In 1894 an Admiralty Warrant authorized Royal Channel Islands Yacht Club vessels to display the Blue Ensign with their own distinctive marks, great value set by such exclusivity. Its first woman member was Lillie Langtry, the eponymous "Jersey Lily."

Born Emily Charlotte Le Breton in 1853 in St. Saviour, the daughter of a clergyman whose extra-marital affairs so scandalized Jersey that he was nicknamed the "Dirty Dean," she was estranged from her husband Edward Langtry. Her good looks attracting constant admirers, she became an actress and society beauty whose affair with the Prince of Wales (later Edward VII) fed the gossip columns of the day. Her first major acting part was in Oliver Goldsmith's *She Stooped to Conquer* in 1881 at the Haymarket Theater, London, and Oliver Wilde created *Lady Windermere's Fan* (1882) for her, famously remarking, "I would rather have discovered Lillie Langtry than America." Several times she crossed the Atlantic to tour with theater companies where her liberated lifestyle provoked comment, not all of it favorable or kind. One American very much taken by her was Judge Roy Bean; he named the Texas saloon bar where he held court sessions the "Jersey Lillie," though he never met her. His reputation as a hanging judge was more image than fact, but like Lillie, he understood that was more valuable than no reputation at all. Dismissed by some as little more than a sexual temptress, her stage work belittled, Lillie Langtry is more recognizable in this age as an early female star with stage presence and business acumen (she endorsed Pears soap) using gumption and guile to get success. Her London debut helped put Jersey on a modern map, and visitors to St. Helier's Jersey Museum can enjoy the few exhibits and John Everett Millais' early portrait of her.

Prelude

The summer of 1914 was interrupted with the heady news that Britain and France were at war, this time as allies. The Channel Islands were never seriously threatened. Guernsey-based French seaplanes successfully sighted and sank U-boats, and although Guernsey had its first airborne invader in the shape of a dirigible airship in 1916, it survived the experience. The islands were considered safe enough to set up a German POW camp at Les Quennevais on Jersey, and by 1915 it had over a thousand inmates. There was great support for the war initially. Over 2,000 had enlisted in the French Army by the end of 1914, and 14,000 volunteers and conscripts signed up for British forces over the four-year duration. Many never returned. The Royal Guernsey Light Infantry was one of those hard hit when hundreds died in a German counter-offensive at Cambrai in November 1917.

On the home front women took jobs vacated by men, but after the war employment roles reverted to type. Old proprieties and gender norms changed nevertheless in the aftermath of 1918. Voting rights for women over the age of 30 and property rights for women were won during the interwar years, consistent with similar reforms in Britain, though not in France until 1944. In the marketplace businesses sought women as consumers on unprecedented levels, demonstrated in the sale of items once exclusive to the rich — cosmetics, fashion clothing and personal accessories — retailed in St. Helier emporia such as De Gruchy, Voison and Le Gallais. Exports of cattle, potatoes and tomatoes, together with tourist revenue, helped pay for the new spending. There was little sign of the depression plaguing parts of Britain during the 1920s and 1930s. New hotels, boarding houses and holiday camps profited while a mild climate and lower taxes lured wealthy retirees to buy up and settle down. New homes strung out in a linear sprawl along main roads submerging older villages. New infrastructure arrived as Victorian rail services along the south Jersey coast between St. Helier and St. Aubin and from St. Helier to Gorey succumbed to bus companies from 1929. Airways and airports opened up. Yet modernity was kept at arm's length in other ways. Church and parish remained bedrock and law-making and law enforcement remained the preserve of an anointed amateur few. Norman-French was still widely spoken, despite the rise of English, and deferential social relationships persisted, despite the informalities engendered by consumerism. Sark's Court of Chief Pleas banned automobiles. An unhurried life still existed, and for those who wished it the modern world remained an outside world.

The knowledge of a new war with Germany in 1939 was unsettling, but all was relatively quiet in the opening six months or so. When Jersey's governor asked London for anti-aircraft and coastal defense guns, the UK government lightly dismissed chances of attack. Hotel and guesthouse proprietors put on a brave face, advertising the "perfect place for wartime holidays" in spring 1940. Nobody anticipated the events to come, although a sense of foreboding must have gripped those who tuned in to radio news during May as *blitzkrieg* hit Belgium, causing evacuation of British forces from Dunkirk beaches and then France. Suddenly on June 16 islanders were urged to send all available seagoing craft to St. Malo and assist in an emergency evacuation of British soldiers. They did not know it but their lives were about to be changed irrevocably.

"The Channel Islands Will Not *Repeat* Not *Be Defended"*

Over 21,000 embattled British troops were shipped out of St. Malo, and as they docked in Jersey locals quickly caught on to the fact they were not for their protection. "To defend every place is to defend no place," Frederick the Great once cautioned, and three days later on June 19, the awful truth arrived in a crisp telegram from London: "the Channel Islands will *not* repeat *not* be defended against external invasion by sea or by air." In an emphatic reversal of tradition, Parliament decided the islands had little strategic value; indeed, if anything, they were a liability. Those wishing to evacuate were urged to do so but had little time to make up their minds. There was a run on the banks as people frantically hurried to withdraw savings. Tens of thousands chose to go (ultimately around half the populace) including those determined to sign up with British forces, but at least one *jurat* urged those of Norman origin to stay, harsh in condemnation of any who would desert native soil. The alarm was acute on Alderney where residents, nearest the enemy action, panicked at the sight of desperate French fleeing advancing Germans. The majority voted to evacuate. A Guernsey lifeboat crew arriving on Alderney June 23 found stray cows bellowing in pain from milk-bloated udders, shooting them to put them out their misery.[16] On Sark, a defiant Sybil Hathaway, seigneur since 1926, called on her tenants to stay and many complied.

The week or so between evacuation and invasion must have seemed an eternity for those opting to stay. The Germans were unaware the islands were undefended. The British kept that a secret to delay their occupation. Hitler wanted them to neutralize any threat posed to a projected attack on Britain itself, and the *Luftwaffe* flew reconnaissance flights to scope the landscape and take photographs. Anticipating resistance, pilots mistook wagonloads of potatoes and tomatoes lined up on quays for military supply convoys and bombed St. Peter Port and St. Helier harbors on June 28, killing 38 civilians and destroying crops and warehouses. Realizing the islands were demilitarized, occupation began during the first four days of July 1940, only three weeks since the St. Malo emergency call. The British monarchy's oldest offshore possession was left to its own fate, tenable in military logistics at that moment but rich in historic irony given the lengths taken for so long to keep it from others.

Occupation and Its Dilemmas

On July 3, 1940, *The Guernsey Star* called for calm, advising readers to obey German orders. The first was for an 11 pm to 5 am curfew. Within weeks automobile use was restricted, British telephone connections severed, checkpoints introduced, and meetings of societies banned. The Germans defined the Channel Islands as *Feldkommandantur 515* or Field Command 51, a sub-district within the wider conquered French administrative region, but allowed island governments to continue. The States formed controlling committees to mediate but members faced criticism (inevitably) when it came to implementing German orders. Permits regulated increasing aspects of life as Hitler's military bureaucracy tightened its grip. Residents confronted fishing restrictions, gasoline rationing, signs with long strange German words, bicycle confiscation (because the Germans needed them), cigarette rationing, and so on. It was inconvenient but less life threatening than the blitz of London. Resistance was not very practical. The Nazi edicts warning the French were not modified for Channel Islands' consumption so the *Gestapo* posted grim notices of crimes and punishments (usually executions) of "Free-French" resistance fighters.

The islanders' reactions to occupation were multitudinous, on a scale from polite protest, sullen defiance, clever subterfuge, resolution to escape (some did), tactical compliance, to varying degrees of collaboration. The dilemma was how to deal with their occupiers. Visitors are asked to reflect on this in the museum that now fills the cold tunnels and wards of a German underground hospital in the center of Jersey. The subterranean complex became a hospital in 1944, having begun as an artillery repair facility and barrack store. Nazi propaganda sought to reassure locals that Germans were really of the same Anglo-Saxon stock as the English, though this ignored the fact that islanders themselves were not. The islanders were mostly of Norman-French origin. A museum video image of the head and shoulders of a handsome young German atop a green uniformed mannequin simulates the sort of casual day-to-day encounter islanders confronted, begging the question: how would *you* greet this fellow if you met him in the street? The sight of "greenfly" (as islanders nick-named them) can hardly have been comforting, but not all Germans were *Gestapo* (state secret police), nor were they all imbued with the same Nazi fervor. There was postwar guilt in expression of friendly feelings, and islander recollections emphasize differentiation between the *Wehrmacht* (German Armed Forces) and malevolent organizations like the *Gestapo*. Germans stationed in Jersey for their part, especially those transferring from combat positions, looked back nostalgically on their posting ("we were enraptured — the flowers, the daffodil fields and all the pine trees"),[17] think-ing themselves on vacation at least in the euphoria of first arrival.

Manipulation of press bulletins was a fact of life. The Nazis were well versed in using media indoctrination. It had played an effective part in seducing Germans to fascism in the first place. On the second anniversary of occupation the *Guernsey Eve-ning Press* (July 1, 1942) advised it was wrong to stereotype Germans as barbaric and praised their conduct. Nazi Party broadcasts meanwhile preached liberation: they had freed islanders from centuries of British imperialism! German was made a com-pulsory part of school curricula and local maps translated parish names into Ger-man equivalents. As information management extended to suppression of British war news, wireless sets were confiscated, though a few well-hidden radios and home-made "crystal sets" still buzzed to the short-wave frequency, listeners devouring snatches of BBC reports. The British government also restricted information, declin-ing to inform Britons of the Channel Islands' occupation, fearful of its demoralizing effect. They announced a "loss of communication." Evacuees meanwhile heard little or nothing of family back home.

Deportation, Internment and Hard Labor

The islands were more important to Hitler than might be thought. He was delighted to have captured a piece of England. The eminent historian Asa Briggs saw decoded *Luftwaffe* messages concerning Channel Islands' airspace as a young man serving in Britain's top-secret project to crack the Nazi "Enigma" communications code at Bletchley Park. He remains convinced that "Jakob," "Gustav" and "Adolf" (as Jersey, Guernsey and Alderney were coded) mattered to Hitler's Third Reich strategically and psychologically.[18] After the *Luftwaffe's* failure to subdue Britain for land invasion in 1940–41, the *Führer* hardened his resolve. His directive of Octo-ber 20, 1941, was ominous in intent, ordering artillery batteries, anti-aircraft batter-ies, searchlights, land mines, anti-tank ditches and walls, underground ammunition stores, and a permanent naval presence. The order amounted practically to fortification forever. Grim round concrete towers encircling the islands at measured distances are still everywhere in evidence.

The same directive called also for deportation and internment of non-native islanders, ostensibly a reprisal for internment of Germans working in Iran. Two thousand islanders were shipped off to France and Germany in 1942, including the American husband of Sybil Hathaway, seigneur of Sark. She won respect for declin-ing to countersign German orders if she disapproved of them but was powerless to prevent this new initiative. Hitler's obsession with Jews gradually surfaced. Jewish authors were cleared from public libraries in the first round and then a registry of Jews was set up. The island leaders cooperated. Destruction of Jewish livelihoods was underway by May 1941 as businesses were closed down, and a more sinister menace surfaced when three Jewish Guernsey women were arrested. One of them, Theresa Steiner, a young music professor from Austria, had fled the Nazis in 1938 to what she thought would be freedom, only to be exposed by Guernsey authorities. Her fate was to be gassed in Auschwitz. Others faced arrest as food shortages increased, often victims of informers seeking favors. The Jersey Heritage Trust lists 20 from Jersey and nine from Guernsey (including Theresa Steiner) who paid a dreadful price.

The German labor agency *Organization Todt* managed the operation of building Fortress Channel Islands. It followed the *Wehrmacht* everywhere on conquests, securing new territory by enslaving labor to work on defenses. The first batch of these forced workers (men and women) began to arrive in the islands in 1942, transported from Nazi-occupied Eastern Europe. The islanders reported shock at their miserable, emaciated appearance and the vicious treatment meted out by whip-swinging OT officials. It was their effort that burrowed into the granite massif for subterranean construction. A converted German command bunker at the La Hougue Bie site on Jersey houses photographs of them and their tormentors, a few faded black and white images giving face to unknown thousands who labored and died in the work camps. There were 12 OT camps on Jersey, another five on Guernsey and four on Alderney. Any islanders who helped them faced punishment. The memorial relates the story of one Louisa Gould, a courageous and probably Jewish grocery shopkeeper from St. Ouen, Jersey, who sheltered an escaped Russian worker for nearly a year during 1943. When a neighbor betrayed her, she was arrested by the Gestapo and interned in France. At some point she was transferred to Ravensbrück concentration camp near Berlin and died in a gas chamber in 1945.

War and Its Discontents

Removed from the bloodshed of battle (the British obviously never made bombing attacks) islanders and their jailers were obliged to form relationships. The situation became complex. A gender imbalance from evacuation and occupation made attractions inevitable between German military and young island women, a concord bound to stir up intensity of feeling and careless talk. Those thought too friendly with soldiers were derided as "jerry bags," a taunt that grew louder in post-war recriminations. As isolation, deprivation and boredom fueled tensions between the two sides, some were tempted to cooperate by betraying those who infringed German regulations. Differentiating between those who informed out of spite, those who were ideological converts, or resigned that the Nazis must win, and those who just wanted to put food on the table is a tough task. It is not inconceivable that some were persuaded by Nazi propaganda (some Britons were) but few were going to admit to it at the end of the war. This resistance vs. collaboration debate has haunted French history in recent times. The official Gaullist memory of heroic resistance in the face of Nazi atrocity is resisted itself by revisionist accounts of French collaborators indifferent to Nazi atrocities. Co-existence meant new social rules and tough compromises.

Morale was deteriorating on both sides by the close of 1943. Household necessities and medicines were scarce, food resources were stretched by high capacity troop deployment, and the inactive troops were bored. German news was restricted as the European battlefront turned against them, following defeat at Stalingrad in 1942–43 by the USSR. The Germans became isolated from their own war. For islanders there was at least the old inter-island rivalry to be played out, and in May 1944 the blue soccer shirts of Guernsey took on the red shirts of Jersey for the annual Muratti Cup as if liberation was the last thing on their minds. Occupation severely disturbed the continuity of life but it did not destroy it.

Anglo-American triumph in Operation Torch (conquest of Italy) changed prosecution of the European war, meaning that the original US preference for an invasion of northern France would be pursued and Allied strategy began to develop Operation Overlord. Intelligence duped the Germans into anticipating Allied assault on the Pas de Calais but through the night and morning of June 5–6, 1944, sleepless islanders heard the distant drone of aircraft. Those with wireless devices discovered with shock that Allied forces had actually landed on Norman beaches, not so far away to the east. *Feldkommandantur 515* sprang into emergency anti-invasion mode with the death penalty for hostile acts. The islanders spent the next week or so in a state of excitement, relishing the thought of liberation, but it did not arrive. It had never been on the D-Day itinerary. High hopes of a swift release turned to acute disappointment, anti-climax and restlessness. Expectations gradually dissolved and for the rest of the year people heard of the slowly advancing Allied front battling eastward toward its Berlin objective but nothing about their own fate. However as Normandy was liberated escape efforts multiplied. Scores bravely left Jersey beaches to attempt the sea crossing, some drowned or were shot but some made it to the Cotentin shore.

The remainder of 1944 was a testing time with German supply lines severely impacted by Allied presence in France. Barges low enough to slide under radar screens were sent but delivery was irregular and sickness and starvation threatened. Finally Red Cross relief arrived in December on the *SS Vega* with canned food and other necessities, but it was for islanders' consumption, not German. Kommandant General von Schmettow acted according to international war convention and had the parcels distributed to islanders, but he ordered house raids to seize any secreted food stocks on the grounds that surpluses must be shared. His soldiers were increasingly desperate, down to eating limpets, seagulls, rabbits, nettle and parsnip stews, the improvised starvation food that the islanders had endured, shooting horses and butchering domestic pets. Meanwhile malnutrition, dysentery and other attendant horrors stalked the forced worker camps with death a merciful release.

Despite the overwhelming odds against them, the German High Command refused to give up the Channel Islands. In February 1945, presumably on Hitler's directive, a career Nazi, Vice-Admiral Friedrich Hüffmeier, replaced Von Schmettow to toughen the defensive will. It was a tall order with German belief in the prospect of victory collapsing. Within a few weeks of his appointment Allied troops crossed the Rhine. At long last in the first week of May 1945, the worst conflict in human history came to an end in Europe. Yet Hüffmeier strung it out to the bitter end; even after the announcement of Hitler's death, German capitulation, and orders from his superior to surrender, he still tried to negotiate armistice terms with the British commander of Operation Nestegg as the liberation was called. Surrender documents were not completed until after VE (Victory in Europe) celebrations in Britain on May 8.

Post-Liberation Reunions and Traumas

The military occupation of the Channel Islands is an exceptional event in modern British history. When it was finally over, emotions were, to say the least, mixed. Some farewells were waved to Germans, shipped out as POWs, those whose considerate acts were remembered. Friendships continued in postwar correspondence and visits. Others harbored painful and bitter memories and considerably less charity. Not all the venom was directed toward the departing jailers. The fraternization of local women with German soldiers was not forgotten or easily forgiven. Maternity counts from liaisons were significant. A crowd of angry women attacked the notorious "Ginger Lou" in a St. Helier street; she had lived well during occupation as the girlfriend of a high-ranking German officer.[19] One collaborator named in the Jersey Underground Hospital museum, Mrs. Baudais, asked to be locked up in the police station for her protection. Nevertheless British investigations found it hard to uncover evidence of traitors and pursue criminal prosecutions. Islanders felt "let down" by Britain on the eve of invasion and liberation did not dispel those opinions. The States' legislation sought to penalize those who had made money out of it all, but a pall of secrecy hangs over collaborator allegations. Islanders are reluctant to dredge up the past for outsiders to scrutinize and criticize. A 1990 decision by Guernsey authorities to deny a venue for a play about Theresa Steiner, the young Jewish music professor killed in the Holocaust, written by former English National Theatre director Julia Pascal, led to renewed accusations that the island wants to hide from its own history.

The evacuees, returning military personnel, and those held as POWs had all had enormously different experiences. After the euphoria of homecomings abated, feelings between these groups could run high. Allegations of desertion were hurled at evacuees and collusion fired back at those who stayed. Traumatized soldiers and POWs felt alienated from everyone who had not tasted the horror of war. Property losses and damage added to the anger. Not everyone came back and war memorials speak for those who had fallen. In time the life force would be recovered, but it never returned to the way it had been; that world was gone forever. Perversely Hitler's occupation helped Anglicization, as a generation of evacuated island children had grown up "Englished" in the UK.

Reconstruction

In an effort to refresh the spirit, new lieutenant governors were speedily appointed for both bailiwicks, but with democratic deficits more conspicuous after the war, especially to those who had been away, calls for reconstruction grew. The practice of those who judged law (*jurats*) also making the law came under fire, and the establishment was pressured to open its doors and admit lawmakers who represented islanders individually. Reforms were worked out in varying ways at different speeds. Jersey began reorganization of its legislature in 1948 when sitting *jurats* and rectors were replaced by a dual system of senators and deputies elected for the island and parishes respectively. However constables continued to sit as "fathers of the parish" and offices remained non-salaried, in keeping with the past. The traditional priority was balancing parochial interests with island needs but increasingly the wider world was the standard to which the islands would be held accountable, a reality not always to their liking. Law enforcement is a case in point. Guernsey employed professional police from 1919, but the medieval constabulary of amateur *centeniers* and *vingteniers* remained the sole method of policing in all but one of Jersey's parishes until the criminal excesses of postwar society forced reform. The parish tradition is not all lost, though; the *Jersey Evening Post* still lists duty *centeniers* with contact telephone numbers for each of the parishes and together with *vingteniers* these non-uniformed worthies may intervene in minor offenses.

If what to do with the old collectivist "parish-states" model is one challenge, the two bailiwicks have had to face another. The notion that voluntary amateurs sitting on various select committees could handle the weighty government issues of the new financial economy and its global implications has come under intense review. Island politicians are now paid professionals, and the Clothier Report in 2000 made substantial restructuring recommendations for the Jersey States. Implementation looks inevitable. The proposal of popularly elected representatives called Members of the States of Jersey (the dual system distinction between senators and deputies scrapped) is still tentative at the time of writing but administration by a ministerial government (not committees) under a central executive (the office of bailiff confined to the judiciary) seems unstoppable. The trends and issues in Guernsey have not been dissimilar, though on a different calendar. The wider electorate chose deputies for decades but *conseillers*, equating with Jersey's senators, were still chosen by the parishes (rather than individual voters) until 1994. The Harwood Report of 2000 for the States of Guernsey has recommended committee downsizing and (like Jersey) a form of cabinet government in an effort to strengthen leadership and modernize accountability. In a 2002 Mori study, 72 percent of those polled in Guernsey thought there were too many committees (37 in fact) and 67 percent on Jersey thought similarly about the Jersey States.[20]

The judiciary is not under review (yet). The *jurats* may have lost their legislative role but they remain an important part of judiciaries in both bailiwicks. In keeping with the tradition in the UK (and USA) a legal training is still not a prerequisite but *jurats* are chosen by electoral colleges to long terms of office, rather different from the UK and USA where all citizens are required to periodically participate for a short term. Channel Islands' *jurats* are not salaried and really are more comparable to British justices of the peace, sitting as non-professional assessors of fact. The bailiff remains the sole judge of law and old judicial customs survive. *Le Clameur de Haro* is a classic example of one such, a call for justice before "Ha-Ro," the first duke of Normandy Rollo. *Le Clameur* is abolished in Normandy but is still resorted to occasionally in the Channel Islands, used in recent times against property developers. The words *Haro, Haro, à l'aide mon Prince, on me fait tort* ("Rollo, Rollo, my Prince, come to my aid") uttered before the Attorney General and two witnesses serve as an immediate injunction, a cease-and-desist command until a court has passed judgment. There are severe penalties for anyone who abuses it.

Alderney, desolated by evacuation in 1940, faced major reconstruction after 1945 and rewrote its constitutional arrangements. The product is the most centralized system in the islands and, locals would claim the most democratic, not least because they did not have to deal with a strong parish tradition. The States of Alderney, activated in 1949, is an elected parliament within the jurisdiction of the Guernsey bailiwick. As for the economy the utilities left by wartime forced labor of piped water and electricity generating stations made a start for revival and the UK Labor Government of 1945–1951 helped by subsidizing house repair and building. The loan was repaid out of profits from a revived agriculture run initially on collectivist principles. Taxes were levied for the first time to enable education, public health and infrastructure. Most of Alderney's current income derives from services provided to outsiders, those who choose to reside, invest or just visit. The laws are designed accordingly. Its public relations hook is "Caring but carefree" and the population had climbed back to around 2,400 in 2001, though with less than 50 percent Alderney-born.

Inimitable Sark

Feudal Sark remains inimitably feudal Sark. The 40 Elizabethan land lots or *ténéments* continue to give those tenants a hereditary right to sit for life on the Chief Pleas, the island parliament. A 1951 reform allowed another 12 people's deputies to be elected triennially for three-year terms. Since the year-round population is only around 600, it promises a direct democracy ahead of anywhere else in the British Isles. On the other hand small parcels of seigneurial land have been leased out over the years and these newer properties do not entitle holders to a seat on the Pleas (nor do they carry the right of carrying muskets for defense of the realm!); indeed few constitutional reforms are anticipated as long as Elizabeth I's 1565 feudal grant is in place. A furor over primogeniture in the later 1990s did force one significant change, however.

Since the fief by definition was granted for defense of the realm and not for commercial gain, land was deemed indivisible, to be left to the eldest son in its entirety. This rule ran foul of the multi-millionaire Barclay brothers, owners of several high profile worldwide businesses, who paid £2.3 million for the leasehold of Brecqhou, a tiny neighboring island, and one of the original Elizabethan *ténéments* under Sark

law. The Barclays wanted to will their newly built £60 million castle home on Brecqhou jointly to all their children but ran into the wall of primogeniture. In a war of
words the resident seigneur, Michael Beaumont, a retired ballistics engineer, was
accused of being a medieval dictator. In Sark's defense it made no sense to break up
land already small in acreage into microscopic tenancies, but under the onslaught of
Barclays' litigation (reputedly to the tune of £1.75m.) and the realization that sooner
or later somebody else would contest the same law, the Chief Pleas buckled and passed
a 1999 inheritance law amendment. Landholders with children may now will their
property to any one of their children, but if they die intestate the eldest child inher-
its regardless of gender.

Traditionalists can content themselves with much that is unaltered. Seigneurs
still hold Sark by hereditary right. The original fee of 50 *sols tournois* under Elizabeth I in 1565 computed at less than £2 a year under Elizabeth II in 2000. The seigneur
is still sole appointee of the *seneschal* (judge) and *prevot* (sheriff). He or she can still
claim *le trezième* by right, a 13th share of the purchase price of land. The privilege
of sole keeper of pigeons is untrammeled by modernity. Water still comes from wells.
There is no airport and cars are still banned. The devious introduction of tractors
exasperated Sybil Hathaway to the point of threatening sale of the island to Guernsey.
The tractors won out (John Deere is a popular choice) but the roads are still unpaved.
The dusty main street has all the look of a bygone rural age and the feudal custom
of *La Branchage* is still observed whereby members of the *Douzaine* or parish council walk the roads annually to determine repairs and censure those who have not
fulfilled their maintenance duties.

Sark still has no income tax. There are no death duties or capital transfer taxes.
The Pleas' income derives from an excise duty, a landing tax (included in every visitor's ferry ticket), a small capital tax and property tax. Defaulters on the latter are
named on the notice board outside the Chief Pleas office for all to see! There is no
divorce law on Sark although divorces granted elsewhere are accepted. Sark's police
remain entirely of the non-uniformed voluntary variety and fortunately serious problems are rare, but they can happen. On August 24, 1990, a French citizen, André
Gardes, believing he was the rightful seigneur, attempted a one-man coup. Armed
with a Mannlich "Bull Pup" rifle (now in the tiny Sark Museum), several explosives,
and over 200 rounds of ammunition, he passed undetected through French, Jersey
and Guernsey security before coming ashore on Sark. Fortunately a duty *vingtenier*
spotted him before he could do any damage, alerted his superior, and with others
overpowered him. After several days of imprisonment in Guernsey, Gardes was
deported back to France.

The New Financial Economy

Two factors above all combined to revolutionize economic prospects in the postwar era — a sympathetic tax structure and the freeing of interest rates on investments.
In the first case consistent flat income tax rates of 20 percent have been good for residents (since 1940 in Jersey) and attracted wealthy British tax exiles. There are no

capital gains, estate or inheritance duties. A tax-free interest policy on funds deposited in island banks brought in the money of non-residents too, a hedge against inflation in the later 1960s and 1970s and a tax shelter. In the second case Jersey Senator Cyril Le Marquand set the investment ball rolling in 1962 with his proposed repeal of a 200-year-old usury law fixing interest rate ceilings of 5 percent. Guernsey and Alderney followed suit and Channel Islands' banking boomed. After Margaret Thatcher's Conservative administration in the UK lifted exchange controls on UK financial capital flows in 1979, the financial economy diversified further. Accountancy businesses, insurance and reinsurance companies, investment funds and fiduciaries handling trusts and company management joined the banks to make a home on the islands. The Guernsey States Economics and Statistics Review of 2000 called fiduciaries "the silent engine room of the Channel Islands' finance industry." At least 60 percent of Jersey's government income at the close of the 20th century derived from revenue from company registration and fees. The beehive-shaped Treasury building in St. Helier is fittingly named Cyril Le Marquand House.

What were once sleepy market garden islands have become cutting edge offshore financial centers. The revolution has been such that both bailiwicks present "rich countries" profiles with over 75 percent of their economies in service sector activities. Billion pound production levels are realized. Jersey's GDP measured £2.9 billion[21] in 2001 and Guernsey £1.3 billion.[22] On both islands the finance and business sector accounted for over 50 percent of recorded profits and paid out the best wages, but in job creation it accounted for less than 25 percent of employment by occupation. The new financial economy has come with a price, not least of which is that the parochial government of the past is to be replaced by professional ministerial parliaments. Further, in a new borderless European economic atmosphere, UK membership of the European Economic Community in 1974 and the European Union in 1993 poses questions about future status. New supranational rules binding European agricultural policy and finance threaten the islands' long-cherished autonomy. Full membership of the EU has been studiously avoided so far through a "special relationship" compromise, whereby the islands comply with parts of Common Agricultural Policy (CAP), but not all of it. Cattle were exempted to ensure maintenance of historic pedigree stock, for example, but finance is a major stumbling block. And in this arena the islands ran foul of the influential Paris-based Organization for Economic Cooperation and Development (OECD) and its multi-government constituents.

Under Scrutiny

Capitalizing on competitors' restrictive business and tax laws, including those of the UK, is the *raison d'être* of the new economy, and the OECD has been very critical of such practices. Both States' assemblies came under international pressure with Jersey and Guernsey included on a "name and shame" OECD blacklist of 35 global tax havens in June 2000, with the Isle of Man. The reporting committee — a multi-governmental body serving under the auspices of OECD named Financial Action

Task Force (FATF)—was not happy about potential erosion of national tax bases and undermining of government finances. It was also nervous about the threat tax havens pose to the legitimacy of tax paying culture. The States' willingness to share information with other countries' tax authorities removed the islands from the blacklist but that was not all.

Tax evasion concerns were exacerbated by FATF charges that offshore tax havens promote money laundering. Apart from involving ill-gotten gain money laundering disturbs money demand and it distorts capital and trade flows. It is a matter of serious international concern. FBI agents investigating international fraud in the 1990s rated the Channel Islands' weak banking regulations (and Isle of Man) as attractive for criminals with cash to launder. A British government investigation resulting in the Edwards Report of 1998 estimated investments in hundreds of billions of pounds, but it did not (could not?) differentiate between what was and what was not legitimate. However the islands are not on the OECD blacklist of money laundering states; in fact, island authorities were complimented for their cooperation with outside criminal investigations. The fact remains, though, that with modern telecommunications, customers need never put in a personal appearance. Implementation of regulatory "know your customer" laws is a challenge. In effect banks must know their customers' customers, not a very practical goal for island businesses marketing themselves internationally on non-disclosure and confidentiality. The recent worries over financing of international terrorism (post–New York World Trade Center bombing) are likely to increase scrutiny and tighten regulations. The islands are not alone. In fairness it is worthy of note that money launderers use onshore means just as readily.

Company registration is another area under scrutiny. The business stretches back to the 1930s but it only attracted major publicity in recent times. Sark particularly has been in the spotlight. As the offshore company registration business grew, non-resident companies (their business operations conducted elsewhere) paid Sark residents to be nominee stockholders and directors. An absence of corporate law and taxes provided incentive. Islanders allegedly pocketed tens of thousands of pounds sterling to join the so-called "Sark lark" and become quasi-stockholders and host board meetings. At one stage media reports claimed that Sark had 23,000 registered companies or about 38 companies per head of population! Angry accusations of subterfuge of European corporate culture were leveled at Sark authorities. Calls for compliance with wider political rules on corporate supervision were partially satisfied when the States prevented free-for-all proliferation with a mandatory payment of exemption status fees by companies whose beneficiaries do not live or reside on the islands. *The Economist* has pointed out that the Channel Islands probably now have tighter corporate controls than Britain, where it is still possible to conceal the identity of the beneficial owner of a company.[23]

Suburban Isles

The postwar fiscal liberalization has worked a remarkable change with government reconstituted and an old usury law founded on money lending as a sin replaced by a no-limits business ethic. The old ways of earning cash are still found on Jersey's potato strips, in steamy hotel kitchens and on construction sites, but the big money is in the financial quarters of St. Helier and St. Peter Port, a keyboard tap away from the rest of the world. Tourist brochures talk up idyllic retreats and rustic scenes, but the new way of life is more suburbanite consumer than it is quaintly rural. The seigneurs are still there but land is no longer the prime economic force. When Elizabeth II visited Jersey in 2001, only a handful of seigneurs were there to give homage.

There are plenty of new controversies. The cost of homes, the number of vehicle registrations and consumer sales all point to a healthy quality of life, but new wealth does not mask old problems. Housing stock is an issue. Prices are tough for the have-nots and draconian laws restrict development, purchase and lease. The struggle between those who want more housing and those who want green fields is ongoing. Space is finite but critics point to the percentage of newly developed land on Jersey as being less than that of traditional farmland and areas protected for natural beauty. Cash has little problem finding its way into the islands, but it is not so easy for would-be immigrants. The islands have been popular destinations for young Britons pursuing out-of-Britain work opportunities for 50 years, a unique offshore phenomenon in itself, but interaction has brought fallout problems such as drug usage. As evidence of its more liberal face, the States support rehabilitation rather than punishment and offer treatment readily. On the other hand hard-to-get permits and restrictive financial requirements closely regulate permanent residency. The status quo is defended.

The English language has prevailed. German occupation in World War II is blamed for exposing evacuees to English, but the tide began long before that. The number of Norman-French speakers at the outset of the 21st century was small with less than 5 percent reportedly fluent in Dgernesiais and those conversant in Jèrriais only a little higher, down from 20 years ago. It is flickering but the signs are it will survive. Efforts to keep it alive persist. An ability to talk in the vernacular may yet win appeal; it is a way of maintaining cultural distance in the face of newcomers, a durable in a hurried age.

---

1. Hugo, Victor, *L'Archipel de la Manche* (La Haule Books, 1985), 89.

2. Hugo, Victor, *The Toilers of the Sea* (Guernsey Press, 1990), 58.

3. Cunliffe, Barry, *Facing the Ocean: The Atlantic and Its Peoples, 8000* B.C.–A.D. *1500* (Oxford University Press, 2001), 211.

4. Lemprière, Raoul, *The Channel Islands* (Robert Hale fifth ed, 1990. First published 1970), 29.

5. Cunliffe, Barry, "Jersey in Prehistory: A Centre Or A Periphery?" Fourth Joan Stevens Memorial Lecture, June 1995 (Societe Jersiaise publication, 1995), 25.

6. Uttley, John, *A Short History of the Channel Islands* (Praeger, 1966) 27–28.

7. Hacquoil, Marleen, "Wace: His Literary Legacy," in Societe Jersiaise online (http://www.societe-jersiaise.org/langsec/wace.html) .

8. Hugo, *L'Archipel de la Manche*, 37.

9. Uttley, 76.

10. Lemprière, Raoul, *History of the Channel Islands* (Robert Hale, 1974), 44.

11. Lemprière, *History*, 51.

12. Uttley, 94.

13. Uttley, 149.

14. Hugo, *The Toilers of the Sea*, 26.

15. Bailiwick of Jersey Report of 2001 Census, "Population and Inter-Census Variations, 1821–2001," Appendix B, Table 1, 92.

16. McLoughlin, Roy, *Living with the Enemy* (Starlight Publishing, 1995), 17.

17. McLoughlin, 186.

18. Briggs, Asa, "Memory and History: The Case of the Channel Islands," Fifth Joan Stevens Memorial Lecture, April 26, 1996 (Societe Jersiaise publication, 1997), 13.

19. McLoughlin, 108.

20. States of Guernsey Website, "Machinery of Government in Guernsey: Research Study by Mori," Feb. 2002 (http://www3.gov.gg/content/).

21. States of Jersey Report, "Jersey in Figures, 2003," published by Statistics Unit, Policy and Resources Dept, Key Indicators (http://www.gov.je/content/popular_docs/jerseyinfigures.pdf), IV.

22. States of Guernsey Report, "Guernsey Facts & Figures, 2002," published by Policy and Research Unit (http://www3.gov.gg/content/online-reports/23-reports/23-guernsey-facts-and-figures-guide.jsp), 3.14.

23. "Hitting Terrorists' Cash: The Financial Front Line," *The Economist*, October 25, 2001.

Appendix 1.

Geographical Descriptions

	Population (2001)	Area (sq. miles)	Description
Great Britain	**58.8 million** (UK census)	**88,745**	**Archipelago off the northwest coast of continental Europe.**
Shetland	21,988	567	Archipelago of 100 islands/islets, 112 miles north of Scotland (60° N). About 15 islands inhabited.
Orkney	19,245	349	Archipelago of 90 islands/islets, 6 miles north of Scotland. About 17 islands inhabited.
Hebrides (Outer and Inner) plus Arran and Bute.	63,000 (OH: 27,000; Skye:14,000; IH & Bute: 16,000; Arran: 6,000)	3,000	Archipelago of 500 islands/islets in the Atlantic Ocean stretching 200 miles north to south off the west Scottish coast. Divided into two groups: Outer Hebrides and Inner Hebrides. Less than 100 are inhabited. Arran and Bute are islands in the Firth of Clyde estuary.
Isle of Man	73,873	221	An island in the Irish Sea equidistant from England, Scotland, Wales and Ireland, includes the Calf of Man, a rocky islet off the southern coast.
Anglesey	66,829	290	An island off the North Welsh coast, connected by bridges to Wales.
Scilly Isles	2,153	6	Archipelago of 55 islands/islets and 90 rocks in the Atlantic Ocean, 28 miles off southwestern England.
Isle of Wight	132,731	147	An island in the English Channel off the southern English coast, separated from the mainland by a narrow channel called the Solent.
Channel Islands	149,878 (Jers. 87,186; Guer. 59,807	78 (Jers. 45; Guer. 24)	A small archipelago in the Gulf of St. Malo, off the Normandy coast of France. Jersey and Guernsey are the principal islands, plus Alderney, Sark, Herm.
Total Other British Isles	530,000 (est.)		

Appendix 2.
Scottish Islands:
Population 1755–2001

	1755	1801	1841	1901	1951	1981	1991	2001
Scotland	**1.2m.**	**1.6m.**	**2.6m.**	**4.5m.**	**5.1m.**	**5.1m.**	**4.9m.**	**5.06m.**
Highlands & Islands	**337,000**	**350,700**	**472,000**	**390,000**	**361,900**	**446,300**	**369,308**	**372,000**
Shetland	15,200	22,379	30,558	28,166	19,352	26,347	22,522	21,988
Orkney	20,774	24,445	30,507	28,699	21,255	19,182	19,612	19,245
Outer Hebrides	N/A	N/A	35,590	46,172	35,591	31,500	29,400	26,502
Inner Hebrides: Skye	11,252	15,788	23,000	13,800	8,632	8,139	11,740*	12,200*
Inner Hebrides: Mull	5,287	8,539	10,000	4,000	2,693	2,605	2,648	2,500
Inner Hebrides: Islay	N/A	N/A	18,000	N/A	N/A	3,814	3,538	3,500
Arran	N/A	5,179	N/A	4,766	N/A	N/A	4,474	4,864
Bute	N/A	6,106	8,078	14,034	12,547	7,733	7,354	7,228

*These figures include mainland Lochalsh. Skye alone 1991: 8,695 (74 percent of Skye & Lochalsh figure).

Sources:
(I) 1755 figures based on Webster, Alexander, *An Account of the Number of People in Scotland in 1755*. An accepted estimate.
(II) Great Britain censuses for 1801–2001.

Appendix 3.

English and Welsh Islands: Population 1750–2001

	1750[1]	1801	1841	1901	1951	1981	1991	2001
England	**5m.**	**8.3m.**	**14.9m.**	**30.5m.**	**41.1m.**	**46.3m.**	**47m.**	**49.1m.**
Isle of Man	20,000	26,000[1]	47,975	54,752	55,123	64,679	69,788	76,315
Scilly	1,500	2,000[1]	2,556	2,092	2,194	1,946	2,048	2,153
Isle of Wight	18,000	23,687	45,640[2]	66,556	95,625	114,879	124,577	132,731
Wales	*450,994*	*587,128*	*1m.*	*2m.*	*2.6m.*	*2.7m.*	*2.8m.*	*2.9m.*
Anglesey	26,900	33,806	50,891	50,606	50,660	66,496	69,149	66,829
Channel Is.	*35,000*	*45,500*	*76,000*	*95,618*	*103,500*	*132,000*	*145,000*	*149,878*
Jersey	20,000	26,000[1]	47,544	52,576	57,310	76,050	84,082	87,186
Guernsey	14,000	18,000[1]	26,693	40,446	43,652	53,313	58,867	59,807

[1]Estimates
[2]1851 figure

Sources:
(I)   1750 figures based on estimates
(II) Great Britain censuses for 1801–2001

Appendix 4.

2001 Census Returns
for the Other Isles

CENSUS: 2001

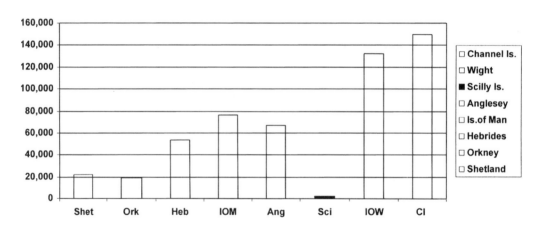

Note: Hebrides figure includes Arran and Bute.

Note: Hebrides figure includes Arran and Bute.

Appendix 5.
Political Profiles

	Key Stages in Socio-Political Development	Current Governance	Capital/Admin. Center
British Isles	*Tribal confederations for millennia. Two-thirds within Roman Empire 43–410. Mix of independent kingships in medieval era. Union of England & Wales 1536. United Kingdom incl. Scotland 1603.*	*UK: constitutional monarchy within European Union, parliamentary democracy. Devolution of power to Scotland and Wales, 1999.*	· *UK Parliament: London;* · *Regional Parliaments for Scotland (Edinburgh) & Wales (Cardiff).*
Shetland	First farmers c.3200 B.C. Iron Age within Celtic and Pictish spheres. Under Norwegian suzerainty (until 1194 as part of Orkney earldom, a.k.a. Nordreys) c. 900–1379. In Scotland from 1468. Part of UK since 1603.	UK insular county: Shetland Islands Council. Part of Orkney and Shetland electoral district for UK Parliament. Unitary constituency for Scottish Parliament within Highlands & Islands Region. Part of Scotland region for EU Parliament.	Lerwick (Shetland Islands Council).
Orkney	First farmers c.3800 B.C. Iron Age within Celtic and Pictish spheres. Orkney earldom under Norwegian suzerainty, a.k.a. Nordreys c. 875–1379. In Scotland from 1468. UK since 1603.	UK insular county: Orkney Islands Council. Part of Orkney and Shetland electoral district for UK Parliament. Unitary constituency for Scottish Parliament within Highlands & Islands Region. Part of Scotland region for EU Parliament.	Kirkwall (Orkney Islands Council).

Key Stages in Socio-Political Development	Current Governance	Capital/Admin. Center
Hebrides First farmers 4th millennium B.C. Northern Hebrides within Pictland & Southern Hebrides in Scots Dalriada A.D. 6th–9th centuries. Part of Gaelo-Norse Kingship of Man and Isles, a.k.a. Sudreys c.850–1266 and Lordship of Isles (1266–1493). Fully integrated in Scotland from 1493. Part of UKsince 1603.	Outer Hebrides is a UK insular county: Western Isles Council. Inner Hebrides split between Scottish councils of Highland and Argyll & Bute. Arran is part of Scottish council of North Ayrshire. For UK Parliament divided between 3 electoral districts and for Scottish Parliament 3 constituencies within Highlands & Islands Region. Part of Scotland Region for EU Parliament.	• Stornoway, Isle of Lewis (Western Isles Council) for Outer Hebrides. • Other islands annexed to mainland regional administrative centers in Inverness (Highland Council); Lochgilphead (Argyll & Bute; and Irvine (North Ayrshire).
Isle of Man First farmers 4th millennium B.C. Iron Age within Celtic sphere. HQ of Gaelo-Norse Kingdom of Man and Isles (a.k.a. Sudreys) under Norwegian suzerainty 800s–1266. English fief 1333–1765. British Crown dependency since 1801. Important constitutional reforms 1947 & 1958. Not part of UK.	Self-governing jurisdiction under supervision of British Home Office. The Manx parliament Tynwald is one of the oldest in the world. Democracy: elections to House of Keys (legislature) from multi and single-seat constituencies on island. Not a member state of the EU.	Douglas: home of Tynwald/Isle of Man Government.
Anglesey First farmers 4000 B.C. Iron Age within Celtic sphere.Under Roman authority A.D. 60–410. HQ of Celtic Kingdom of Gwynedd 500s–1283. English shire from 1283. Part of English annexation of Wales 1536 and UK 1603.	UK insular county: Anglesey County Council. Unitary constituency (named in Welsh *Yns Môn*) for UK Parliament and Welsh National Assembly. Part of Wales Region for EU Parliament.	Llangefni (Anglesey County Council).
Isles of Scilly First farmers 3 millennium B.C. Iron Age in orbit of Roman Britain & within Celtic sphere. English fief 1114–1831 & incl. in Duchy of Cornwall 1337. Part of UK 1603.	Council of the Isles of Scilly functions under auspices of UK county of Cornwall. Part of St. Ives constituency for UK Parliament. Part of South-West England Region for EU Parliament.	Hugh Town, St. Mary's Isle (Council of the Isles of Scilly).

	Key Stages in Socio-Political Development	Current Governance	Capital/Admin. Center
Isle of Wight	First farmers 4th millennium B.C. Iron Age in Celtic sphere. Under Roman authority A.D. 44–410. Within orbit of various Germanic kingdoms 500s–1000s. Anglo-Norman feudal lordship c.1070–1490. Part of UK 1603.	UK insular county: Isle of Wight Council. Unitary constituency for UK Parliament. Part of South-East England Region for EU Parliament.	Newport (Isle of Wight Council).
Channel Islands	First farmers 5th millennium B.C. Iron Age in Celtic sphere. Part of Roman Gaul 56 B.C.–A.D. 5th century. Within orbits of Frankish & Breton influence 500s–900s. Norman fiefdom from 933 & partof cross-Channel Norman-French realm from 1066.Under British Crown suzerainty from 1204 but with self-government rights confirmed by successive monarchs. Important constitutional reforms 1948–49. Not part of the UK.	The Channel Islands comprise two self-governing democratic jurisdictions under supervision of the British Home Office. • The States of Jersey (executive, legislature, and judiciary). • The States of Guernsey (executive, legislature and judiciary). Guernsey has dependencies of its own — principally Alderney and Sark (both with their own local government). Not member states of the EU.	• St. Helier: home of States of Jersey Government. • St. Peter Port: home of States of Guernsey Government.

Appendix 6.
20th Century Economic Profile

	Summary: 1900	*Summary: 2004*	*1998: GDP per capita, % of UK*	*Rank*
UK	*World's premier industrial urban economy.*	*#4 in World GDP ranking. 73% of GDP: services; 20%: manufacturing.*	100	
Shetland	Herring/mackerel/cod commercial fishing; lace and wool textiles; subsistence farming/fishing a.k.a. crofting.	Offshore oil bonanza 1970s (still 20% of GDP 2000); fish farming (aquaculture) growing.	90	3
Orkney	Commercial cereal crop cultivation & livestock raising for beef/dairy/exports strong; fishing; crofting.	Offshore oil boost in 1970s; public sector services; growth in food processing, finance.	69	4
Hebrides	Crofting strong/pre-capitalist; some textiles, commercial fishing, whisky distilling, tourism.	Local resource focus: fish farms, distilleries, tourism, wind farms for electricity, offshore oil exploration.	58	7
Isle of Man	Mining of copper, zinc, lead, silver; agriculture; fishing; tourism.	Offshore financial center: banks, reinsurance, fiduciaries over 50% of GDP.	93	2
Anglesey	Quarrying (by 1900 copper mining boom over); livestock/dairy; Anglo-Irish transit route services.	Port and minerals still impt; food processing, pharmaceuticals, fish farming.	58	7
Scilly	Horticulture: cut-flower exports; commercial fishing	Natural history tourism contributes most income; some horticulture.	59	6
Isle of Wight	Agriculture (livestock focus); quarrying; small fishing/boat building firms; tourism.	20th century boost in flying boats, hovercraft, space rockets declined. Public sector services, tourism biggest sectors.	60	5

	Summary: 1900	Summary: 2004	1998: GDP per capita, % of UK	Rank
Channel Islands	Agriculture (cattle & potatoes for export); horticulture, fishing; textiles; quarrying; manufacturing; tourism.	Offshore financial center: banks, insurance, reinsurance, fiduciaries over 50% GDP. Tourism.	102	1

Sources:
Office for National Statistics (UK); Dept. of Treasury IOM Govt; States of Jersey/Guernsey economic reports.

Selected Reading List

Many islands either do not have full histories or they are no longer in print. The following list includes recent publications that either focus on the islands or include significant historical information about them.

Chapter 1: Shetland

Ballantyne, John, and Brian Smith. *Shetland Documents 1580–1611*. Shetland Times Press, 1994.

Barnes, Michael. *The Norn Language of Orkney and Shetland*. Shetland Times Press, 1998.

Bathurst, Bella. *The Lighthouse Stevensons*. HarperCollins, 1999.

Fojut, Noel. *A Guide to Prehistoric and Viking Shetland*. Shetland Times Press, 1993.

Graham, John L. *Shetland Dictionary*. Shetland Times Press, 1999.

Graham-Campbell, James, and Colleen E. Batey. *Vikings in Scotland: An Archaeological Survey*. Edinburgh University Press, 1998.

Holbourn, Ian Stoughton. *The Isle of Foula*. Birlinn Ltd, 2001.

Howarth, David. *The Shetland Bus: A World War II Epic of Escape, Survival and Courage*. Lyons Press edition, 2001.

Marwick, Ernest W. *The Folklore of Orkney and Shetland*. Birlinn Ltd, 2000.

Miller, James. *The North Atlantic Front: The Northern Isles at War*. Birlinn Ltd, 2003.

Turner, Val. *Ancient Shetland*. Batsford Books, 2003.

_____. *The Shaping of Shetland: Developments in Shetland Landscape Archaeology*. Shetland Times Press, 1998.

Willis, Douglas. *Crofting*. John Donald Publishers, 1991.

Chapter 2: Orkney

Anderson, P.D. *The Life and Times of Orkney*. John Donald Publishers, 1999.

Barnes, Michael. *The Norn Language of Orkney and Shetland*. Shetland Times Press, 1998.

Brown, George Mackay. *Magnus*. Canongate Books, 1998.

Cunliffe, Barry. *Facing the Ocean: The Atlantic and Its Peoples, 8000 B.C.–A.D. 1500*. Oxford University Press, 2001.

Graham-Campbell, James, and Colleen E. Batey. *Vikings in Scotland: An Archaeological Survey*. Edinburgh University Press, 1998.

Gray, Alison. *Circle of Light: The Catholic Church in Orkney Since 1560*. John Donald Publishers, 2000.

Marwick, Ernest W. *The Folklore of Orkney and Shetland*. Birlinn Ltd, 2000.

Palsson, Hermann, and Paul Edwards, translation. *Orkneyinga Saga*. Penguin Classics edition, 1981.

Piggott, Stuart. *Scotland Before History*. Polygon Press, 1992.

Ritchie, Anna. *Neolithic Orkney in Its European Context*. MacDonald Institute for Archaeological Research, 2000.

_____. *Orkney*. Mercat Press, 1996.

_____. *Prehistoric Orkney*. Batsford Books, 1995.

Thompson, E. *The New History of Orkney*. Mercat Press, 2001.

Thompson, W.P.L. *History of Orkney*. Mercat Press, 1987.

Chapter 3: The Hebrides

Armit, Ian. *The Archaeology of Skye and the Western Isles*. Edinburgh University Press, 1996.

Bray, Elizabeth. *The Discovery of the Hebrides: Voyagers to the Western Isles, 1745–1883*. Birlinn Ltd, 1996.

Burl, Aubrey. *From Carnac to Callanish*. Yale University Press, 1993.

Caldwell, David. *Islay, Jura and Colonsay: A Historical Guide*. Birlinn Ltd, 2001.

Cooper, Derek. *The Road to the Isles: Travellers in the Hebrides 1770 to 1914*. Macmillan, 2002.

Currie, Jo. *Mull: The Island and Its People*. Birlinn Ltd, 1996.

Dodgson, Robert A. *From Chiefs to Landlords*. Edinburgh University Press, 1998.

Graham-Campbell, James, and Colleen E. Batey. *Vikings in Scotland: An Archaeological Survey*. Edinburgh University Press, 1998.

Grimble, Ian. *Clans and Chiefs*. Birlinn Ltd, 2000.

_____. *Scottish Islands*. BBC Books, 1985.

Hughes, Mike. *The Hebrides at War*. Birlinn Ltd, 2001.

Hutcheson, Rosalind. *Lordship to Patronage: Scotland 1603–1745*. Edinburgh University Press, 1983.

Levi, Peter, ed. *Samuel Johnson and James Boswell: A Journey to the Western Islands of Scotland* and *The Journal of a Tour to the Hebrides*. Penguin Classics, 1984.

Low, Mary. *Celtic Christianity and Nature: The Early Irish and Hebridean Traditions*. Polygon Press, 1996.

MacDonald, R. Andrew. *Kingdom of the Isles*. Tuckwell Press, 1997.

Macleod, John. *Highlanders: A History of the Gaels*. Hodder and Stoughton Sceptre Books, 1996.

McLellan, Robert. *The Isle of Arran*. David and Charles, 1970.

McLennan, George. *Scots Gaelic: A Brief Introduction*. Argyll Publishing, 1998.

McPhee, John. *The Crofter and the Laird*. Noonday Press, 1969.

Mithen, Steve. *Hunter-Gatherer Landscape Archaeology: The Southern Hebrides Mesolithic Project 1988–1998*. MacDonald Institute for Archaeological Research, 2001.

Rixson, Dennis. *The Small Isles: Canna, Rum, Eigg and Muck*. Birlinn Ltd, 2001.

Sharpe, Richard, translation. *Adomnán of Iona: Life of St. Columba*. Penguin Classics, 1995.

Storrie, Margaret. *Islay: Biography of an Island*. Islay: The Oa Press, 1981.

Thompson, Francis. *Lewis and Harris: History and Prehistory on the Western Edge of Europe*. Luath Press, 2004.

_____. *The Western Isles of Scotland*. Batsford Books, 1988.

Wiener, Christine. *Arran and Bute*. Stuart Forsyth, 1995.

William, Ronald. *The Lords of the Isles: Clan Donald and the Early Kingdom of the Scots*. House of Lochar, 1997.

Willis, Douglas. *Crofting*. John Donald Publishers, 1991.

Chapter 4: Isle of Man

Belchem, John, ed. *A New History of the Isle of Man, Vol. 5: The Modern Period 1830–1990*. Liverpool University Press, 2001.

Broderick, George, translation. *Cronica Regum Mannie et Insularum: Chronicles of the Kings of Man and the Isles*. Manx National Heritage, 1996.

Burrow, Stephen. *The Neolithic Culture of the Isle of Man: A Study of the Sites and Pottery*. Archaeopress, 1997.

Cesarini, D., and T. Kushner, eds. *The Internment of Aliens in Twentieth Century Britain*. Frank Cass, 1993.

Dickinson, J.R. *The Lordship of Man Under the Stanleys: Government and Economy in the Isle of Man, 1580–1704*. Carnegie, 1996.

Graham-Campbell, James, ed. *Cultural Atlas of the Viking World*. Facts on File, 1994.

Kermode, David G. *Offshore Island Politics: The Constitutional and Political Development of the Isle of Man in the Twentieth Century*. Liverpool University Press, 2001.

Kinvig, R.H. *The Isle of Man: A Social, Political and Cultural History*. Liverpool University Press, 1975.

Mongan, Norman. *The Menapia Quest, Two Thousand Years of the Menapii: Seafaring Gauls in Ireland, Scotland, Wales and the Isle of Man, 216 B.C.–A.D. 1990*. Herodotus Press, 1995.

O'Breaslain, Diarmuid, and Brian Stowell. *A Short History of the Manx Language*. Clochan, 1996.

Rhys, John. *Manx Folklore*. Oakmagic Publications, 2003.

Robinson, V., and D. MacCarroll, eds. *The Isle of Man: Celebrating a Sense of Place*. Liverpool University Press, 1990.

Chapter 5: Anglesey

Hughes, Wendy. *Anglesey: Past and Present.* Careg Gwalch, 1999.

Lynch, Francis. *Gwynedd: A Guide to Ancient and Historic Wales.* Stationery Office Books, 1995.

_____. *Prehistoric Anglesey: Archaeology of the Island to the Roman Conquest.* 2nd ed. Anglesey Antiquarian Society, 1991.

Ramage, Helen. *Portrait of an Island: Eighteenth Century Anglesey.* Anglesey Antiquarian Society, 1987.

Rowlands, John. *Copper Mountain.* Republished by Stone Science Anglesey, 2002.

Senior, Michael. *Anglesey: The Island's History.* Careg Gwalch, 1996.

Thorpe, Lewis, translation. *Gerald of Wales: The Journey Through Wales & The Description of Wales.* Penguin Classics, 1978.

Chapter 6: Scilly

Ashbee, Paul. *Ancient Scilly: From the First Farmers to the Early Christians.* David & Charles, 1974.

Bowley, R.L. *The Fortunate Islands: Story of the Isles of Scilly.* Bowley Publications, 1990.

Brandon, Robin. *Isles of Scilly.* Imray, Laurie, Norie and Wilson, 1999.

Thomas, Charles. *Exploration of a Drowned Landscape: Archaeology and History of the Isles of Scilly.* Batsford Books, 1985.

Vyvyan, C.C. *The Scilly Isles.* Robert Hale, 1953.

Chapter 7: Isle of Wight

Hockey, S. F. *Insula Vecta: The Isle of Wight in the Middle Ages.* Phillimore, 1982.

Hyland, Paul. *Wight: Biography of an Island.* Victor Gollancz, 1984.

Mills, A.D. *Place Names of the Isle of Wight: Origins and Meanings.* Paul Watkins, 1996.

Moore, Pam. *The Industrial Heritage of Hampshire and the Isle of Wight.* Phillimore, 1989.

Searle, Adrian. *The Isle of Wight at War, 1939–45.* Dovecote Press, 2000.

Shuter, Jane. *Carisbrooke Castle.* Heinemann Library, 2000.

Chapter 8: The Channel Islands

Bunting, Madeleine. *The Model Occupation: The Channel Islands Under German Occupation, 1940–1945.* Pimlico, 2004.

Burns, Bob, Barry Cunliffe, and Heather Sebire, eds. *Guernsey: An Island Community of the Atlantic Iron Age.* Oxford University School of Archaeology, 1996.

Cox, Geoffrey Stevens. *St. Peter Port, Guernsey, 1680–1831: The History of an International Entrepôt.* Boydell Press, 1999.

Cruickshank, Charles. *The German Occupation of the Channel Islands.* Sutton Publishing, 2004.

Everard, Judith, and J.C. Holt. *Jersey 1204: The Forging of an Island Community.* Thames & Hudson, 2004.

Forty, George. *German Occupation of the Channel Islands.* Pen and Sword Books/Leo Cooper, 2002.

Hugo, Victor. *The Toilers of the Sea.* Guernsey Press, 1990.

Johnson, Peter, ed. *The Archaeology of the Channel Islands.* Phillimore, 1986.

Jones, Roger, ed. *John Skinner's Visit to the Channel Islands August 1827.* Seaflower Books, 2000.

Le Feuvre, David. *Jersey, Not Quite British: The Rural History of a Singular People.* Seaflower Books, 1993.

Lemprière, Raoul. *History of the Channel Islands.* Robert Hale, 1974.

_____. *The Channel Islands*, 5th edition. Robert Hale, 1990.

Le Ruez, Nan. *Jersey Occupation Diary: Her Story of the German Occupation, 1940–45.* Seaflower Books, 2003.

Marr, L. James. *The History of Guernsey: The Bailiwick's Story.* Phillimore, 1982.

McLoughlin, Roy. *Living with the Enemy.* Starlight Publishing, 1995.

_____. *Sea Was Their Fortune: A Maritime History of the Channel Islands.* Seaflower Books, 1997.

Ogier, D.M. *Reformation and Society in Guernsey.* Boydell Press, 1997.

Patton, M. *Jersey in Prehistory.* Aris & Phillips, 1987.

Williams, Caroline. *From Sail to Steam: Studies in the Nineteenth Century History of the Channel Islands.* Phillimore, 2000.

Index